Constructive Drinking

This volume is sponsored by the International Commission on the Anthropology of Food.

Constructive Drinking

Perspectives on Drink from Anthropology

Edited by Mary Douglas
Visiting Professor, Princeton University

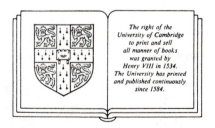

The right of the
University of Cambridge
to print and sell
all manner of books
was granted by
Henry VIII in 1534.
The University has printed
and published continuously
since 1584.

Cambridge University Press
Cambridge
New York   New Rochelle   Melbourne   Sydney

Editions de la Maison des Sciences de l'Homme
Paris

Published by the Press Syndicate of the University of Cambridge
The Pitt Building, Trumpington Street, Cambridge, CB2 1RP
32 East 57th Street, New York, NY 10022, USA
10 Stamford Road, Oakleigh, Melbourne 3166, Australia
and
Editions de la Maison des Sciences de l'Homme
54 Boulevard Raspail, 75270 Paris, Cedex 06

First published 1987
Reprinted 1988

Printed in Great Britain by
Antony Rowe Ltd, Chippenham, Wiltshire

British Library cataloguing in publication data

Constructive drinking: perspectives on
drink from anthropology.
1. Drink of alcoholic beverages
2. Drinking customs
I. Douglas, Mary   II. International
Commission on the Anthropology of Food
394.1'3   GN411.5

Library of Congress cataloguing in publication data

Constructive drinking: perspectives on drink from anthropology.
"Sponsored by the International Commission on the
Anthropology of Food" – P. preceding t.p.
Includes index.
1. Drinking of alcoholic beverages – Cross-cultural
studies.   2. Drinking customs – Cross-cultural studies.
3. Alcoholism – Cross-cultural studies.   I. Douglas,
Mary.   II. International Commission on Anthropology of
Food and Food Problems.   [DNLM: 1. Alcohol Drinking.
2. Anthropology.   3. Cross-Cultural Comparison.
WM 274 C758]
HV5047.C65   1987   394.1'3   86–33388

ISBN 0 521 33504 3
ISBN 2 7351 0177 0 (France only)

Contents

Contributors to this volume

Yochanan Altman is a Senior Research Lecturer at North East London Polytechnic, England and a Senior Associate Member of St Antony's College, Oxford. He obtained degrees (BA and MA) in Psychology from Bar-Ilan University, Israel and a PhD in anthropology from Middlesex Polytechnic, England. For the last five years he has been working with Gerald Mars on second economies of the Soviet Union.

Paul Antze is an Assistant Professor with the Division of Social Science at York University, Toronto, Canada. A graduate of the Committee on Social Thought at the University of Chicago, he describes his research interests as including social theory, symbolic anthropology and ethno-psychiatry. He is presently completing a book on the relationship between belief systems and the therapeutic process in modern self-help organizations.

Elizabeth Bott is a social anthropologist and a psycho-analyst. She received a PhD from the London School of Economics published as the book *Family and Social Network* in 1957; second edition, 1972 (Free Press). Other publications include the results of fieldwork in Tonga, *Tongan Society at the Time of Captain Cook's Visits* and "Rank and authority in the Kingdom of Tonga"; psychological commentary, "Hospital and Society"; and psycho-analytic papers "Clinical reflections on the negative therapeutic reaction" and "Some developments from the work of Melanie Klein."

Anne Tyler Calabresi is writing a book on the life of Tuscan farmers who are still working under the *mezzadria*, an ancient share-cropping tenure which goes back to about AD 1200. Since 1970 she has made four long fieldwork visits and many shorter trips to Tuscany for the research. She worked on this project (of which the chapter in this volume is the first piece to be published) when a visiting fellow of Lucy Cavendish College 1980–1.

Thomas Crump, currently lecturer in the Dept. of Anthropology at University of Amsterdam, received his PhD from the University of London for his research in the Highlands of Chiapas. His recently published book, *The*

Phenomenon of Money (Routledge & Kegan Paul) is an anthropological approach to money.

Lisa Gurr is a graduate of the Anthropology Dept. at Northwestern University. She knows Paris well and is an enthusiast of French detective fiction.

Joseph Gusfield is professor of sociology at University of California at San Diego. He has written extensively in areas connected with the study of social movements, sociology of law, economic development, with special reference to India and on alcohol studies. His published books include *Symbolic Crusade: Status Politics and the American Temperance Movement* (1963) and *The Culture of Public Problems: Drinking-Driving and the Symbolic Order* (1981).

Haim Hazan is a Senior Lecturer in Anthropology at the Dept. of Sociology and Anthropology at Tel-Aviv University. He received his PhD degree in 1976 from University College London. He is the author of *The Limbo People: A Study of the Constitution of the Time Universe Among the Aged* (Routledge & Kegan Paul 1980).

Dwight Heath is Professor of Anthropology and Program Director, "Social Science Research Training on Alcohol" at Brown University. He earned his PhD in Anthropology at Yale University. While conducting ethnographic and ethno-historical research on a variety of topics, his interest in alcohol use among tribes and peasants in different parts of the world developed. His experiences and research resulted in several books on alcohol and led to being a consultant to international organizations and governments. Books: *Cross-Cultural Approaches to the Study of Alcohol* (with M. W. Everett and J. O. Waddell), *Alcohol Use and World Cultures* (with A. M. Cooper), and *Cultural Factors in Alcohol Research and Treatment of Drinking Problems* (with J. O. Waddell and M. D. Topper).

Hillel Levine is a professor of sociology and religion at Boston University and Director of the United States Holocaust Memorial Council. He taught Sociology and Religious Studies at Yale and at Harvard where he received his PhD. He is currently involved in research on eighteenth-century Polish Jewry and the modernization of consciousness. He serves as a Consulting Editor to the *American Journal of Sociology*.

Gerald Mars directs the Centre for Occupational and Community Research at North East London Polytechnic, England, and he is a Senior Associate Member of St Antony's College, Oxford. He is a social anthropologist interested in the study of occupations, crime and subterranean economy, and he is the author of *Cheats at Work: an Anthropology of Workplace*

Crime (1983); and joint author with M. Nicod, *The World of Waiters* (1984).

Ndolamb Ngokwey is a Lele, African anthropologist, educated first at the Lubumbashi University and then at UCLA where he was awarded a PhD in anthropology. After doing fieldwork near Salvador, Brazil, on the role of the social support network in the health seeking process in an urban setting, and teaching and researching in Zaire, he is now working at UNICEF in the République du Cap Vert.

Farnham Rehfisch is Senior Lecturer in Anthropology at the University of Hill, England. After acquiring a BA at the University of California-Berkeley and an MA from the University of London, he continued his research in Edinburgh at the School of Scottish Studies and later at the University of Khartoum. His fieldwork extended from what is now Nigeria (formerly British Cameroons) to the Tinkers of Scotland, followed by a study of Ombudsman of Sudan.

Mary Anna Thornton, a Mellon Humanities Fellow, is a graduate at the Anthropology Department at Northwestern University. She spent a year in Eastern Austria as a Fulbright scholar.

I

INTRODUCTORY

1. A distinctive anthropological perspective

Mary Douglas

The scope of this volume

This volume is designed to amplify the claim that anthropologists have a distinctive perspective on drinking. According to Dwight Heath[1] few anthropologists before the 1970s would set out deliberately to study patterns of thought and action concerning drink. In spite of this lack of concentration on the subject they had nevertheless written a great deal on alcohol. This was because whatever other concerns inspired their ethnographic project they could not avoid taking note of the importance of drinking in the lives of the people they lived among. The record they thus constituted was based on "felicitous by-products of field research". In consequence, anthropologists have a frankly different focus on alcohol. They do not necessarily treat it as a problem. In effect, Dwight Heath's earlier review of the anthropological literature on alcohol up to 1970 shows the anthropologists bringing their own professional point of view to bear interestingly upon the same materials studied by specialists on alcohol abuse. The research of the latter is inevitably focused upon pathology. Their research on drinking has been instituted precisely because of grave problems; their assumptions and methods are problem-oriented. Dwight Heath argued that the anthropologists' evidence suggests that the medical and sociological research exaggerates the problems. In concentrating on the excess and abuse of alcohol, they are tending to express a strong bias of western culture and one which Joseph Gusfield has shown[2] to be particularly entrenched in America. From the wider comparative standpoint of anthropology, "problem drinking" is very rare and alcoholism seems to be "virtually absent even in many societies where drunkenness is frequent, highly esteemed and actively sought".[3] Even in the United States where there is so much concern about alcohol abuse, the most pessimistic estimate is that alcohol-related troubles afflict fewer than 10 percent of those who drink.

Anthropologists bring several challenges to the assumptions of other writers on alcohol. They challenge the common view that some races are, because of their biological inheritance, peculiarly vulnerable to ill effects from alcohol. They challenge the view that alcohol leads to anomie. They would be more satisfied with the notion that a state of anomie leads to alcoholism and they are prepared to face the theoretical problems involved in

3

defining anomie. They find no clear relation between the use of alcohol and a tendency to aggressive or criminal behavior. They dispute that drunken behavior exemplifies a relaxation of cultural constraints before the levelling effects of nature: Drunkenness also expresses culture in so far as it always takes the form of a highly patterned, learned comportment which varies from one culture to another: pink elephants in one region, green snakes in another. The general tenor of the anthropological perspective is that celebration is normal and that in most cultures alcohol is a normal adjunct to celebration. Drinking is essentially a social act, performed in a recognized social context. If the focus is to be on alcohol abuse, then the anthropologists' work suggests that the most effective way of controlling it will be through socialization. In an ideal comparative program in which anthropologists and medical researchers collaborate, the former would provide systematic analysis of the quantity and incidence of rules governing drinking. The comparative project would involve comparing degrees of alcohol imbibed by an average individual against the local pattern of rules about where, when, and what to drink, and in whose company. Predictions about alcoholism would have to be based on an analysis of these patterns of rules, a very complex and technical task.

Meanwhile, some immediate difficulties with the dichotomy proposed by Dwight Heath spring to mind. What is meant by "problem drinking"? How severe must a problem be before it gets counted into the statistics? What is meant by "alcoholism" or by "alcohol-related troubles"? Are we to take the native view of troubles? In which case the incidence of drinking trouble is likely to be assessed by natives as lower in a heavy-drinking culture than by the medical sociologists. And what about the bias of the latter? Do they vary from one generation to the next in their assessment of the evil effects of demon rum? Do the experts from wine-producing countries take a lighter view of the dangers than experts from the grain-based alcohol regions? In what was described as a forum for debate which any scholar from other fields must envy, *Current Anthropology* recently published a remarkable discussion of these questions.[4] Robin Room, writing as Science Director of the Alcohol Research Group Institute of Epidemiology and Behavioral Medicine[5] summarized his own experience of the contrast between anthropologists and two other classes of persons. On the one hand indigenous peoples in positions of responsibility in the Caribbean or in Papua, New Guinea tend to join their concern about the severity of the alcohol problem with that of doctors and epidemiologists. This is especially the case for regions undergoing urbanization and rapid change. On the other hand, the anthropologists tend to downgrade the issue. Robin Room confirmed more or less the same dichotomy, using Dwight Heath's 1975 paper as a main point of reference. Whereas Dwight Heath argued that the anthropologists had got a more balanced perspective, Robin Room reversed the values in favor of the epidemiologists. All the ticklish issues of professional bias were publicly examined by experienced anthropologists who have concentrated in the last decade or more upon problems of alcoholism. The upshot was agreement that in this important field of inquiry the two kinds of specialists should not let their work run in parallel tracks. In future, social and cultural studies of alcohol use should be matched by medical studies. This is the point to which this volume is addressed.

To become as systematic as the epidemiologists, cultural anthropology will need to develop some new tools. It seems clear that the discussion in *Current Anthropology* ran into the sand at two points. First, changing observer's bias as between different generations of researchers only becomes important over a long time span or if a subject is changing so swiftly that the new frames of reference have to be taken into account. This has not been the case with the anthropologists' study of alcoholism, as Dwight Heath's second review article (published here) confirms. He has updated his original review to cover the 1970–80 decade. The answers show more sophistication and subtlety, but the questions raised are recognizably the same. It is just as well to lay the issue of professional bias aside, since it is impossible to research and since other more measurable matters need to be studied anyway. Second, native attitudes to alcohol problems are part of the subject of inquiry and cannot be treated as parameters for measuring degrees of trouble. It would seem that there is at present no way of establishing a cultural level of tolerance for alcohol against which to ask the questions implicit in the debate in *Current Anthropology*: do cultural constraints dictating a restricted framework for drinking enable more individuals to absorb more alcohol with less apparent physical effect? Does cultural training which enables individuals to hold their drink more easily protect their livers from damage? Most likely not. Does the individual breaking out of a set of cultural constraints drink more deeply and more dangerously than one whose heavy drinking is culturally expected and approved? What difference does the surrounding culture's attitude to drunkenness make to the prospects of an addict's cure?

In a comparison of drinking habits among two Southwest Indian tribes, Kunnitz and Levy suggest that the cirrhosis mortality rates, which are much lower among Navaho than among the Hopi, reflect the Hopi condemnation of drinking and their rejection of the addict, while the Navaho rather expect young men to be heavy drinkers and never force them into isolation or fail to welcome them back into the community.[6] On much the same lines an interesting literature on Jewish attitudes to alcohol seeks to explain the break between the traditional Jewish sobriety and the heavy alcohol addiction of Jews in New York.[7] Does the assimilation of Jewish immigrants to American norms account for Jewish alcoholism in America? The answer is: No, not assimilation to some other cultural norm, but distance from traditional orthodoxy and from all that the ceremonial participation does to enable Jews to reenact solidarity and to renew the moral authority of their faith.

This kind of explanation covers both the New York Jews and the New York Irish. As Richard Stivers has said, Catholicism offers nothing like the same ritual control of personal behavior as Judaism. Its specialized and therefore isolated clergy preach temperance and stay outside of the public drinking places where their flock tends to gather: the Catholic Church "is not a viable reference group in terms of drinking".[8] Its ceremonies do not incorporate drinking within the ritual frame. Ringing the changes on the same interest in the boundaries of religious authority, important studies of Latin American drinking patterns introduce the element of power and status advantage. Among Mexicans before the conquest, drinking pulque was a rite of corporate identification. In modern Mestizo society drinking is part of the individual's competition to assert himself, with feats of consumption being supported by insults and drunken fighting. Whereas by contrast, within the Indian community "prescribed drunkenness never gave rise to addiction, social problems, or guilt".[9]

This considerable literature on the social conditions affecting alcoholism may perhaps overplay the idea of community as the answer to alcohol problems. Community authority, community rituals, community solidarity, they seem to bring drinking under control. But sometimes the form of the community is aggressively competitive, and the drinker who follows its customs puts his health at risk. Clearly this approach needs a precise method for comparing community structure. Though several anthropologists have experimented with such methods and are confident of their value, nothing has been done to use cultural analysis[10] to examine problems of alcoholism. These methods of estimating the relative strength of various forms of social control would be eminently practicable for comparative studies of alcohol use.

Two other approaches to the relation between culture and alcohol carry very different moral and academic intentions. The first, the project in the sociology of sociability, was started by David Reisman in the mid 1950s inspired by George Simmel and based on a Chicago seminar on play and leisure. What was obviously an extremely stimulating collaboration for those involved, was summed up in 1968 as a chronicle of frustration and achievement.[11] Their inquiries into parties and informal social networks continually bumped against the lack of theoretical work in the comparison of culturally received ideas. They needed some measure or concept of levels of sociability but the cultural anthropologists' contribution was not in evidence. Another thing that is very striking about this literature on parties and drinking is that practically nothing is said about the drinks. The same applies to the writing by anthropologists on the ethno-science of drinking. In this literature the anthropologists seem to earn the reproaches of their medical colleagues for their unwillingness to recognize pathology where it seems obvious, and for their horror of ethnocentric judgments.[12] James Spradley, in *You Owe Yourself a Drunk: An Ethnography of Urban*

Nomads (1970)[13] says it was written with "the wish to provide social justice for the skid row alcoholic". It starts with the clarion call: "The American city is convulsed with pain." These ethnographies of bars and flops[14] fall in some unsatisfactory place between genres, not nearly as interesting to read as a novel, not any use at all for getting justice, nor even for raising the level of understanding of the problems of alcoholism.

The drinks themselves are one of the important gaps in the subject of alcoholism which this anthology is not intended to remedy. We can only signpost it and take care to describe how some of the drinks are made and how their manufacture enters into the economy. Fortunately, the French anthropologists[15] are taking a great interest in fermentation processes from the points of view of nutrition, biochemistry and economic organization. As their work on palm wine and maize beer is extended by others, this particular omission in our knowledge will gradually be rectified.

At first it seemed that an anthropological collection would emphasize the relation between physical, evolutionary, and socio-cultural processes. Many questions about drinking arise on the border of society and biology. For example, in many civilizations women are habitually excluded from taking strong alcohol. One might look for an ancient wisdom which protects the vulnerable foetus by a general rule applied to all females. If that line is followed what could be said about the sources of such rules? Are they explicitly based on gynecology or do they result from a happy convergence of medical and social ideas? If women for whatever reason tend to be excluded from alcohol, one can be curious about the health value of the other drinks that would, in a carefully partitioned society, be classed as peculiarly appropriate for women. If the classification has purely social functions, thirsty women or women wanting to celebrate might be driven in default to very unhealthy alternatives. Water is often contaminated; tea and coffee are not perfect health drinks. Furthermore, protection of women from dangerous foods is not universally practiced. Do we expect to find women drinking alcohol freely only when the social norms are broken down? "Gin, gin was mother's ruin", runs the old vaudeville chorus. It is tempting to go straight from these reflections to theories of social pathology, assuming that a stable society would have worked out all the best solutions, and that the breakdown of mores by industrialization or invasion or migration will have produced indiscriminate feeding, drinking and alcohol abuse. It was looking for a chapter on women's drinking or to any work that would give a rounded view of the nutritional and toxic aspects of drinking in general, that I was referred to Dwight Heath's review of the anthropological work on alcohol. A subsequent search in the literature led me to decide that it is premature to attempt to study the interface of biology and culture when the drinks themselves have not even been catalogued and their properties are not known. Nor have the cultural aspects of drinking been adequately studied. It is difficult to find any survey of all the drinks used in a given population, to say nothing of the relation between them. In view of this I have merely indicated certain fields that are ready for systematic research.

Phenomenologists keep saying that the world is socially constructed. Where drinks are concerned, there are at least three distinct ways in which that happens. First, drinks give the actual structure of social life as surely as if their names were labels affixed upon expected forms of behavior. Second, the manufacture of alcohol is an economic activity of consequence. Third, the ceremonials of drinking construct an ideal world. To develop these three functions of drinking I have been able to draw on accounts of some exotic drinks, some alcoholic and others not, but I have not attempted to include all of those wonderful brews which anthropologists encounter.

Drinks construct the world as it is

For Joseph Gusfield drinking is a form of ritual. Very much a symbolic interactionist he treats alcohol and coffee as two opposing pointers. Coffee cues the shifts from playtime to worktime and alcohol cues the transition from work to playtime, as every American reader will recognize in their own drinking behavior. What we are not so well aware of is that this is a relatively new pattern, dependent on a major shift in the division of labor. The big distinction in contemporary western culture is that between work and leisure, a segregation that holds across classes and sexes and occupations. Gusfield points out that in the pre-industrial work pattern men worked in all-male teams, as construction workers still do. In that pattern, the dominant cleavage is between work and home, work being associated with males and home with females. In this case, drinking alcohol, strong drink at that, is not separated from work, and by that token, it does not belong in the home.

Drinks also act as markers of personal identity and of boundaries of inclusion and exclusion. Gerald Mars gives a brief account of longshoremen's drinking patterns in which exclusion from the tavern takes on the darkest possible aspect. On the docks men are judged by how well they carry their drink and by how generously they spend on drink. Belonging to a gang as an insider means everything, more regular work, higher earnings, mutual aid and a comfortable place in the tavern. A man's progress up the ranks from outsider to established insider depends on his role as a drinking companion as much as upon skills and devotion to work. How warm and friendly this inclusion sounds by contrast with its sinister side. The outsiders drink, though not in the tavern; they carry a bottle of wine or cheap rum which they call 'screech' and they draw their fellow drinkers to the parking lot by a nod or a wink. All that this boundary between insiders and outsiders means for entitling a worker to negotiate boldly with the foreman, to speak up against exploitation and to take other risks at work is eloquently brought out. Just because alcohol in this setting is the gate of access to all that is most desired, a person suffering social rejection would understandably turn to compensatory drinking, to possess at least the symbol of what he does not have. This suggests a vein for research among the social uses of alcohol: the more that alcohol is used for signifying selection and exclusion the more might we expect its abuse to appear among the ranks of the excluded. Again it suggests that much of the anthropologists' work is among people whose drinking behavior follows a generally inclusive pattern. This in itself may account for their finding that alcoholism is rarer than in western industrial society, where selective hospitality[16] promotes competitive individualism.

Exclusion takes many forms, some very subtle. Connoisseurship in the matter of wines is in itself a field for competition. We must take note of the exclusionary potential represented by the serried ranks of vintage and lesser wines in Europe. Amazing in itself is the trained palate that can recognize and name the vineyard, the year, even the growth of particular wines. Apparently, the top wine taster needs to keep his palate in form by never relaxing his specialized daily practice, like a violinist and quite unlike a language speaker who can always pick up the nuances of a language once learnt well. Dorothy Sayers attributed to Peter Wimsey these skills when she had him win the bet with Freddie Arbuthnot at the Egotists' Club by naming blindfold the vintage years of seventeen wines. Then he was admittedly in good form. But when two imposters both presented as Lord Peter tried to buy military secrets, the Comte de Reuil unmasked them by a wine tasting contest in which the real Lord Peter easily triumphed. "Even the most brilliant forger can scarcely forge a palate for wine."[17] So, connoisseurship has power for identifying the person as well as the wine. Not knowing may deliver one into the hands of manipulators. Connoisseurship also has its own power for social domination. Who could afford to let the hotel waiter get the upperhand and yet, how much expertise is needed to stop the waiter from forcing a humiliating dependence upon himself?[18] These essays treat drinking as a medium for constructing the actual world. The drinks are in the world. They are not a commentary upon it, nor a surface nor a deep structure model of its relations. They are as real as bricks and mortar. They are examples of things that constitute the world, they enter into bundles of other real things, with times and lists of names and calendrical connections. Sampling a drink is sampling what is happening to a whole category of social life.[19] We have to show that what is being categorized at any tavern meeting or home reunion is a part of a social ordering.

Of course anthropologists do not suppose that extreme poverty makes this refined signalling and constructing impossible. Anne Calabresi's account of a Tuscan farmer's wine-making and wine-drinking settles this decidedly. A lyrical tranquility and sweet order transforms the hardships of daily life in the farm. We learn how the grapes fit into the series of fruits, and of how fruits contrast as luxuries with the vegetables and cereals on the farm; the pride in quality and the frugal use. The every day ordinary table wine, which is watered and drunk with meals, contrasts with the *Vin Santo* used for special occasions and for consecration at Mass. It is rare to have a description of how this venerable drink is actually made, and a surprise to learn that after the juice fermented within the grape, the final process is so quick and the actions so simple.

With only one source of alcohol, Ndolamb Ngokwey shows how the Lele distinguish many kinds of palm wine and allocate them to different social categories building their sense of community around it. As anthropologists we do not idealize community or suppose that it always prevents individual competitiveness. Often the community channels the competition. Farnham Rehfisch's account of competitive beer drinking illustrates the agonistic role of drinking in making partnerships and gaining personal reputation. Looking at the social uses of drinks reveals sensitive mechanisms for redefinition of roles. Mary Anna Thornton's essay is a rare account of the whole range of drinks used in a given community to express the whole range of social relations. She finds that an Austrian village polarizes social events towards two opposite types, the one exemplifying degrees of intimacy and the other, degrees of formal celebration. Each type of event is matched by its associated family of drinks. The insight enables her to make a convincing ascent from ethnographic catalogue to a higher level of abstraction.

At this point we should ask how the anthropologist can make a systematic comparison of cultural attitudes to put side by side with biomedical information. The answer is to resist the temptation to plunge deeper and deeper into a search for bias-free data. Success depends on having a researchable problem about cultural comparison, to find appropriate abstractions and counting and calculating techniques for expressing them. The drinking habits we have described here are all fraught more or less intensely with social concerns. In the Austrian countryside drinking sekt together guarantees nothing about mutual support, whereas drinking schnapps does. In the Tuscan farmhouse, *Vin Santo* is brought out only on very special occasions. Frenetic gulping of screech in the car lot outside contrasts dramatically and tragically with comfortable beer drinking in the warm dockside tavern. The whole subject of inclusion and exclusion is probably ripe to be handled by the information theoretic approach developed by Jonathan Gross and colleagues on food habits.[20]

In a culture that knows only one drink, signifying friendship, or two drinks, one signifying insider and the other signifying outsider status, a heavy weight of concern is likely to pile upon the boundary of shared drinking. We could start to prognosticate alcohol addiction adding to the despair of the person who finds himself already an outsider and about to be excluded from the round of drinks. The Austrian case presented here is relatively simple, with only two main kinds of drinks. When there are many kinds of drinks, each partitioning a piece of social knowledge and helping to articulate a diversified social universe, we could also risk prognosticating intolerance of drunkenness – if a great deal of information had to be coded on to drinks a high value would be set on the physical and mental controls needed for sending and reading the messages. So we would expect that the more discriminated social information that is carried in the drinking code, the less tolerance in the community for abuse of alcohol and so the more mutual monitoring and effective control. As to the research, the sheer amount of information that is carried by a complete range of available drinks could be calculated and related to expectations about performance. Various applications of information theory could be used for providing the objective background to cultural behaviour that will help medical researchers assess social factors conducive to alcoholism

Drinking constructs an ideal world

The essays in this collection have not been chosen to illustrate false constructions of the world. However, we shall not have met the demands of the subject if we only insist on how drinks really constitute the world by being the occasions of gatherings of particular sorts and by serving as brightly colored material labels of events. There is also a sense in which drinks perform the other task of ritual. They make an intelligible, bearable world which is much more how an ideal world should be than the painful chaos threatening all the time. To bring out this aspect as a separate ritual construction we have four essays.

Paul Antze takes up the ancient relation between religion and alcohol. His chapter on Alcoholics Anonymous shows how this prestigious organization works like a religious cult, following the rituals of conversion and incorporation described by anthropologists in other societies.

Elizabeth Bott's cool style, introducing the orders of rank and power and authority in the island realm of Tonga, is in itself like the unobtrusive, methodical preparation for the Kava ceremony. Two myths about the origin of the ceremony yield to the analysis by which she uncovers envy, fratricidal hatred, and unspeakable desires to kill with poison. The myths deal with the destruction and restoration of a brother and son: they state the passionate problems of enmity and rivalry in a ceremonially abstracted form: the tale is reenacted with the pounding of the Kava root and its solution in water and distribution as a soothing drink. By the ceremony, the Tongans transcend emotions and enhance their consciousness of belonging in a larger society. The passions she is writing about are not the strange fantasies of an exotic people. She is a psychoanalyst as well as an anthropologist and she is telling us that she recognizes our dreams in their ceremonies. The Tongan construction of a world in which victims can be restored to life and in which rivals can tolerate each other's presence is a version of the sociability which David Reisman's research team were trying to identify.

In something of the same spirit, Haim Hazan's friends in the old people's Day Centre in the East End of London create a myth and a ceremony that holds grim realities at bay. Coming together daily to enjoy a free lunch, tea, meetings, entertainment and welfare counselling, they know very well they are destitute. They are the left-behind poor. Hazan has shown elsewhere[21] that their adaptation to their plight is to deny their past. Throwing themselves hectically into the life of the Centre, they make its egalitarian mutual aid the only reality. The present which they collectively construct denies the external world of family neglect and physical decay. The process of construction revolves around making tea, sharing it out with sugar and biscuits on a strictly equal basis. Tea time is the focus of dramatic confrontations. They must practice exclusiveness upon one another to enforce conformity to their adopted values. They rally to protect their fragile world of short, repetitive cycles from the hostile march of time in the outside world. The strict order and peace of their own tea time contrasts with the disagreeable hustle and discontent of the staff-regulated lunchtime. Lunch is a sign that points towards the inexorable slide to decay and change, the world they strive to exclude. Partaking of tea, they collude to hold time still. These tricks of consciousness, contrived but unacknowledged, are hard for ethnographers to reach. To do their work they have to be hidden from even the performers. But every novelist knows that this is how the structure of time and place and personality is conveyed, if he knows his craft at all. Lisa Gurr's essay considers Simenon's signalling of the distinctions in a peculiar and diverse world she calls Maigret's Paris. For the sake of a continuous stream of stories over three decades Maigret's Paris has to have a time-defying quality. This chapter plays an important part in this book in drawing our attention to the difference between ideal types and fictional types. Deconstructing of an ideal world by kava drinking or by tea drinking is not a deception or fiction like Simenon's ideal Paris. The difference between these ideal worlds defined by kava and tea and those imaginary worlds of fiction is clear. We have classed the former here as ideal, in distinction to the worlds where screech is the unpleasing alternative to beer or sekt the formal alternative to merry toasts in schnapps, not because they are false. They are not false worlds, but fragile ones, momentarily upheld and easily overturned. They are more precarious than worlds constructed upon a stable distribution of power and that is the only reason for putting them in a separate section

Alcohol entrenches the alternative economy

The last section deals analytically with the place of alcohol in three kinds of political economy. Alcohol production and distribution as an industry is peculiarly conducive to monopoly. It provides a uniform product, its manufacture offers large economies of scale, it has low carrying costs and is highly in demand. In the Polish case, described by Hillel Levine, demand for alcohol was used as a means for economic control, to prop a rich but vulnerable section of the economy by insulating it from modernization. Contrast this with the role of alcohol in developing an alternative economy, almost an alternative currency, in the history of the Chiapas Highlands in Mexico, recorded by Thomas Crump. Here is an instance of how the black market in rum succeeded in mobilizing resources that would otherwise seem to have been blocked. The combination of owning a trucking business, having some spare investment capital and supplying bootleg rum at locally affordable prices (by escaping tax) created new centers of power, working against the institutions which would have excluded Indians from economic development.

In Poland in the seventeenth and eighteenth century, the Jews found themselves squeezed between peasants and landlords in a system of newly consolidated agrarian feudalism. The landlords instituted a monopoly of the manufacture and distribution of alcohol, for which they licensed Jewish entrepreneurs. The export of grain from Poland to urbanizing Europe had been a prime source of profit in the sixteenth century, but a century later the lesson of commercial organization had been learned so well that along with price fluctuations, Polish farming had to compete with more efficient agriculture and food provisioning in Europe. Through the seventeenth and eighteenth century, the magnates were concentrating their holdings of land and the terms of trade were such that the lower nobility were losing out to the upper nobility and the peasants were losing out even more to the lower nobility. Their new conditions of serfdom were more constraining and degrading than anywhere else in Europe. At this point, already complaining of the low productivity of his peasants, the lord was making greater quantities of intoxicants available to them. It may have partly been because "Drunken peasants are more easily beaten into sullen obedience." But more significantly, the gentry saw their interest in preventing the monetization of the economy. They did not want a labor market based on rent and wages rather than on feudal service. When the ideal was an autarchic productive unit in which only the lord would have dealing with the outside world, the manufacture of alcohol on the estate was a mechanism for siphoning off spare cash. If the peasants could accumulate a little cash, it was better to provide ways of spending it that reverted to the landlord. Some estates actually required serfs to buy a stipulated minimum of alcohol as part of their feudal obligations. This attempt to create a closed monetary system opened a niche for commerce, otherwise carefully excluded. And here the Jewish communities were enrolled. The Jews foresaw quite correctly that by accepting concessions to organize the monopoly of production and sale of alcohol they would antagonize and become targets for peasants' wrath. The history of Polish alcohol shows the unfolding tragedy of Polish anti-Semitism in its early stages.

The current interest in the alternative or black economy must turn more and more towards the anthropology of drink. These essays correct the perspective of sociological and medical writers, whose focus is so strongly upon personal degradation of individual alcoholics. Anthropologists do not frivolously disregard these questions. But to end this section and the volume on the cheerful note struck by Heath's reviews of the subject, consider how wine enlivens the alternative economy that flourishes in Soviet Georgia. Soviet authorities disapprove of Georgian traditions of hospitality as a vast misuse of resources. But they are powerless to prevent a pattern of drinking that sustains private networks and softens the austerities of bureaucracy while creating much needed channels for the flow of resources in a real alternative economy.

Acknowledgments
This volume began with the meetings of six panels on food at the Tenth Congress of the International Union of Anthropological and Ethnological Sciences in Delhi in 1978. This was the first session of the Congress at which the newly formed ICAF (the International Commission on the Anthropology of Food), which was founded and chaired by Ravindra Khare, took responsibility for organising panels on food and food problems. There was no panel on drink, but a few papers addressed the topic. Making these the basis of a collection, soliciting additional articles and other editorial processes have taken much too long. I am grateful to the earliest contributors for their patience. I also thank Dr. Lita Osmundsen, who, as Director of the Wenner Gren Foundation, has always been a generous supporter of ICAF. Grateful acknowledgments are also due to Dr. Arjun Appadurai, who started the volume and to Andrew Leslie and Helen McFaul who have given steadfast help.

Notes
1 Heath, Dwight, 1975, "A critical review of ethnographic studies of alcohol use," in R. Gibbons, Y. Israel, H. Kalant, R. Popham, W. Schmidt, and R. Smart (eds.) *Research Advances in Alcohol and Drug Problems*, vol. 2, John Wiley & Sons, N.Y.
2 Gusfield, Joseph, 1963, *Symbolic Crusade: Status, Politics and the American Temperance Movement*. University of Illinois Press, Urbana, Il., *idem*, 1981, *The Culture of Public Problems: Drinking, Driving and the Symbolic Order*, University of Chicago Press, Chicago.
3 Heath, 1975, *op.cit.*, p. 57.
4 Room, Robin, 1984, "Alcohol and ethnography: a case of problem defiation?" in *Current Anthropology* 25, no. 2, April, 1984:169–91.
5 Room, Robin, 1984, *ibid.*, p. 169.
6 Kunitz, S. J. and Levy, J. E., 1971, "The epidemiology of alcoholic cirrhosis in two southwestern Indian tribes," in *Quarterly Journal of Studies on Alcohol* 32, no. 3: 706–20, Sept. 1971.
7 Snyder, Charles, 1978, *Alcoholism and the Jews*, Acturus Paperbacks, S. Illinois University Press, Carbondale, Il. *idem*, 1982, "Alcoholism among Jews in

Israel: a pilot study," in *Quarterly Journal of Studies on Alcohol* 43, no. 7: 623–54, July.

8 Stivers, Richard, 1976, *A Hair of the Dog: Irish Drinking and American Stereotypes*, Pennsylvania State University Press, University Park, p. 87.

9 MacMarshall, ed., 1979, *Beliefs, Behaviors and Alcoholic Beverages: A Cross Cultural Survey*, University of Michigan Press, Ann Arbor, Michigan, p. 49.

10 Douglas, Mary, 1970, *Natural Symbols*, Barrie & Rocklife; *idem*, 1982, *In the Active Voice*, R. K. P. Gross, J. & Rayner, S. 1984. *Measuring Culture*, Columbia University Press. Mars, Gerald, 1982, *Cheats at Work*, Allen & Unwin.

11 Reisman, David, 1960, "The vanishing host," *Human Organisation* 19, no. 1, Spring: 17–27; *idem*, 1960, "Sociability, permissiveness, and equality," in *Psychiatry* 23, no. 4: 323–40; *idem*, 1964, "The sociability project: a chronicle of frustration and achievement," in *Sociologists at Work*, Phillip Hammond, ed., Basic Books, N.Y.

12 Fox, Richard, 1978, "Ethnicity and alcohol use," by A. S. Brown, in *Medical Anthropology* 2, no. 4: 53.

13 Spradley, James, 1970, *You Owe Yourself a Drunk: An Ethnography of Urban Nomads*, Little, Brown & Co., N.Y., p. viii.

14 Cavan, Sherri, 1966, *Liquor License: An Ethnography of Bar Behavior*, Aldine Publishing Co., Chicago. Dollard, John, 1945, "Drinking mores of the social classes," in *Alcohol, Science and Society*, Quarterly Journal of Studies on Alcohol, New Haven, Conn. Roebuck, J. B., and Krese, W., 1976, *The Rendezvous: A Case Study of an After Hours Club*, Free Press, N.Y. Stone, Gregory, 1962, "Drinking styles and status arrangements," in *Society, Culture and Drinking Patterns*, J. Pittman and C. Snyder, eds., Wiley, N.Y. pp. 121–45.

15 de Lestrange, Marie-Therese, 1981, "La consommation de 'bière de mil' à eyolo, village Bassari du Senegal oriental," in *Objets et Mondes* 21, no. 13:107–14. Fournier, Dominique, "Le pulque et le sacrifice humain Chez les Azteques," *L'Imaginaire du Vin*, ed. Jeanne Lafitte, Marseille, 1983.

16 Douglas, Mary, ed., 1984, *Food in the Social Order: Studies of Food and Festivities in Three American Communities*, Russell Sage Foundation, Basic Books, N.Y.

17 Sayers, Dorothy, 1972, *Lord Peter, A Collection of All the Lord Peter Wimsey Stories*, Harper and Row, N.Y.

18 Mars, Gerald and Nicod, Michael, 1984, *The World of Waiters*, George Allen and Unwin, London.

19 Goodman, Nelson, 1978, "When is art: samples," ch. 4 in *Ways of Worldmaking*, Hackett Publishing Co., Indianapolis.

20 Gross, Jonathan, 1984, "Measurement of calendrical information in foodtaking behavior," in *Food in the Social Order, op.cit.*

21 Hazan, Haim, 1980, *The Limbo People: A Study of the Constitution of the Time Universe Among the Aged*, Routledge & Kegàn Paul Ltd., London.

2. A decade of development in the anthropological study of alcohol use: 1970–1980

Dwight B. Heath

In recent years, there have been striking advances in the study of beliefs and behaviors that relate to alcoholic beverages, and this is especially true with respect to anthropological perspectives. Even practitioners of the so-called "hard sciences" acknowledge that social and cultural factors must be taken into account, together with physiological and psychological factors, when one attempts to understand the interaction of alcohol and human behavior. This has been the case because, as Marshall succinctly phrased it, "The cross-cultural study of alcohol presents a classic natural experiment: a single species (*Homo sapiens*), a single drug substance (ethanol), and a great diversity of behavioral outcomes" (1979a:1). Unfortunately, few observers had paid systematic attention to the anthropological study of drinking until the middle of this century, although the output of such studies has, with remarkable regularity, doubled every five years since then (Heath 1976a: 52–56).

Introduction

This is an appropriate context for taking brief stock of recent developments in anthropological studies of alcohol use, and of some theoretic and practical implications of such research.[1] This article summarily reviews work from 1970 through 1980; as such it is most valuable as a complement to my earlier survey (Heath 1975). For the convenience of colleagues who may use them in juxtaposition as reference materials, the organization is similar: however, there is little redundancy, so the earlier paper is an important introduction to key concepts and theories. Unlike the earlier paper, this makes no pretense at comprehensive coverage of the relevant sources: unpublished papers and reports are not cited, nor is work in progress; when several authors have written on the same subject, I cite only a few of the more substantive works, and when the same author is redundant, I have also been selective.

An anthropological perspective

The scope of this discussion is intentionally broad, reflecting the wide range of methodological approaches and topical concerns that are generally sub-sumed under the academic rubric of "anthropology" in the contemporary United States. This includes not only *ethnography* and *sociocultural anthro-pology* but also *archaeology, physical anthropology, linguistics,* and *folk-lore.* My presentation here will also reflect some non-anthropological categories that are of special substantive or conceptual importance to others in the broadly transdisciplinary community of scholars who are interested in *alcohol studies.*

There has been a striking proliferation of activity in this field since 1970. At the suggestion of Sol Tax, with funding from the National Institute on Alcohol Abuse and Alcoholism and administrative support from the Smith-sonian Institution's Center for the Study of Man, I planned a Conference on Alcohol Studies and Anthropology to be held in conjunction with the IX In-ternational Congress of Anthropological and Ethnological Sciences. When I became severely ill, Jack Waddell and Mike Everett joined me in sharing the burden of organizing and chairing the Conference, and they also took part in the subsequent editing of the proceedings. Representatives of several disciplines from many countries took part, and our goal was achieved: to assess interdisciplinary contributions toward the cross-cultural study of alcohol use, in both behavioral and physiological terms. Unfortunately, the publisher had not planned adequately for a project on the vast scale of the *World Anthropology* series, so the papers, both read and revised in 1973, were not published until three years later, but the book (Everett, Waddell and Heath 1976) serves as a kind of mile-stone nevertheless, both in terms of stock-taking and in suggesting new directions.

In that book, I summarized the long-term development of anthropologi-cal studies on alcohol, within a chronological framework (Heath 1976a); a more thorough evaluation of the same large, diverse, and widely scattered literature, written later but ironically published earlier, combined a samp-ling of worldwide variation in links between drinking and other aspects of culture on the one hand, and relevant concepts and theories on the other (Heath 1975). In both of those reviews, it was noted that the uneven quality of ethnographic studies of drinking was in part due to the fact that no one had gone to the field with the intention of focusing attention on the subject. This meant that not only were analyses and interpretations done *post facto*, but even the data were usually collected incidentally, as serendipitous by-products of fieldwork that had other emphases. This is no longer the case, although much more could still be done to increase the quantity and quality of detailed reporting.

Anthropological viewpoints had gained widespread recognition among professionals of many other disciplines, perhaps most dramatically with Horton's (1943) pioneering cross-cultural study, which is still one of the most cited sources on the big question "why do people drink to get drunk?"

The lines between anthropology and sociology were appropriately unclear, to the point where specialists in alcohol studies probably more often think of sociologists than of anthropologists when they refer to socio-cultural factors (e.g., Bales 1946, Snyder 1958, McCarthy 1959, Pittman 1967).

In the mid-1970s, however, the distinctive contributions that anthropologists could make gained recognition. One crude but useful index of this is the fact that contributions to the encyclopedic five-volume *The Biology of Alcoholism* included Ablon (1976a) on family structure and behavior, a chapter on tribal societies (M. Bacon 1975a), and another on anthropological perspectives (Heath 1965b). An important contribution to acceptance may have been Madsen's *The American Alcoholic* (1974). Better known among clinicians than among the author's anthropological colleagues, this book combines an ambitious multidisciplinary review of the nature–nurture controversy about alcoholism with a detailed study of how and why the self-help group Alcoholics Anonymous seems to be at least as "successful" (in lessening drinking problems) as clinical facilities staffed by various kinds of health professionals. Anthropologists are increasingly being invited to contribute to conferences and anthologies on the subject, and to do research, evaluation, consulting, and related work on alcohol-related topics. One of the few postdoctoral research-training programs sponsored by the US National Institute on Alcohol Abuse and Alcoholism had anthropology at its core,[2] and the venerable Finnish Foundation for Alcohol Studies recently employed an anthropologist (Peltoniemi 1980).

Two areas in which the practical relevance of transcultural understanding are immediate are the provision of services for the health and welfare of minority populations, and assessing the different nature and rates of occurrence of problems among various populations. Early reviews of multiethnic clinical settings (Westermeyer 1974a, 1975a), together with a comparison of how Indian and other populations use alcoholism facilities (Westermeyer and Lang 1975), led to a useful elementary handbook for clinicians (Westermeyer 1976c). Normative approaches were the focus of a conference on the prevention of drinking problems (Harford *et al.* 1980), and the mutual relevance of work by sociocultural researchers and those engaged in treatment of problem drinkers was explored at another (Heath, Waddell and Topper 1981). In the latter connection, Ablon (1979) made a special plea for anthropologists to bring their skills to bear on current social problems.

Without in any way belittling the importance of human suffering that does occasionally stem from toxic or other effects of alcohol, however, it deserves mention that a long-term strength of anthropological studies has been that they have paid attention not only to "alcohol*ism*" but rather to alcohol as an artifact and to the complex of attitudes, values, and actions that are associated with it. A major finding, in cross-cultural perspective, is that alcohol-related problems are really rare, even in many societies where drinking is customary, and drunkenness is commonplace. This simple observation, unsurprising to anthropologists, takes on special significance in contrast with the situation in most Western and other urban and industrialized societies. Researchers, clinicians, and others who pay attention to alcoholic beverages in those contexts focus their attention almost exclusively on pathological outcomes of drinking, whether in terms of economic cost, physical or mental disability, social disruption, or in other terms. The ethnographic viewpoint, therefore, has not only added to our understanding of the range of variation in human beliefs and behaviors with respect to alcohol, but to the fundamental realization that many of the outcomes of its use are mediated by cultural factors rather than chemical, biological, or other pharmaco-physiological factors. Similarly, the importance of drinking as a "normal" (and not necessarily "deviant") behavior has rarely been recognized in other disciplines. The same is true with respect to the fact that drinking can have negligible – or even positive – effects as well as deleterious ones. Such an "unbiased phenomenological approach" has been hailed by a major spokesman in the field of alcohol studies (S. Bacon 1978) as both distinctive and exceptionally promising, especially in contrast with the "problem-emphasis" that dominates in other approaches.

A variety of events in recent years might be interpreted as markers of the coming-of-age of alcohol studies in anthropology. In some fields of study, the publication of a "reader" has been viewed as a milestone: Marshall's (1979a) compilation is welcome for bringing much of the diverse and widely scattered literature on worldwide variant beliefs and behaviors about alcoholic beverages into a convenient volume, and his brief "Conclusions" (pp. 451–47) are sound generalizations based on the diverse human experience with alcohol. It is sometimes also regarded as a critical event when an organization is formed and/or a newsletter issued. An informal Alcohol and Drug Study Group, begun in 1979, affiliated with the American Anthropological Association in 1980; it issues an occasional *Newsletter* (1980–) and promises to thrive under the joint leadership of Genevive Ames, Linda Bennett, and Miriam Rodin. We were fortunate in early having a major bibliographic tool (Popham and Yawney 1967); its updated successor is more thoroughly indexed, to include concepts, theories, and issues as well as peoples and places (Heath and Cooper 1981).

In this chapter, I will briefly review selected publications to show directions in which anthropologically grounded research on alcohol developed between 1970 and 1980, and to illustrate the themes noted in my earlier more comprehensive review: Prehistory and history; "Ethnic groups" in Western societies; Non-Western literate societies; Non-literate societies; Cross-cultural studies; Human biology; Aspects of culture; Theoretical and practical concerns; and Conclusions.

Prehistory and history

A remarkable fact about alcohol is how simple it is to make; the process of fermentation occurs naturally, even without human intervention. Minor refinements assured that wines and beers were developed early in prehistory in many parts of the world, and have been easy to obtain throughout history. Like ethnographers, historians are interested not only in how people have used alcoholic beverages, but also in the diverse and often emotionally loaded roles that such drinks have played in various times and places.

Several highlights in the world history of alcohol are touched on in Tongue's (1978) brief account; Popham (1978) was similarly broad in his history of the tavern as a social institution. The Alcohol and Temperance History Group (1980–   ) has been formed as a network of colleagues with shared interests, and their semi-annual newsletter is a useful guide to publications and research in progress with respect to both drinking and temperance.

A review article on fermented drinks throughout antiquity (Ghalioungui 1979) has broad scope, whereas Darby *et al.* (1977) provide in-depth analysis of beer and wine as part of their comprehensive account of Egyptian foodways. A curious volume purports to prove that the beneficent references to drinking that occur in the Bible all relate to unfermented grape juice (Wilkerson 1978), and Chalke (1978) suggests that people of that time may have already recognized the dangers of woman's drinking while pregnant, citing the mention that Samson's mother had "refrained from drink." Cohen (1974) shows how interpretations of the drunkenness of Noah have changed through time.

Robert Popham has performed a labor-of-love in editing notes left by far-ranging pioneer in alcohol studies, E. M. Jellinek; random comments on drinkers and alcoholics in ancient Rome (Jellinek 1976), and an imaginative suggestion that much of the importance that alcohol has had throughout culture-history may derive from its symbolic association with blood (Jellinek 1977). On the classical period in Greece, a series of papers by O'Brien (especially1980a,b) have met with predictable controversy in their well documented inference that Alexander the Great suffered progressive drinking problems and died in withdrawal. Emboden's (1977) account of the evolution of the cult of Dionysus links intoxication and shamanism, and Stanislawski (1975) adds a dimension of economic geography to that discussion.

Pre-colonial historical studies in Latin America include an analysis of economic, political, and religious meanings of maize beer in the Inca Empire of the Andes region (Morris 1979); similar in scope is Paredes (1975) on the Aztecs, and Gonçalves *et al.* (1977) on the Mayas, both of Mexico and Central America.

On the colonial and modern periods, Lomnitz's (1976) account of the Mapuche Indians in Chile is one of few attempts to trace the changing meanings and uses of alcohol in a non-Western society during four centuries. A detailed and well documented analysis of eighteenth-century Indian peasants in Mexico (Taylor 1979) contradicts many of the stereotypes that have been generally accepted about drinking there, including pre-Columbian prohibition and post-conquest dissipation. The economic strength of Jesuit-managed estates in colonial Peru rested in large part on their production of wine (Cushner 1980).

Historical studies on alcohol in Europe and the United States have often emphasized the political and normative ambivalence that were associated with the movements for temperance and prohibition (e.g., Engelmann 1979, Harrison 1971, Blocker 1979). Others have focused on the saloon as a multipurpose social institution (e.g., West 1979). A broad-brush attempt to portray the United States in its first fifty years as "the alcoholic republic" (Rorabaugh 1979) is interesting, despite simplistic psychologizing and sociologizing. Pinson's (1980) account links socioeconomic class and beverages earlier. An anthology devoted to various aspects of "the black drink," as used by Indians in the southeastern US (Hudson 1979), deserves mention – not because it is an alcoholic beverage, but because so many people seem to think it is. Waddell's (1980a) survey demonstrates the relations between alcoholic and other intoxicants in the aboriginal southwest.

During the 1970s, there were also a few efforts to look at alcohol in historical perspective in other parts of the world. Pan's (1975) synthesis of the literature on colonial Africa will be the cornerstone for any future work, and the work of M. and L. Marshall (1975, 1976) brought diverse sources to bear on the introduction and diffusion of alcohol in Micronesia.

"Ethnic groups" in Western societies

The confusion surrounding "ethnicity" is at least as great in alcohol studies as it is in sociology and anthropology, and it would be redundant to reiterate here my criticism of the logical inconsistency of the categories that are often used (Heath 1975: 7–12). Nevertheless, it would be counterproductive to ignore normal usage when reviewing the literature that is cast in those terms. Although Native American populations (including American Indians and Eskimos), as well as various sub-populations in other parts of the world, are in close and sustained contact with Western societies, they are treated below in a section on "Non-literate societies," as groups who did not have written language before subjection to colonial powers.

The significance of sociocultural factors in relation to drinking and its outcomes is, in the minds of many, vividly demonstrated by the contrast between Jews and Irish Americans. The classic formulation by Bales (1946) has had an enormous impact far beyond academic social science, emphasizing Orthodox intrafamilial introduction of children to wine in a sacred, ritual context in contrast with the Irish pattern in which children are not supposed to drink but adolescents then are confronted with "proving their manhood" in the convivial secular context of the pub.

Since the 1970s, an interesting change has taken place with respect to our view of alcohol and the Jews (Snyder 1978), and the implications are significant in terms of the esteem enjoyed by sociocultural interpretations of drinking. The stereotype that Jews were somehow "immune" to drinking problems has been progressively rejected, as more Jews join Alcoholics Anonymous, seek various kinds of treatment for alcohol-related ills, and so forth. A variety of interpretations have been offered, focusing on this apparent epidemiological shift as an artifact of cultural change (Blume *et al.* 1980), for example: that attenuation of religious orthodoxy has weakened the ritual significance of drinking, that loosening of family ties has undercut the parental norm of moderation in response to peer-pressures for heavier drinking among young people, that Jews have "acculturated" to Gentile patterns of business and sociability in which drinking plays secular roles, that Jewish problem drinkers were around all along but are now more visible as the stigma has lessened, health insurance pays for detoxication and treatment, and so forth. Each of these seems plausible, and systematic research is in order. From an anthropological point of view, however, it is both important and gratifying to note that all of the hypotheses are fundamentally grounded in sociocultural variables. An anthology by Blaine (1980) combines historical and modern perspectives; a recent small-scale survey (Glassner and Berg 1980) fits the earlier patterns, in which religious and symbolic associations were cited as crucial in preventing alcoholism among Jews, although clinical evidence (Blume and Dropkin 1980) supports the view of change. The self-styled "Black Hebrews," migrants from Texas to Israel, appear to have institutionalized sobriety as an important ethnic boundary-marker (M. Singer 1980), and a psychiatrist has suggested that traditional Jewish attitudes toward drinking might fruitfully be taught to others in the interest of preventing alcoholism (Zimberg 1977). In Israel, it was long believed that problem drinking was rare except among Yemenites (Hes 1970), but an international multidisciplinary conference has been convoked in Jerusalem in 1981 to discuss alcohol and other drug issues more broadly.

The Irish tend to be second only to the Jews in terms of the attention paid to their drinking patterns. A basic source is Stivers's (1976) careful social history, including the crucial mass migration to the United States; in more recent decades, hard-drinking in accordance with the stereotype has become a sort of badge of ethnic pride (Stivers 1978). Drinking played various roles in the old country before the famine (Barrett 1978), with moonshining an important part of the peasant economy (Dawson 1977).

Recent community studies show that alcohol-related psychiatric problems are frequent among men in Ireland (Brody 1973, Scheper-Hughes 1979), and Burns (1980) shows continuity of the boisterous pattern among Irish-American adolescents. In chronicling the interpersonal strains in middle-class Irish-American families, Ablon and Cunningham (1981) suggest that heavy-drinking may be as much a symptom as a cause; O'Carroll's (1979) focus on abusive drinking as a reaction to psychosexual and authoritarian tensions imposed by Catholicism may be related.

Spanish-speakers have become a large and vocal segment of the population in many parts of the United States, under various names (Hispanos, Latinos, Hispanics, Chicanos, etc.), and much has been written about the need for adaptation of health and welfare services in ways that would be "culturally congenial." Unfortunately, much of that literature traffics in stereotypes that ignore the considerable diversity found among Spanish-speakers of different national and cultural backgrounds; an outstanding exception to that shortcoming is Gordon's (1981) comparison of Dominicans, Puerto Ricans, and Guatemalans in a US city. A useful anthology was compiled by Trotter and Chavira (1977); selected ethnographic studies include Dobkin and Feldman (1977), M. Gilbert (1978), and Gordon (1978b); and a review of the literature by Hall *et al.* (1977).

Italian-Americans have been important not only because of their numbers in the population, but also because of their traditional widespread use of wine as a workaday beverage. Independent surveys in two cities emphasize changes in drinking patterns over three generations (Blane 1977; Salvatore 1979). Armenian-Americans are of special interest to students of alcohol because virtually all drink but few have alcohol-related problems; normative and attitudinal patterns strikingly similar to those earlier emphasized among Jews are probably salutary (Freund 1979). Polish-American drinking and the role of ethnic social clubs have changed over three generations, in an area of little social mobility (Freund 1980). Recreational use of alcohol and other drugs among Portuguese-American immigrants show different kinds of variation across generations (Cabral 1980).

Comparative ethnic studies pose special methodological problems. The survey approach of Greeley *et al.* (1978, 1980) appears to yield quantitatively rigorous data, except that most of their elaborate series of hypotheses hinge on responses to single questions. Boscarino's (1980) comparison of the differential frequenting of bars by four groups is an imaginative effort in which marketing research supports hunches derived from ethnographic-observational studies.

Non-Western literate societies

Apart from sociocultural consideration, so-called "Mongoloid" populations are of interest in alcohol studies because of the controversy over possible "racial" differences in susceptibility to the physical effects of ethanol, discussed briefly under "Human biology," below. Many anthropologists and others recognize the fallacy of assuming uniformity among populations that are labeled "Islam," "Chinese," "Japanese," and so forth, but such conventional usage continues to dominate in many kinds of writing.

The relation of alcohol to Islam has been of interest because abstinence on religious grounds is important to some Muslims, whereas others wax eloquent about both drinking and drunkenness. A brief volume (Badri 1976) shows minor variations in ideal patterns, focusing on the Koran and related texts, rather than on behavior. Despite strict prohibition, the growth of alcohol-related problems is being recognized in Saudi Arabia (Al-Qthami 1978), and in Bahrein (Alsafar 1974, Magruder 1978).

India's experiment in nationwide prohibition has ended, and attempts by various states appear generally unsuccessful. In a single North Indian village (Shukla 1978), there is marked variation in alcohol use among the castes, ranging from abstinence to many frequent and integral roles in social and ceremonial life.

Some intensive studies of drinking in Japan, both rural and urban, are underway; a brief account views "bar culture" as an alarming response to recent impact of conflicting Western values (Gedig 1979). Drinking in all parts of contemporary China remains undescribed but "traditional" views are reported for Chinese in Hong Kong (K. Singer 1972), including medicinal and social uses, tempered by "Confucian moderation."

Non-literate societies

One of the special strengths of anthropology has been its consistent concern with documenting the range of variation in terms of human experience, revealing beliefs and behaviors that sometimes diverge widely from what is too often naively presumed to be "human nature." The study of alcohol is one of the fields in which selected ethnographic cases have gained widespread familiarity and have often been cited by specialists in other academic disciplines and in clinical and service fields. Part of the reason for this lies in the fact that, although most societies have alcoholic beverages, few have anything that might be called "alcoholism" or even frequent "drinking problems," even when drinking and drunkenness are common. Another part of it lies in the fascinating diversity with which beverage alcohol is regarded sometimes as a food, other times as a tranquilizer, by some groups as a sacred substance and by others as sacrilegious, as an aphrodisiac or as a poison, and so forth. Similarly, some societies embrace drunkenness as a religious state whereas others consider it disgusting; for some it absolves one of responsibility for what would otherwise be serious offenses, and for others it is a crime in itself; or drinking may be viewed as an invaluable aid to sociability at the same time that drunkenness is feared for the violence that accompanies it.

A bibliography on alcohol and world cultures (Heath and Cooper 1981) has the advantage of being thoroughly indexed by place and by "tribal" name as well as by topic. M. Bacon (1976b) explains to non-specialists why this literature is important, and Marshall's anthology (1979a) makes readily accessible much of the best work published since 1960. The books and articles referred to in this section only in gross regional terms are, in many instances, referred to in slightly more detail in subsequent topical and theoretical sections.

On Africa, Pan's (1975) monograph is an outstanding summary of data from the colonial period; Haworth (1980) calls for more studies to complement his own WHO-sponsored survey in Zambia. The important roles of homebrew in native communities were analyzed in some detail for the Uduk (James 1972), the Hide (Eguchi 1975), LoBir (Hagaman 1980), Yoruba (Obayemi 1976), Chiga (Omori 1978), Buganda (Pollnac and Robbins 1972, M. Robbins 1977, M. and L. Robbins 1980); beer gardens in urban South Africa are functionally analogous in many respects (Wolcott 1974, 1975).

Oceania holds special interest because the initial introduction of alcoholic beverages is relatively recent, and the reactions of various populations have been strikingly different. Historical perspective is available for Micronesia (M. Marshall and Marshall 1975, 1976), and parts of Polynesia (Lemert 1976, Gluckman 1974). Helpful bibliographies and a review article distinguish between alcoholic beverages and kava, a traditional drink widespread in Oceania (often mistakenly presumed to be alcoholic) and important in social and ceremonial rituals (M. Marshall 1974, 1976, Freund and Marshall 1977).

Contemporary drinking and associated behavior are often linked with traditional patterns (e.g., Nason 1975, M. Marshall 1979b, T. Schwartz and Romanucci-Ross 1974, Urbanowicz 1975). In Australia, alcohol is often viewed as having a catastrophic impact on the aboriginal population (e.g., Australia 1977), in much the same way as in North America; similarly, alternative interpretations sometimes occur (e.g., Collmann 1979); interethnic variation in drinking and violence is a recent focus in New Zealand (Graves *et al.* 1979a, 1979b). A conference on various aspects of alcohol use among many peoples of Papua New Guinea (summarized in M. Marshall 1981) will contribute substantially to the ethnographic literature.

Concerning tribal populations in Asia, there has been a great deal written about other drugs but little about alcohol in recent years (Rao and Rao 1977, Westermeyer 1971, Shukla 1978).

On Latin America, virtually every ethnography has some allusion to drinking and drunkenness. Increasingly sophisticated methods and more focused research have yielded interesting insights in virtually all regions.

Good examples from the Caribbean include Beaubrun 1975, Angrosino 1974, Manning 1979; from the Andes, Lomnitz 1973, 1976, Medina and Marconi 1970, Heath 1971, Carter 1977, Wagner 1978; on the Chaco, Pagés 1976; from Central America, Prestan 1975, N. Schwartz 1978; and in contemporary Mexico, Kennedy 1978, Kearney 1970, Lutes 1977, Siverts 1972, and Zeiner *et al.* 1979.

As is the case with respect to many other aspects of culture, the literature on native North American peoples is extremely rich on both alcohol use and its policy implications. An outstanding bibliography, well indexed and annotated, makes the literature on Indians of the United States easily accessible (Mail and McDonald 1980). An impressionistic history (R. Thomas 1981) fits more with popular stereotypes (discredited in Westermeyer 1974b) than with the rich ethnographic literature (nicely summarized, e.g. in May 1977, Leland 1980, Heidenreich 1976). An especially ambitious survey (Leland 1976), mustered the data as they refer to several specific criteria of addiction, and discredits "the firewater myth," the widespread belief that Indians are inherently more vulnerable to the intoxicating and debilitating effects of alcohol because of "racial" differences. Brief reviews are also available emphasizing health (Baker 1977) and mental health (Brod 1975).

On Arctic and Sub-Arctic populations, a convenient collection of articles is available (Hamer and Steinbring 1980); a projected worldwide International Arctic Rim Conference on Alcoholism (1978) was not held but the publication of some preliminary drafts of papers signals increasing recognition of problems shared across national boundaries. The Honigmanns (1970) contributed another to their series of excellent analyses of drinking in isolated multiethnic Arctic towns, and a posthumous essay (J. Honigmann 1980) explores the ways in which the evolution of his personal viewpoint allows for alternative interpretations of data collected throughout his professional career. Illustrative of other recent work in the area are Durgin, 1974, Savishinsky 1971, 1977, Kraus and Buffler 1979, and the highly controversial interethnic study of Klausner *et al.* (1979, 1980).

For the Northwest, see Jilek (1974, 1981) and Jilek-Aall (1974, 1981) linking social and psychological views. Various aspects of drinking among different Plains tribes are explored by May 1976, Kenmitzer 1972, Fairbanks 1973, Stratton *et al.* 1978, and others; in the Northeast, see Stevens 1981.

On various Southwestern tribes, a collection of original papers is available (Waddell and Everett 1980), and an unusually detailed comparative study (Levy and Kuntz 1974). Good topical studies include, e.g., Levy and Kunitz 1971a, b, 1981, Leland 1975, Everett 1980, Waddell 1975, 1976a, b, 1979, Ferguson 1976a, b, Nelson 1977, Escalante 1980, Brown 1980.

Cross-cultural studies

Different usages of the term "cross-cultural" persist, as discussed in the earlier review (Heath 1975: 19–23), and drinking remains one of the topics most often studied in terms of controlled comparison and by the correlational "holocultural" methods made feasible by the Human Relations Area Files. M. Bacon provided two brief reviews of the latter approach (1973, 1980), suggested some interesting aspects of sex differences in drinking (1976b), and outlined the "dependency-conflict theory" (1974), showing how drunkenness tends to occur most often in societies that combine indulgent and dependent child-training with demands for individualism and independence among adults. Barry, who collaborated with her on the original dependency study, defended it (1976) against a challenge (summarized in Boyatzis 1976), from McClelland *et al.* (1972), whose "power theory," also cross-cultural in both its derivation and application, stresses that men drink alcoholic beverages in order to assuage their need for feelings of power. Just as many others have raised serious questions about the appropriateness of extrapolating indices that relate to individual psychology and applying them to cultural patterns in other realms of behavior, Mäkelä (1979), is critical of this approach to the interpretation of drinking. Stull (1975) is similarly critical of such studies; in his work on drunkenness and stress, Schaefer (1976) suggested some methodological refinements. With a specific concern to minimize social problems in complex societies, others found that the per-capita level of consumption of absolute alcohol has greater predictive and explanatory value (in relation to the epidemiology of alcohol-related morbidity) than do norms about drinking (summarized in Whitehead and Harvey 1974); that view is expanded and refined, still using holocultural methods, to demonstrate the value of synthesizing "the sociocultural model" with "the distribution-of-consumption model" (Frankel and Whitehead 1981).

An ambitious attempt to collect comparable data on alcohol-related problems has been initiated in Mexico, Zambia, Scotland, United States, and Canada, under the auspices of World Health Organization (Moser 1977). Leland's (1976) survey of North American Indian groups provides little support for the view that they have special susceptibility to alcohol, and Schaefer (1981) agrees, including recent physiological and biochemical studies as well.

Unusual and imaginative efforts at controlled comparison among large and pluralistic cultures, with an emphasis on beliefs and behaviors about alcohol, include Frankel (1980) on China, US, and USSR, and Maghbouleh (1979) on Western Christianity, Hindu-Buddhism, Judaism, and Confucianism. More limited comparisons include Navajo, Hopi, and Apache Indians in southwestern United States (Levy and Kunitz 1974); Navajo, Taos, Papago and Apache in the same area (Waddell 1980c), various

Eskimo populations (J. Honigmann 1980), changes in two Bolivian communities (Heath 1971), and a violent Mexican village with a peaceful one (Cinquemani 1975).

Human biology

Like anthropology, the field of alcohol studies is inherently multidisciplinary, or transdisciplinary. Ethanol, the principal active component in alcoholic beverages of whatever type, is a relatively simple chemical substance, of which the pharmacological properties were thought to be well known until recent years. The fact that its effects on individuals within various populations are so varied has made it an exceptional focus of concern for those who deal with both bio-medical and psycho-social influences and consequences of human behavior.

"Race"

Although some observers are intensely involved in trying to understand differences with respect to the interactive effects of alcohol and behavior among individuals within their own society, others focus on differences among populations. One of the most controversial topics in alcohol studies these days has to do with apparent ethnic variation in sensitivity to the short-term physiological effects of ethanol. A familiar example of this is "the firewater myth," already briefly noted above; although the stereotypical "folk wisdom" was discredited for a while (see, e.g., MacAndrew and Edgerton 1969, Leland 1976), the issue has been reopened in a broader sense. Because detailed reviews of this complex literature are already available (Reed 1978, Schaefer 1979, 1981), it should be sufficient here simply to note that some investigators have reported significant differences between or among populations (such as "Whites," "Orientals," "Indians," "Eskimos," etc.) with respect to the rapidity with which alcohol is metabolized within the body, frequency of subjective discomfort from drinking, increased heart-rate and/or facial flushing in response to alcohol, and so forth. Among those who have noted major physical differences among populations in response to alcohol are Agarwal *et al.* 1981, Fenna *et al.* Farris and Jones 1978, Ewing *et al.* 1974, 1979, Reed *et al.* 1973, 1976, Goedde *et al.* 1979, Mizoi *et al.* 1979, Marinovich *et al.* 1976, Wolff 1972, 1973, Seto *et al.* 1978, Zeiner *et al.* 1979; enzymatic differences are often cited, including differences in quantity or form of endogenous alcohol dehydrogenase; some link physiological differences to psychological attitudes about drinking (e.g., Sanders *et al.* 1980). Among those who found no significant difference are Bennion and Li 1976, Hanna 1978, Schaefer 1978. This kind of research is controversial and has often been clouded by charges of "racism" (Hanna 1976); furthermore, many of the studies are marred by various methodological shortcomings (J. Gilbert and Schaefer 1977, Schaefer 1981). Adams's (1980) imaginative linkage between caffeine and alcohol deserves broader cross-cultural testing.

Nutrition and health

It is ironic that beverage alcohol, abhorred by some peoples as a poison, is embraced by others as a staple food, a specific medicine, or a general tonic. There is no question that large quantities ingested over long periods of time are toxic to several organ systems in the human body, but light or infrequent use can be healthful. An interesting range of data on beliefs and practices that relate alcohol to nutrition and health came to light during the 1970s.

In a worldwide survey of fermented foods, Steinkraus (1979) noted that they often have *in*creased nutritional value in comparison with their components; this occurs through the concentration of proteins from free-floating micro-organisms. Although less detailed in their analyses, several ethnographic and historical observers emphasized the food-value of traditional homebrews: e.g., Hagaman (1980) among the LoBir of Guinea, Morcos and Morcos (1977) on ancient Egypt, Roy (1978) among tribal populations in India, and Spring and Buss (1977) throughout English history.

Changes in drinking patterns can affect health. The US Indian Health Service (1977:1) "considers alcoholism to be one of the most significant and urgent health problems facing the Indian and Alaskan Native people today." Levy and Kunitz (1974) found remarkable continuity of epidemiological indices over a long period of time, however, even among the Navajo who have a reputation for frequent drunkenness and who have a high rate of alcohol-related morbidity and mortality. Kunitz and Levy (1974) point out that the Navajo have adapted the "disease concept of alcoholism," considering heavy drinking to be a symptom – not a root-cause – of illness; with other colleagues, they (Kunitz *et al.* 1971) also showed how contrasting attitudes and patterns of drinking result in markedly different rates of liver cirrhosis among Navajos and Hopis. Cirrhosis is often considered a primary diagnostic feature of alcoholism, not only by physicians in clinical settings but also by epidemiologists as the basis for large-scale estimations of prevalence among populations. For this reason, it is striking that American Indian women (who drink much less than Indian men or whites) have such an unusually high rate of cirrhosis mortality (Johnson 1978, 1979); there is no ready explanation at this time. Most recent studies of health among Eskimos and many general studies of American Indians and Australians Aborigines include at least brief mention of alcohol-related problems as highly visible and presumably important. Emphases include not only physical and mental health but also exceptionally high rates of accidental death, suicide, homicide, arrest, and so forth. Without in any way minimizing the extent of human suffering that does derive from drinking, it seems important to note that most of such viewing-with-alarm is based on brief visits in which no attempt is made to understand the meanings and values that are attached to drinking, or to compare those rates over time. When Levy *et al.* (1969) considered Navajo homicide in historical perspective, for example, they found little change during more than a century in which drinking and drunkenness have increased enormously; similarly, Eskimo suicides may be proportionately no more frequent now than they were before alcohol was introduced (Foulks 1980).

The interrelations of cultural change and alcohol use are not so simple as some might imagine. MacPhail *et al.* (1979) point out that Black South Africans suffer less from iron overload after having switched from homebrew to commercially produced beers. An epidemic of clay-eating among Australian Aboriginal women may have been both an adaptation and a protest when men spent the family food-budget on beer (Eastwell 1979). An interesting historical sidelight is the fact that the concept of addiction emerged within the United States only during the past century, and that it was applied to alcohol before it was extended to other drugs (Levine 1978). The changing use of alcohol as medicine throughout US history is traced by Williams (1980).

Aspects of culture

Many colleagues as well as laypersons have difficulty recognizing the variety of important insights that can be gained from paying attention to alcohol use, even without any special emphasis on alcoholism. As artifacts that are always hedged about with certain prescriptive and proscriptive norms, often the focus of considerable emotion, alcoholic beverages play a wide range of roles in various cultures. For example, where alcohol is an important food, patterns of sharing can help in understanding social organization; symbolic, religious, and other beliefs associated with such beverages are often important. The technology of production is varied, and the substance is often used in economic and political transactions. Communications in alcohol-related contexts can be distinctive, and drinking has a special association with sex and with recreation in many societies. Because alcohol is so intricately imbedded in sociocultural context, it often is revealing to note changes in related beliefs and behaviors. Recent studies illustrative of each of these topics will be noted in this section.[3]

Social organization

The ways in which family organization affects and is affected by alcohol use have been reviewed by Ablon (1976a), who also explored them in some depth among urban middle-class Americans (1976b, with Cunningham 1981). Special emphasis on family rituals as they affect intergenerational transmission of drinking problems, again in urban USA, has been a long-term concern of the multi-disciplinary team of Wolin *et al.* (e.g., 1980). The implication of family in the contrasting patterns of Irish and Jewish drinkers has been noted above, in the section on "'Ethnic groups' in Western societies;" brief notes on "Family and group disruption" follow.

With respect to castes or "ethnic categories," Shukla (1978) outlines differences in the use of alcohol and other drugs by various segments of a highly stratified North Indian village. Public beer-gardens provide a special context where racial segregation is minimized in South Africa (Wolcott 1974), whereas Alcoholics Anonymous ironically serves as a social club for East Indian migrants who do not want to mix with local Blacks in Trinidad (Angrosino 1974). Two communities in Bolivia responded to land reform in ways that resulted in diametrically contrasting shifts in patterns of inter-ethnic drinking, with each changing to what had previously obtained in the other (Heath 1971). Many authors make the point succinctly put by Jilke-Aall (1974:358): "Drinking for an Indian becomes symbolic of white status and prerogatives." Social class implications figure importantly in studies of some public drinking establishments (LeMasters 1975, A. Thomas 1978), and sexual preference in others (e.g., Read 1980). In a Mexican village, the "folk-wisdom" was contradicted when DeWalt (1979) found that heavy drinking was positively correlated with both wealth and adoption of modern methods in agriculture and other realms.

Self-concept and sex roles are themes that recur in varied analyses of drinking. Economic aid may prove detrimental rather than beneficial if it undermines the identity of Naskapi men (R. Robbins 1973). In much the same way, American women may be drinking more recently in response to conflict about their roles (e.g., Beckman 1978), and, in a more general sense, status inconsistency appears to be a good predictor of increased drinking for both sexes (Parker *et al.* 1978). Anomie, sometimes thought to be too imprecise a concept to be helpful in sociocultural analysis, is often cited as part of the context in which native peoples around the world develop drinking problems; Jilek (1981) identifies "anomic depression" as a psychiatric illness and shows how the Salish developed a culturally congenial response. Leland (1978) explores a generally neglected topic, how women respond to men's drinking. The discussion of "Dependence and power" below is relevant in this connection.

Whatever the problems that sometimes result from drinking, the act of drinking is usually viewed as a pleasant and sociable one. In many ethnographic reports, heavy emphasis is laid on the socially integrative functions of alcohol. Among American Indians on Skid Row, Brody (1970) found that drinking "unites Indians as Indians"; in a similar context, bottle-sharing was similarly frequent and socially significant among white "winos"

(Spradley 1970). Among the Buganda, the traditional homebrew is integral to many social relationships in ways that a modern liquor distilled from it is not (M. Robbins 1977). An Australian Aboriginal population use liquor effectively as a means of building social credit (Collmann 1979); so do the Papago (Waddell 1973, 1975) and the Giriama (Parkin 1972). Maize beer "is the most important thread in the loose fabric of LoBir life" (Hagaman 1980: 205), and women earn social status on the basis of their skill at making it. The importance of socialization while drinking is emphasized as providing a sense of *communitas* for Swiss villagers (Gibson and Weinberg 1980), and, similarly, Haas and Joralemon (1978) feel that that aspect deserves more attention from sociologists who ignore it when describing bars, pubs, or taverns. In imaginative culture-historical speculation about the symbolism of drinking, Jellinek (1977:864) even suggests that, "Through drinking together, people are able to identify with each other, to form symbolic blood covenants; by drinking alone, one is able to achieve power, a resurgence of life."

Beliefs and religion

Indigenous alcoholic beverages often play major roles in ritual and other kinds of relations with the supernatural; some examples are described and analyzed by Shukla (1978), James (1972), Hagaman (1980), Omori (1978), Morris (1979), Carter (1977), Parkin (1972), among others. In a generalized discussion of ancient history, Jellinek (1977) suggests that alcoholic beverages may have displaced water and milk in various cultures to become the ritual symbol par excellence, noting that its use gives a feeling of power, and "drunkenness can be a kind of shortcut to the higher life." By contrast, Armenian adherence to an ethic of "the golden mean," emphasizing temperance in all things, may in part account for the low rate of drinking problems among that population where some drinking is virtually universal (Freund 1979). Converts to charismatic sects in the US often abruptly cut their use of alcohol and other drugs (Galanter 1981); conversion to more traditional forms of Protestantism can have the same outcome for Northern Athabascans (Hippler 1974) or for Zapotecs (Kearney 1970), and the Native American Church ("Peyote cult") is therapeutic for many American Indian problem drinkers (Albaugh and Anderson 1974, Pascarosa *et al.* 1976). An account of Apache drinking stresses that certain norms of "proper behavior" are best met in that context (Everett 1980), whereas an account of Passamaquoddy drinking emphasizes that their world view imputes drunkenness to demonic possession (Stevens 1981). Sobriety demanded in connection with a spirit-quest or ceremonial dances sometimes serves, whether by design or not, as an effective indigenous therapy for individuals who had been heavy drinkers (e.g., Jilek 1974, 1981).

Technology

Techniques of production of traditional fermented beverages are often described in considerable detail (e.g., Hagaman 1980, Scourfield 1974), but Desta (1977) in Ethiopia was surprised nevertheless to find alcoholic content close to that of industrially produced beers. Locating the origin of grape wine is cited as remaining "a problem of historical-ecological anthropology" (Forni 1976), but Allchin (1979) suggests that distillation may have begun in India, rather than southwestern Asia as had been generally believed.

Economic and political aspects

Although it is easy to produce, beverage alcohol can also be an important economic good. High value in low volume is an important consideration when raw materials are processed far from markets, and liquids have the additional advantage of easy divisibility. Taxation and/or monopoly can be manipulated by powerful individuals, and the social aspect of most drinking means that it can be used discreetly to create social capital.

All of these considerations and more are nicely analyzed in an Australian Aboriginal setting (Collmann 1979); Waddell makes most of the same points in his cumulative studies on the Papago (esp. 1980b), and others report similar meanings and uses elsewhere (e.g., Bartlett 1980, Suuronen 1973). The impact of economic changes beyond the local community, as relates to alcoholic beverages, can also be various, as described among seventeenth-century Canary Islanders (Steckley 1980), the nineteenth-century Akan (Dumett 1974), Italian and French wine-producers (Loubère 1978) and South Africans (Onselen 1976); temperance movements and Prohibition had longer and deeper impacts on some Western nation-states than is often realized (e.g., Everest 1978, Blocker 1979, Fahey 1980). As the Giriama shifted from palm-wine production, largely a redistributional economic system, to copra for an international market, entrepreneurship accentuated familial and individual differences in wealth (Parkin 1972); much the same thing happened when the Chiga began to sell sorghum rather than using it for the beer that had been so important in intra-community exchanges (Omori 1978).

Communication

Although it has not been tested in cross-cultural perspective, an interesting finding in small groups of US whites is that the rate of drinking varies in direct proportion to the rate of talking *at high rates of talking*, but, at low rates, the relationship is inverse (Burley *et al.* 1978). Elaborate linguistic styles and urban folklore in a Black bar are described by Bell (1975). An unusual effort to trace the role of alcohol through a nation's literature has been undertaken in Poland (Godlewski 1978–   ). The "ethnoscience" approach has been applied to types of beer (Hage 1972), Skid Row inhabitants (Spradley 1970), drinkers (Siverts 1972, Topper 1980), drinking styles (Hill 1980, Leland 1975) and tasks of a cocktail waitress (Spradley and Mann 1975); analysis of "verbal action-plans" illuminates the logic of Navajo drinking (Topper 1976, 1980).

Sex and recreation

Many people seem to consider alcohol to be aphrodisiac in small doses, although it is unequivocally a depressant drug in large amounts. It is also associated with leisure and other forms of recreation in many societies (Lex 1980). One study reverses the stereotypical cause-and-effect relationship and suggests that increased leisure results in increased drinking (Juhász 1973). The links between marihuana, beer, and song are analyzed for the Tsonga (Johnston 1973, Jones 1975). Bach and Schaefer (1979) report that the rate of drinking is inverse to the tempo of country music in some US bars. Drinking and "getting rowdy" are both a pastime and a sort of informal initiation for adolescent Irish-American males (T. Burns 1980); a similar pattern obtains among Athapaskan Indians (K. Little 1979) and among migrants to the city from various Plains Indian groups (Hill 1978). Drinking plays an important part in social clubs of Blacks in Bermuda (Manning 1979), and of Cape Verdeans in USA (Cabral 1980); the commercial bar as a kind of social club can be seen among men who emphasize their homosexuality (Read 1980) or among others who emphasize their "blue-collar" social status (Le Masters 1975, A. Thomas 1978); the "after-hours club" combining illegal drinking with sexual liaison is presumably a widespread urban phenomenon but the nearest we have to a description in social science terms is in USA (Roebuck and Frese 1976).

Change

As with any other aspect of culture, drinking and its associated meanings and values are subject to change, whether by indigenous dynamics or in response to intrusive forces.

In much of the ethnographic literature, there is an emphasis on the ways in which transcultural contacts have influenced drinking, with sharp increases in alcohol consumption often associated with pressures of acculturation, deculturation, and so forth. Many writers do little more than describe a variety of alcohol-related problems in a community, presuming that they are either new or recently increasing, and uncritically attribute them to "cultural stress," "anomie," or some such. American Indians, unskilled and having difficulty adjusting to an alien ambience, often drink heavily and are arrested for public drunkenness or other alcohol-related offenses (e.g., Ablon 1971, Brod 1975, Waddell 1976b). This idea is developed in somewhat more detail by Jilek (1981), who describes "anomic depression" and how people medicate themselves with alcohol. Also relevant in this context is the fact that some of the bars which are almost exclusively frequented by Indians serve a variety of informational and adaptive functions for clients who have recently migrated to the city (Price 1975, Fiske 1979).

One long-term observer of contemporary Eskimo life suggested that fundamental structural aspects of the international economic system may be operating to increase drinking problems among dependent peoples, pointing to *lumpenproletarianization*, alienation from the means of production (Brody 1977). Although application of that terminology is new in such a context, alcohol was used as a tool of colonial conquest by the Dutch in South Africa (Onselen 1976), English and Americans on the North American frontier (Mosher 1975, Heaston 1971), and others. "Cultural imperialism" from the West is even cited as an explanation of the sharp increase in alcohol-related problems in postwar Japan (Gedig 1979). The "frontier mentality" is viewed as part of the reason why all of the groups in culturally pluralistic new towns in the Arctic drink so heavily (Honigmann and Honigmann 1970).

Obviously, not all changes in drinking patterns are deleterious, however. Adolescent Navajo males drink in ways that combine old ways with new ones copied from Anglos (Topper 1974); their age-mates on Truk engage in drinking-parties that Marshall (1979b) views as a functional substitute for traditional war. Among some immigrant groups, studies over three generations reveal a gradient of change in both consumption and ideas about alcoholic beverages (Blane 1977, Salvatore 1979, Freund 1980). Even migrants to USA sometimes drink less rather than more (Gordon 1978b); the same author (1981) shows how changes in drinking patterns are by no means uniform among "Hispanics," but vary markedly among men from Dominican Republic, Guatemala, and Puerto Rico. Although Irish-American drinking patterns and their outcomes are similar to ancestral ways, the rationale seems to have shifted markedly (Stivers 1976, 1978). Economic and nutritional changes that have affected or been affected by small-scale domestic production of alcoholic beverages have already been discussed above, as have long-term historical studies. Occasional cases illustrate that drinking, like any other learned behavior, may be subject to short-term change as well (e.g., Heath 1971).

Theoretical and practical concerns

Thematic and conceptual categories differ markedly within the discipline of anthropology, and in the emerging field of alcohol studies. In attempting to review recent developments in some of the most important categories from the point of view of each, I will pay special attention to "social problems" because they are a focus of concern to many who deal with drinkers, and to symbolism as a broad category that should interest some anthropologists who might otherwise doubt that drinking had any relevance to them, at least in academic terms. Brief notes on epidemiology show how anthropological perspectives have sometimes been helpful and sometimes grossly misunderstood in relation to public health. The subheadings "Ambivalence," "Functional interpretations," and "Dependence and power" relate to concepts, theories, or approaches to the understanding of alcohol and human behavior, with respect to which social and behavioral scientists have had considerable impact in a field that is largely dominated by biological and medical specialists.

"Social problems"

It is a striking pattern that most non-anthropological writers who deal with alcohol tend to focus primarily on various problems that they consider derive from its use, whereas most anthropologists tend to focus more on the use. This does *not*, as some might imagine, reflect a difference between "practical" and "scientific" approaches, or between "applied" and "pure" concerns. It results at least as much from the often ignored fact that most societies that use alcohol are virtually free of alcohol-related troubles. For that matter, even the most pessimistic estimates are that no more than 10 percent of those in the United States who drink have serious problems as a result. In smaller societies, with fewer technological and other hazards and with relatively lower-proof beverages – quite apart from any question of "norms," "social integration," and so forth – it is rare to find people who feel that drinking causes problems. This does not, of course, deter well intentioned outsiders from being concerned about alcohol-related problems. For example, the boisterous behavior that many Indians enjoy (Hill 1978, K. Little 1979) is viewed with alarm by many others. Too few studies have attempted to discern what kinds of events or symptoms are labeled problematic by various populations (Heath 1981); exceptions to this include Hill (1980), Westermeyer (1981), Lang (1979).

A variety of economic, political, and acculturational stresses and outcomes have been described above, but it seems not particularly helpful to attempt to attribute any significant portion of them to drinking or drunken comportment. The World Health Organization's first multinational study on drinking focuses on "Community Responses to Alcohol-Related Problems" (Moser 1977). The cultural insensitivity of a psychiatric consultant to that program is reflected in his title "Drinking problems putting the Third World on the map" (Edwards 1979).

Aggression and criminality. An important and recurrent theme emphasized by anthropologists in this connection is the caveat that statistical data distort both the nature and scale of such problems. A simple illustration has to do with the "alarming" fact that over half of arrests of American Indians are alcohol-related. This becomes much less alarming when one recognizes a number of other relevant facts (summarized in Mail 1980). Indian reservations were given local option when Federal prohibition of alcoholic beverages to Indians was finally repealed in 1953, and most voted to remain "dry" (Fuller, 1975, P. May 1976). This means that mere possession of a beer is a crime. Similarly, the custom of drinking outdoors makes Indians especially liable to arrest where the minor crime of "drinking in public" is enforced – and racial prejudice may sometimes be expressed that way by White policemen. The pattern of always emptying a bottle (rather than saving any contents) may increase the frequency of public inebriation (a crime in many jurisdictions); ironically, another contributing factor may well be the habit of drinking fast to avoid detection.

This is not to deny that some important crimes are highly correlated with drinking. Some of the most vocal critics of Prohibition, wherever it has been attempted, have been primarily concerned that, unless strictly enforced, it can become a model for popular disregard of law. The failure of police to control moonshining in Ireland (Dawson 1977) or in Canada (Gervais 1978), or to control rum-running in USA (Englemann 1979, Kobler 1973) were important factors leading to the liberalization of access.

It is often presumed that rates of homicide and suicide increase as alcohol consumption increases within a population, although evidence for this is not compelling in most nation-states, nor among native populations that are well documented (e.g., Levy and Kunitz 1974, Westermeyer and Brantner 1972). A comparison of "wet" and "dry" Indian reservations in the United States showed that those where alcohol was legally available have *lower* rates than those where it was banned (P. May 1976). In colonial Mexico, drunkenness was alleged in a few homicides – although some peasant defendents appear to have claimed it as an extenuating factor (Taylor 1979). Those who have paid special attention to homicide and suicide in various sociocultural contexts emphasize that they see no reason to posit any causal link on the basis of the high frequency with which victims have alcohol in their blood. It is not clear to what extent alcohol is justifiedly implicated in many instances of deviant behavior, or to what extent people take advantage of "time-out," the cultural convention that accepts drunken comportment that deviates – within limits – from usual norms of behavior (MacAndrew and Edgerton 1969, Hill 1978). Among contemporary Eskimos, it has been suggested that alcohol may "allow the expression of denied pent-up interpersonal hostilities which are usually repressed" (Foulks 1980: 158); it is not clear what light Wolf's (1980) ethically questionable experiment shed on this.

In many Western cultures, there is a frequent association also between alcohol and aggression, whether expressed verbally or physically. Although this is the case in relatively few other cultures, it is invariably a focus of attention where it occurs. The general hypothesis that men's principal reason for drinking is to satisfy their need for a feeling of power (McClelland *et al.* 1972) might lead us to expect more alcohol-related aggression, but a tempering factor may lie in Boyatzis's (1975) suggestion that distilled liquor makes men more violent than fermented beverages, even when the blood-alcohol level is the same.[4]

Among Hare Indians, the cultural form favoring emotional suppression is interpreted as resulting in the explosive expression of aggression when men go on occasional binges (Savishinsky 1971). Several other Native American and Native Canadian populations, including various Indian tribes, Eskimos, and Aleuts by whatever designation, are summarily said to have a similar pattern, although documentation is often lacking, and it is difficult to evaluate such comments when they occur in association with other stereotypic statements that are patently inaccurate.

Aggression is common enough in public drinking places in urban New Zealand that investigators focused on inter-ethnic variation (Graves *et al.* 1979 a,b). In the US, ethnicity was not significant among the several factors that Graham *et al.* (1980) analyzed in relating frequency of aggressive acts to barroom environments. The links between drinking and violence are explored in Mesoamerica (Cinquemani 1975), and Trukese drinking parties are described as a functional replacement for war (Marshall 1979b).

Familial and group disruption. This category is, in a sense, the obverse of an earlier discussion of the socially integrative functions of drinking. Again, it may be an ethnocentric bias, based on the dismal evidence of Western urban societies, that has led many students of alcohol to expect that problems of social relations will loom large in the study of drinking. As with so many of the other "social problems," familial and group disruption may loom much larger in the eye of a short-term visitor from a Western culture than among members of an integral community.

Because drinking is, for most people in the world, inherently a social act, the progressive isolation that typifies the stereotypical Western alcoholic rarely occurs elsewhere, and drinking and drunkenness more often conform to known and shared norms. Nevertheless, when culturally inappropriate drinking or drunken comportment does occur, it unquestionably strains the social fabric, especially when it results in economic or other deprivations for kin and others. Among the Cheyenne and Arapaho, for example, frequent drunkenness and neglect on the part of parents seem to result in severe emotional deprivation among children (Albaugh and Albaugh 1979). On Truk, the issue of prohibition became an important focus of conflict between young men and the elders (M. Marshall 1975).

A striking indirect support for the ethnologist's generalization that – in worldwide perspective – familial and group disruption are rare in relation to drinking derives from a microcosmic study that was phrased in somewhat different terms. When comparing the rate of incidence of alcohol-related problems (of various kinds) among several Indian tribes in Oklahoma, Stratton *et al.* (1978) found that they occur in inverse proportion to the "communal orientation" of the tribal cultures.

Anxiety, anomie, tension. Ever since the first holocultural study based on what have become the Human Relations Area Files, many colleagues in other disciplines who know little else about anthropology accept the finding that *"the primary function of alcoholic beverages in all societies is the reduction of anxiety"* (Horton 1943: 223, italicized in original). Although his methodology was weak, and his conclusions have subsequently been challenged with considerable success (for a review, see Schaefer 1976), psychological and sociological evidence lends varied support for the proposition that a cardinal value of alcohol is as a tranquilizer. As such, it has many advantages: it is relatively inexpensive, easy to administer in doses that most people readily learn to estimate with considerable accuracy, and is both non-addictive and relatively harmless when taken in small quantities (i.e., under 3 oz. daily). In support of his thesis that optimism has strong evolutionary value, Tiger (1979) also suggested that intoxicants are universally valued for their ability to relieve stress.

Although anthropologists rarely make specific reference to Horton's thesis or to "the tension-reduction hypothesis," as do other professionals in alcohol studies, they often write as if such a view were axiomatic. Beyond the several cases mentioned above with reference to migration, acculturation, and other kinds of stress, several populations are said to drink heavily in response to anxiety, anomie, and tension from various sources. Among the Lumbees, migrants are said to drink more because of the stress of urban life and job-dissatisfaction (Beltrame and McQueen 1979); among various Alaskan Native populations, the stresses of "population size," "cash economy," and "Westernization" are cited (Foulks and Katz 1973); Eastern Cherokees are similarly distressed (French and Hornbuckle 1979); Australian Aborigines as "marginal men" (Lickiss 1971); various urban Indians in Chicago (Littman 1970), and so forth.

A few interesting exceptions to the pattern are noteworthy, including Taylor's (1979) well documented refutation of the widely held view that Mexican Indian communities disintegrated after the Spanish conquest and that a majority of the peasants were hopelessly and aimlessly drunk for years. Some observers were surprised when Levy and Kunitz (1974) demonstrated that "degree of acculturation" did not correlate significantly with quantity or frequency of drinking among Navajos; Stull (1973) explicitly rejects the popular assumption that individuals labeled "modern" differ in drinking from "traditionals," citing evidence from the Papago.

The role of anomie becomes especially important when one addresses the issue of culturally congenial programming of health services. It is widely recognized that efforts at prevention, diagnosis, and treatment of drinking problems should be adjusted in relation to the sociocultural context of the clientele (Heath, Waddell, and Topper 1981). Only recently, however, have there been varied and sustained efforts on the part of public agencies to make them available (e.g., Ferguson 1976b, Shore and Fumetti 1972, Trotter and Chavira 1977, Westermeyer 1976c). Unfortunately, even with the best intentions, "hidden agendas" often interfere with the efficacy of such efforts (Levy and Kunitz 1981). Another important development in this connection is the increasing recognition of the values of indigenous therapies (e.g., Trotter 1979, Jilek 1981, Pascarosa and Futterman 1976), and of inventive reworkings of institutions *by* members of other cultures (e.g., Jilek-Aall 1981, Hippler 1974).

Symbolism

Whatever reason people may have for drinking alcoholic beverages, few would say – and fewer believe – that thirst plays a major role in many societies. In part, it was the associated meanings that brought alcohol to the attention of ethnographers long before anyone set out to conduct research with drinking as a conceptual or theoretic focus of concern.

An imaginative "just-so story" approach to the symbolism of alcohol in broad culture-historical perspective was offered by Jellinek (1977), who posits it as successor to water and blood as the quintessential symbol, "the stream of life." His account is not just hypothetical; plausible linkages are made to toasting, the obligation to accept a proffered drink, and other wide-spread and emotionally charged customs. Related to this view, although somewhat less global, is Emboden's (1977) account of the evolution of the cult of Dionysus, emphasizing links between the god of wine and shaman-istic traditions.

The implication of alcoholic beverages in religious symbolism is by no means limited to societies in which the substance itself is deified, however. Carter (1977) calls drinking a foundation of sacred ritual among the Aymara; beer is an offering and has other sacred values among the LoBir (Hagaman 1980), and the Quechua (C. Wagner 1978); cactus wine is focal to Papago rain ceremonies (Waddell 1976a); and so forth. It is no surprise that religion is also the basis for strongly negative views toward alcohol in some groups: the Native American Church ("Peyote cult"; Pascarosa *et al.* 1976), Unification Church ("the Moonies"; Galanter 1981), and a number of ascetic Protestant sects which managed to equate it with "evil" among several Micronesian populations (M. Marshall and Marshall 1976):

We have already referred to alcohol as an ideal prestation from aspiring low-level patrons in small communities (e.g., Waddell 1980b, Collmann 1979); it is similarly an important part of the balanced reciprocity that often obtains in parties associated with reciprocal labor-exchange (e.g., Haga-man 1980, Kennedy 1978).

Not all symbolic associations are unequivocal, however, and ambivalence is often reflected in the meanings attributed to alcohol. Maghbouleh (1979) relates attitudes toward alcohol to attitudes toward witchcraft and asceticism in Western Christianity, Hindu-Buddhism, Judaism, and Confucianism. Although drinking and drunkenness are accepted among the Cheyenne, they refer to "the drunk" as a bogey-man to intimidate children (A. Strauss 1977). Within Western cultures, strong love–hate/vitality–death feelings are expressed with respect to alcohol in country and rock music (Beckley and Chalfant 1979), and implied in Finnish films (Partanen 1980), British and US films and television shows (Cook and Lewington 1979, Lowery 1980), and in advertising (e.g., Key 1973).

Epidemiology

There is a vast literature on the epidemiology of alcoholism, but little of it has direct bearing on sociocultural concepts or methods (Lint 1976). Some of the more dramatic formulations are of interest as, for example, the assertion that alcoholism is "one of the most significant and urgent health problems facing the Indian and Alaskan Native People today" (US Indian Health Service 1971:1).

Many anthropologists, in recent years, have become co-opted into what they believe is an overwhelming preoccupation with quantification in behavioral research. Without in any way denigrating the potential value and importance of quantitative data in some respects, it seems important also to point out that qualitative data also have potential value and importance. What may not be so widely recognized and appreciated is the fact that colleagues in many other disciplines are increasingly turning to non-quantitative methods and data (Heath 1980a,b). Illustrative of this is recent experimentation with "the informant method" for estimating the prevalence of alcohol-related problems within a population (Smart *et al.* 1980). Based on directed interviews with a panel of key-informants, this "novel" approach is being hailed in alcohol studies for both economy and efficiency – in comparison with social surveys – in dealing with populations of various sizes (Bonilla *et al.* 1979, Liban and Smart [1980]). Anthropologists might wonder why epidemiological methods are so important in alcohol studies; whereas most anthropologists who study alcohol tend to focus on belief and behavior, paying at least as much attention to "normal" as to "deviant" patterns, most others who study alcohol tend to focus on "alcoholism," variously defined, by implying that habitual drinking is invariably associated with some kind of problem or kinds of problems.

An unforeseeable outcome of this difference has been discussion, in recent years, of a supposed controversy between those who subscribe to "the sociocultural model" and defenders of "the distribution-of-consumption model," alternately called "the single-consumption model."

For many years, most practitioners of "the sociocultural model" conceived of it as a model for understanding beliefs and practices related to alcohol use, with an emphasis on norms, attitudes, values, and socialization to them (see, e.g., Heath 1978, 1980c; Parker and Harman 1978, 1980; Parker *et al.* 1978). Such a model seems appropriate for understanding customary drinking patterns in any society, regardless of what degree of prevalence or importance "problem-drinking" or "drinking problems" may have with respect to a given population. By contrast, practitioners of "the distribution-of-consumption model" viewed that as a model for understanding the prevalence of "problem drinking" within a population, with a universally applicable mathematical formula yielding neat quantitative results regardless of any specific details about alcohol use and related norms (see, e.g., Lint 1976, Schmidt and Popham 1978, 1980). They hold that the per-capita consumption of alcohol follows a log-normal ("reverse-J" curve in every population, so that as total consumption increases, so do the averages (mean, mode, and median).

The supposed controversy centers on the relative efficacy of "the sociocultural model" and "the distribution-of-consumption model" as guidelines for "prevention" (a code-word in alcohol studies that can be glossed approximately as "lessening the deleterious effects of drinking"). Those who have made substantive contributions in terms of "the sociocultural model" have, in fact, rarely made prescriptive (or proscriptive) recommendations with respect to the manipulation of drinking practices. Some others have done so, however, with reference to data collected and described in terms of "the sociocultural model," and they have emphasized education about alcohol, easier access to it, and a diminished mystique about it as being effective ways of lessening the occurrence of drinking problems. These guidelines have been dismissed as naive and idealistic by some critics (e.g., Whitehead and Harvey 1974, Mäkelä 1975, Frankel and Whitehead 1981). Those same critics are more impressed by the apparent simplicity and surety that, to lessen the damaging effects of alcohol, overall consumption should be decreased. Taxation, rationing, price-indexing, fewer outlets and shorter hours for sales, and other restrictive regulations are recommended by adherents to "the distribution-of-consumption model."

All of this might seem irrelevant to a discussion of "Epidemiology" if it weren't for the fact that "the single distribution model" with which there is ostensibly a controversy, has been used as basis for a mathematical formula to estimate the number of alcoholics within a population. It is awkward to defend oneself against things one never said, but anthropologists who are not familiar with this peculiar and narrow usage of the term "socio-cultural model" should be forewarned.

A solid contribution to epidemiological methods that better fits what most anthropologists would think of as a sociocultural model is Westermeyer's (1976b) experiment using a variety of social indicators as indirect indices of alcohol-related problems among American Indians.

In spite of the anomalous nature of much of the material discussed here, there are some interesting studies that relate epidemiology of drinking problems to other sociocultural factors (e.g., Stratton *et al.* 1978, Kunitz *et al.* 1971). There are also studies that relate the occurrence of other diseases to alcohol consumption (e.g., Fritz 1976, Dobkin de Rios 1979) as well as some that link homicide, suicide, and other forms of violence with drinking (e.g., Klausner *et al.* 1980, P. May 1976).

Ambivalence

To a readership interested in anthropological, sociological, and transcultural psychiatric perspectives, it may seem strange to have such a topical heading in the context of the others used in this chapter, but it is conceptually significant in the history of alcohol studies. Among the few explicit and unequivocal hypotheses offered to account for different incidence of alcohol-related pathologies in societies, most have emphasized a normative viewpoint. For example, ". . . in any group or society in which the drinking customs, values, and sanctions – together with the attitudes of all segments of the group or society – are well established, known to and agreed upon by all, and are consistent with the rest of the culture, the rate of alcoholism will be low" (Ullman 1958: 50, italicized in original). An important qualification was added to that statement by Blacker (1966: 68) who inserted before the mention of rate, ". . . and are characterized by prescriptions for moderate drinking and proscriptions against excessive drinking." In an attempt to reconcile these views (which they linked with several other works that described drinking patterns in normative terms) under the rubric "sociocultural model" on the one hand, with the "single consumption model" (see "Epidemiology," above) on the other, Whitehead and Harvey (1974:63) added yet another qualification to the Ullman–Blacker formulation, specifying ". . . norms (social, legal, etc.) that keep per-capita consumption low enough that few persons in that society will consume in excess of 10 cl. of absolute alcohol per day."

Another sociologist may have laid the idea to rest (Room 1976) with his reminder that the values and attitudes in question have never been seriously addressed by researchers, and that the consensus implied in those formulations probably never prevails anyway. It is also salient that many societies which unambivalently endorse drinking and some which also approve of drunkenness are fearful or suspicious of what drunks may do to themselves or to others; a couple of examples are the Papago (Waddell 1973) and the Winnebago and Santee (Hill 1974).

And there is probably as much profound truth as there is wry humor in Mäkelä's (1975:345) observation that "alcohol research as a behavioral science is particularly active in ambivalent societies," by which he meant those in which attitudes toward drinking and drunkenness are unclear or inconsistent.

Functional interpretations

As unfashionable as it may be in sociology, anthropology and psychiatry today, it would be misleading not to discuss the important role that functional interpretations continue to play in many discussions about alcohol and human behavior. It may be significant that *explicitly* functional interpretations are offered with relatively less frequency than was the case before 1970, but the theme remains a major one in implicit terms.

Authors use various terminologies, but a strain of functional bias prevails, whether from the perspective of the individual actor or of the sociocultural system. For example, anthropologists on hand to observe the first legal drinking on Manus had been told by local Whites that it would wreak havoc with traditional values, but they found remarkable "fit" instead (Schwartz and Romanucci-Ross 1974). On Eta in Micronesia, drinking parties are an "integral part of life," despite official sanctions against them, and an anthropologist describes how they preserve traditional values and provide an outlet for tensions caused by political and social change (Nason 1975). In Australia, "Heavy alcohol intake was a partly adaptive response to the life problems of Aborigines" (Kamien 1975: 297). Among the Tarahumara, institutionalized beer-exchange is important in so many aspects of human relations that a multidisciplinary team called it "a specifically biosocial adaptation" (Paredes *et al.* 1970). After reviewing the extensive literature on alcoholism as a mental health problem among Native Americans, Brod (1975) concluded that the crucial individual motive is that "drunkenness can provide fantasy solutions to culture-bound problems." Also with reference to American Indians, Littman (1970) offers the view – heretical among most recovering alcoholics and treatment personnel – that abstinence may not be an appropriate goal of treatment inasmuch as alcohol "promotes psychological and social integration in an alien culture."

Illustrative of mixed feelings is an author who explicitly rejects a "functionalist" approach in favor of an "interactionist" one, in order to demonstrate that heavy drinking is not necessarily problematic as is usually presumed, but rather ". . . heavy drinking is, in many ways, functional for the drinker" (Brissett 1978:8). Although much has been written about the functions of drinking, and some about the functions (for the drinker) of drunkenness, Dennis (1975) is probably the first to analyze in any detail the functions (for the community) of drunken individuals; in a Zapotec town, he skillfully shows how they play various politically and dramaturgically significant roles.

Dependence and power

There was an era in anthropology, within living memory, when key controversies were closely followed even by those whose major interests were not crucially affected by either side. In contemporary alcohol studies, such a controversy is sometimes attributed to those who point to "dependency vs. power" as alternative primary motives for heavy drinking. Such a phrasing does violence to the formulation of M. Bacon *et al.* (1965), whose careful cross-cultural study emphasized "conflict over dependency" (resulting from permissive-dependent child-training followed by demands that one act independently later in life) as highly correlated with drunkenness. The "power" side of the supposed controversy is not misrepresented: McClelland *et al.* (1972: 334) put it very succinctly: "Men drink primarily to feel stronger. Those for whom personalized power is a particular concern drink more heavily."

When invited to compare and contrast the viewpoints, Barry (1976) and Boyatzis (1976) agreed that complementarity obtains, rather than conflict or contrast. M. Bacon (1974) summarized the dependency-conflict research, and also pointed out some other interesting insights that had come from that project but that have been generally ignored (1976b). An analysis of drinking among Australian Aborigines is among the few that specifically cites the relevance of that view (Lickiss 1971). The Papago are said to use alcohol to maximize personal power with an ethos of egalitarianism support (Waddell 1975), and some Australian Aborigines seem to also (Collmann 1979). The Salish say they drink to feel "power from outside," and consider it symbolic of White status and prerogatives (Jilek-Aall 1974: 358); Cutter *et al.* (1973:389) suggest that "inhibition is more important than power in predicting drinking behavior."

Conclusions

In one sense, a chapter such as this may be used primarily as a guide to the bibliography on certain limited topics. In another sense, it can be useful as an introduction to some of the important concepts and issues that link alcohol and human behavior. The dense patchwork of brief allusions to a great many sources, without careful discussion of any, often results in a paper that is useful to some individuals, interesting to a few and significant only in terms of the author's time-budget. But one who has digested this vast and diverse corpus should be able to articulate at least a few important points about the relevance of alcohol studies to anthropology, promising directions for future work in the field, and some implications that ought to be of interest to behavioral scientists and to health service practitioners as well.

Despite the significant increase in societies among which drinking beliefs and behaviors have been described, there is no reason to revise some of the most significant generalizations that derive from cross-cultural study of the subject:

1   In most societies, drinking is essentially a social act and, as such, it is embedded in a context of values, attitudes, and other norms.
2   These values, attitudes, and other norms constitute important socio-cultural factors that influence the effects of drinking, regardless of how important biochemical, physiological, and pharmacokinetic factors may also be in that respect.
3   The drinking of alcoholic beverages tends to be hedged about with rules concerning who may and may not drink how much of what, in what contexts, in the company of whom, and so forth. Often such rules are the focus of exceptionally strong emotions and sanctions.
4   The value of alcohol for promoting relaxation and sociability is empha-sized in many populations.
5   The association of drinking with any kind of specifically associated problems – physical, economic, psychological, social relational, or other – is rare among cultures throughout both history and the con-temporary world.
6   When alcohol-related problems do occur, they are clearly linked with modalities of drinking, and usually also with values, attitudes, and norms about drinking.
7   Attempts at Prohibition have never been successful except when couched in terms of sacred or supernatural rules.

It is gratifying that "observational methods" were considered important enough to be included in planning for the WHO multinational study of alcohol-related problems (Heath 1977), and "the ethnographic method" has been widely endorsed – by administrators and policy-makers as well as by social scientists – as able to provide valuable data that would not otherwise be available with respect to alcohol and other drugs (Akins and Beschner 1980). These facts suggest that one of the traditional strengths of anthropology may be better appreciated by others than it is by some col-leagues within the discipline (Heath 1980a). The value of quantitative data may again be appreciated by more anthropologists as the newly founded National Institute on Ethnography and Social Policy issues a newsletter and becomes an effective interest-group. It was a sociologist who praised the contribution of anthropologists to alcohol studies as evoking "... an almost unusual optimism that scholarship based upon logics and data, rather than upon stereotypes of special disciplines or popular belief, can in fact emerge in this subject-matter field" (S. Bacon 1978:146).

It is also gratifying that more anthropologists are paying attention to al-cohol and its diverse meanings and roles in cultures, and that some are suf-ficiently interested to learn about other approaches so that transdisciplinary

communication is enhanced and multidisciplinary collaboration is facilitated. This is not to imply that "alcohology" should become a new subdisci-
pline within anthropology, but that more and better contributions to the
literature result in more and better opportunities for anthropologists to
work on a subject that is of increasing interest to a wide range of public and
private agencies throughout the world.

It also seems appropriate in this context to mention a few specific gaps
that remain in the literature, and questions that remain important. Despite
the continuing importance that is placed on drinking and drunkenness as
learned behaviors, there have been few attempts to study in detail the ways
in which young people learn what they do "know" about alcohol and its
effects. In those countries where social surveys are commonplace, increasing numbers of questionnaire-surveys reveal increasingly early and more
frequent drinking on the part of young people, and some questions are
raised about the relative impact of parental and peer modeling and
responses, but the processes of enculturation on the subject are almost
never addressed.

The nature of "addiction" has been given much less attention in this context than would be the case if I were addressing another readership. It is
probably significant that, in a few societies, some individuals appear to be
physically and/or psychologically dependent on alcohol, to the extent that
they suffer the withdrawal syndrome if deprived of it. The physiology of this
was thought to be understood, until a few years ago, but it is again highly
controversial. Related to this is the issue of "commonality," exploring what
there may be in common among those behaviors that are often called
"addictions" or "like addictions," including gambling, heavy eating, and so
forth; the anthropological view that this is a meaningless question (Agar
1981) has not yet had much impact.

"The racial question" in alcohol studies involves the sorting out of biological, pharmacological, and nutritional factors on the one hand, and
psychological and sociological factors on the other, an ideal context for collaboration between anthropologists and biomedical researchers. The fact
that possible "racial" differences in tolerance to alcohol are again highly
controversial – after a brief period (about 1945–70) in which recognition of
significant cultural differences drew attention away from such concerns –
raises questions that are of interest in terms of intellectual history as well as
in terms of the interplay of genetic and sociocultural factors. It is ironic that
a rigorous genealogical analysis within a meaningful breeding-population
has not yet been used, despite meticulous attention to various kinds of
"hard science" indicators such as genetic markers, sophisticated analysis of
physiochemistry of the subjects, and so forth; for that matter, dietary factors have also been inappropriately ignored in most such studies.

Although the obvious link is rarely made in the alcohol literature, the
same complex interplay of "nature and nurture" is important in addressing

the question of heritability of alcoholism, which unquestionably "runs in families." Far from being neglected, the subject has received considerable attention, but the most systematic research has been comparison of twins who had been reared apart from their parents and from each other. The work by Wolin and his colleagues (e.g., 1980) on intra-family dynamics is an imaginative new approach to this question; anthropologists who devise others would find a receptive hearing.

Those who are not familiar with the literature may be surprised at how few data are available in terms of microscopic descriptions of drinking and related behavior. Many of the ethnographic studies, useful as they are for comparative purposes, have the typical limitation of being cast in terms of modal patterns, sometimes with little attention to the range of variation. This is as true within the heavily studied Western societies as it is in others so that, for example, we know little about how fully 30 percent of adults in the United States, who do not have more than one drink per year, manage to abstain in an ambience that is often characterized as strongly favoring drinking. For that matter, neither do we know much about some issues that medical anthropology should be able to illuminate such as how a significant portion of problem drinkers manage to conceal much of their drinking and many of their problems until some critical event (Topper 1981); physicians, counselors, and other treatment-oriented personnel agree that early identification would be enormously helpful but that it is extremely rare. Presumably anthropological approaches could have immediate practical value in identifying behavioral symptoms and adaptive strategies that could serve as early-warning signals; on the pros and cons of cultural relativity in alcohol studies, see Waddell 1981.

In fact, there is enormous variation in the nature of "drinking problems." The fact that the American Medical Association ((1956) resolved to label "alcoholism" a "disease" or "illness," and later (1980) a "handicap" or "disability" has diminished the relevance of sociocultural factors from the point of view of many who find such resolutions helpful in diminishing the stigma that was often associated with alcohol-related troubles. Whatever the economic, political, and ideological values of "the disease concept" and "the handicap concept" may be, individuals who seek help for themselves or for persons close to them seem most concerned with specific kinds of "inappropriate" behavior, and, although few alcoholics claim to be "cured," many have learned to alter their behavior in ways that they and others find more congenial. If we knew more about the several kinds of behavior that various populations identify as problematic, programs of education and prevention might be more effective, treatment facilities could reach out to clients before enormous damage had been done, and so forth. It is evident that the "establishment" views about the nature of drinking problems are often markedly discrepant from popular views, and those anthropologists who have pressed to point out the differences have had significant impact, even in the face of massive bureaucracy (e.g., Spradley 1970).

The emphasis on practical applications of anthropology to alcohol-related problems reflects both a recognition that drinking is often implicated in a variety of economic, psychological, and social as well as physical pathologies especially in societies where commercially produced beverages are readily available. It also reflects a series of concerns that have been articulated by various populations, but that few anthropologists have addressed; this means that work on those subjects might both satisfy the popular criterion of "contemporary relevance" and stand a good chance of being recognized by colleagues in other professions. For many anthropologists, these are important considerations, that are difficult to meet in the selection among topics that have traditionally been studied.

Emphasis on "social problems" in terms of promising areas for future research should not obscure the fundamental and most important finding that anthropologists have so far contributed to alcohol studies – the fact that most of the peoples who drink – like most of the individuals in Western society who drink – do so without suffering in any discernible way. Solitary drinking, often viewed as a crucial symptom of problem drinking, is virtually unknown in most societies. Among the data from most societies are details on sex differences, age differences, and differences among other social categories that may be important, as well as differences among individuals within any category. Whether the focus is beliefs or behaviors with respect to alcohol, greater attention to detail in reporting would be helpful for analysis and for comparisons, as well as for increasing the credibility of such studies. Qualitative and quantitative approaches should be complementary rather than contrastive; open-ended (or "emic") material can be grouped into categories for quantitative analysis in the same way that a series of multiple-choice responses to a survey-instrument can be devised for coding. A major advantage of doing such "lumping" after-the-fact is that the categories are more likely to be meaningful, i.e., valid, than those that are done before responses are elicited. Another advantage is that the "raw" data are not lost, but can be used for illustrative purposes, for more intensive analysis by other means, or by other analysts as new questions and methods emerge.

The contributions of anthropology to alcohol studies have been many and varied (Heath 1975, 1980c, Room 1979, Sargent 1976). They are recognized and appreciated by colleagues in many disciplines and throughout the world. Links between alcohol and other cultural items, whether in terms of ideology, social relations, materiél, or other respects, can reveal important insights about sociocultural systems. There are ample opportunities for a wide range of research, and those who choose to apply their skills to practical problems in this connection will find interested colleagues and laypersons almost everywhere.

Notes

1 This paper was originally submitted for publication in July 1981. Several important developments have taken place in the anthropological study of alcohol use
since then, but, in keeping with Dr. Douglas's preference, I have made only
minor stylistic revisions rather than expanding the scope of the chapter. A
slightly revised version has appeared with permission of both editors and publishers, as "Drinking and Drunkenness in Transcultural Perspective: An Over-
view," in *Transcultural Psychiatric Research Review*, vol. 23, no. 1, pp. 7–42;
and vol. 23, no. 2, pp. 103–26, 1986.
2 This chapter was written while the author was Program Director of "Social
Science Research Training on Alcohol," a postdoctoral grant 5 T32 AA 07131,
awarded by the National Institute on Alcohol Abuse and Alcoholism.
3 It should be obvious that mention of a book or article in my discussion of recent
work relevant to particular "Aspects of culture" or "Theoretical and practical
concerns" does not necessarily reflect the same emphases that the original
author(s) had in mind.
4 Readers who are not familiar with the literature on pharmacological and physiological effects of alcohol may be surprised that this "commonsense" view differs
from that of most specialists. In alcohol studies, much stress is put on the role of
"absolute alcohol," noting that "a drink is a drink is a drink." A shot of liquor
(containing about 1.5 oz. at 90 proof) is equivalent, in ethanol content, to a glass
of wine (about 5 oz. at 12 percent), a bottle of beer (about 12 oz. at 5 percent), or
a serving of sherry (about 3 oz. at 20 percent). Each contains approximately 0.6
oz. of absolute alcohol, which, incidentally is roughly the amount that an
average healthy person weighing 60 kg. can metabolize in an hour.

References

Ablon, Joan, 1971. Cultural conflict in urban Indians. *Mental Hygiene* 55: 199–205
    1976a. Family subculture and behavior in alcoholism: A review of the literature.
    In: B. Kissin and H. Begleiter (eds.), *The Biology of Alcoholism: volume 4,
    Social Aspects*. Plenum, New York, pp. 205–42
    1976b. Family behavior and alcoholism. In: M. Everett, J. Waddell, and D.
    Heath (eds.), *Cross-Cultural Approaches to the Study of Alcohol: An Inter-
    disciplinary Perspective*. Mouton, The Hague, pp. 133–60
    1979. Research frontiers for anthropologists in family studies: A case in point,
    alcoholism and the family, *Human Organization* 24: 196–200
Ablon, Joan, and William Cunningham, 1981. Implications of cultural patterning
    for the delivery of alcoholism services: Case studies. In: D. Heath, J. Waddell,
    and M. Topper (eds.), *Cultural Factors in Alcohol Research and Treatment of
    Drinking Problems*. Journal of Studies on Alcohol Supplement 9, New Bruns-
    wick, NJ, pp. 185–206
Adams, Walter Randolph, 1980. The interaction of caffeine and alcohol in Native
    American populations. *The Digest* 3 (1): 23–44

Agar, Michael, 1981. The commonality quest: The search for parallels between drug use and other behaviors. *Newsletter of the Alcohol and Drug Study Group* 3: 3–5

Agarwal, Dharam P., Shoja Harada, and H. Werner Goedde, 1981. Racial differences in biological sensitivity to ethanol: The role of alcohol dehydrogenase and aldehyde dehydrogenase isoenzymes. *Alcoholism* (New York) 5: 12–16

Akins, Carl, and George Beschner (eds.), 1980. *Ethnography: A Research Tool for Policymakers in the Drug and Alcohol Fields*. National Institute on Drug Abuse, Rockville, MD

Albaugh, Bernard, and Patricia Albaugh, 1979. Alcoholism and substance sniffing among the Cheyenne and Arapaho Indians of Oklahoma. *International Journal of the Addictions* 14: 1001–07

Albaugh, Bernard, and Philip Anderson, 1974. Peyote in the treatment of alcoholism among American Indians. *American Journal of Psychiatry* 131: 1247–50

Alcohol and Drug Study Group, 1980– . *Newsletter*

Alcohol and Temperance History Group, 1980– . *Newsletter*

Allchin, F. R., 1979. India: The home of distillation? *Man* (n.s.) 14: 55–63

Al-Qthami, H., 1978. Alcohol and drugs in Saudi Arabia. In: *Proceedings of the Alcohol and Drug Problems Association of North America*. Washington, D.C., pp. 10–12

Alsafar, J. A., 1974. Alcoholism in Bahrain. *Drinking and Drug Practices Surveyor* 9: 8 *et seq.*

American Medical Association, 1956. *Manual on Alcoholism*. American Medical Association [Chicago]
   1980. *Proceedings of the House of Delegates. Council on Scientific Affairs, 34th Interim Meeting* [Chicago]

Angrosino, Michael V., 1974. *Outside is Death: Alcoholism, Ideology and Community Organization among the East Indians of Trinidad*. Medical Behavior Science Monograph, Overseas Research Center, Wake Forest University, Winston-Salem, NC

Australia, House of Representatives, Standing Committee on Aboriginal Affairs, 1977. *Alcohol Problems of Aboriginals: Final Report*. Australian Government Publishing Service, Canberra

Bach, Paul J., and James M. Schaefer, 1979. The tempo of country music and the rate of drinking in bars. *Journal of Studies on Alcohol* 40: 1058–64

Bacon, Margaret K., 1973. Cross-cultural studies of drinking. In: P. Bourne and R. Fox (eds.), *Alcoholism: Progress in Research and Treatment*. Academic Press, New York, pp. 171–92
   1974. The dependency-conflict hypothesis and the frequency of drunkenness: Further evidence from a cross-cultural study. *Quarterly Journal of Studies on Alcohol* 35: 863–76
   1976a. Alcohol use in tribal societies. In: B. Kissin and H. Begleiter (eds.), *The Biology of Alcoholism: volume 4, Social Aspects*. Plenum, New York, pp. 1–36
   1976b. Cross-cultural studies of drinking: Integrated drinking and sex differences in the use of alcoholic beverages. In: M. Everett, J. Waddell, and D. Heath (eds.), *Cross-Cultural Approaches to the Study of Alcohol: An Interdisciplinary Perspective*. Mouton, The Hague, pp. 23–33
   1980. Cross-cultural perspectives on motivations for drinking. In: R. Munroe, R.

Munroe, and B. Whiting (eds.), *Handbook of Cross-Cultural Human Development*. Garland Press, New York, pp. 14–32

Bacon, Margaret K., Herbert Barry III, and Irvin L. Child (eds.), 1965. A Cross-Cultural Study of Drinking. *Quarterly Journal of Studies on Alcohol Supplement 3*, New Haven

Bacon, Selden, 1978. Commentary. *Medical Anthropology* 2 (4): 137–46

Badri, M. B., 1976. *Islam and Alcoholism*. American Trust Publications, Indianapolis

Baker, J. M., 1977. Alcoholism and the American Indian. In: N. Estes and M. Heinemann (eds.), *Alcoholism: Development, Consequences and Interventions*. C. V. Mosby, St. Louis, pp. 194–203

Bales, Robert F., 1946. Cultural differences in rates of alcoholism. *Quarterly Journal of Studies on Alcohol* 6: 480–99

Bartlett, Peggy F., 1980. Reciprocity and the San Juan fiesta. *Journal of Anthropological Research* 36: 116–30

Barrett, James R., 1978. Why Paddy drank: The social importance of whiskey in pre-famine Ireland. *Journal of Popular Culture* 11: 156–66

Barry, Herbert, III, 1976. Cross-cultural evidence that dependency-conflict motivates drunkenness. In: M. Everett, J. Waddell, and D. Heath (eds.), *Cross-Cultural Approaches to the Study of Alcohol: An Interdisciplinary Perspective*, Mouton, The Hague, pp. 249–64

Beaubrun, Michael H., 1975. Cannabis and alcohol: The Jamaican experience. In: V. Rubin (ed.), *Cannabis and Culture*. Mouton, The Hague, pp. 485–94

Beckley, Robert E., and H. Paul Chalfant, 1979. Contrasting images of alcohol and drug use in country and rock music. *Journal of Alcohol and Drug Education* 25: 44–51

Beckman, L. J., 1978. Sex-role conflict in alcoholic women: Myth or reality? *Journal of Abnormal Psychology* 87: 408–17

Bell, Michael, 1975. Running Rabbits and Talking Shit: Folkloric Communications in an Urban Black Bar. PhD (Folklore), University of Pennsylvania, Philadelphia

Beltrame, Thomas, and David V. McQueen, 1979. Urban and rural Indian drinking patterns: The special case of the Lumbee. *International Journal of the Addictions* 14: 533–48

Bennion, Lynn, and Ting-Kai Li, 1976. Alcohol metabolism in American Indians and whites. *New England Journal of Medicine* 294 (1): 9–13

Blacker, Edward, 1966. Sociocultural factors in alcoholism. *International Psychiatry Clinics* 3 (2): 51–80

Blaine, Allan (ed.), 1980. *Alcoholism in the Jewish Community*. Commission on Synagogue Relations, New York

Blane, Howard T., 1977. Acculturation and drinking in an Italian-American community. *Journal of Studies on Alcohol* 38: 1324–46

Blocker, Jack S. (ed.), 1979. *Alcohol, Reform and Society: The Liquor Issue in Social Context*. Greenwood Press, Westport, CT

Blume, Sheils B., and Dee Dropkin, 1980. The Jewish alcoholic: An under-recognized minority? *Journal of Psychiatric Treatment Evaluation* 2:1–4

Blume, Sheila B., Dee Dropkin, and Lloyd Sokolow 1980. The Jewish alcoholic: A descriptive study. *Alcohol Health and Research World* 4 (4): 21–26

Bonilla, Juan A. *et al.*, 1979. *Estudio del Uso de Alcohol y los Problemas del Alcoholismo en Honduras Usando el Método de E. M. Jellinek.* Ministerio de Salud Pública y Asistencia Social, Tegucigalpa

Boscarino, Joseph, 1980. Isolating the effects of ethnicity on drug behavior: A multiple classification analysis of barroom attendance. *Addictive Behaviors* 5: 307–12

Boyatzis, Richard E., 1975. The effect of alcohol consumption on the aggressive behavior of men. *Quarterly Journal of Studies on Alcohol* 35: 959–72

   1976. Drinking as a manifestation of power concerns. In: M. Everett, J. Waddell, and D. Heath (eds.), *Cross-Cultural Approaches to the Study of Alcohol: An Interdisciplinary Perspective.* Mouton, The Hague, pp. 265–86

Brissett, Dennis, 1978. Toward an interactionist understanding of heavy drinking. *Pacific Sociological Review* 21: 3–20

Brod, Thomas M., 1975. Alcoholism as a mental health problem of Native Americans: A review of the literature. *Archives of General Psychiatry* 32: 1385–91

Brody, Hugh, 1970. *Indians on Skid Row.* Northern Science Research Group, Department of Indian Affairs and Northern Development Publication 70–2, Ottawa

   1973. *Innishkillane: Change and Decline in the West of Ireland.* Allen Lane, Penguin Press, London

   1977. Alcohol, change and the industrial frontier. *Etudes/Inuit/Studies* 1 (2): 31–46

Brown, Donald N., 1980. Drinking as an indicator of community disharmony: The people of Taos Pueblo. In: J. Waddell and M. Everett (eds.), *Drinking Behavior among Southwestern Indians: An Anthropological Perspective.* University of Arizona Press, Tucson, pp. 83–102

Burley, Peter M., Colin MacLeod, and John Gemmil, 1978. Effects of social interaction on rate of alcohol consumption. *Psychological Reports* 42: 49–50

Burns, Thomas F., 1980. Getting rowdy with the boys. *Journal of Drug Issues* 10: 273–86

Cabral, Stephen L., 1980. "Time-out": The recreational use of drugs by Portuguese-American immigrants in southeastern New England. *Journal of Drug Issues* 10: 287–99

Carter, William E., 1977. Ritual, the Aymara, and the role of alcohol in human society. In: B. du Toit (ed.), *Drugs, Rituals, and Altered States of Consciousness.* A. A. Halkema, Rotterdam, pp. 101–10

Chalke, H. D., 1978. Strength of Samson. *British Journal of Alcohol and Alcoholism* 13: 98–99

Cinquemani, Dorothy K., 1975. Drinking and Violence among Middle American Indians. PhD (Anthropology), Columbia University, New York

Cohen, H. Hirsch, 1974. *The Drunkenness of Noah.* University of Alabama Press, University

Collmann, Jeff, 1979. Social order and the exchange of liquor: A theory of drinking among Australian Aborigines. *Journal of Anthropological Research* 35: 208–24

Cook, Jim, and Mike Lewington (eds.), 1979. *Images of Alcoholism.* Educational Advisory Service, and Maudsley Hospital, London

Cushner, Nicholas P., 1980. *Lords of the Land: Sugar, Wine, and Jesuit Estates of Coastal Peru, 1600–1767.* State University of New York Press, Albany

Cutter, Henry S. G., John C. Key, Emil Rothstein, and Wyatt C. Jones, 1973. Alcohol, power, and inhibition. *Quarterly Journal of Studies on Alcohol* 34: 381–89

Darby, William J., Paul Ghalioungui, and Louis Grivetti, 1977. *Food: The Gift of Osiris* (2 volumes). Academic Press, London

Dawson, Norma M., 1977. Illicit distillation and the revenue police in Ireland in the eighteenth and nineteenth centuries. *Irish Jurist* 12: 282–94

Dennis, Philip A., 1975. The role of the drunk in a Oaxacan village. *American Anthropologist* 77: 856–63

Desta, Belachew, 1977. A survey of the alcohol content of traditional beverages. *Ethiopian Medical Journal* 15: 65–68

DeWalt, Billie R., 1979. Drinking behavior, economic status, and adaptive strategies of modernization in a highland Mexican community. *American Ethnologist* 6: 510–30

Dobkin de Rios, Marlene, 1979. Mexican migrant tubercular patients' attitudes concerning alcohol. *Journal of Psychedelic Drugs* 11: 347–50

Dobkin de Rios, Marlene, and Daniel J. Feldman, 1977. Southern Californian Mexican-American drinking patterns: Some preliminary observations. *Journal of Psychedelic Drugs* 9: 151–58

Dumett, Raymond E., 1974. The social impact of the European liquor trade on the Akan of Ghana (Gold Coast and Asante), 1875–1910. *Journal of Interdisciplinary History* 5: 69–101

Durgin, Edward C., 1974. Brewing and Boozing: A Study of Drinking Habits among the Hare Indians. PhD (Anthropology), University of Oregon, Eugene

Eastwell, H. D., 1979. A pica epidemic: A price for sedentarism among Australian ex-hunter-gathers. *Psychiatry* 42: 264–73

Edwards, Griffith, 1979. Drinking problems: Putting the Third World on the map. *Lancet* 2 (8139): 402–04

Eguchi, Paul K., 1975. Beer drinking and festivals among the Hide. *Kyoto University African Studies* 9: 69–90

Emboden, William, 1977. Dionysus as a shaman and wine as a magical drug. *Journal of Psychedelic Drugs* 9: 187–92

Englemann, Larry, 1979. *Intemperance: The Lost War against Liquor*. Free Press, New York

Escalante, Fernando, 1980. Group pressure and excessive drinking among Native Americans. In: J. Waddell and M. Everett (eds.), *Drinking Behavior among Southwestern Indians: An Anthropological Perspective*. University of Arizona Press, Tucson, pp. 183–204

Everest, Allan S., 1978. *Rum across the Border: The Prohibition Era in Northern New York State*. Syracuse University Press, Syracuse

Everett, Michael W., 1980. Drinking as a means of proper behavior: The White Mountain Apaches. In: J. Waddell and M. Everett (eds.), *Drinking Behavior among Southwestern Indians: An Anthropological Perspective*. University of Arizona Press, Tucson, pp. 148–77

Everett, Michael W., Jack O. Waddell, and Dwight B. Heath (eds.), 1976. *Cross-Cultural Approaches to the Study of Alcohol: An Interdisciplinary Perspective*. Mouton, The Hague

Ewing, John A., Beatrice A. Rouse, and R. M. Aderhold, 1979. Studies of the mechanism of Oriental hypersensitivity. In: M. Galanter (ed.), *Currents in Alcoholism:* volume 4. Grune and Stratton, New York, pp. 45–52

Ewing, John A., Beatrice A. Rouse, and E. D. Pellizzari, 1974. Alcohol sensitivity and ethnic background. *American Journal of Psychiatry* 131: 206–10

Fahey, David M., 1980. Brewers, publicans, and working-class drinkers: Pressure group politics in late Victorian and Edwardian England. *Histoire Sociale/Social History* 13: 85–104

Fairbanks, Robert A., 1973. The Cheyenne-Arapaho and alcoholism: Does the tribe have a legal right to a medical remedy? *American Indian Law Review:* 1: 55–77

Farris, John J., and Ben Morgan Jones, 1978. Ethanol metabolism in male American Indians and whites. *Alcoholism* (New York) 2: 77–81

Fenna, D., L. Mix, O. Schaefer, and J. A. L. Gilbert, 1971. Ethanol metabolism in various racial groups. *Canadian Medical Association Journal* 105: 472–75

Ferguson, Frances N., 1976a. Stake theory as an explanatory device in Navajo alcoholism treatment response. *Human Organization* 35: 65–78

   1976b. Similarities and differences among a heavily arrested group of Navajo Indian drinkers in a southwestern American town. In: M. Everett, J. Waddell, and D. Heath (eds.), *Cross-Cultural Approaches to the Study of Alcohol: An Interdisciplinary Perspective*. Mouton, The Hague, pp. 161–71

Fiske, Shirley J., 1979. Urban Indian Institutions: A reappraisal from Los Angeles. *Urban Anthropology* 8: 149–72

Forni, G., 1976. The origin of grape wine: A problem in historical-ecological anthropology. In: M. Arnott (ed.), *Gastronomy: The Anthropology of Food and Food Habits*. Mouton, The Hague, pp. 67–78

Foulks, Edward F., 1980. Psychological continuities: From dissociative states to alcohol use and suicide in Arctic populations. *Journal of Operational Psychiatry* 11: 156–61

Foulks, Edward F., and Solomon H. Katz, 1973. The mental health of Alaskan natives. *Acta Psychiatrica Scandinavica* 49: 91–96

Frankel, Barbara, 1980. Human nature, addictions, and the geography of disorder in three cultures. *Journal of Drug Issues* 10: 165–201

Frankel, B. Gail, and Paul C. Whitehead, 1981. *Drinking and Damage: Theoretical Advances and Implications for Prevention*. Rutgers Center of Alcohol Studies Monograph 14, New Brunswick, NJ

French, Lawrence, and Jim Hornbuckle, 1979. Indian stress and violence: A psycho-cultural perspective. *Journal of Alcohol and Drug Education* 25: 36–43

Freund, Paul J., 1979. *Armenian-American Drinking Patterns: Ethnicity, Family, and Religion*. Working Papers on Alcohol and Human Behavior 5, Department of Anthropology, Brown University, Providence, RI

   1980. *Polish-American Drinking: An Historical Study in Attitude Change*. Working Papers on Alcohol and Human Behavior 9, Department of Anthropology, Brown University, Providence, RI

Freund, Paul J., and Mac Marshall, 1977. Research bibliography of alcohol and kava studies in Oceania: Update and additional items. *Micronesica* 13: 313–17

Fritz, W. B., 1976. Psychiatric disorders among natives and non-natives in Saskatchewan. *Canadian Psychiatric Association Journal* 21: 393–400

Fuller, Lauren L., 1975. Alcoholic beverage control: Should the remaining reservations repeal Prohibition under 18 U.S.C. 1161? *American Indian Law Review* 3: 429–44

Galanter, Marc, 1981. Sociobiology and informal controls of drinking: Findings from two charismatic sects. *Journal of Studies on Alcohol* 42: 64–79

Gedig, G., 1979. Imperialisme culturel et alcoolisme au Japon: Historique et evolution des mentalités. *Alcool ou Santé* 151: 15–24

Gervais, Charles H., 1978. *The Rumrunners: A Prohibition Scrapbook*. Firefly Press, Thornhill, Ontario

Ghalioungui, P., 1979. Fermented beverages in antiquity. In: C. Gastineau, W. Darby, and T. Turner (eds.), *Fermented Food Beverages in Nutrition*. Academic Press, New York, pp. 4–18

Gibson, James A., and Daniela Weinberg, 1980. In vino communitas: Wine and identity in a Swiss Alpine village. *Anthropological Quarterly* 52: 111–21

Gilbert, J. A. L., and O. Schaefer, 1977. Metabolism of ethanol in different racial groups. *Canadian Medical Association Journal* 116:476

Gilbert, M. Jean, 1978. *Five-Week Alcoholism Ethnography Conducted in Three Spanish-Speaking Communities*. ERIC Reports 261

Glassner, Barry, and Bruce Berg, 1980. How Jews avoid alcohol problems. *American Sociological Review* 45: 647–63

Gluckman, L. K., 1974. Alcohol and the Maori in historical perspective. *New Zealand Medical Journal* 79: 553–55

Godlewski, Grzegorz, 1978– . Alkohol w literaturze polskiej: [several parts]. *Problemy Alkoholizmu* 25: 13–16 [*et ff.*]

Goedde, H. W., S. Harada, and D. P. Agarwal, 1979. Racial differences in alcohol sensitivity: A new hypothesis. *Human Genetics* 51: 331–34

Gonçalves de Lima, Oswaldo, José Francisco de Mello, Ivan Leoncio D'Albuquerque, Franco Delle Monache, Giovanni Battista Marini-Bettolo, and Mario Sousa, 1977. Contribution to the knowledge of the Maya ritual wine: Balché. *Lloydia* 40: 195–200

Gordon, Andrew J. (ed.), 1978a. Ethnicity and Alcohol Use. *Medical Anthropology* 2 (4): [entire issue]

   1978b. Hispanic drinking after migration: The case of Dominicans. *Medical Anthropology* 2 (4): 61–84

   1981. The cultural context of drinking and indigenous therapy for alcohol problems in three migrant Hispanic cultures: An ethnographic report. In: D. Heath, J. Waddell, and M. Topper (eds.), *Cultural Factors in Alcohol Research and Treatment of Drinking Problems*. Journal of Alcohol Studies Supplement 9, New Brunswick, NJ, pp. 217–40

Graham, Kathryn, Linda LaRoque, Rhoda Yetman, T. James Ross, and Enrico Guistra, 1980. Aggression and barroom environments. *Journal of Studies on Alcohol* 41: 277–92

Graves, Theodore, Nancy B. Graves, Iulai Ah Sam, and Vineta N. Semu, 1979a. *Drinking and Violence in a Multi-Cultural Society*. South Pacific Research Institute Research Report 21 [Auckland]

   1979b *Patterns of Public Drinking in a Multi-Ethnic Society: A Systematic Observational Study*. South Pacific Research Institute Research Report 20 [Auckland]

Greeley, Andrew M., and William C. McCready, 1978. A preliminary reconnaissance into the persistence and explanation of ethnic subcultural drinking patterns. *Medical Anthropology* 2 (4): 31–51

Greeley, Andrew M., William C. McCready, and Gary Thiesen, 1980. *Ethnic Drinking Subcultures*. Praeger, New York

Haas, Laurel M., and Don Joralemon, 1978. Single stranger, self and saloon. *Anthropology UCLA* 9: 17–35

Hagaman, Barbara L., 1980. Food for thought: Beer in a social and ritual context in a West African Society. *Journal of Drug Issues* 10: 203–14

Hage, Per, 1972. Münchner beer categories. In: J. Spradley (ed.), *Culture and Cognition: Rules, Maps, and Plans*, Chandler, San Francisco, pp. 263–78

Hall, Douglas C., Kathleen Chaikin, and Barrie Piland, 1977. *Review of the Problem Drinking Behavior Literature Associated with the Spanish-Speaking Population: volume 3*. Stanford Research Institute, Menlo Park, CA

Hamer, John, and Jack Steinbring (eds.), 1980. *Alcohol and Native Peoples of the North*. University Press of America, Lanham. MD

Hanna, Joel M., 1976. Ethnic groups, human variation, and alcohol use. In: M. Everett, J. Waddell, and D. Heath (eds.), *Cross-Cultural Approaches to the Study of Alcohol: An Interdisciplinary Perspective*. Mouton, The Hague, pp. 235–44

1978. Metabolic responses of Chinese, Japanese, and Europeans to alcohol. *Alcoholism* (New York) 2: 89–92

Harford, Thomas C., Douglas A. Parker, and Lillian Light (eds.), 1980. *Normative Approaches to the Prevention of Alcohol Abuse and Alcoholism*. National Institute on Alcohol Abuse and Alcoholism Research Monograph 3, Rockville, MD

Harrison, Brian, 1971. *Drink and the Victorians: The Temperance Question in England, 1815–1872*. Faber and Faber, London

Hawarth, Alan, 1980. The need for the study of abuse of alcohol and other drugs in Africa. In: A. Kiev, W. Muya, and N. Sartorius (eds.), *The Future of Mental Health Services*. Excerpta Medica, Amsterdam, pp. 191–202

Heaston, Michael D., 1971. Whiskey regulation and Indian land titles in New Mexico Territory, 1851–1861. *Journal of the West* 10: 474–83

Heath, Dwight B., 1971. Peasants, revolution, and drinking: Interethnic drinking patterns in two Bolivian communities. *Human Organization* 30: 179–86

1975. A critical review of ethnographic studies of alcohol use. In: R. Gibbins, Y. Israel, H. Kalant, R. Popham, W. Schmidt, and R. Smart (eds.), *Research Advances in Alcohol and Drug Problems: volume 2*. John Wiley and Sons, New York, pp. 1–92

1976a. Anthropological perspectives on alcohol: An historical review. In: M. Everett, J. Waddell, and D. Heath (eds.), *Cross-Cultural Approaches to the Study of Alcohol: An Interdisciplinary Perspective*. Mouton, The Hague, pp. 41–101

1976b. Anthropological perspectives on the social biology of alcohol: An introduction to the literature. In: B. Kissin and H. Begleiter (eds.), *The Biology of Alcoholism, volume 4: Social Aspects*. Plenum Press, New York, pp. 37–76

1977. *Observational Studies into Alcohol-Related Problems*. World Health Organization Project on Community Responses to Alcohol-Related Problems Background Document, Geneva

1978. The sociocultural model of alcohol use: Problems and prospects. *Journal of Operational Psychiatry* 9: 55–66

1980a. Ethnographic approaches in alcohol studies and other policy-related fields. *Practicing Anthropology* 3: 19 *et ff.*

1980b. Comment on "Ethnography and applied policy research." *Practicing Anthropology* 3: 35–36

1980c. A critical review of the sociocultural model of alcohol use. In: T. Harford. D. Parker, and L. Light (eds.), *Normative Approaches to the Prevention of Alcohol Abuse and Alcoholism*. National Institute on Alcohol Abuse and Alcoholism Research Monograph 3, Rockville, MD, pp. 1–18

1981. Determining the sociocultural context of alcohol use. In: D. Heath, J. Waddell, and M. Topper (eds.), *Cultural Factors in Alcohol Research and Treatment of Drinking Problems*. Journal of Studies on Alcohol Supplement 9, New Brunswick, NJ, pp. 9–17

Heath, Dwight B., and A. M. Cooper, 1981. *Alcohol Use and World Cultures: A Comprehensive Bibliography of Anthropological Sources*. Addiction Research Foundation Bibliographic Series 15, Toronto

Heath, Dwight B., Jack O. Waddell, and Martin D. Topper (eds.), 1981. *Cultural Factors in Alcohol Research and Treatment of Drinking Problems*. Journal of Studies on Alcohol Supplement 9, Smithsonian Institution and Journal of Studies on Alcohol, New Brunswick, NJ

Heidenreich, C. Adrian, 1976. Alcohol and drug use and abuse among Indian-Americans: A review of issues and sources. *Journal of Drug Issues* 6: 256–72

Hes, J. P., 1970. Drinking in a Yemenite rural settlement in Israel. *British Journal of Addictions* 65: 293–96

Hill, Thomas W., 1974. From hell-raiser to family man. In: J. Spradley and D. McCurdy (eds.), *Conformity and Conflict: Readings in Cultural Anthropology* (2nd edition). Little, Brown, Boston, pp. 186–200

1978. Drunken comportment of urban Indians: "Time-out" behavior? *Journal of Anthropological Research* 34: 442–67

1980. Life styles and drinking patterns of urban Indians. *Journal of Drug Issues* 10: 257–72

Hippler, Arthur E., 1974. An Alaskan Athabascan technique for overcoming alcohol abuse. *Arctic* 27: 53–67

Honigmann, John J., 1980. Perspectives on alcohol behavior. In: J. Hamer and J. Steinbring (eds.), *Alcohol and Native People of the North*. University Press of America, Lanham, MD, pp. 267–85

Honigmann, John J., and Irma Honigmann, 1970. *Arctic Townsmen: Ethnic Backgrounds and Modernization*. Canadian Research Centre for Anthropology, Saint Paul University, Ottawa

Horton, Donald J., 1943. The functions of alcohol in primitive societies: A cross-cultural study. *Quarterly Journal of Studies on Alcohol* 4: 199–320

Hudson, Charles M. (ed.), 1979. *Black Drink: A Native American Tea*. University of Georgia Press, Athens

International Arctic Rim Conference on Alcohol Problems, 1978. *Selected Papers*. National Council on Alcoholism – Alaska Region, Anchorage

James, W. R., 1972. Beer, morality and social relations among the Uduk. *Sudan Society* 5: 17–27

Jellinek, E. M., 1976. Drinkers and alcoholics in ancient Rome. *Journal of Studies on Alcohol* 37: 1718–41

1977. The symbolism of drinking: A cultural-historical approach. *Journal of Studies on Alcohol* 38: 849–66

Jilek, Wolfgang G., 1974. Indian healing power: Indigenous therapeutic practices in the Pacific Northwest. *Psychiatric Annals* 4: 13–21

1981. Anomic depression, alcoholism and culture – congenial Indian response. In: D. Heath, J. Waddell, and M. Topper (eds.), *Cultural Factors in Alcohol Research and Treatment of Drinking Problems*. Journal of Studies on Alcohol Supplement 9, New Brunswick, NJ, pp. 159–70

Jilek-Aall, Louise, 1974. Psychosocial aspects of drinking among Coast Salish Indians. *Canadian Psychiatric Association Journal* 19: 357–61

1981. Acculturation, alcoholism, and Indian-style Alcoholics Anonymous. In: D. Heath, J. Waddell, and M. Topper (eds.), *Cultural Factors in Alcohol Research and Treatment of Drinking Problems*. Journal of Studies on Alcohol Supplement 9, New Brunswick, NJ, pp. 143–58

Johnson, Sandie, 1978. *Cirrhosis mortality among American Indian women: Rates and ratios, 1975*. Alcohol Epidemiological Data System Working Paper 6, Rockville, MD

1979. *Cirrhosis mortality among American Indian women: Rates and ratios, 1975 and 1976*. Alcohol Epidemiological Data System Working Paper 11, Rockville, MD

Johnston, Thomas, F., 1973. Dagga use among the Shangana-Tsonga of Mozambique and the modern Transvaal. *Zeitschrift für Ethnologie* 98: 277–86

Jones, A. D., 1975. Cannabis and alcohol usage among the Plateau Tonga: An observational report on the effects of cultural expectation. *Psychological Record* 25: 329–32

Juhász, P., 1973. Pathogenic factors eliciting neurosis in the inhabitants of a Hungarian village in the years following the formation of agricultural cooperatives. *International Journal of Social Psychiatry* 19: 173–79

Kamien, Max, 1975. Aborigines and alcohol: Intake, effects and social implications in a rural community in western New South Wales. *Medical Journal of Australia* 1: 291–98

Kearney, Michael, 1970. Drunkenness and religious conversion in a Mexican village. *Quarterly Journal of Studies on Alcohol* 31: 132–52

Kenmitzer, Luis S., 1972. The structure of country drinking parties on Pine Ridge Reservation, South Dakota. *Plains Anthropologist* 17: 134–42

Kennedy, John G., 1978. *Tarahumara of the Sierra Madre: Beer, Ecology, and Social Organization*. A H M Publishing, Arlington Heights, IL

Key, Wilson Bryan, 1973. *Subliminal Seduction: Ad Media's Manipulation of a Not so Innocent America*. Prentice-Hall, Englewood Cliffs, NJ

Klausner, Samuel Z., Edward P. Foulks, and Mark H. Moore, 1979. *The Inupiat, Economics, and Alcohol on the Alaskan North Slope*. Center for Research on the Acts of Man, Philadelphia

1980. *Social Change and the Alcohol Problem on the Alaskan Northern Slope*. Center for Research on the Acts of Man, Philadelphia

Kobler, John, 1973. *Ardent Spirits: The Rise and Fall of Prohibition*. G. P. Putnam's Sons, New York

Kraus, Robert F., and P. A. Baffler, 1979. Sociocultural stress and the American Natives in Alaska: An analysis of changing patterns of psychiatric illness and alcohol abuse among Alaska Natives. *Cultural and Medical Psychiatry* 3: 111–51

Kunitz, Stephen J., and Jerrold E. Levy, 1974. Changing ideas of alcohol use among Navaho Indians. *Quarterly Journal of Studies on Alcohol* 35: 243–59

Kunitz, Stephen J., Jerrold E. Levy, C. L. Odoroff, and J. Bollinger, 1971. The epidemiology of alcoholic cirrhosis in two southwestern Indian tribes. *Quarterly Journal of Studies on Alcohol* 32: 706–20

Lang, Gretchen Chesley, 1979. Survival strategies of Chippewa drinkers in Minneapolis. *Central Issues in Anthropology* 1: 19–40

Leland Joy H., 1975. Drinking Styles in an Indian Settlement: A Numerical Folk Taxonomy. PhD (Social Sciences), University of California, Irvine

1976. *Firewater Myths: North American Indian Drinking and Alcohol Addiction.* Rutgers Center of Alcohol Studies Monograph 11, New Brunswick, NJ

1978. Women and alcohol in an Indian settlement. *Medical Anthropology* 2 (4): 85–119

1980. Native American alcohol use: A review of the literature. In: P. Mail and D. McDonald (compilers), *Tulapai to Tokay: A Bibliography of Alcohol Use and Abuse among Native Americans of North America.* HRAF Press, New Haven, pp. 1–56

LeMasters, E. E., 1975. *Blue-Collar Aristocrats: Life Styles at a Working-Class Tavern.* University of Wisconsin Press, Madison

Lemert, Edwin M., 1976. Koni, kona, kava: Orange beer culture of the Cook Islands. *Journal of Studies on Alcohol* 37: 565–85

Levine, Harry Gene, 1978. The discovery of addiction: Changing conceptions of habitual drunkenness in America. *Journal of Studies on Alcohol* 39: 143–74

Levy, Jerrold E., and Stephen J. Kunitz, 1971a. Indian reservations, anomie, and social pathologies. *Southwestern Journal of Anthropology* 27: 97–128

1971b. Indian drinking: Problems of data collection and interpretation. In: M. Chafetz (ed.), *Proceedings of the First Annual Alcoholism Conference.* National Institute on Alcohol Abuse and Alcoholism, Rockville, MD, pp. 217–36

1974. *Indian Drinking: Navajo Practices and Anglo-American Theories.* Wiley, New York

1981. Economic and political factors inhibiting the use of basic research findings in Indian alcoholism programs. In: D. Heath, J. Waddell, and M. Topper (eds.), *Cultural Factors in Alcohol Research and Treatment of Drinking Problems.* Journal of Studies on Alcohol Supplement 9, New Brunswick, NJ, pp. 60–72

Levy, Jerrold E., Stephen J. Kunitz, and Michael W. Everett, 1969. Navajo criminal homicide. *Southwestern Journal of Anthropology* 25: 124–52

Lex, Barbara W. (ed.), 1980. The Recreational and Social Uses of Dependency-Producing Drugs in Diverse Social and Cultural Contexts. *Journal of Drug Issues* 10 (2): [entire issue]

Liban, Carolyn B., and Reginald G. Smart [1980]. *The Value of the Informant Method for Studying Drinking Habits.* Addiction Research Foundation, Toronto

Lickiss, J. Norelle, 1971. Alcohol and Aborigines in cross-cultural situations. *Australian Journal of Social Issues* 6: 21–216

Lint, Jan de, 1976. The epidemiology of alcoholism with specific reference to sociocultural factors. In: M. Everett, J. Waddell, and D. Heath (eds.), *Cross-Cultural Approaches to the Study of Alcohol: An Interdisciplinary Perspective.* Mouton, The Hague, pp. 323–40

Little, Kenneth W., 1979. Nobody knows the good times: Drinking in Athapaskan communities. *Journal of Anthropology at McMaster* 5: 126–79

Littman, Gerard, 1970. Alcoholism, illness, and social pathology among American Indians in transition. *American Journal of Public Health* 60: 1769–87

Lomnitz, Larissa, 1973. Influencia de los cambios poíticos y económicos en la ingestión del alcohol: El caso mapuche. *América Indígena* 33: 133–50

1976. Alcohol and culture: The historical evolution of drinking patterns among the Mapuche. In: M. Everett, J. Waddell, and D. Heath (eds.), *Cross-Cultural Approaches to the Study of Alcohol: An Interdisciplinary Perspective.* Mouton, The Hague, pp. 177–98

Loubère, Leo A., 1978. *The Red and the White: A History of Wine in France and Italy in the Nineteenth Century.* State University of New York Press, Albany

Lowery, Shearon A., 1980. Soap and booze in the afternoon: An analysis of the portrayal of alcohol use in daytime serials. *Journal of Studies in Alcohol* 41: 829–37

Lutes, Steven V., 1977. Alcohol Use among the Yaqui Indians of Potam, Sonora, Mexico. PhD (Anthropology), University of Kansas, Lawrence

MacAndrew, Craig, and Robert Edgerton, 1969. *Drunken Comportment: A Social Explanation.* Aldine, Chicago

MacPhail, A. P., M. O. Simon, J. D. Torrance, R. W. Charlton, T. H. Bothwell, and C. Isaacson, 1979. Changing patterns of dietary iron overload in Black South Africans. *American Journal of Clinical Nutrition* 32: 1272–78

Madsen, William, 1974. *The American Alcoholic: The Nature–Nurture Controversy in Alcoholic Research and Therapy.* Charles C. Thomas, Springfield, IL

Maghbouleh, Mitra D., 1979. *Psychocultural Dimensions of Alcoholism, Witchcraft, Ethnic Relations, and Asceticism: A Comparative Study* (3 volumes). Social Science Research Reports 56, School of Social Sciences, University of California, Irvine

Magruder, K. M., 1978. Alcohol Problems in Bahrain. PhD (Anthropology), University of North Carolina, Chapel Hill

Mail, Patricia D., 1980. American Indian drinking behavior: Some possible causes and solutions. *Journal of Alcohol and Drug Education* 26: 28–39

Mail, Patricia D., and David R. McDonald, 1980. *Tulapi to Tokay: A Bibliography of Alcohol Use and Abuse among Native Americans of North America.* HRAF Press, New Haven, CT

Mäkelä, Klaus, 1975. Consumption level and cultural drinking patterns as determinants of alcohol problems. *Journal of Drug Issues* 5: 344–57

1979. Holocultural generalizations and historical fluctuations in aggregate drinking. *Drinking and Drug Practices Surveyor* 15: 11–14

Manning, Frank E., 1979. *Black Clubs in Bermuda: Ethnography of a Play World.* Cornell University Press, Ithaca, NY

Marinovich, N., O. Larsson, and K. Barber, 1976. Comparative metabolism rates of ethanol in adults of Aboriginal and European descent. *Medical Journal of Australia* 7 (Special Supplement 1): 44–46

Marshall, Mac, 1974. Research bibliography of alcohol and kava studies in Oceania. *Micronesica* 10: 299–306

1975. The politics of prohibition on Namoluk Atoll. *Journal of Studies on Alcohol* 36: 597–610

1976. A review and appraisal of alcohol and kava studies in Oceania. In: M. Everett, J. Waddell, and D. Heath (eds.), *Cross-Cultural Approaches to the Study of Alcohol: An Interdisciplinary Perspective.* Mouton, The Hague, pp. 103–18

(ed.), 1979a. *Beliefs, Behaviors, and Alcoholic Beverages: A Cross-Cultural Survey.* University of Michigan Press, Ann Arbor

1979b. *Weekend Warriors: Alcohol in a Micronesian Culture.* Mayfield, Palo Alto, CA

1981. *A Summary of the IASER Conference on Alcohol Use and Abuse in Papua New Guinea.* IASER Discussion Paper 37, Institute of Applied Sociology and Economic Research, Boroko

Marshall, Mac, and Leslie B. Marshall, 1975. Opening Pandora's bottle: Reconstructing Micronesia's early contacts with alcoholic beverages. *Journal of the Polynesian Society* 84: 441–65

1976. Holy and unholy spirits: The effects of missionization on alcohol use in eastern Micronesia. *Journal of Pacific History* 11: 135–66

May, Philip A., 1976. Alcohol Legalization and Native Americans: A Sociological Inquiry. PhD (Sociology), University of Montana, Missoula

1977. Explanations of Native American drinking: A literature review. *Plains Anthropologist* 22: 223–32

McCarthy, Robert G. (ed.), 1959. *Drinking and Intoxication: Selected Readings in Social Attitudes and Controls.* Free Press, Glencoe, IL

McClelland, David C., William N. Davis, Rudolf Kalin, and Eric Wanner, 1972. *The Drinking Man.* Free Press. New York

Medina C., Eduardo, and Juan Marconi, 1970. Prevalencia de distintos tipos de bebedores en adultos mapuches de zona rural en Cautín. *Acta Psiquiátrica y Psicológica de América Latina* 16: 273–85

Mizoi, Y., I. Ijiri, Y. Tatsuno, T. Kijima, S. Fujiwara, J. Adachi, and S. Hishida, 1979. Relationship between facial flushing and blood acetaldehyde levels after alcohol intake. Pharmacology, *Biochemistry and Behavior* 10: 303–11

Morcos, S. R., and W. R. Morcos, 1977. Diet in ancient Egypt. *Progress in Food and Nutrition Sciences* 2: 457–71

Morris, C[raig], 1979. Maize beer in the economics, politics, and religion of the Inca Empire. In: C. Gastineau, W. Darby, and T. Turner (eds.), *Fermented Food Beverages in Nutrition.* Academic Press, New York, pp. 21–34

Moser, Joy, 1977. Community responses to alcohol-related problems: A World Health Organization research proposal. *Alcoholism* (New York) 1: 267–70

Mosher, J. F., 1975. *Liquor Legislation and Native Americans: History and Perspective.* Boalt Hall School of Law, University of California, Berkeley

Nason, James D., 1975. Sardines and other fried fish: The consumption of alcoholic beverages on a Micronesian island. *Journal of Studies on Alcohol* 36: 611–25

Nelson, Leonard, 1977. Alcoholism in Zuni, New Mexico. *Preventive Medicine* 6: 152–66

Obayemi, Ade M. U., 1976. Alcohol usage in an African society. In: M. Everett, J. Waddell, and D. Heath (eds.), *Cross-Cultural Approaches to the Study of Alcohol: An Interdisciplinary Perspective*. Mouton, The Hague, pp. 199–208

O'Brien, John Maxwell, 1980a. The enigma of Alexander: The alcohol factor. *Annals of Scholarship* 1: 31–46

1980b. Alexander and Dionysus: The invisible enemy. *Annals of Scholarship* 1: 83–105

O'Carroll, M. D., 1979. The Relationship of Religion and Ethnicity to Drinking Behavior: A Study of North European Immigrants in the United States. D.P.H., School of Public Health, University of California, Berkeley

Omori, Motoyoshi, 1978. Social and economic utility of *omuramba*: The Chiga sorghum beer. *Senri Ethnological Studies* 1: 89–104

Onselen, Charles van, 1976. Randlords and rotgut, 1886–1905: An essay on the role of alcohol in the development of European imperialism and South African capitalism. *History Workshop* 2

Pagés Larraya, Fernando, 1976. Modos culturales del beber en los aborígenes del Chaco. *Acta Psiquiátrica y Psicológica de América Latina* 22: 21–45

Pan, Lynn, 1975. *Alcohol in Colonial Africa*. Finnish Foundation for Alcohol Studies Monograph 22, Helsinki

Parades, Alfonso, 1975. Social control of drinking among the Aztec Indians of Mesoamerica. *Quarterly Journal of Studies on Alcohol* 36: 1139–53

Parades, Alfonso, Louis J. West, and Clyde C. Snow, 1970. Biosocial adaptation and correlates of acculturation in the Tarahumara ecosystem. *International Journal of Social Psychiatry* 16: 163–74

Parker, Douglas A., and Marsha S. Harman, 1978. The distribution of consumption model of prevention of alcohol problems: A critical assessment. *Journal of Studies on Alcohol* 39: 377–99

1980. A critique of the distribution of consumption model of prevention. In: T. Harford, D. Parker, and L. Light (eds.), *Normative Approaches to the Prevention of Alcohol Abuse and Alcoholism*. National Institute on Alcohol Abuse and Alcoholism Research Monograph 3, Rockville, MD, pp. 66–88

Parker, Douglas A., Elizabeth S. Parker, Thomas C. Harford, and Jacob B. Brody, 1978. Status inconsistency and drinking patterns among men and women. *Alcoholism* (New York) 2: 101–05

Parkin, David J., 1972. *Palms, Wine, and Witnesses: Public Spirit and Private Gain in an African Farming Community*. Chandler, San Francisco

Partanen, Juah (ed.), 1980. *Finnish Intoxication on the Screen*. Reports of the Social Research Institute of Alcohol Studies 143, Helsinki

Pascarosa, Paul, and Sanford Futterman, 1976. Ethnopsychedelic therapy for alcoholics: Observations on the Peyote Ritual of the Native American Church. *Journal of Psychedelic Drugs* 8: 215–21

Pascarosa, Paul, Sanford Futterman, and Mark Halsweig, 1976. Observations of alcoholics in the Peyote Ritual: A pilot study. In: F. Seixas and S. Eggleston (eds.), *Work in Progress on Alcoholism*. Annals of the New York Academy of Sciences 273, New York, pp. 518–24

Peltoniemi, Teuvo, 1980. Antropologia ja alkoholitutkimus. *Suomen Antropologi* 2: 77–82

Pinson, Ann, 1980. *The New England Rum Era: Drinking Styles and Social Change in Newport, Rhode Island, 1720–1770*. Working Papers on Alcohol and Human Behavior 8, Department of Anthropology, Brown University, Providence, RI

Pittman, David J. (ed.), 1967. *Alcoholism*. Harper and Row, New York

Pollnac, Robert B., and Michael C. Robbins, 1972. Gratification patterns and modernization in rural Buganda. *Human Organization* 31: 63–72

Popham, Robert E., 1978. The social history of the tavern. In: Y. Israel, H. Kalant, R. Popham, W. Schmidt, and R. Smart (eds.), *Research Advances in Alcohol and Drug Problems: volume 4*. Plenum Press, New York, pp. 225–302

Popham, Robert E., and Carole D. Yawney (comps.), 1967. *Culture and Alcohol Use: A Bibliography of Anthropological Sources* (2nd edition). Addiction Research Foundation Bibliographic Series 1, Toronto

Prestan Simon, Arnuflo, 1975. *El Uso de la Chicha y la Sociedad Kuna*. Instituto Indigenista Interamericano Ediciones Especiales 72, México

Price, John A., 1975. US and Canadian Indian urban ethnic institutions. *Urban Anthropology* 4: 35–52

Rao, S. V. A. Satyanarayana, and C. R. Prasad Rao, 1977. Drinking in the tribal world: A cross-cultural study in "cultural theme" approach. *Man in India* 57: 97–120

Read, Kenneth E., 1980. *Other Voices: The Style of a Male Homosexual Tavern*. Chandler and Sharp, Novato, CA

Reed, T. Edward, 1978. Racial comparisons of alcohol metabolism: Background, problems, and results. *Alcoholism* (New York) 2: 83–88

Reed, T. Edward, Harold Kalant, and Robert J. Gibbins, 1973. Ethnic and sex differences in responses to alcohol. *Behavior Genetics* 3: 413–17

Reed, T. Edward, Harold Kalant, Robert J. Gibbins, Bushan M. Kapur, and James G. Rankin, 1976. Alcohol and acetaldehyde metabolism in Caucasians, Chinese and Amerinds. *Canadian Medical Association Journal* 115: 851–55

Rios: see: Dobkin de Rios

Robbins, Michael C., 1977. Problem-drinking and the integration of alcohol in rural Buganda. *Medical Anthropology* 1 (3): 1–24

Robbins, Michael C., and Linda C. Robbins, 1980. An optimization analysis of alcohol use in rural Buganda. *Human Organization* 39: 261–62

Robbins, Richard H., 1973. Alcohol and the identity struggle: Some effects of economic change on interpersonal relations. *American Anthropologist* 75: 99–122

Roebuck, Julian B., and Wolfgang Frese, 1976. *The Rendezvous: A Case-Study of an After-Hour Club*. Free Press, New York

Room, Robin, 1976. Ambivalence as a sociological explanation: The case of cultural explanations of alcohol problems. *American Sociological Review* 41: 1047–65

1979. Priorities in social science research on alcohol. In: M. Keller (ed.), *Research Priorities on Alcohol*. Journal of Studies on Alcohol Supplement 8, New Brunswick, NJ, pp. 248–68

Rorabaugh, W. J., 1979. *The Alcoholic Republic: An American Tradition*. Oxford University Press, New York

Roy, J. K., 1978. Alcoholic beverages in tribal India and their nutritional role. *Man in India* 58: 298–326

Salvatore, Santo, 1979. *Intergenerational Shifts in Drinking Patterns, Opinions, Behaviors, and Personality Traits of Italian Americans*. Working Papers on

Alcohol and Human Behavior 6, Department of Anthropology, Brown University, Providence, RI

Sanders, Barbara, George P. Danko, and Bernadette Ching, 1980. Cardiovascular responses of Oriental and Caucasian men to alcohol: Some psychological correlates. *Journal of Studies on Alcohol* 41: 496–508

Sargent, Margaret, 1976. Theory in alcohol studies. In: M. Everett, J. Waddell, and D. Heath (eds.), *Cross-Cultural Approaches to the Study of Alcohol: An Interdisciplinary Perspective*. Mouton, The Hague, pp. 341–52

Savishinsky, Joel S., 1971. Mobility as an aspect of stress in an Arctic community. *American Anthropologist* 73: 604–18

1977. A thematic analysis of drinking behavior in a Hare Indian community. *Papers in Anthropology* 18 (2): 43–59

Schaefer, James M., 1976. Drunkenness and culture stress: A holocultural test. In: M. Everett, J. Waddell, and D. Heath (eds.), *Cross-Cultural Approaches to the Study of Alcohol: An Interdisciplinary Perspective*. Mouton, The Hague, pp. 287–322

1978. Alcohol metabolism and sensitivity reactions among the Reddis of south India. *Alcoholism* (New York) 2: 61–70

1979. Ethnic differences in response to alcoholism. In: R. Pickens and L. Heston (eds.), *Psychiatric Factors in Drug Abuse*. Grune and Stratton, New York, pp. 219–38

1981. Firewater myths revisited: Review of findings and some new directions. In: D. Heath, J. Waddell, and M. Topper (eds.), *Cultural Factors in Alcohol Research and Treatment of Drinking Problems*. Journal of Studies on Alcohol Supplement 9, New Brunswick, NJ, pp. 99–117

Scheper-Hughes, Nancy, 1970. *Saints, Scholars, and Schizophrenics: Mental Illness in Rural Ireland*. University of California Press, Berkeley

Schmidt, Wolfgang, and Robert E. Topham, 1978. The single distribution theory of alcohol consumption: A rejoinder to the critique of Parker and Harman. *Journal of Studies on Alcohol* 39: 400–19

1980. Discussion of "A critique of the distribution of consumption model of prevention." In: T. Harford, D. Parker and L. Light (eds.), *Normative Approaches to the Prevention of Alcohol Abuse and Alcoholism*. National Institute on Alcohol Abuse and Alcoholism Research Monograph 3, Rockville, MD, pp. 89–105

Schwartz, Norman B., 1978. Drinking patterns, drunks, and maturity in a Petén town (Guatemala). *Sociologus* (n.s.) 28: 35–53

Schwartz, Theodore, and Lola Romanucci-Ross, 1974. Drinking and inebriate behavior in the Admiralty Islands, Melanesia. *Ethos* 2: 213–31

Scourfield, Elfyn, 1974. *Farmhouse Brewing*. Bulletin of the National Museum of Wales 17, Amgueddfa

Seto, A., S. Tricomi, D. W. Goodwin, R. Kolodney, and T. Sullivan, 1978. Biochemical correlates of ethanol-induced flushing in Orientals. *Journal of Studies on Alcohol* 39: 1–11

Shore, James H., and Billee von Fumetti, 1972. Three alcohol programs for American Indians. *American Journal of Psychiatry* 128: 1450–54

Shukla, B. R. K., 1978. Religious and convivial use of intoxicants in a north Indian village. *Eastern Anthropologist* 31: 511–20

Singer, K., 1972. Drinking patterns and alcoholism in the Chinese. *British Journal of Addictions* 67: 3–14

Singer, Merrill, 1980. The function of sobriety among Black Hebrews. *Journal of Operational Psychiatry* 11: 162–68

Siverts, Henning (ed.), 1972. *Drinking Patterns in Highland Chiapas*. Universitets-forlaget, Bergen

Smart, Reginald G., Guillermina Natera, and Juan Alemandares Bonilla, 1980. *A Trial of a New Method for Studying Drinking and Drinking Problems in Three Countries of the Americas*. Addiction Research Foundation Substudy 1115, Toronto

Snyder, Charles R., 1958. *Alcohol and the Jews: A Cultural Study of Drinking and Sobriety*. Yale Center of Alcohol Studies Monograph 1, Free Press, Glencoe, IL

    1978. Preface to this edition. In: *Alcohol and the Jews*. Southern Illinois University Press, Carbondale

Spradley, James P., 1970. *You Owe Yourself a Drunk: An Ethnography of Urban Nomads*, Little, Brown, Boston

Spradley, James P., and Brenda J. Mann, 1975. *The Cocktail Waitress: Woman's Work in a Man's World*. John Wiley and Sons, New York

Spring, Josephine A., and David H. Buss, 1977. Three centuries of alcohol in the British diet. *Nature* 270: 567–72

Stanislawski, Dan, 1975. Dionysus westward: Early religion and the economic geography of wine. *Geographical Review* 65: 427–41

Steckley, George F., 1980. The wine economy of Tenerife in the seventeenth century: Anglo-Spanish partnership in a luxury trade. *Economic History Review* 33: 335–50

Steinkraus, Keith H., 1979. Nutritionally significant indigenous foods involving an alcoholic fermentation. In: C. Gastineau, W. Darby, and T. Turner (eds.), *Fermented Food Beverages in Nutrition*. Academic Press, New York, pp. 36–57

Stevens, Susan M., 1981. Alcohol and world view: A study of Passamaquoddy alcohol use. In: D. Heath, J. Waddell, and M. Topper (eds.), *Cultural Factors in Alcohol Research and Treatment of Drinking Problems*. Journal of Studies on Alcohol Supplement 9, New Brunswick, NJ, pp. 122–42

Stivers, Richard, 1976. *A Hair of the Dog: Irish Drinking and American Stereotype*. Pennsylvania State University Press, University Park

    1978. Irish ethnicity and alcohol use. *Medical Anthropology* 2 (4): 121–35

Stratton, R., A. Zeiner, and A. Paredes, 1978. Tribal affiliation and prevalence of alcohol problems. *Journal of Studies on Alcohol* 39: 1116–77

Strauss, Anne A., 1977. Northern Cheyenne ethnopsychology. *Ethos* 5: 326–57

Stull, Donald D., 1973. Modernization and Symptoms of Stress: Attitudes, Accidents, and Alcohol Use among Urban Papago Indians. PhD (Anthropology), University of Colorado, Boulder

    1975. Hologeistic studies of drinking: A critique. *Drinking and Drug Practices Surveyor* 10: 4–10

Suuronen, Kerttu, 1973. *Traditional Festive Drinking in Finland According to Responses to an Ethnographical Questionnaire*. Social Research Institute of Alcohol Studies Report 76, Helsinki

Taylor, William B., 1979. *Drinking, Homicide, and Rebellion in Colonial Mexican Villages*. Stanford University Press, Stanford

Thomas, Anthony E., 1978. Class and sociability among urban workers: A study of the bars as social club. *Medical Anthropology* 2(4): 9–30

Thomas, Robert K., 1981. The history of North American Indian alcohol use as a community-based phenomenon. In: D. Heath, J. Waddell, and M. Topper (eds.), *Cultural Factors in Alcohol Research and Treatment of Drinking Problems*. Journal of Studies on Alcohol Supplement 9, New Brunswick, NJ, pp. 29–39

Tiger, Lionel, 1979. *Optimism: The Biology of Hope*. Simon and Schuster, New York

Tongue, Archer, 1978. 5,000 years of drinking. In: J. Ewing and B. Rouse (eds.), *Drinking – Alcohol in American Society: Issues and Current Research*. Nelson-Hall, Chicago, pp. 31–38

Topper, Martin L., 1974. Drinking patterns, culture change, sociability and Navajo "adolescents." *Addictive Diseases* 1: 97–116

   1976. The cultural approach, verbal action plans, and alcohol research. In: M. Everett, J. Waddell, and D. Heath (eds.), *Cross-Cultural Approaches to the Study of Alcohol: An Interdisciplinary Perspective*. Mouton, The Hague, pp. 379–402

   1980. Drinking as an expression of status: Navajo male adolescents. In: J. Waddell and M. Everett (eds.), *Drinking Behavior among Southwestern Indians: An Anthropological Perspective*. University of Arizona Press, Tucson, pp. 103–47

   1981. The drinker's story: An important but often forgotten source of data. In: D. Heath, J. Waddell, and M. Topper (eds.), *Cultural Factors in Alcohol Research and Treatment of Drinking Problems*. Journal of Studies on Alcohol Supplement 9, New Brunswick, NJ, pp. 73–86

Trotter, Robert T., II, 1979. Evidence of an ethnomedical form of aversion therapy on the United States-Mexican border. *Journal of Ethnopharmacology* 1: 279–84

Trotter, Robert T., II, and Juan Antonio Chavira (eds.), 1977. *El Uso del Alcohol: A Resource Book for Spanish Speaking Communities*. Southern Area Alcohol Education and Training Program, Atlanta

Ullman, Albert D., 1958. Sociocultural backgrounds of alcoholism. *Annals of the American Academy of Political and Social Science* 315: 48–54

United States, Indian Health Service, Task Force on Alcoholism [1977]. *Alcoholism: A High Priority Health Problem*. Indian Health Service, Washington, DC

Urbanowicz, Charles F., 1975. Drinking in the Polynesian Kingdom of Tonga. *Ethnohistory* 22: 33–50

Waddell, Jack O., 1973. "Drink, friend!" Social contexts of convivial drinking and drunkenness among Papago Indians in an urban setting. In: M. Chafetz (ed.), *Proceedings of the First Annual Institute on Alcohol Abuse and Alcoholism*, Rockville, MD, pp. 237–51

   1975. For individual power and social credit: The use of alcohol among Tucson Papagos. *Human Organization* 34: 9–15

   1976a. The role of the cactus wine ritual in the Papago Indian ecosystem. In: A. Bharati (ed.), *Rituals, Cults, Shamanism: The Realm of the Extra-Human: volume 2*. Mouton, The Hague, pp. 213–28

   1976b. From tank to townhouse: Probing the impact of a legal reform on the drinking styles of urban Papago Indians. *Urban Anthropology* 5: 187–98

1979. Alcoholic intoxication as a component of the Papago Indian system of experiential reality. *Journal of Ultimate Reality and Meaning* 2: 4 ff.

1980a. The use of intoxicating beverages among native peoples of the aboriginal Greater Southwest. In: J. Waddell and M. Everett (eds.), *Drinking Behavior among Southwestern Indians: An Anthropological Perspective*. University of Arizona Press, Tucson, pp. 1–32

1980b. Drinking as a means of articulating social and cultural values: Papagos in an urban setting. In: J. Waddell and M. Everett (eds.), *Drinking Behavior among Southwestern Indians: An Anthropological Perspective*. University of Arizona Press, Tucson, pp. 37–82

1980c. Similarities and variations in alcohol use in four Native American societies in the Southwest. In: J. Waddell and M. Everett (eds.), *Drinking Behavior among Southwestern Indians: An Anthropological Perspective*. University of Arizona Press, Tucson, pp. 227–37

1981. Cultural relativity and alcohol use: Implications for research and treatment. In: D. Heath, J. Waddell, and M. Topper (eds.), *Cultural Factors in Alcohol Research and Treatment of Drinking Problems*. Journal of Studies on Alcohol Supplement 9, New Brunswick, NJ, pp. 18–28

Waddell, Jack O., and Michael W. Everett (eds.), 1980. *Drinking Behavior among Southwestern Indians: An Anthropological Perspective*. University of Arizona, Tucson

Wagner, Catherine A., 1978. Coca, Chicha, and Trago: Private and Communal Rituals in a Quechua Community. PhD (Anthropology), University of Illinois, Urbana

West, Elliott, 1979. *The Saloon on the Rocky Mountain Mining Frontier*. University of Nebraska Press, Lincoln

Westermeyer, Joseph J., 1971. Use of alcohol and opium by the Meo of Laos. *American Journal of Psychiatry* 127: 1019–23

1974a. Cross cultural studies of alcoholism in the clinical setting. *American Journal of Drug and Alcohol Abuse* 1: 89–105

1974b. "The drunken Indian": myths and realities. *Psychiatric Annals* 4 (11): 29 ff.

1976a. Cross-cultural studies of alcoholism in the clinical setting: A review and evaluation. In: M. Everett, J. Waddell, and D. Heath (eds.), *Cross-Cultural Approaches to the Study of Alcohol: An Interdisciplinary Perspective*. Mouton, The Hague, pp. 359–78

1976b. Use of a social indicator system to assess alcoholism among Indian people in Minnesota. *American Journal of Drug and Alcohol Abuse* 3: 447–56

1976c. Clinical guidelines for the cross-cultural treatment of chemical dependency. *American Journal of Drug and Alcohol Abuse* 3: 315–22

1981. Research on treatment of drinking problems: Importance of cultural factors. In: D. Heath, J. Waddell, and M. Topper (eds.), *Cultural Factors in Alcohol Research and Treatment of Drinking Problems*. Journal of Studies on Alcohol Supplement 9, New Brunswick, NJ, pp. 44–59

Westermeyer, Joseph J., and John Brantner, 1972. Violent death and alcohol use among the Chippewa in Minnesota. *Minnesota Medicine* 55: 749–52

Westermeyer, Joseph J., and Gretchen Lang, 1975. Ethnic differences in use of alcoholism facilities. *International Journal of the Addictions* 10: 513–20

Whitehead, Paul C., and Cheryl Harvey, 1974. Explaining alcoholism: An empirical test and reformulation. *Journal of Health and Social Behavior* 15: 57–65

Wilkerson, D., 1978. *Sipping Saints*. Fleming II. Revell, Old Tappan, NJ

Williams, Sarah E., 1980. The use of beverage alcohol as medicine, 1790–1860. *Journal of Studies on Alcohol* 41: 543–66

Wolcott, Harry F., 1974. *African Beer Gardens of Bulawayo: Integrated Drinking in a Segregated Society*. Rutgers Center of Alcohol Studies Monograph 10, New Brunswick, NJ

1975. Feedback influences on fieldwork, or: A funny thing happened on the way to the beer garden. In: C. Kileff and W. Pendleton (eds.), *Urban Man in South Africa*. Mambo Press, Gwelo [Rhodesia], pp. 99–125

Wolf, Aron S., 1980. Homicide and blackout in Alaskan Natives: A report and reproduction of five cases. *Journal of Studies on Alcohol* 41: 456–62

Wolff, Peter H. 1972. Ethnic differences in alcohol sensitivity. *Science* 175: 449–50

1973. Vasomotor sensitivity to alcohol in diverse Mongoloid populations. *American Journal of Human Genetics* 25: 193–99

Wolin, Steven, J., Linda A. Bennett, Denise L. Noonan, and Martha A. Teitelbaum, 1980. Disrupted family rituals: A factor in the intergenerational transmission of alcoholism. *Journal of Studies on Alcohol* 41: 199–214

Zeiner, Arthur R., Alfonso Paredes, and H. Dix Christensen, 1979. The role of acetaldehyde in mediating reactivity to an acute dose of ethanol among different racial groups. *Alcoholism* (New York) 3: 11–18

Zimberg, Sheldon, 1977. Sociopsychiatric perspectives on Jewish alcohol abuse: implications for the prevention of alcoholism. *American Journal of Drug and Alcohol Abuse* 4: 571–79

II

DRINKS CONSTRUCT THE WORLD AS IT IS

3. Passage to play: rituals of drinking time in American society

Joseph R. Gusfield

A number of years ago I led an undergraduate class discussion of Aldous Huxley's novel *Brave New World*. Huxley's work was an anti-Utopian vision of a future world in which human hedonism ran rampant at the expense of human qualities of spirit, independence and creativity. All material needs and desires and all sensual gratifications were satisfied. I began the discussion by asking a student if he would like to live in Huxley's future society. "No", he replied, "but I'd sure like to visit on week-ends."

That answer has seemed to me to encapsulate a characteristic of the modern, organizational society: its division of time into periods of different quality as well as function. To use the week-end as a contrast to the week implies a routinized scheduling of time in which a period of work and a period of play exist as contrasts. In the response of that undergraduate, the week-end becomes a release from the rules and the tasks of daily routine.

The clock is as much a symbol of modern civilization as shoes, print and the steam engine. Contemporary industrialized societies are time-bounded. The hour, the day and the week are definite and fixed units. Punctuality and attention to time, subdivided into minutes and even seconds, is a fundamental part of social organization (Zerubavel, 1981). Earlier, pre-industrial, societies reckoned their time divisions by more natural rhythms prescribed by sunrise and sunset, religious calendars of festival, Sabbaths and feast days; by the ebb and flow of the bodily energy (Dumazedier, 1968, pp. 248–54; Le Goff, 1980, pp. 43–52). As life moved into cities and work into factories and organizations, predictability and constancy came to be prized (Reid, 1976; E. P. Thompson, 1967). Time was cut up into smaller units and the flow of time secularized and made into routine, fixed elements.

It is in this context that I want to consider the symbolic uses of drinking in the time frames of American life. While many societies have distinguished periods of play from periods of other activity, the conception of leisure as a definite and bounded part of time is a feature of the industrial and post-industrial world of work.[1] This very distinction, between work and leisure must be viewed as a development of industrialized society and its normal definition and division of time (Dumazedier, 1968; Marrus, 1974, pp. 1–10). Leisure is an historically emergent category, dependent on the separation of work from home and thus from one period of the day to another. In the routinized, secularized and disciplined activity of the factory modern life has found its metaphor, a metaphor dramatized and characterized in Chaplin's classic film *Modern Times*.

With industrial labor there came a new conception of time. Instead of working in spurts and splutters, with long bursts and short rests, the daily round was transformed into a regular and repeated process, with beginnings and endings clearly stated and enforced, with a specified length of work defined in units of time ("the hourly wage" or "the monthly salary") and with a definite work-week (E. P. Thompson, 1967; Gutman, 1977, pp. 3–79). Historians of nineteenth-century Europe have written about "Saint Monday" as a form of resistance to the appearance of fixed schedules of work. The high degrees of absenteeism by workers at the beginning of the week seems analogous to the many Saint days by which work was punctuated in an earlier, less secular and less rationalized work-time (Kaplow, 1981; Reid, 1976). With the rigid time schedules of industrial organization everyday life becomes as a set of impermeable membranes and the flow of time experienced as a passage from one period to another; from organization to home; from work to play.

As a characteristic of modern life, leisure must be seen in its contrast to the demands of work. The different contexts of time are also different contexts of comportment; areas of life in which contrasting attitudes exist toward the activities and objects of attention. Leisure is not-work; work is not-leisure. The terms separate areas of self-control required at work from those expressed at play: supervision; standardization and utilitarian forms of thought and criteria of action from areas of release, of spontaneity; of action for its own satisfactions. Boundaries must be maintained but within the confines of leisure there is a wider range of choices and behaviors. The culture of time in modern life is symbolized in the slogan of some American labor unions in their struggle for the eight-hour day in the 1890s: "Eight Hours of Work; Eight Hours for Sleep; Eight Hours for What We Will" (Rosenzweig, 1983).

Day and night; week and week-end; work and vacation – these comprise much of the rhythm of our lives (Melbin, 1978). Work and play; workplace and home; organization and community – these comprise much of the shifts we pass through in the course of daily existence. Spontaneity, disorder, relaxation, freedom, equality – these are some of the terms of description for the time and area of play and leisure. Leisure has its meaning in modern life in the contrast to work – to the controlled, disciplined, orderly, hierarchical nature of organizational tasks. The world of work requires and demands from us behavior that stands often in opposition to the license and leeway of playful motivations and attitudes. Routine involves us in fixed boundaries of time, in a limitation of choice of activity and in a definite sequence of behavior (Zerubavel, 1981, pp. 44–49).

The great threat to organization is disorganization: the failure to conduct ourselves in accordance with rules. Leisure provides, in the British phrase, a "free time". To mix the two domains becomes a danger to the serious side and an opposition to the playful. If play and leisure constitute counter-cultures of release from the discipline and ruled nature of "serious" work they are not completely unruled. Social organization governs both the dominant culture and the release from its claims (Rieff, 1966, pp. 1–28). What the rationalistic, modern impulse has demanded is that the hedonistic, the playful, the irresponsible, the non-serious not be permitted to enter the domain of the "serious" areas of making a living and earning a livelihood.

In the agenda of every-day life we pass from one arena to another. We go through the time periods in spatial passage. We travel from organization to home; from work to play. It is the thesis of this chapter that alcohol, in the particular historical context of the United States, has developed symbolic properties which serve to facilitate this passage in a generally, though not always, orderly manner. This paper is an analysis of the symbolic meaning of alcohol in the temporal organization of daily and weekly life for a large segment of the American population.

The symbolism of food and drink

Culture as language. It has been conventional in anthropology to think of drinking as a ritual act, used as an adjunct to religious rituals or a focal point of Dionysian rites (Heath, 1975; Jellinek, 1977). From this and other perspectives alcohol has been analyzed for its tension-reducing properties or its unifying effects in rituals of solidarity. Such approaches have studied drunkenness rather than drinking. The occurrence of limited, recurrent occasions of drinking rather than drunkenness is closer to the subject of this chapter. It is drinking as a cultural object that occupies my attention.

My use of culture and its embodiment in food and drink is a perspective of the understanding of meanings. From this viewpoint, culture can be seen as symbol systems with which life is organized into an understandable set of actions and events (Gusfield, 1981). Clifford Geertz has stated this in an excellent fashion:

> both so-called cognitive and so-called expressive symbols or symbol-systems have, then, at least one thing in common: they are extrinsic sources of information in terms of which human life can be patterned – extrapersonal mechanisms for the perception, understanding, judgment and manipulation of the world. Culture patterns . . . are –"programs"; they provde a template or blueprint for the organization of social and psychological processes . . . (Geertz, 1973, p. 216).

That food and drink are used as symbols of social position and status is an

old theme in Sociology. Thorstein Veblen's classic study of conspicuous consumption and status symbols created a mode of analysis which has been the staple of sociological studies of consumer behavior since its original publication in 1899 (Veblen, 1934). More recently the study of food and drink has been as attentive to the text – the content of consumption – as to its context – the setting and the participants (M. Douglas 1984, pp. 1–39). Mary Douglas makes the distinction between the interest in food as material and as symbolic by referring to eating as a "field of action. It is a medium in which other levels of categorization becomes manifest" (ibid., p. 30). In her own analyses of British meals and of the Judaic rules of *kashruth* she has demonstrated how what is eaten and how it is eaten constitute a mode of communication and can be read as a cultural object, embodying the attributes of social organization or general culture (M. Douglas, *Purity and Danger*, 1966)

Others have made use of somewhat similar orientations to the study of food. Sahlin's distinction between animals that are improper to eat and those proper to eat in Western societies laid emphasis on the "human-like" qualities atttributed to "pets", such as dogs, horses and cats as compared to those perceived as less than human, such as pigs, sheep and cows (Sahlins, 1976). Barthes' analysis of steak as a male food or sugar as symbolic of a "sweet time" again show the use of food as a system of signs and symbols capable of being read for their meaning; what they say as well as what they denote as material sustenance (Barthes, 1973, 1979; also see Farb and Armelagos, 1980, Ch. 5). Lévi-Strauss' *The Raw and the Cooked* is, perhaps, the seminal work in this approach to the study of food as a symbol and as a medium of communication (Lèvi-Strauss, 1969).

In his recent analysis of taste and social structure, Pierre Bourdieu presents both an empirical study of consumer habits and an interpretive theory which, applied to food and drink, sees in the content of meals and foods, the communication and representation of more general orientations to life styles. In his surveys of the French population, Bourdieu found sharp differences in both the foods eaten and the nature of meals among various classes and occupational groups. Among the working classes, the emphasis in eating is on the material and the familial. Guests not closely related to the household are seldom invited. The sequence of courses is unimportant. The changing of plates is minimal. The food itself is heavy and filling; a focus on plenty. There is a sharp division between male food and female food and a lack of concern for food as creating health or beauty of body. Among petite-bourgeoisie and the bourgeoisie, the opposite is the case. The meal is an occasion for social interaction; it is regulated in manners and sequences; it is pre-occupied with considerations of health and aesthetic consequences (Bourdieu, 1984, pp. 177–200).

Bourdieu reads these empirical differences as the existence of distinctive tastes; part of fundamental and deep-seated styles of life. In emphasizing the meal as an occasion of social relationships, the bourgoisie deny the primary, material function of eating and maintain the integration of familial with the more disciplined areas of life. Order, restraint and propriety may not be abandoned. In this they express a dimension of the bourgeois' orientation to society as a matter of refinement and regulation, of a "stylization of life" which "tends to shift the emphasis from substance and function to form and manner, and so to deny the crudely material reality of eating and of the things consumed or ... the basely material vulgarity of those who indulge in the immediate satisfactions of food and drink" (Bourdieu, 1984, p. 196).

In the light of these analyses of food, the relation between alcohol and the passage from one realm to another is to be studied as text, that is as a statement or language through which a message is being communicated. This does not preclude its status as expressive of a way of experiencing life and expressing culture. At the same time, to understand that message it needs to be understood in a context. That context is both interactive – where it is occurring and on what kinds of occasions – and historical – the meanings that the past and the particular society have given it. The styles of one group cannot be understood in isolation from their contrasts. Neither can the uses and meanings of alcohol in the passage from work to play be understood apart from its connotations in American history.

The meanings of alcohol in American culture

Alcohol in American culture. Political conflicts over the use and availability of alcoholic beverages have been a persistent part of American history. The efforts of the Temperance and Prohibition movements to limit and eradicate the use and the availability of alcohol through persuasion and through law are a salient piece of American politics (Gusfield, 1963; 1986, ch. 8). Even after Repeal of the Prohibition amendment alcohol has remained a "dangerous commodity", limited in its legitimate use to adults, to specific hours and provided by licensed sellers.

Before the 1830s, while drunkenness was observed and condemned, it had an accepted place in American life in both work and play. With the emergence of industrial organization, the separation of work as an area of sobriety and play as an area of permissible insobriety became more common (Tyrell, 1979; Rorabaugh, 1979).The development of leisure as a contrast to work did much to reinforce the disapproval of drinking as daytime activity. The prohibition against drinking on the job was much like that which occurred in Britain with industrial development: "The frequency of early nineteenth-century protest against working-class drunkenness is as much an indication that the ancient inseparability of work and recreation has become inconvenient as that drunkenness had itself become more prevalent" (Harrison, 1971, p. 40).

In the United States, the association of alcohol with leisure is part of a unique pattern of drinking. Societies differ in the periodicity and manner of drinking as they do in many other forms of behavior. The French drink wine at any time of day. The Finns consume alcohol on the week-end and in large quantities, to get drunk (Beauchamp, 1980). Americans also confine alcohol to certain periods of the day, to certain days of the week, to certain areas of the locality. When these norms are breached, the resulting behavior is cause for disapproval, ridicule and more punishing sanctions.

Whether the use of alcohol is rejected or not, the concept of a proper time for drinking contains a recognition of time frames. There are appropriate settings in time, space and activity for drinking and inappropriate ones where drinking is to be avoided. The phrase, "It's time for a drink" is used to mark the conclusion of work activities. As studies of behavior in bars has shown, that part of the folk conception of "competent drinkers" lies in not crossing the boundaries that separate acceptable places of drinking and drunkenness from unacceptable ones (LeMasters, 1975; Gusfield, Kotarba and Rasmussen, 1981). To appear on time for work and perform adequately; to carry out one's obligations as husband or father is crucial to the notion of social competence.

There is a time for work and a time for play; a time for drunkenness and a time for sobriety. Day and night, weekday and week-end, work-time and leisure time; these mark the boundaries of ordinary separation of abstinence-time from drinking-time in a wide range of American groups and sub-cultures.

The meanings of alcohol in American culture. Why alcohol? What is the content of the message conveyed by drinking that makes it a fit object to symbolize and ritualize the transition from work to play?

On one level it exists as a sign. Already segregated and separated from work, it is an index to the appearance of a nighttime attitude. The sight of containers of wine, beer and/or whiskey testifies to the time period itself, just as the increased flow of traffic serves to announce the end of the workday to observers of the highway.

But there are deeper meanings to the use of alcohol in American life that stem from its character as a source of conflict and ambivalence in American life. In their comparative study of drunkenness in a large sample of societies, McAndrew and Edgerton coined the term "time out" to describe the way in which drinking in American culture symbolizes and introduces a degree of cultural remission (McAndrew and Edgerton, 1969; Cavan, 1966). By "cultural remission" I refer to the conventionalized relaxation of social controls over behavior. The very derogation of drinking among large segments of American society creates its meaning as quasi-subterranean behavior when practiced within those segments.

As an object, as a form of food, alcohol is believed to be a disinhibitor (Levine, 1978). Some anthropologists, like McAndrew and Edgerton, attribute the disinhibiting qualities of alcohol to the social definitions of drink and drunkenness rather than to its physio-chemical properties. Whatever the correctness of those views, alcohol appears in American society deeply connected with mood-setting. It is a mood which contrasts with the serious and the work-a-day world.

Several attributes associated with alcohol help to enhance the belief in its mood-setting properties and enhance its ability to symbolize the passage from work to play. One is the "cover" which alcohol provides to the exposure of the self to public judgments. By shifting the burden of explaining embarrassing moments from a reflection of the self to the effects of alcohol, drinking provides an excuse for lapses of responsibility, for unmannerly behavior; for gaucheries, for immoral and improper actions. "I was not myself" is the plea the morning after. In this fashion, the use of alcohol places a frame around action which mitigates effects in other spheres of life.

Secondly, there is the festive character of alcohol use. Work, especially in the modern formal organization, demands an attitude of serious attention to task. To again refer to an American idiom, "It's no party" is a way of contrasting the festive, fun-oriented attitude with the nature of the regulated, goal-oriented life of organized work. The spontaneity of leisure is not the measured tones of daily labor.

Third, alcohol is an accompaniment of social solidarity. Precisely because it possesses a meaning of contrast to organized work, it is a dissolver of hierarchy. In Victor Turner's term 'communitas', it is a contrast to structure, a commitment to values of human similarity and anti-structure (Turner, 1969, 1977). This again highlights its fitness as a marker of time and space for the transformation of the person from a socially bound and limited player of roles into someone of self-expression.

Alcohol in the ritual transformation of space and time

The calendrical movement is also a movement of social space and social time, as distinguished from chronological space and chronological time. What is contrasted are styles of behavior which constitute the meanings of a space and a time change. Another way of seeing such changes is as a transformation of frame in which alcohol performs the function of keying events into a new frame.

Framing and keying. Frameworks of thought and perception enable participants in social action to define the behavior allowable and expected within an area – a space – and within a swath of time. With the carpets rolled up and the chairs and tables placed against the wall, the dining room becomes a dance floor. To "mistake" a dance floor for a dining room is to make a grievous social error. The frame provides the interpretations that enable the actor and the observer to know what set of rules apply because he can now define the meaning of the situation. A clear example of frames is exemplified in the behavior of art models. Posing in the nude during a "sitting", they generally robe themselves during rest periods. To be "working" rather than "playing" is to place action in a different frame and generate a different set of meanings to a situation.

In our every-day lives we shift frames continuously: the shift from work to play being one of the major transformations of daily life. Such shifts are facilitated by stylized, ritualized ways of making the change. Goffman has referred to such social devices through an analogy with music as "keying": "I refer here to the set of conventions by which a given activity, one already meaningful in terms of some primary framework, is transformed into something patterned on this activity but seen by the participants to be something quite else" (Goffman, 1974, pp. 43–44).

Such keys, continues Goffman, operate as cues to establish the beginnings and endings which bound the transformation in time. I will use the concepts of frame and key to describe the uses of alcohol in establishing time frames of play. In non-mechanical work, wine is sometimes used, especially late in the workday, in conjunction with work, such as meetings. It turns a work activity into a more social occasion.

I am also using the concept of keying to include devices and conventions by which new settings and new frames are created within new activities. A related concept, used by an observer of the beer party in an African society, refers to the significance of beer as a "context marker" (Karp, 1980, p. 90). Reference to beer drinking in announcements of mortuary ceremonies indicates a commensal aspect of the occasion.

Alcohol as a keying device. The sharp segregation of areas of life from one another in modern societies makes the journey from work to home a liminal period – a transition that is ambiguously framed. From Arnold van Gennep to Victor Turner the concept of *rites de passage* has been an object of special attention among anthropologists. It has been used to describe the characteristic rituals which mark movement from one status to another, from one stage in the life cycle to another (Van Gennep, 1960; V. Turner, 1969, 1977). To see liminality in the journey from work is to analogize the tension and danger associated with liminality in primitive societies to the modern round of the daily and weekly shifts in modern life.

Within the American context, drinking en route to home, to begin the evening or on the threshold of entry into the home is a frequent event among groups where drinking is accepted. I am not describing bouts of drunkenness but the contained and circumscribed "social drinking" which may occur in bars or at home. What is significant is the meaning of drinking as an aftermath to the work period and a prelude to the leisure period. The "cocktail hour" embodies the symbolism of a time period between work and leisure. The term itself connotes a means of ending a period of time and thus a transformation into another. Within the workplace, the expression "It's time for a drink" is used among fellow-workers to signal the end of the workday and the beginning of another style of behavior. It is a way of announcing that one frame – of work – is now ended and another – of play – is about to begin.

The festive character of the occasion is a matter of its frame. Commercial bars have created a new term in recent years to describe the period of drinking of the "cocktail". They use the expression "Happy Hours" to connote the period of time at the end of work-day, usually 4–6 p.m., and its attendant shifts in style. Here too the special nature of the time is further symbolized in the lowering of prices during "Happy Hours". In recent years the expression, TGIF, has emerged in American English. It is an acronym for "Thank God It's Friday", and clearly bestows the meaning of cultural remission on the week-end. It too is celebrated by drinking.

The ritual in which work colleagues celebrate the end of the day or the end of the week is again illustrative of the meaning of drink as solidifying personal relationships. It serves as a cue to permit non-hierarchical relations, unregulated by the structures of organization. At another level it signals the exposure of the self to others within an atmosphere which is also protective. One of the norms of action within the drinking group is a lesser attention to calculations of economic fairness and justice. The buying of rounds is one way in which an exact measure of *quid pro quo* is replaced by a moral economy in which money must not be "the measure of all things" (E. P. Thompson, 1978; Rosenzweig, 1983). In "rounds" each person takes responsibility for payment of the drink of all members of the group, no matter what his own consumption will be or has been (Gusfield, Kotarba and Rasmussen, 1981).

In another passage of mood, the drink is consumed on first entering the home or shortly after. Here again the demand for transforming the person from a work-oriented to a family-oriented person presents the problem of how this is achieved. Change of dress is another way of changing the person and is another, perhaps substitute, ritual through which the transformation is marked.

Note that the form of drinking described here is not that of drunkenness or unlicensed behavior. Such celebrations are not marked by the drunken behavior and licensed deviation from norms that has often been associated with Saturnalia ceremonies, such as the Christmas office party or the New Year's Eve party (Gusfield, 1963). Alcohol may not be consumed in large amounts at all. It is its use as cue to a changed agenda of behavior that is the function under study here.

Alcohol and the meal: priorities and sequences. The gulf that separates work from play; abstinence from drink and alcohol from industry appears as well in the hierarchy of drinks. Beer and wine, low alcohol content drinks, have a wider use, in more settings, than does whiskey or gin. Hard liquor is segregated even more than "softer" drinks containing less alcohol.

This hierarchy must be understood in analyzing the symbolism of alcoholic beverages in the meal. One rule of taste is that the alcohol served before the meal may be of higher "proof" than that served during the meal. Whiskey or gin may be offered and accepted as a prelude to the meal but not as an accompaniment to the meal. Beer or wine may be offered as well and may also be used as part of the meal. The higher the alcohol content, the less it is viewed as a nutrient. Eating as a physical activity is to be separated, to some degree, from eating as a social occasion.

The prelude to the meal, more characteristic of middle-class homes on occasions of receiving guests, serves a mood-setting function as well as marking the transition from one home to another and, sometimes, the passage from work to play. Food offered in the form of *hors d'oeuvres* (literally, "outside the main work") is part of the setting of a mood of friendly interaction to which the alcohol contributes both as cue and as disinhibitor.

It is important to note the change which eating appears to have undergone in American life during the past 100 years. Riesman's study of American cookbooks shows a shift from instructions in utilitarian cooking to those teaching the use of exotic foods that display the taste and wide knowledge of the hosts (Riesman, 1950, pp. 148–52). This seems close to Bourdieu's differentiation of working-class and bourgeois uses of eating, although the class lines are probably not as clearly defined as in Bourdieu's description (see pp. 76–77, 85). In this shift from utilitarian use of foods to an aesthetic attitude, the continuity between work and leisure is diminished and the experience of eating transformed into an occasion of play. In the American context, the use of alcohol, especially of spirits, defines the non-substantiality of the meal as a fun time rather than a refueling stop.

Alcohol as activity. The cultural definition of alcohol as a liquid which develops and sustains personal and solidary human relationships is significant in cueing occasions. The drinking occasion is a contrast to the rational and hierarchical attitudes of persons as dramatic actors and actresses; as players of roles. In the drinking arena first names are required and organizational placements tabooed. Here again Victor Turner's distinction between structure and communitas is useful. Structure is rule-bound and role-oriented. Relationships between persons are mediated and regulated by their position in the structure: employee and supervisor; doctor and patient; clerk and customer. These are the identities by which we frame relationships. In play such attributions have less claim on our attention and on our behavior.

The ability to shift moods and frames is daily demanded of us in modern life. We are moved to adjust to changes of scene and frame. Sometimes this requires us to act differently toward the same people, as with colleagues outside the work-place. Sometimes it requires us to act differently toward different people, as in going from work-place to home. The drinking situation enables us to provide liminal time; a way of passing from the ordered regulation of one form of social organization to the less-ordered, deregulated form of another.

Here the presence of alcohol takes on another meaning: its unpredictability. Insofar as alcohol is believed to relax inhibitions, the outcomes of that disinhibition are never clearly contained even by rules of appropriate drinking behavior. One of the contingencies of drinking arenas is that the social organization may come unglued. While drinking can promote fellow-feeling it can also be a catalyst to angry words, denunciations and the exposure of those secrets by which social organization is held in place. *In vino veritas* but social order cannot stand too much *veritas*. In enhancing disorder and unpredictability there is also risk and danger. That in itself suggests the meaning of alcohol in developing the frame of anti-structure; of passage from serious to the playful; from predictable order to risky role-release.

Coffee: the passage to work. In the folklore of drinking there is the belief that coffee is an agent of sobriety. It is what the drinker should drink if he wishes to achieve sobriety quickly. Common talk pictures coffee as the antithesis to alcohol. It is the liquid with which one wakes-up in the morning. It is what the workers and the professionals drink on "breaks" or sip alongside their work. Although physiologists disclaim the ability of coffee to eradicate the effects of alcohol, it persists as the symbol of contrast – the food with which we return from the world of leisure to the world of work.

It is the appearance of coffee that symbolically ends the party as it does the meal. As breakfast food, coffee is the "eye-opener"; the food that recalls the coffee drinker to the serious mien of the work-place. Coffee stimulates; alcohol relaxes. Its symbolic properties produce its ritualistic usage.

Abstinence and drinking: the symbiosis of contrasts

In America the segregation of the use of alcohol to the period of leisure is largely a product of the nineteenth century. Colonial America did not generally perceive alcohol as inherently evil. Its consumption was not limited to special times and places (Landers and Martin, 1982). Its impropriety as an adjunct to "serious" utilitarian pursuits arises with industrial and organizational development. The shift from alcohol as the "goodly creature of God" to "Demon rum" was, however, not simply a response to economic development. The ambivalent and remissive meanings of alcohol owe much to the work of the American Temperance and Prohibition movements in creating the public awareness of alcohol as a "dangerous commodity" (Gusfield, 1963; 1984).

Alcohol is a point of tension, ambivalence and conflict in American life unlike its status in most industrial societies. Only in Finland, Norway and

Sweden have anti-alcohol movements been as politically salient as in the United States. The many political battles over the regulation of sales; the special restrictions on time of sale, especially to adolescents; the numerous legal measures enacted to limit its availability and use all attest to public ambivalence. The Prohibition amendment was a major restriction on American consumption habits. Even after Repeal alcohol continued to be a restricted commodity and its sale regulated by legal constraints. For large segments of the American population the use of alcohol is minimal and the descriptions of the passage through daily life above are maps to a non-existent island. It is a Brave New World which many neither wish to live in nor to visit.

Neither is the idea of leisure as play or as cultural remission a uniform feature of American life. Until this point I have used the concepts of leisure and play almost synonymously. That usage is misleading in a way that hides the contrastive character of alcohol in American life. Leisure is a chrono-logical concept – the absence of work and the time period of choice, of "what we will". Play is, as I am using the concept, leisure characterized by spontaneity, by unscheduled action, by a blurring of social boundaries and by activity which is chiefly unproductive from an economic viewpoint.[2] It is "fun time" and opposite in quality and style to the serious activities of life.

It is possible for leisure to be conducted in ways indifferent to or even an-tagonistic to play and certainly to cultural remission. The distinction made by Zerubavel between profane time and sacred time, following Durkheim, recognizes that leisure may be a time of considerable self-commitment, discipline and contemplation, hardly meriting the description of playful-ness. Such sacralizing of leisure is apparent in the Sabbath of major re-ligions (Zerubavel, 1985, Ch. 4; 1984, passim.).

The advent of leisure and the possibilities of play raise problems as well as opportunities. There are diverse possibilities in the continuity of discon-tinuity between realms of the spirit as there are between periods of the day. For the deeply religious, the secular world of work may push one to wear a mask which abjures the sacred world of spiritual and/or mystical attain-ments. Leisure permits the expression of a self for whom the very term "play" is an abomination. To be absent from work is to be able to enter a different world; to be released to God. The cultural remission is not from order but from the profane world to the sacred.

Both the transition from work to play and from the secular to the sacred are transformations of discontinuity. They involve shifts in the styles of thought and behavior that constitute contrasts with the personality and character of the work arena. For many others, work and leisure may be more closely associated. A sermon by a nineteenth-century American min-ister illustrates the attitude of continuity. In "Christian Recreation and Un-christian Amusements" Reverend Theodore Cuyler cautioned against the attitude that "wants stimulation and excitement". Condemned enjoyments, such as the theater, do not strengthen us for the work of the following day and lack spiritual value (Gusfield, 1963, pp. 30–31).

Reverend Cuyler's sermon represents only one form of continuity between leisure and work; one in which leisure is judged on its implications for work. Equally significant is the characteristic life style in which routine, discipline, and scheduling remain central to the daily agenda of life. That playful orientation toward activity in which carelessness and disorder are prized is anathema for this philosophy. The meaning of play as release from the dominance of the "serious" side of life is unattractive and even immoral from the perspective of continuity.

This sense of opposition between drinker and non-drinker as a contrast of cultural themes may also have its analogies elsewhere than the American situation. Pierre Bourdieu, utilizing a survey of the French population, finds a similar set of distinctions:

> in abstaining from having a good time and having it with others, the would-be *petit bourgeois* betrays his ambition of escaping from the common present, when, that is, he does not construct his whole self-image around the opposition between home and the cafe, abstinence and intemperance, in other words between individual salvation and collective solidarities (Bourdieu, 1984, p. 183).

Bourdieu's description of the French *petite bourgeoisie* differs from the American in at least two respects. First, the contrast is situated in a context of class differentiation. In the American case the opposition, once religious and ethnic, has become more characterological and generational (Gusfield, 1963). It cuts across the categories of class and ethnicity. Secondly, in the French case the contrast is a more general one between an emphasis on the here and now, on the utilitarian values of food and drink in the working class and the emphasis on refinement, on escape from the mundane and the useful among the *petite bourgeoisie*. In the American case, abstinence from alcohol is associated with a utilitarian and religious perspective toward leisure. As Bourdieu also points out, in the French case, among the bourgeoisie foods are also sources of pleasure but with less emphasis on the physical character of food than on its commensal and taste-symbolizing aspects. The individualism is a deeper one in the American context. The person is the dependable source of social control and the group, the crowd, the peer is the mechanism of temptation and disorder. What the antipathy to cultural remission displays in the American context is a fealty to and dependence on the importance of self-control and a distrust of the ability of social and institutional restraints to regulate and constrain human behavior. It is the prized image of the person who resists temptations and limits worldly desires for spiritual rewards that the abstinence ethic means in the American setting (Levine, 1979; Nissenbaum, 1980).

American culture and the symbolism of drinking

One of the streams of thought in Temperance literature of the nineteenth century was the "all or none" character of drinking (Gusfield, 1963; Levine, 1978). The argument for abstinence was for total abstinence on the grounds that a little would become more and would grow beyond control. The habitual drunkard, the chronic alcoholic, are the tangible reminders of what constitutes the deviant person and the grim prophecy of what that deviance is and does. The belief extends to limited drinking in the assertion that release from social controls cannot be a moderated, regulated and controlled affair. Once Pandora opens the box, the spirits that flow out from it cannot again be captured and encaged.

The identification of modern life with rational and systematic thought and action has been a major theme of contemporary sociological theory. The rationalization of the institutional framework in the form of organizational structures has been the structural side to the cultural *geist* of rationality and regulation. At the same time that industrialization and capitalism emerged from the cocoon of history the dialectical opposition to both of them emerged as well. A romantic resistance to rationality has been a recurrent theme in modern life (Spitzer, 1983; Lears, 1981; Bell, 1976; Gouldner, 1980).

Such orientations toward modern life are represented as well in the divergent conceptions of the value of alcohol and those who hold them. One fears exactly what the other seeks. A Romantic approach prizes the end of the day and the discontinuity which it makes possible. Those who accept it look with favor on the "time-out" as a bounded and limited space and time in which a more authentic self can achieve expression. The use of alcohol symbolizes a temporal life style and accentuates the transformation out of the posture of social controls and self-imprisonment.

But the meaning of alcohol as symbolizing and signalling a remission of social controls is both underlined and shaped by the contrasting condemnation of its use and of the relaxation of control that it presages. The existence of a once-dominant and still vital culture of continuity between leisure and work gives the behavior of drinking an even clearer sense of a "break" in the styles of life that mark the daily routines of work and organizational tasks.

Despite these wide divergences in life styles and conceptions of leisure represented in the presence or absence of alcohol in transforming social activities, there is an underlying uniformity of meaning. Both groups – abstainers and users – and those overlapping have a similar understanding of what the presence of alcohol symbolizes. The cognitive understandings are the same even though the evaluational stances are in conflict. The conflict is not possible without the common "agreement" on the definition of the situation. Both see in the use of alcohol the same transformation of the frame from work to play.

This symbiosis within conflict is apparent in two other frameworks for the relation of work to play in which alcohol plays a symbolic role. One is found in certain occupations in which pre-industrial forms of organization and culture still exist. In construction industries, for example, there often persists a definition of work as male activity (LeMasters, 1975, esp. Ch. 2). Drinking is more likely to occur within the work period. Beer and whiskey, but not wine, may be used during worktime in any quantity and not always be seen as antithetical to the day's activities. Such occupational worlds have only partially "surrendered" to the routinized and controlled arenas of bureaucratic organization and factory discipline. Here the idea of a regulated order of space and time has not fully been institutionalized. Work and play are not yet impermeable.

The opposite is also both possible and, perhaps, increasingly found in modern organization and among upper echelons of control. This form is the intrusion of play into work (Riesman, 1950). Here work forms take on something of the character of informal sociability. The serving of wine at committee meetings is one such mode in which the meeting is placed, though ambiguously, in the frame of a social occasion. The use of alcohol at business luncheons serves both to remove something of the intrusion of work into "private time" and also to provide a framework of conviviality and social equality where it may be useful to the work of achieving a consensus among possibly conflicting members.

In both of these examples – the construction industries and organizational management – the meaning of alcohol is homogeneous to the others discussed above. What differs is the content of the rituals in the drinking acts. The meanings follow the same code; speak in the same language.

In the perpetual struggle of the individual toward self-expressiveness and social integration, the conflict between work and play, day and night, gains intensity. Release is both a boon and a danger. The alcoholic is the obverse of the workaholic. (Note how the word has been adapted to both poles.) The alcoholic becomes one of the symbols of a fear of falling; of a threat in the personal drama of success and failure that is the key story of American careers. The workaholic is the opposite. Here the danger lies in the inability to let go; to enjoy release from role. That one is pathology and the other only troubling is the difference between cultural subordination and dominance.

Drinking in America remains a point of political, legal and social conflict. While it retains meanings of cultural remission, the society is able to institute social controls that generally bound and limit the "time out" character of play. While the use of alcohol continues to be seen as possessing unpredictable danger, its use is generally institutionalized into conventional areas and activities. It is further testimony to the ability of drinkers to regulate and restrict the periods and arenas of cultural remission, "to visit on weekends." That others find "playing" with social controls threatening to their own self-control and to the social organization is testimony to the fear that the "wild man" in us is uncontainable. Once let loose he may not show up for church on Sunday or for work on Monday.

Notes

1 This should not be construed to imply that pre-industrial Western societies did not recognize a difference between periods of work and periods of not-work. Certainly the ubiquitous holidays, Saint days and recreational events would be inconsistent with that notion (Burke, 1978).
2 I realize that the concept of play is also used in more restricted forms in which it refers to concentrated and disciplined activity, as in games. Here the activity is both freely chosen and unrelated to practical, work-oriented goals. As in my usage, it is "not serious" though it may demand attentiveness and absorption (Caillois, 1979, Ch. 1).

References

Barthes, Roland, 1973. *Mythologies*. London, Paladin
   1979. Towards a psychosociology of contemporary food consumption, in R. Forster and O. Ranum, *Food and Drink in History*. Baltimore and London, Johns Hopkins University Press
Beauchamp, Dan, 1980. *Beyond Alcoholism: Alcohol and Public Health Policy*. Philadelphia, Pa., Temple University Press
Bell, Daniel, 1976. *The Cultural Contradictions of Capitalism*. New York, Basic Books
Bourdieu, Pierre, 1984. *Distinction*. Cambridge, MA, Harvard University Press
Burke, Peter, 1978. *Popular Culture in Early Modern Europe*. New York, Harper Torchbooks
Caillois, Roger, 1979. *Man, Play and Games*. New York, Schocken Books
Cavan, Sherri, 1966. *Liquor License*. Chicago, Aldine Publishing Co.
Douglas, Mary, 1966. *Purity and Danger*. London, Routledge & Kegan Paul
   1971. Deciphering a Meal, in C. Geertz, ed. *Myth, Symbol, and Culture*. New York, W. W. Norton, pp. 61–82
Douglas, Mary, ed., 1984. *Food and the Social Order*. New York, Russell Sage Foundation
Dumazedier, Joffre, 1968. Leisure, in David Sills, *Encyclopedia of the Social Sciences*. New York, The Macmillan Co. Vol. 9, pp. 248–54
Farb, Peter and Armelagos, George, 1980. *Consuming Passions: The Anthropology of Eating*. New York, Pocket Books
Geertz, Clifford, 1973. *The Interpretation of Cultures*. New York, Basic Books
Goffman, Erving, 1974. *Frame Analysis*. New York, Basic Books
Gouldner, Alvin, 1980. *The Two Marxisms*. New York, Oxford University Press
Gusfield, Joseph, 1963. *Symbolic Crusade: Status Politics and the American Temperance Movement*. Urbana, University of Illinois Press
   1981. *The Culture of Public Problems: Drinking, Driving and Their Symbolic Order*. Chicago, University of Chicago Press

1984. "Prevention": Rise, Decline and Renaissance, in E. Gombereg, H. White, and J. Carpenter, *Alcohol and Society Revisited*. Ann Arbor, Mich., University of Michigan Press

1986. Epilogue, in J. Gusfield, *Symbolic Crusade*, 2nd Edition. Urbana, Ill., University of Illinois Press

Gusfield, Joseph, Kotarba, Joseph, and Rasmussen, Paul, 1981. Managing competence: an ethnographic study of drinking-driving and barroom behavior, in T. Harford, ed., *Social Drinking Contexts*. Washington, D.C., Health and Human Services

Gutman, Herbert, 1977. *Work, Culture and Society in Industrializing America*. New York, Vintage Books

Harrison, Brian, 1971. *Drink and the Victorians: The Temperance Question in England, 1815–1872*. Pittsburgh, University Press

Heath, Dwight, 1975. A critical review of ethnographic studies of alcohol use, in R. Gibbins, ed., *Research Advances in Alcohol and Drug Problems*, Vol. 2. New York, John Wiley and Sons

Jellinek, E. M., 1977. The symbolism of drinking. *Journal of Studies on Alcohol* 38: 852–66

Kaplow, Jeffrey, 1981. La fin de la Saint-Lundi. *Temps Libre* 2: 107–18

Karp, Ivan, 1980. Beer drinking and social experience in an African society, in Ivan Karp and Charles Bird, eds., *Explorations in African Systems of Thought*. Bloomington, Indiana University Press

Landers, Mark, and Martin, James, 1982. *Drinking in America*. New York, The Free Press

Lears, T. J. Jackson, 1981. *No Place of Grace: Antimodernism and the Transformation of American Culture, 1880–1920*. New York, Pantheon Books

Le Goff, Jacques, 1980. *Time, Work and Culture in the Middle Ages*. Chicago, University of Chicago Press

LeMasters, E. E., 1975. *Blue-Collar Aristocrats: Life Styles in a Working-Class Tavern*. Madison, University of Wisconsin Press

Levine, Harry G., 1978. Demon of the middle class: self-control, liquor and the ideology of temperance in 19th-century America (Unpublished PhD dissertation, Department of Sociology, University of California, Berkeley)

Lévi-Strauss, Claude, 1969. *The Raw and the Cooked*. New York, Harper and Row

MacAndrew, Craig, and Edgerton, Robert, 1969. *Drunken Comportment*. Chicago, Aldine Pub. Co.

Marrus, Michael, 1974. *The Emergence of Leisure*. New York, Harper and Row

Melbin, Murray, 1978. Night as frontier. *American Sociological Review*, 43 (Feb.), 3–22

Nissenbaum, Stephen, 1980. *Sex, Diet and Debility in Jacksonian America*. Westport, Conn., Greenwood Press.

Reid, Douglas, 1976. The decline of Saint Monday, 1766–1876. *Past and Present*, 71: 76–101

Rieff, Phillip, 1966. *The Triumph of the Therapeutic*. New York, Harper Torchbooks.

Riesman, David, 1950. *The Lonely Crowd*. New Haven, Yale University Press

Rorabaugh, William, 1979. *The Alcoholic Republic: An American Tradition*. New York, Oxford University Press

Rosenzweig, Roy, 1983. *Eight Hours for What We Will: Workers and Leisure in an Industrial City, 1870–1920.* New York, Oxford University Press

Sahlins, Marshall, 1976. *Culture and Practical Reason.* Chicago, University of Chicago Press

Spitzer, Steven, 1983. The rationalization of crime control in capitalist society, in S. Cohen and A. Scull, eds., *Social Control and the State.* Oxford, Martin Robertson

Thompson, E. P., 1967. Time, work-discipline and industrial capitalism. *Past and Present* 38: 56–97

1978. Eighteenth-century English society: class struggle without class? *Social History*, 3 (May)

Turner, Victor, 1969. *The Ritual Process.* Chicago, Aldine Pub. Co.

1977. Variations on a theme of liminality, in Sally Moore and Barbara Meyerhoff, eds., *Secular Ritual.* Amsterdam, Van Gercum and Co., pp. 36–52

Tyrell, Ian, 1979. Temperance and economic change in the ante-bellum north, in Jack Blocker, Jr., ed., *Alcohol, Reform and Society.* Westport, Conn., Greenwood Press

Van Gennep, Arnold, 1960. *The Rites of Passage.* Chicago, University of Chicago Press

Veblen, Thorstein, 1934. *The Theory of the Leisure Class.* New York, Modern Library

Zerubavel, Eviatar, 1981. *Hidden Rhythms.* Chicago, University of Chicago Press

1985. *The Seven Day Circle: The History and Meaning of the Week.* New York, The Free Press

4. Longshore drinking, economic security and union politics in Newfoundland

Gerald Mars

Introduction

This chapter examines two different styles of drinking practised by long-shoremen in the Port of St John's in Newfoundland, Canada. These two styles are linked to regular membership in a longshore gang or to exclusion from such membership. Those excluded are called "outside" men and it is their fate to work only on odd occasions when a vacancy occurs in a gang or a sudden rush of work means that gangs of outside men are needed.

There are marked differences in the way these two classes of longshore-men drink. These can be seen in the rate they drink, the locale they occupy and even the beverages they choose. Regular men drink in taverns close to their wharf; they sit with their regular workmates and drink beer: outside men, even though working on the same wharves, usually drink in the open air or sit in parked cars and they drink rum or wine in smaller groups that vary in membership.

It is only through a comparative examination of these drinking styles that we can understand how drinking is more than merely a leisure activity – a way of passing time and of spending money. We can see how styles of drink-ing not only reflect basic differences between two groups of men but how they contribute to and re-affirm these differences. We come to see that un-derstanding their drinking can allow us to understand much more than we would otherwise know about the processes of exclusion and of incorpor-ation that these men adopt. We will see how power governing access to and the dispersal of material goods is mediated and controlled through drinking and how and in what ways the very political life of the union is sustained by it.

Drinking is so important to nearly all longshoremen that it is common to find it used as a basis of assessments. Men are judged as men by how well they carry their drink and by how generously they spend their money on drink. There is a correspondingly strong suspicion of the small minority of men who do not drink. When early in fieldwork I asked a group of long-shoremen why someone who was married, young, fit and hardworking – all well regarded qualities in a workmate – was nonetheless an outside man, the answer given was that he was a "loner". When I queried what form this took, I was told "He doesn't drink – that's what I mean by a loner."

But to understand these dimensions of longshore life we must first learn more about the system by which work is allocated, what it means to a man to be selected or rejected from membership in a gang and the role that drink and drinking play in this process.

The two classes of longshoreman

A man makes himself available to be hired as a gang member by standing in a horseshoe-shaped group from which he can be selected by a hiring fore-man. This "shape up" method of hiring occurs each time a boat docks and men are individually selected in groups of twenty plus. Shape up hiring appears to be much more casual than it is and seems to give massive power to the foreman since unemployment is high in Newfoundland and there are always more men "shaping up" than there are vacancies. In fact this power is considerably modified *so long as the men can act collectively*. In return for regular re-hiring, the gang offer the foreman a consistent level of output. This "security/effort bargain" is then played out in individual terms. If the foreman drops a man the gang wants, they can threaten to slow up; similarly if the foreman hires a man the gang rejects, they can similarly threaten. In this way power over the gang's constituency effectively passes from the foreman to the gang. And in this transition all members of the gang benefit as long as they are considered acceptable to their co-workers.

There are thus two very different classes of dockworker – "regular men" with some security who are regularly re-hired and "outside men" who "fill in", and who are only erratically employed. Membership in a gang there-fore offers considerable advantage. This is apparent not only in the higher level of earnings enjoyed by regular men, but also in the provision of what can be called "insurance facilities" that a gang offers its members. A gang will collect funds for a sick member, for instance, or donate blood for an injured one. Members will defend each other against attacks on their indi-vidual or collective reputations and will protect and support each other in obtaining and distributing pilfered cargo (Mars, 1972). And not least they offer a secure leisure time social group based on drinking in the gang's tavern. All of these advantages are denied to outside men.

As might be expected, men are not lightly offered membership in a gang. Though a man might be regularly hired it takes some considerable time before he can regard himself as fully enmeshed in a gang's system of rights and duties. Often, when discussing their gangs with regular longshoremen, it became apparent that each gang always contains marginal members, and, further, that a marginal man's limited service in a gang is only one factor contributing to his marginality. A more important factor derives from *rela-tive* seniority in a gang: a new member in a gang always remains marginal until, in effect, his mantle of marginality can be taken on in turn by an even newer arrival.

This practice of "relative marginality" which acts irrespective of actual time served, contributes to the gang's autonomous identity. In restricting the grant of full member status, more-established gang members emphasize their own collective identity, and the exclusiveness of their individual memberships within it. At the same time they benefit materially (in drink receipts as well as in prestige), to a disproportionate extent because a flow of obligations is, as it were, always offered up from a constantly renewed prestige level at the gang's base. Members of this low prestige level then rise as they become progressively integrated.

The gradations of membership in the gang and the understanding that men need to work some time before their acceptance, serve some of the functions of an apprenticeship; men in the St John's dock have to learn the social as well as the technical requirements of their job. Indeed, the articulation of social and technical factors in dock work means that technical competence by itself represents only a relatively small proportion of the total requirements of a work role. To these requirements must be added the need for men to learn the social requirements involved in non-work roles as, for instance, that of drinking companion.

The role that drink plays is so basic in linking work and non-work roles and one so taken for granted by longshoremen that it can easily be missed by a casual enquirer. When – early in fieldwork – I was giving a questionnaire designed to find out about leisure, I hardly ever elicited replies about drinking. After several interviews with no mention of it, I gave the questionnaire to a man well known for his drinking. He, too, made no mention of his pastime; he said instead that he always went fishing in his leisure time! "Don't you *ever* go drinking with your buddies?" I asked in some exasperation. "Hell!" he replied, "I didn't think you counted drinking! *Everyone* always drinks with their buddies!"

The two styles of drinking

Regular men's drinking groups

Regular longshoremen in St John's do their drinking in about ten taverns, all along or close to the waterfront, and their choice depends on the wharves where they most regularly work. Furness Withy men, for instance, drink in one of two taverns close to their wharf. This correspondence of work and drinking extends beyond choice of tavern. In sitting together – men arrange themselves according to gang membership and job within the limitations of layout allowed by the seating – mostly at small round or square tables designed for four. Thus holdsmen who work in pairs in the ships holds tend to sit together and if two separate tables are occupied by holdsmen the pair system will tend still to be in evidence; sitting with them might be one or both winchmen and perhaps the signaller with whom they normally interact at work.

In a similar manner, stowers who sort cargo in the shed also sit together, often with the shed based fork truck driver, and they too reveal in the tavern differences which divide and unite them at work. Stowers normally work in two groups and both groups similarly divide up in the taverns. If, however, stowers and holdsmen enter a tavern together or find themselves the only members of their gang there, then they sit together, perhaps later to move to another table of closer colleagues. Otherwise, seating arrangements follow closely the technical and pilferage groupings of normal gang working more fully described elsewhere (Mars, 1972: 1974). The physical and social isolation of skidsmen – a pair of men who work by themselves on the quayside – is also reflected in their isolation from the drinking groups. If they do drink with the gang, they might initially sit with men from the two main groups but they rarely sit as long as other members and often find some excuse either to move from the tavern or to another table.

Talk is lively in the taverns and is almost entirely involved with work; its episodes, its prospects or about relationships with co-workers and with management. Such conversations frequently affect seating arrangements. On one occasion when a skidsman was drinking with a group of his gang's stowers, the problems that had arisen with that day's cargo of vegetables were discussed for about a quarter of an hour. Men often discuss in minute detail difficulties experienced on the previous boat, and on this occasion the skidsmen, who were unable to make any relevant contribution, early left the table. At another time a holdsman at a table with stowers from his gang found the conversation turning to criticism of holdsmen for allegedly hoisting overweight slings – that is slings containing cargo in excess of management/union agreements – when discussion became heated the isolated holdsman withdrew.

One important topic of conversation is about the arrival of boats. Since arrival times are not posted, men are dependent on contacts for information and ignorance can mean a loss of work. Discussion in the taverns of future, expected and delayed work serves, therefore, to distribute or restrict this important information to selected members of a gang. Information is usually obtained first of all by a foreman from the company office and he then passes it to his "key men" – that is, by definition, to his most secure men – who then pass it to less secure gang members.

Differences in security and therefore of prestige within a gang are also apparent in taverns through conversation. The jibes of longshoremen are frequently directed against the two low-status categories, bachelors and old men. Such jibes are usually initiated by more secure members of a gang, and new members are not expected to speak out in this way (Gluckman, 1963). Prestige is also "visible" in the observation of who buys drinks which does not follow the English "round" system, where each buys in turn for all other members. Instead, men buy their drinks, predominantly beer, for themselves and for one, maybe two or perhaps three, companions at the same table. When tables are set together the same arrangements apply. The buying of drinks is not symmetrical; the most recent and most marginal tend to buy more than their arithmetical share whilst others, particularly old-established key members of a gang, buy less.

It is common to find that tavern drinking groups contain men away from work through sickness or injury. These men make their way to the tavern when they expect to find the gang there. They are not expected to buy drinks but will instead be "treated" while off work. I have observed men obviously too injured or sick to work, nonetheless hobbling towards their gang's regular tavern to meet their workmates at the end of a shift. These "off work" appearances reinforce an absentee's temporarily weakened ties to his gang, and help to ensure the maintenance of his membership. When such a man re-presents himself at a shape up, he can hope that his work-mates will maintain support for him were he to be dropped by the foreman. As longshoremen describe it, "We will know him at the shape up."

Men in this situation are in an especially marginal position in the taverns and this becomes more pronounced the longer they are away from work. Unable to reciprocate in the buying of drinks, they are in a weak position to enter into the many discussions that can well become heated. Belligerence in argument demands at least prestige equality and this is not likely to be maintained when a man is unable to balance his receipt of drinks from others. The contribution of such men to discussion is, therefore, usually muted; especially since absence from work, even for a week or so, restricts the knowledge of day-to-day work events on which pivot so much tavern conversation and on which most personal gossip is based.

These different degrees of integration within a gang are also reflected in men's presence or absence from the drinking groups; exceptionally mar-ginal as well as exceptionally secure gang members both tend to absence. The most marginal members of a gang are casually employed outside men. Gangs often contain men "filling in" for regulars who are injured, are sick or who have taken a day or two off. If a temporary gang member regularly belongs to another gang on the same wharf, he is likely to drink with his temporary hosts at the tavern after work. If, however, he is permanently an outside man, "filling in" where he can with no regular gang attachment, then he is extremely unlikely to be found at the tavern.

By a seeming paradox, the most secure gang members also tend to absence from the taverns. The greatest security of all is that enjoyed by hatch checkers, who count and check the cargo. With a special relationship to the foreman, to whom their scarce skill (based on relatively scarce lit-eracy) makes them especially valuable, they also uniquely benefit from the system of gang reciprocities – particularly from pilfering. Accordingly they are rarely found in the taverns. One hatch checker known to join with selected friends (including the anthropologist) in a nip in the privacy of his home, was nonetheless regarded by his workmates as a lifelong teetotaller – and this, despite more than twenty years work on one wharf! "Some of them drink a lot and I'd rather keep out of it", he explained. Few men in the gangs can decide or afford to keep out of taverns.

There is a further category of men absent from the taverns. These are many of the Union activists – outspoken members of gangs who "speak for the premises" in both gang and wharf-wide disputes with management. These men are the "link pins" between gang and Union organization, and their role and structural situation will be considered in greater detail later. Some aspects of their situation are described elsewhere (Mars, 1979).

Drinking on the dock, though it occurs, is not frequent and men who need refreshment tend to drink water or Cola. This is partly because drunkenness is prohibited by management and men have been fired from particular boats for being drunk but principally it is because effective social controls come from the men themselves who exert a pressure towards sobriety. Men who are drunk are likely to prove a danger in dockwork, and there are some ten or twelve outside men who everyone knows owe their demotion to being too often drunk on the dock. When this occurs on an odd occasion, men cover up for such a fellow worker (often literally so – he will be hidden under a tarpaulin, for instance, well away from prying eyes until he recovers). But if it occurs too often word will pass to the foreman that such a man is "too much of a lush to be carried" and there will be no collective support when he is dropped from the shape up.

Outside men's drinking groups

Outside men, of course, lack both the economic and the social advantages that come from gang membership. And since they can never tell when and with whom they will work from day to day, they lack the basis of reiterated membership in any regular grouping. The composition of their drinking groups reflects this erraticism so that the men a man drinks with one day are unlikely to be the same on another.

Outside men never drink in the taverns. This is because of the way they use drink to repay obligations and to balance reciprocities. Instead of passing beers between themselves as regulars do, they all drink from a single bottle of wine or cheap rum (called Screech) which they pass among themselves. These drinks are only obtainable from licensed liquor stores or from up-market cocktail bars not found near the waterfront.

Nor can drinking take place in the home, which in Newfoundland is the power base of the women. Instead, among outside men, it is carried on in parked cars, or if the weather is good and the police not too vigilant, in groups in the open – a practice which is illegal and which lowers the prestige of all longshoremen in the wider St John's society.

The routine of drinking is formally maintained and is always the same. The host who has either supplied the bottle or, more usually when this is a shared enterprise, the largest share, is responsible for the constituency of the group. He nods, winks or beckons to six or eight of his selected co-drinkers who leave whoever they are talking to and follow him. When a group is thereby gathered the host, with a watchful eye for the police and with much furtive looking over shoulders, will then produce from a pocket the bottle and a small glass – about the size of a large egg-cup. He then passes both bottle and glass to his principal guest and under the casual but watchful eyes of the group the guest then partly fills the glass, empties it and returns both glass and bottle to his host. The process then continues with the next guest and so on throughout the group. Such groups are selected almost entirely on the basis of repaying what is owed – usually for tips about the arrival times of boats, for knowledge of a sudden need for men at a par-ticular wharf or in anticipation of such information to come.

Though a bottle of cheap wine (Pinky) costs the same as three beers and cheap rum costs the same as twelve beers, both wine and rum are more easily divided than if a man had merely spent the same amount of money on a crate of beer. It is also less cumbersome and certainly is less expensive in terms of the numbers that can be entertained. One man with one bottle of spirits has control of approximately 20 units of social credit and each drink – as a specific unit of credit – is publicly issued before an audience. An incre-ment of obligation is thereby publicly obtained or repaid each time bottle and glass are passed – and seen to pass – from host to guest.

Sometimes a host will entertain several groups from the same bottle. When he thinks enough drink has been expended on a particular group he recorks the bottle, replaces it in his pocket and the group then disperses. A host is then free to collect together a new group, which might well, and often does, include some members of the previous group. By this means a man with a bottle can control and balance different degrees of obligation and reciprocity which he feels are relevant to different individuals and he can make very delicate adjustments between them. A particularly favoured workmate can, for instance, be "given the wink" to attend two, or perhaps even three, consecutive sessions, whilst a less favoured obligator can be dis-pensed with after only one. A host controls the rate of drinking in his groups by holding on to bottle and glass for greater or lesser periods between hand-outs. He is, therefore, in position to control the length of time members talk together, and in this way a man with a bottle has some control over how long he is able to occupy the centre of the social stage.

Union activists

Despite the importance of drinking as a norm and the need for social integration in the gangs we find that most gangs contain at least one person who never drinks. Often these are members of Alcoholics Anonymous or of minority religious sects that forbid alcohol. How can their presence be explained?

The significance of non-drinking became apparent when discussing with longshoremen and managers the characteristics of gang spokesmen. These are men who speak out for the gang against the foreman. For reasons which have been explained elsewhere (Mars, 1972), they are predominantly stowers. They may speak out against a foreman to his face or against holdsmen for the hoisting of over-weight slings – a common tendency of holdsmen who are more amenable to the pressures of foremen who always aim to speed a ship's turnround. Sometimes, however, a spokesman may make an approach direct to a wharf superintendent or to a manager.

All these activities can be dangerous. Even an indirect attack on a foreman via the holdsmen can well result in a spokesman being victimised at subsequent shape ups. There are enough cases of this having happened for men to be well aware of its likelihood, and a man's only defence against it is the collective support of his gang. We thus find that spokesmen are those who are highly secure as gang members – confident of gang support when it is necessary. Or they are men who are hardly integrated at all and have nothing to lose by speaking out. Speaking out can thus give them the chance of gaining group support.

There is general agreement that there are five, non-exclusive classes of stower who require such support because they speak out. First, a union executive member in the gang will be expected to speak when necessary. Second, if a gang contains no executive member, one in an adjacent gang, will be expected to speak if asked. Third, a secure member – one with long service in a gang – might occasionally so act. A fourth category comprises marginal gang members – often new men not fully accepted as gang members. The fifth comprises men regarded as established spokesmen for the gangs. They are not usually executive members, though some have a record of election attempts, and they speak almost as much for men in other gangs as for their own gang. It is this group within the wider group of spokesmen who tend to be termed "agitators", the same label being used both by management and by Union Executive members.

When such agitators were considered, twelve men other than executive members were identified by cross-checking with different informants. Though nine were thought secure members of their gangs – all having been members for more than five years – eight of these were considered personally unpopular with their workmates. It was then discovered that of these eight, *six were non-drinkers*, most being members of Alcoholics Anonymous.

The position of agitators as secure members of regular gangs can, therefore, be regarded as highly anomalous: most fail to satisfy the norm of general sociability and some the specific norm of being a drinker. Yet, despite these defects, their position in the gangs is secure – so secure that foremen are unable to remove them and – as in a case noted elsewhere (Mars, 1972, pp. 7/25) – a wharf superintendent remarked of one: "He's a real bastard – always causes trouble. If we could get rid of him that would be a peaceful gang."

One explanation for the anomalous security of such spokesmen lies in a wider understanding of men's integration in their gangs. Normally gang members must conform to norms of what constitutes an adequate workmate. By the normal processes of socialization and the assertion of social controls, as well as by passing through the process of relative seniority, most men eventually become acceptable as full gang members and are then enmeshed in the system of rights and duties which this involves, including participation in drinking. "Agitators", however, obtain the rights of gang membership – or at least the principal right of gang support against being unhired at the shape up – but in return their reciprocal payment is made in a different coin. Their social duties can be understood, not as generalized participators in the overall social life of the gang in which drinking looms large, but specifically as suppliers of a dangerous service on behalf of the rest of their fellows. Their role, however, as non-drinkers is one that cannot be understood without understanding the role of drinking and its place in the integration of men within gangs.

Summary, conclusions and implications

Regular men can only offset their individual vulnerability in the shape up by combining in united work gangs. Such combination allows them a degree of control over their own constituency. The gangs, however, contain men integrated within them to different degrees, and this creates differences in level of obligation between relatively marginal and relatively integral gang members. Further imbalance of obligations arises also from the nature of the jobs that men perform in a gang, as well as their role in the system of pilferage.

By interpreting behaviour in terms of exchange within and between different spheres of activity, however, we see that unbalanced obligations derived from one sphere may be balanced by action in another. When gangs are examined as drinking groups, it is found that obligations and reciprocities from the dock are carried through to drinking and vice versa. At the same time gangs provide a mechanism for excluding unwanted and marginal co-workers; thus they not only supply a ready means of balancing obligations but also create new obligations by, for instance, granting the special drinking licence or other kinds of material support granted to men who are too sick to work. In so acting, the gang's drinking group articulates the spheres of leisure, insurance, family and work.

A comparison was made with the drinking behaviour of outside men, who develop obligations and balance their reciprocities within a wider ranging network of contacts not derived from the work they perform in gangs. Outside men's obligations, being more widely dispersed, are reflected in a pattern of drinking that adapts to varied intensities at different times and between different individuals since, within their more tenuous networks and unlike regular men, they can well be overall patrons one day and clients the next. Regular men's obligations, on the other hand, deriving from a relatively closed field and being more stable, are reflected in drinking groups that are themselves more stable and are essentially stratified, exclusive of outsiders and mutually supportive.

Examination of the nature, process and functions of the integration in the gangs reveals men's need to conform to a gang's norms if gangs are collectively to sponsor and support their members. It was found, however, that some men obtain rights to such membership but do not conform to gang norms – their obligations are repaid in a different coin. These are men, often personally unpopular as co-workers and a high proportion of whom do not drink, who act as spokesmen for the gang in the dangerous task of opposing management. Such men establish the basis of political activity in the Union by providing spokesmen services that go beyond the limits of their own gang affiliation.

Both main kinds of drinking, therefore, show marked differences but they also show a distinct similarity. If we compare these styles with the drinking described by Dennis, Henriques and Slaughter (1969) in the mining village of Ashton, we can learn more about the role played by drinking in St John's. In both St John's and Ashton the same norms surround drinking behaviour and both communities support the same ideal masculine image. But as Douglas and Isherwood (1980) point out in discussing Ashton, it is the systematic destruction of capital there, backed by this ideal of masculinity, that makes for an equality of interests.

In such a bounded occupational community it is considered essential for a solid front to be maintained against management. Since differences in wealth would lead to differences in interests there is pressure to avoid them and it is this that lies behind the social pressure to thriftlessness and capital destruction that is such a marked feature of both communities.

In Ashton the community is divided into different drinking "leagues" linked to differences in earnings and dependent on stages of the life cycle – the older people are, the less they earn. In St John's similar "leagues" exist that also limit expenditure to "same level" groupings, though there they derive from the inadequate overall demand for casual labour.

Outsiders find it difficult to understand such non-acquisitive behaviour. In what is considered a consumer society such pockets of people dedicated to capital destruction seem atavistic or even anti-social. But there is surely some benefit in a community that at least offers an alternative world view and that is based on integrative support and fellowship. One ex-longshoreman who had unusually moved from the waterfront to the Civil Service jaundicedly expressed to me the difference he found in terms of different drinking styles:

> "Oh – the Civil Servants only drink rarely and then they eke their money out – they calculate every piece of expenditure. If a beer's 60 cents a bottle in one place (laugh) they'll move to a 50-cents place! Oh – a longshoreman will always have a dollar in his pocket. Not these fellers."

References

Dennis, N., Henriques, F., and Slaughter, C., 1969. *Coal is Our Life: an Analysis of a Yorkshire Mining Community*. Tavistock, London

Douglas, M., and Isherwood, B., 1980. *The World of Goods. Towards an Anthropology of Consumption*. Penguin, Harmondsworth

Gluckman, M., 1963. Gossip and scandal. *Current Anthropology* 4: 307–15

Mars, G., 1972. An Anthropological Study of Longshoremen and of Industrial Relations in the Port of St John's Newfoundland, Canada. PhD thesis, University of London

Mars, G., 1974. Dock pilferage: a case study in occupational theft. In Rock, P. and McKintosh, M., eds., *Deviance and Social Control*. Tavistock, London

Mars, G., 1979. The stigma cycle: politics in a dockland union. In Wallman, S., ed., *The Anthropology of Work*. Academic Press

5. *Sekt* versus *Schnapps* in an Austrian village

Mary Anna Thornton

In the *Wiener Becken*, an area of eastern Austria, drinking is done from morning till evening at all levels of society, and is the primary focus of all social gatherings. Although the everyday pattern of drinking is guided by the serving of meals, which may be accompanied by mineral water, fruit juices, soft drinks, coffee, tea, wine, or beer (see Appendix), as the social importance of occasions increases, the serving of drinks becomes less associated with eating and more expressive of celebration. The two kinds of drinks which carry the greatest social meaning, sekt and schnapps, polarize social occasions in two directions: the one, increasingly calendrically fixed and formulaic, and the other increasingly spontaneous and intimate. In the direction of formality, sekt marks the celebration of traditional holidays; in the direction of spontaneity, schnapps seals bonds of intimacy. This contrast between sekt celebrations and schnapps celebrations corresponds to an opposition of formality to intimacy which can be traced through many aspects of life in the *Wiener Becken*.

The *Wiener Becken*, or Viennese Basin, a broad plain extending south from Vienna and sheltered on three sides by mountains, once supported an agriculturally based society of two distinct classes, aristocratic land-owner and peasant farmer. Industrialization has since altered class demography. Currently, the population is divided into three flexible occupational levels of increasing prestige and income: subsistence farming often augmented by special skills; clerical work or industrial labor augmented by light farming and gardening; and professional employment independent of any agricultural work. Despite a socialist government and universal public education, mutual distrust and dislike is still tangible between country and city, and between laborer and professional. For example, the Viennese are maligned throughout the countryside as presumptuous aristocrats while the farmers are scorned by their metropolitan neighbors as country bumpkins. Patterns of speech help keep occupational class boundaries distinct. A striking distinction in word pronunciation, sentence intonation, and grammatical construction separates the language spoken by professionals, which approximates to High German, from that spoken by farmers and laborers, which is referred to as *Dialekt* and which varies drastically from region to region. Many people are able to speak High German and *Dialekt*, altering their speech to fit the immediate situation.

Differences in work and leisure activities also maintain country/city and labor/professional distinctions. Unpredictable weather and crop and livestock maturation cause farm work to follow a pattern of sporadic, intense labor. Big jobs like bringing in the hay, slaughtering livestock, and processing meat, are completed with the help of extended categorical kin groups. Family and friends depend upon a direct exchange of goods and services, helping one another with the harvest and sharing storage space and pasturage as well as foodstuffs. Individuals dependent on this sort of social group show little desire to relocate. Newlyweds often live for several years with one set of parents while building a nearby house with the help of the rest of the group. Social gatherings necessarily follow work cycles; kin and close friends enjoy breaks from labor at home or in a nearby *Lokal* (similar to a pub). The interdependence and intimacy among members of such a rurally based co-operative group are underscored by the use of kin titles as well as by the use of the familiar address pronoun *du*.

The professional class, by contrast, is characterized by individual independence, formality, and a greater interest in hobbies, fashion, and "culture." Doctors, lawyers, or government officials draw a high salary and have less economic reason to depend upon colleagues or extended family. Social activities which attract high-income individuals include high-priced formal functions like fancy-dress balls and theater or opera as well as status sports like yachting, sailing, or resort skiing. Members of this occupational class use the formal address pronoun *Sie* among colleagues more than do their working-class cousins. Clerical or industrial workers often come from a farming family but are interested in working their way out of the rural system of exchanged goods and labor and into a higher range of cash salaries. Their lifestyles vary between the two extreme modes described above and depend upon their precise position within the community.

My own experience with the Austrians began with several Alpine mountaineering trips during a study semester in Italy. When I returned to live near Vienna a few years later, I discovered that Austrian social life included the formality of fancy-dress balls as well as the informality of mountain huts that I already knew. Under a Fulbright teaching assistantship, I spent a year living with a family which occupied a small apartment house on farmland outside of an industrial city, Wiener Neustadt. Past generations of the family had been farmers and the current generation was made up of mostly clerical or industrial workers; they had city jobs as well as horses and hay fields and spent much of their time helping their grandfather, a part-time leather worker, with his farm. A great uncle had a larger farm and did some butchering on the side. One brother had risen into the higher echelons of society as a government official, but though welcome at the table, he rarely shared a full meal with us. I spent time on the farm, in the town grammar school where I taught, and at the University of Vienna.

The inhabitants of the province in which the *Wiener Becken* is located are renowned as the most hospitable in Austria, so natives told me. Their unstinting hospitality and insistence upon the gracious acceptance of all offerings turned most social occasions into bouts of copious eating and drinking. Hosts press more food and drink on guests than they could ever physically require and find refusals insulting.

The rules of etiquette which govern alcoholic drinks fall into host, guest, and group categories. Hosts are expected to accept guests regardless of inappropriate timing of impromptu visits and to provide unlimited quantities of some pleasing beverage. Most households buy beer and wine in bulk. Running out of the drink chosen by the guest causes the host embarrassment. A guest should finish whatever he is given. Any social gathering is characterized by the host pressing beverages upon the guests, the guests feigning refusal, and the host eventually winning. Sometimes, but quite unusually, a guest does refuse the offering of an alcoholic beverage. The host then toasts the guest and drinks a glass alone. All members of any social gathering must appropriately acknowledge one another through the proper performance of greeting and leave-taking, toasting (eye-contact and a simultaneous first sip are most important), and through the proper use of formal and informal language. Full participation by each member of the group is expected. This includes a mutually consistent tempo of drinking and sharing in conversation. The more informal the gathering, the more bluntly these rules are enforced through teasing or criticism. Drinking alcohol alone is frowned upon.

Being more associated with thirst-quenching than with celebration, non-alcoholic drinks are little constrained by sociability rules. They therefore can be drunk alone without risking offense. Plain fruit juice is most widely given to infants, but when mixed with mineral water, becomes a popular drink for older children or thirsty adults. Cola and other carbonated beverages are also drunk by all ages throughout the day in order to slake thirst. Plain mineral water is drunk only when dictated by health concerns. Tap water, though pure, is scarcely considered potable. My habit of drinking plain water with meals was thought very odd. Coffee is consumed every morning as a wake-up drink and used as a stimulant throughout the day, often being served in the evening rather than or in addition to wine, especially if some members of the group must drive home. (Stiff insurance penalties follow accidents and drunk-driving charges.) Occasionally, tea is taken during the day as an alternative to coffee.

The different celebratory functions of sekt and schnapps polarize social events. All alcoholic drinks can be separated into two classes, one headed by sekt, the other by schnapps. Use of the schnapps class of drinks is cued by a desire to promote co-operation between individuals, whereas the use of the sekt class of drinks marks culturally recognized holidays. The two most socially important drinks do not directly accompany food; lower order drinks often do. Sekt and schnapps cannot be served in place of one another, wine and beer drinks can in certain circumstance be interchanged, and hot rum and hot wine drinks are highly interchangeable, although determinably different in significance. Non-alcoholic drinks are socially meaningless and are not aligned in this way (see Fig. 5.1). Beverages belonging to the schnapps class of drinks are shared within limited networks of social co-ordination, whereas those belonging to the sekt class are exchanged in circumstances that do not imply personal commitment. The difference is best demonstrated by an analysis of the uses of sekt and schnapps.

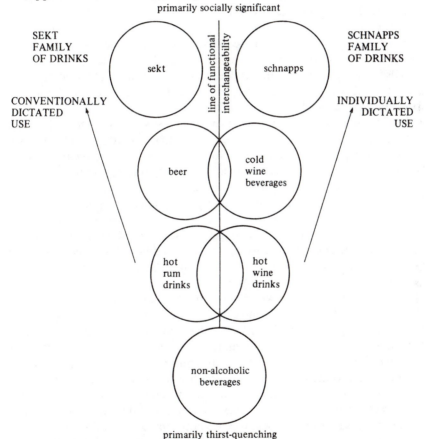

Fig. 5.1: Polarization and interchangeability of beverages.

The drinking of sekt is dictated by tradition and marks conventional national, town, or personal holidays which are celebrated the same way by nearly everybody each year, for example New Year's, *Fasching* (Shrovetide), town or city balls, birthdays, or anniversaries. From year to year, household to household, and ball to ball, the celebration is conducted in a similar fashion. Sekt is commercially available in many price categories, it always looks much the same, tastes much the same, and is served in much the same way. The celebration of this sort of holiday as well as the drinking of sekt is formal. Rather than promoting intimacy, it repeatedly confirms cultural traditions. Most Austrian households celebrate these holidays in the conventional way, regardless of social standing. New Year's Eve, the culmination of the calendrical cycle, is usually celebrated by drinking a great deal of sekt, often amongst many strangers in rather impersonal large dancing establishments. Sekt is consumed in a similar fashion during formal balls, where stranger dances with stranger, making brief and superficial contact with many different people.

In contrast with the calendrically directed serving of sekt, the drinking of schnapps is never dictated by time of the day or day of the month. Its use is always associated with interests shared by individuals or groups of individuals. When people find themselves in situations in which isolation is undesirable and a dependence on others is reassuring, new personal bonds are formed and often sealed with a drink of schnapps.

The importance of schnapps in creating and sustaining intimate bonds is underscored by the complex of beliefs and individual tastes which influence its use. Schnapps can have many flavors and colors but it is always a strong liquor or sweet liqueur derived from fruits, vegetables, herbs, tree saps, berries, or other eclectic natural ingredients. It can be store-bought or home-made, but the home-made variety is considered superior, and commercial sorts can be doctored to suit personal tastes. Schnapps is believed to be both soothing and envigorating and is used to alleviate stomach ailments, fatigue, and physical weakness. An element of play is introduced into social events with the drinking of schnapps, manifested in ribald songs, drinking games, and elaborate practical jokes. When schnapps is served, barriers of formality are down; people do silly, otherwise socially unacceptable things which heighten group camaraderie. A host is proud of his selection of schnapps and watches guests closely for their reactions when they sample it. Guests, in turn, show marked interest in the schnapps they are drinking, commenting upon its quality and enquiring after its origin. By contrast, sekt is served and drunk with little comment on its quality.

Sekt is always bought commercially, and when it is served, much less interest is directed toward it by either guest or host. Whereas sekt is always stored in the same green, gold-topped bottles and served in conventional fluted glasses, schnapps bottles and glasses come in different shapes, sizes and colors. Men tend to favor conventional shot glasses, while women often have their own tiny handblown flasks, which are decorated with bumps, bubbles, and swirls in the glass. In the most intimate of groups, one glass might be used by everybody. Sekt would never be served so informally.

Schnapps is significantly absent during stock holiday celebrations which half a town (in the case of the ball), or an entire nation (in the case of New Year's Eve), celebrates in much the same way. It appears only during celebrations within selective and sometimes transitory groups of individuals who are on an intimate footing with one another or would like to be. Whereas sekt is often served to a large number of people at once, schnapps is usually shared among a small group and sometimes between only two. For example, housewives often share a clandestine shot of schnapps while taking a break from chores, at the same time roundly cursing the onerous duties which everyone else leaves to wives and mothers. Thus, they reinforce their own uniqueness as a smaller, more intimate group within larger society. Similarly, after returning from formal celebrations, or after shutting the door on the last formal guests, the most intimate friends or family group often share a round of schnapps. Sudden, evanescent friendships are often struck and sealed with schnapps during ski trips, the typical Austrian winter holiday.

An offer of a glass of schnapps can also be used as an ingratiating gesture. For example, the head of the family with which I lived was a recognized breeder of a certain race of pony. The entire family was once invited to a distant acquaintance's farmhouse, wined, dined, and repeatedly offered home-made schnapps. It turned out that our gracious host was angling for a favorable evaluation of two ponies which lacked official papers. The ploy was only partially successful: the ponies were too ragged to merit a high rating, but the owner had managed to make a friend of a potentially useful authority. On the ride back from the farmhouse, the family chuckled over his attempts to pass off his nags as good ponies, but they spoke very highly of his schnapps and of his hospitality.

Sekt and schnapps are brought out the least often of all drinks, sekt because it is drunk only to celebrate infrequent, calendrically fixed holidays, schnapps because it is drunk as an accompaniment to relatively rare moments of high conviviality. Although this division in the uses of alcoholic beverages is most marked between sekt and schnapps, it is still discernible through a close look at the preparation and uses of more commonly served drinks. Wine, the prized product of local farmers, belongs in the schnapps class of beverages, as its use is more symptomatic of close social relations than either rum or beer, the drinking of which tends to follow calendrical or seasonal patterns, much like sekt.

The opposition between cold wine and beer drinks is quite clear and follows the same division as that between sekt and schnapps. Wine is produced from either white or red grapes or from a mixture of apples and pears; white is most popular and is produced within the province, often by large establishments; red is produced in other provinces and is drunk rarely; apple/pear wine (*Most*) is produced even by small farmers and is often intended primarily for home consumption. Wine usually accompanies the meal, unless the food traditionally "calls" for beer. If consumed alone, beer accompanies summer sport or seasonal farm and construction work, whereas wine nearly exclusively accompanies social relaxation. Beer is always bought at the store; wine is often ordered from the farmer and fetched or delivered personally. A family may have had a long association with the particular farmer who produces its preferred wine. The production of beer is considered the forte of foreigners (western Austrians or Germans); the production of wine is their own province's forte. The purity and healthiness of the local wine is contrasted with the adulteration and inferiority of foreign wines. Beer figures rarely in this sort of comparison.

The distinction between hot rum and hot wine beverages is not quite so obvious but similar. Both drinks are served on cold evenings or during breaks in cold-weather outdoor sports and so are conceivably functionally interchangeable, yet there are telling distinctions. Both rum and wine are common to any but the most impoverished Austrian pantry, but rum is commercially bought and a common cooking ingredient, whereas wine is rarely used in cooking. Hot rum drinks are commonly purchased in a commercial establishment, whereas hot wine drinks are often prepared at home. Rum is unceremoniously dumped from the bottle (which often stands on the table) into hot tea or other liquids, but wine is first mixed into other ingredients and then heated, stirred, and spiced, often with the help of those who are to drink it. Rum is distributed through extensive, impersonal networks. Wine, by contrast, is tendered with personal care to small, intimate social groups.

In summary, those drinks which fall into the sekt class are marketed commercially and served according to widely acknowledged conventions of taste or of season, while the class of schnapps drinks are more often prepared and served with care at home or in the community.

Tracing the uses of various sorts of drinks throws into relief boundaries which guide the actions of individuals in the *Wiener Becken*. The distinction already remarked between those drinks which facilitate close personal ties and those which support formal cultural traditions carries through into patterns of intimacy and formality embedded consistently throughout *Wiener Becken* society.

The most obvious examples of this configuration are forms of address. *Sie* is used to address strangers or acquaintances and can persist as a form of address between individuals for years if a sufficient level of intimacy, which would warrant the use of *du*, is never reached. A switch from the formal to the informal pronoun is a marked occasion and rarely goes by without at least a toasting of wine. The use of the sekt class of drinks would be entirely inappropriate in such a situation, but schnapps, which is saved for just such a breaking down of formality, is particularly appropriate and will be used if a high level of camaraderie has been reached. Traditionally, the toast of *Bruderschaft* was celebrated (and sometimes still is) with a linking of arms and a simultaneous downing of a shot of schnapps. I was told that, long ago, through such a pledging of brotherhood, men would seal a pact of mutual defense. That particular practice is considered antiquated and amusing now, but the switch from *Sie* to *du* still signifies an increase in intimacy and mutual dependence and is not undertaken lightly.

The occupational structure provides another example of an emerging pattern of increasing formality and independence. Farmers need to develop a strong network of dependable helpers in order to insure that they can bring in their crops and care for their farm animals. A circle of close kin and intimate friends reinforced through repeated reciprocal hosting of wine and schnapps drinking affairs insures the strong bonds which spell farming success. People who are economically more independent are less in need of help with chores. They lead an appropriately more flexible social life with a wider but on average less intimate circle of friends and acquaintances. Professionals do not need to be dependent upon one another in their work much at all. Colleagues may be social strangers and treat one another with great formality. Members of this occupational group are just as likely to maintain strong personal bonds with immediate family, with childhood friends, or with members of a social club as with their work partners. A sharing of schnapps between professional colleagues would be uncalled for unless more specific grounds for collaboration existed, whereas members of a farm labor group are bound to toast one another with schnapps occasionally by virtue of their close social relations.

The different sorts of drinking establishments also display distinct levels of intimacy and formality. Least formal is the cramped, crowded *Lokal*. Intimate social groups go to boisterous *Lokal*s or come into being there, even if only to last the night. Benches surround the tables, forcing physical intimacy between the customers. Small groups of twos or threes who find themselves at the same or adjoining tables often make friends with their neighbors and share wine, schnapps, jokes, and game-playing the rest of the evening. In a loud and rowdy *Lokal*, maintenance of formality is nearly impossible. At the opposite end of the spectrum is the coffeehouse, where formality is the rule and easily maintainable in the restrained atmosphere. A wide choice of beverages is available here, including both schnapps and sekt, although a coffee drink is the usual choice. Chairs and spacious quarters encourage physical distance. Dress is formal, talk is hushed, and movements circumscribed. Loud, inappropriate behavior is punished by stares and negligent service. Restaurants with bars, called Gasthäuser, maintain various levels of formality and fill in the rest of the structure. Large establishments of the last sort sometimes include dance floors and are the sorts of places where one might celebrate holidays, in particular New Year's Eve. In contrast to the *Lokal*, where predominantly schnapps and wine are drunk, in a dance establishment, sekt is a favorite. Here, restraint between tables is maintained. At a New Year's Eve function I attended, an inebriated Yugoslavian, obviously a recent immigrant, roamed from table to table attempting to insinuate himself with the guests. He was ridiculed and rejected. In a *Lokal*, a place on the bench would have certainly been provided for him and his bad German would have made him the life of the party.

Student bars present an interesting departure from these repeated patterns of formality and intimacy. Young academics are apt to reject formality, and to force intimacy by insisting on the use of *du*. The bars they frequent are rather absurd hybrids, part elegant coffeehouse and part boisterous *Lokal*. Here, masses of uniformly unorthodoxly dressed people cram into dark, smoky rooms filled with delicately baroque tables and chairs. Harried, perspiring waiters in tuxedos dash about, alternately serving Turkish coffee, wine, schnapps, or mixed drinks with American names.

Rules of household behavior parallel the pattern set by the various sorts of drinking establishments and dictate who is allowed in which rooms. The bedroom is reserved for spouses, the kitchen for intimate friends and kin, and the front room for acquaintances who hold the weakest bonds with the family. Children pass unrestrained from room to room, regardless of the social status of the adults who might be present. Paralleling the situation in drinking establishments, the kitchen is cramped and often furnished with benches, while the front room is spacious and equipped with chairs and roomy couches. Good friends are welcome in the kitchen, where the atmosphere is intimate but not so intimate as the bedroom, but they would never venture into the bedroom itself. New acquaintances are entirely unwelcome in the kitchen, whereas gatherings of family or close friends traditionally take place there. The term of address most used in the front room is the formal *Sie*; anything but *du* would sound ridiculous in the bedroom, since only spouse or children are allowed in anyway. A mixed group of acquaintances and friends using both forms of address might socialize in the kitchen if ties are strong enough, and in the course of such an afternoon or evening, the familiar *du* is likely to become a more common form of address than the formal *Sie*. Exactly where in the house which sort of drink would be served is difficult to predict, as it would depend on the lay-out of any particular dwelling (a small apartment might have a very abbreviated kitchen/dining room/front room arrangement, whereas a spacious home would have clearly delineated entertaining areas). Yet it is certain that sekt would be served in the most formally appointed area, with guest and host seated and composed, whereas schnapps might be brought out anywhere, conceivably even when guests are standing in the hallway or out of doors – whenever and wherever the mood strikes.

The alpine system of mountain huts carries forward the role of schnapps in expressing interdependence and commitment within small groups. The low hut is usually a modern hotel which offers single rooms as well as dormitory-like sleeping rooms and is accessible by car, bus, or train. The next highest hut is smaller, more rustic, has fewer single and more group sleeping rooms, and it might have a mattress room, the cheapest quarters

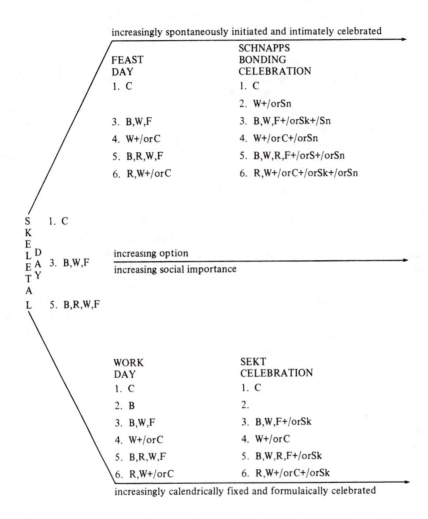

Fig. 5.2: Four possible elaborations of an everyday "skeletal" drinking pattern.

Key

1. breakfast
2. morning
3. midday meal
4. afternoon
5. evening

B beer
C coffee
F fizzy non-alcoholic drinks
R hot rum drinks
Sk sekt
Sn schnapps
W wine

preferred by "real" mountaineers, in which mattresses are strewn about the floor. Most fit people can ascend to a middle hut without much difficulty, but it is recommended that one hike in groups. The high hut is near the mountain peak, often hedged in by snow, and sometimes only accessible by trained mountaineers using safety equipment. A trip to a high hut ought not to be attempted alone or without certain equipment, and the climbing party may need to be roped together. The high hut is tiny and often family-run, and usually the only available sleeping quarters in it are dormitory and mattress rooms. Intimacy is unavoidable. By far the favorite drink of hikers and mountaineers is schnapps. Precious space in the rucksack is always set aside for the small flask of schnapps which carries its own shot glass as a cover. Friendships are made quickly along the way or in the hut, often with the aid of schnapps, among members of any age or occupational group. Here, help is offered unconditionally, physical safety comes before formalities, and rules of intimacy and reciprocity are strictly held to.

The mountaineer's climb from low huts to high huts parallels the movement of individuals from the formal fringes of a loosely bonded group to an intimate center. If resourceful enough, the mountaineer who can reach the low or middle huts can climb to the high hut as well. Along the way, he might meet other mountaineers whose equipment he'd like to borrow, who are planning a similar route, or whom he plainly finds pleasant, and the whole group might rope up in order to negotiate the risky last leg of the journey, the successful completion of which they will celebrate in the intimate atmosphere of the high hut – with schnapps, of course.

6. Varieties of palm wine among the Lele of the Kasai

Ndolamb Ngokwey

Each evening in the forest or savannah paths leading to Lele[1] villages, the traveler who visits Lele country for the first time can see groups of males returning home, carrying calabashes of palm wine, and engaging in lively conversations. Or perhaps he will hear a powerful voice singing, expressing the simple joy of living. The traveler can also come across a man, apparently tipsy, thinking aloud, thundering against the injustice and ingratitude of mankind, returning lonely from his fields, also carrying his calabashes of wine.

And each evening in each Lele village, he can observe all these calabashes changing hands, circulating, sent or brought by male adults to their wives, mothers, sisters, or to elderly or sick friends and relatives. With all this general flow of wine, the visitor should not be surprised if tempers get hot, if there are a couple of arguments in one corner or the other of the village, between spouses, co-wives, good friends, or not so good friends. And if there is no mourning in the village or any other ritual restrictions, the visitor should not be surprised if the general gaiety accompanying the consumption of wine is expressed in energetic dancing till late at night. At this point, the traveler (and hopefully the reader) would have guessed that, among the Lele, palm wine is not simply a drink, intended only for quenching thirst. The aim of this chapter is to describe these other meanings and uses and to try to make sense of palm wine drinking by examining its relationships with some other important aspects of Lele culture.

Palm wine and water are the major beverages in traditional Lele culture. A typical Lele adult drinks more wine than water. Some even say that they never drink water. Such a claim is probably exaggerated. Nevertheless, water is not the favorite, nor the most commonly used beverage among the Lele. The Lele attitudes towards palm wine drinking appear in the prejudices and stereotypes they have of their neighbors, the Cokwe and the Ndjembe, with regard to palm wine or to drinking in general. The Ndjembe, who live south of the Lele region, are perceived as too sober; they seldom drink. This, according to the Lele, is not so much because the Ndjembe are virtuous as because they do not know how to grow palm trees and tap them for wine. Contrary to this disparaging Lele prejudice, it appears that the meagerness of palm wine production among the Ndjembe has more to do with ecological conditions than with any alleged technological incompetence. Indeed the Ndjembe live in a less well-forested area; palm trees grow better in forests and on moist soils.

In contrast to the sober Ndjembe, the Cokwe are perceived by the Lele as drinking too much. Although they do not master the technique of palm wine production either and are considered too lazy to do anything else besides what they can do best – hunting, the Cokwe still can get or buy palm wine from the Lele. Further they produce gin by distilling fermented maize. The Cokwe are perceived as drinking too much, everywhere, and all the time. This intemperance is worsened, according to a well-known saying, by the fact that "the Cokwe always get drunk on somebody else's knife."[2] The knife referred to is the one used for tapping wine. In other words, the Cokwe get drunk on Lele wine, since they do not usually produce it themselves.

The Lele often wonder how the Ndjembe can live with so little wine. They must have very calm and boring evenings. How can they dance heartily after drinking only water? The Lele also wonder how the Cokwe can conduct a normal life while drinking so much. How can they work while almost always drunk? All these Lele prejudiced perceptions and stereotypes of their neighbors describe more their own standards of wine consumption than the actual drinking habits of the Ndjembe or the Cokwe. These stereotypes are in fact self-defining devices, used for cultural identification and moral definition. From them we learn that the Lele value temperance and condemn extreme drinking behaviors: excessive sobriety as well as permanent drunkenness. We also learn that they value sharing palm wine, but in the context of reciprocity, that is, they expect every male adult to produce wine and share it. We also learn that the Lele associate drinking and leisure on the one hand, and sobriety and work on the other hand. These points will be discussed further.

Palm wine is obtained by tapping the base of the crown of a palm tree. The sap that escapes from the incision is converted into palm wine by chemical processes triggered by various micro-organisms (Bassir 1962; 1968; Maduagwu and Bassir 1979). Palm wine is produced by men only. In fact, everything to do with palm trees, or for that matter trees in general, is the exclusive concern of men (Douglas 1963:31). The technology of palm wine production involves knowing when the tree matures, climbing it, making incisions, attaching a calabash to collect the wine, and tending the palm tree daily until it is dead.

According to the Lele, the quantity and the quality of wine produced by a palm tree depend upon the nature of the seed, upon the way it is planted, upon the "arm" of the planter and upon the "arm" of the first person to tap the tree. The Lele believe that some people have an "arm" for planting fruitful seeds, or inaugurating the production of abundant and excellent wine. They are often called upon by those who know their "luck" with palm trees. Except for these few gifted people, most Lele try to control the wine production of their palm trees by following certain practices traditionally known to be effective or having worked for them previously. Some drink wine and/or smoke before tapping a palm tree; some pass the meal immediately preceding the first tapping. Most avoid water and all avoid soap.

Drinking times and contexts

The Lele draw palm wine twice daily, in the morning and in the evening. But as Douglas notes, "wine [is] not normally brought back to the village until the evening, unless there [is] a special call for wine to offer to a visitor, or to feed a newly delivered mother" (1963:31).

The evening or late afternoon is the most appropriate time to drink palm wine. The choice of the evening as contrasted to daytime is best understood when paralleled to another contrast: work vs. leisure. Drinking and working are incompatible activities. The most appropriate drinking time is leisure time, or at least after work or during non-working time.

Agriculture, hunting, weaving, house-building, and productive work in general, exclude palm wine drinking. The only instances of work during which a Lele could be seen drinking are small tasks such as making combs or carving bowls, which the Lele do in their "spare time" and do not really consider work. An anthropology of work seeking to analyze Lele conceptualizations of work and evaluations of different subcategories of work would have to look at Lele drinking behavior. Palm wine drinking thus marks the transition from the working period of the day to the relaxed atmosphere of the evening.

The Lele do not usually drink palm wine while eating, although they may drink *after* a meal "to help the food sink." Social events (births, marriages, installation of a new polyandrous wife etc.) are, of course, occasions for drinking. Wine is also offered as a form of tribute for visiting traditional chiefs and as an almost mandatory sign of hospitality for administrative officials and military or police officers. But the daily context of palm wine drinking for males are the *mapalu*. The *mapalu* are small cleared areas in the forest or savannah where groups of three or more people meet after drawing palm wine and before returning to the village.

These "drinking clubs," as Torday called them (Douglas 1963:53) are exclusively for men, and they are comprised of friends, relatives and their guests. As a practical matter, they often include those whose palm trees are relatively close.

By allowing daily interactions and informal discussions on various personal and communal matters, these meetings are socially important. They have aspects and play functions of other more formalized, but irregular meetings called *mabandja*. The *mabandja* meetings are convoked on special occasions and may include the whole village, or a particular group within the village: male adults, a generation, the local section of a clan or lineage, etc. These meetings are convoked to discuss specific problems concerning the attendants: an epidemic, the reception of a distinguished guest, deteriorating relationships with a neighboring village, tensions within the clan, etc. All these features of *mabandja* contrast with the meetings of the drinking clubs. The meetings at the *mapalu* are not convoked; they are daily. They have no specific points of discussion; they are informal and private, and they take place in the forest or the savannah. Drinking wine is the main objective of the meetings.

The contrast between *mapalu* and *mabandja* meetings highlights once again the parallel contrast between work and leisure. Indeed, it indicates that there is no palm wine drinking during meetings in which some kind of economic or political *work* is being done: discussions concerning the distribution of goods, deteriorating relationships, etc.

Yet due to their regularity, informality, and private nature, the drinking clubs often accomplish the kind of work expected from the *mabandja*. As forums to continue consideration of questions unsettled in general discussions, they help clarify the issues and bring about a consensus in one way or another. But the encounters organized around palm wine do not only serve to exchange information; they are also the locus of exchange of services and goods.

Types of wine

The Lele distinguish qualities of palm wine according to the type of palm tree, the maturation of the palm tree, the freshness of wine and the taste of the wine. As will be clear, the taste depends mostly upon these other factors.

According to types of palm trees, the Lele distinguish wine from the palm trees *mabondu* and wine from the palm trees *mayanda*. Palm trees *mabondu* are the most common. They are grown in the forests or near the village. The variety *mayanda* is rare in Lele region and is usually taller than the *mabondu*. The type of wine produced by the *mayanda* variety is very strong, stronger than the more common *mabondu* wine. It is also reputed to cause headaches. *Mayanda* wine is light in the stomach; *mabondu* wine is heavy and fattening.

According to the maturation of the palm tree, the Lele distinguish between wine drawn from a newly cut tree (*nkepu*), wine drawn from a matured tree (*long*), and wine drawn from a tree at the end of its production (*hambo*). Wine tapped from a mature tree in full production is preferred by everybody. The other two types are drunk for lack of better. They are watery and known to provoke diarrhea. Especially when a palm tree tends toward the end of its production of palm wine, the aroma is spoiled by the obnoxious smell of larvae that develop in the rotting tree.

According to the freshness of the wine, the Lele distinguish *nhabu*, tapped the very day of its consumption from *kole*, wine left from yesterday. Most people prefer fresh wine; stale wine is drunk for lack of better. It is usually not offered to important guests or on formal occasions. It is watery, too strong and known to cause headaches.

According to taste, the Lele distinguish two types of fresh wine: *mana ma piya* or *mana ma bolu* (sweet wine or weak wine) and *mana ma kabo* or *mana mamanono* (angry, fierce wine or strong wine). The sweet wine is usually reserved for women and children. Male adults prefer the "fierce" wine which is more acidic and contains more alcohol. The attributes of strength and fierceness applied to wine translate well the Lele idea of masculinity.

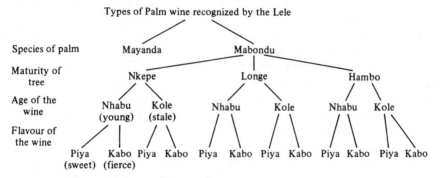

Fig. 6.1: Types of palm wine among the Lele.

The Lele use roots with their wine most of the time. These roots are either chewed while drinking, or soaked in the beaker or in the calabash itself. These roots are primarily used to "strengthen" the wine. By getting stronger and becoming bitter, the wine responds to the ideal wine preferred by male adults. But the roots are not used only as flavorings. Apart from enhancing the flavor of the wine, some of these roots also have medicinal properties; they help prevent common colds and other minor ailments. Almost all of these roots are reputed to have aphrodisiac properties. Notwithstanding the chemical characteristics of these roots, it is worthwhile to note that the parallel established, at the symbolic level, between the strength of wine, the strength of the body (its resistance to minor ailments), and the strength of sexual desire and performance corresponds to the Lele ideal of masculinity. Indeed, women do not use these roots. Plain sweet wine is the most appropriate for them.

Drinking manners

It is unmannerly to drink palm wine while standing or to stand near someone drinking it. The drinker and the persons near him/her must sit down or kneel, and be generally relaxed. Spitting while drinking is very rude. The Lele say that the ill-mannered Cokwe spit all the time and everywhere.

Although some people, especially the young adults, use glasses, most Lele still prefer to use wooden cups, beakers or folded leaves, which supposedly keep the natural flavor of the wine better than glasses. A folded leaf is to be held in the left hand when drinking. I could not find any local interpretation of this rule, nor any indication that the Lele see it as symbolic. Perhaps it is just a matter of practical convenience; it is easier to hold the leaf in the left hand while the right hand either folds it or pours wine in.

Everybody is advised to bring his own cup or leaves. If you wait for other people's cups, a saying goes, you will end up drinking dregs.[3] The drinkers will lend you their cups only when they have had enough themselves, leaving you only the dregs at the bottom of the calabash. Moreover, the whole content of a folded leaf, cup, beaker or glass has to be drunk all at once. To the Lele, this is not only the normal and polite way of drinking palm wine, but also the best way of really appreciating it and tasting its richness.

In the *mapalu*, everybody drinks the wine brought in. In some drinking clubs, there are people designated to serve wine; in others, everyone serves his own wine. Wine is served according to seniority; older people must be served before younger people. Anyone serving wine in the context of the drinking club or in any other context has to drink it first, or at least taste it. This shows that there are no "harmful substances" or "sorcery" in the wine.

Drunkenness is socially disapproved of, for it indicates a lack of self-control and an egoistic lack of sharing; it indicates that one had drunk alone and too much, without sharing. Drinking in a group should thus prevent one from getting drunk, although it is not always successful. The individual who tends to drink too much will be warned by the other members of the group against the negative behavioral disruptions which accompany drunkenness; they will also remind him of his obligation to save wine for those who stayed in the village: the elderly, the sick and the women. Numerous stories depict the disruptive effects of drunkenness on the individual as well as on the community.[4]

Relative tipsiness is tolerated in men but not in women. The daring and uninhibited attitudes and behaviors which accompany it correspond to the Lele idea and ideal of masculinity whose dominant aspect is *tamo*: a mixture of aggressiveness, assertiveness, and machismo, congruent to the Lele warrior tradition. The common saying "wine is a second man"[5] suggests precisely that it can enhance one's "manhood" by suppressing all inhibitions and restraints.

Palm wine, health and illness

Palm wine enters in Lele medical notions and practices. Some qualities or varieties of palm wine are reputed to cause diseases, or at least to be closely linked to diseases. As mentioned earlier, *nkepu* can provoke diarrhea. Hernia and headaches can be caused by the variety *mayanda* and by stale wine. The Lele also say that *hambo* wine can provoke rheumatism and hernia. But all these types and varieties of wine are drunk rarely and, as we have seen for lack of better. *Long*, the preferred fresh wine, tapped from a mature tree in full production, is believed to be highly nutritious.[6] The evidence of its nutritional value for the Lele is the weight gained and the general healthy appearance of palm wine drinkers. This is why it is prescribed as the only drink during certain illnesses such as the psychosomatic *mukund* (Ngokwey 1980) or as the privileged drink for pregnant women, postpartum mothers and most convalescents.

Palm wine is also highly recommended in case of hemorroids, diarrhea, and threat of miscarriage. The popular rationale for the recommendation of wine in case of diarrhea and threat of miscarriage is that water would accelerate the "flow" of diarrhea or of the miscarriage; in contrast, palm wine being less liquid, would prevent it.

Palm wine is also used to drink some medicines, such as the exceptionally bitter ones. In the past, it was used in the concoction drunk as poison ordeal, or as "medicine" in the initiation ritual of antisorcery movements (Ngokwey 1975:109). Palm wine is forbidden in case of rheumatism, hernia, tuberculosis and migraines, because it is considered somewhat instrumental in the onset of these conditions.

Summary and conclusion

Lele rules and practices concerning palm wine re-produce cultural values, notions, and categories. The value of solidarity, for example, is expressed and strengthened in palm wine sharing among males and between them and the females, sick and elderly. But solidarity operates in a context of reciprocity and responsibility. For example, every male is expected to produce wine and share it with others. No able male should be totally dependent upon the others for his wine or for the cup used to drink it.

The categories of work and leisure are symbolically distinguished by the absence or presence of palm wine drinking. The opposition between wine and water is a very important one. The two beverages have to be kept apart; bad wine is basically watery. Wine is provided by men, water by women. Wine is produced through human action on nature; water is simply fetched. Male-produced wine is used to contain the flow of female ruptured membranes.

The differentiation of masculinity and femininity, which is a central theme in Lele culture, appears clearly. As just noted, everything to do with palm wine production is the exclusive concern of men. The provision of water, in contrast, is an exclusively women's activity. The consumption of wine varies also along sexual lines. First, in the locus of consumption itself: men drink mostly in the forest or savannah *mapalu*; women drink in the village. Second, in the quantity and quality consumed: men are expected to drink more wine than women. Men drink "strong" wine, women drink "soft" wine. Tipsiness and its accompanying aggressiveness are tolerated in men; sobriety and self-restraint are expected of women. Culturally meaningful differences between the sexes are thus expressed and re-affirmed in palm wine drinking.

Notes

1 The Lele live in the Kasai region of the Republic of Zaire. For more information, see Douglas 1963. In this paper, I will examine only palm wine drinking in the "traditional" rural context, excluding then drinking behavior in urban settings where palm wine can indeed be bought. The ethnographic information contained in this paper is available to any Lele who lives in a village, or who, as myself, spends holidays in the village. In 1974 and 1976, I did fieldwork among the Lele and, although palm wine was not the central concern of my research, I had the chance to observe it more systematically and consciously. I wish to thank here all my informants, and particularly Kuka Mingombo who helped me later on in administering a questionnaire aimed at checking some of my data on the subject.

2 *Bacoke ba mak waki pal bakana.*

3 *Kwa bel wal a ikopu, unyu bitula bia mbenda.*

4 See de Heusch (1972) for similar stories in other Bantu cultures.

5 *Mana mi nguak nung ndjua mpende.*

6 Biochemical analysis has established the nutritional value of palm wine which provides calories, proteins, vitamins B1, B2, C and various minerals (Bassir 1968:45).

References

de Heusch, L., 1972. *Le roi ivre ou l'origine de l'état.* Paris, Gallimard

Douglas, M., 1963. *The Lele of the Kasai.* London, IAI

Bassir, O., 1962. Observations on the fermentation of palm wine. In *West African Journal of Biological Chemistry*, 6(2)

   1968. Some Nigerian wines. In *West African Journal of Biological and Applied Chemistry*, 10(2)

Maduagwu, E., and Bassir, O., 1979. Microbial nitrosamine formation in palm wine: In Vitro N-Nitrosation by cell suspensions. In *Journal of Environmental Pathology and Toxicology*, 2

Ngokwey, N., 1975. *Imanya: Un mouvement antisorcellerie chez les Bashilele.* Mémoire de Licence en Sociologie. Lubumbashi, Université Nationale du Zaire

1980. Possessions: Analyse des somatisations du sacré chez les Bashilele du Kasai. *Cahiers des religions Africaines*, 13 (25)

7. Vin Santo and wine in a Tuscan farmhouse

Anne Tyler Calabresi

In October Adamo and Maria go about their farm in shirtsleeves, picking the last fruit from the trees and the first ripe clusters from the vines as they wait for the moment to gather in all the grapes and begin the production of the new wine. Waiting for the *vendemmia*, after the months of care and attention to the vines, the pruning, fertilising, hoeing, cultivating, tying up of new shoots, the spraying on of copper sulfate, the continual anxiety about the weather, is a tense, expectant moment on the farm, but a cautiously happy one if the grapes have developed well and the weather remains fine. The warmth of the season increases the pleasure of bringing in the fruit. The light is softer and hazier than under the dry glaze of the high summer sun. The air is as thick and white in the morning as the bloom on the skin of the yellow grapes. Pears, apples, figs, late peaches and the grapes are warm to the touch on vines and branches; dessert is festooned about the farm.

Fruit, in all its forms, is the luxury of the farm compared to the necessities of olive oil and bread, and although it is not needed for survival, it is a source of health and pleasure. Very much is carefully put away for the winter – little is eaten as it is picked, and part of the satisfaction of the fruit harvest is in the anticipation of future enjoyment. The apples and pears are stored on bamboo racks in a dry, cool storeroom; and many of the figs are dried on trays of woven twigs in the sun. Tomatoes are pulled up, plant and all, and hung in the storeroom from a line which is threaded through two old wine bottles at each end to discourage the mice who walk the tightrope anyway. "*Acrobati*", Maria calls them in disgust. Some of the best bunches of grapes are also hung up to dry in the storeroom, saved to sweeten holiday breads, called the *schiacciata al 'uva* and to be eaten on New Year's eve to bring good luck. "*Chi mangia l'uva a capodanno, ha i quatrini tutto l'anno*" (He who eats grapes on New Year's day, has money all year long).

Adamo and Maria eat fruit sparingly, to make it last as long as possible, yet many meals at the end of the winter are finished without it. Few apples remain after March and there is a gap until the May strawberries and the apricots and cherries of June, a gap filled occasionally by oranges from the market. But in October there is always a generous supply even after the perfect fruit has been carefully husbanded, for the ripest fruit as well as that which has been damaged, bruised or pecked by the birds can be used for the table. There is always a surfeit of the reliable hardy figs which are filling and have a high sugar content. In Roman times Cato suggested issuing a smaller ration of wheat for bread to his farm workers when the figs were plentiful. When Maria was a child, a piece of bread with figs was breakfast. Even now a ripe fig, its skin bursting at the base, is a particular treat in a diet containing so little sugar. Adamo's pears too seem sweet as honey. "Some people like their fruit a bit tart," he said one day at lunch, as he cut a big brown pear with his knife and the juice ran out over his fingers, "he who pleases may eat apples, or cherries, or even peaches, when they are hard, but pears have no flavor before they are ripe. They taste like wood." The wine grapes, purple, amber and especially the white, are also surprisingly sweet, with slippery skins which slide off the body of the grape in the mouth. A few bunches only are taken for the table as the grapes are valued more for their wine, and they are left on the vine until the precise moment comes for gathering them.

As is often the case after a cold spring or summer, even the early hothouse days of October had not been enough to ripen the grapes by the middle of the month. Every advancing day brought the chance of a change in the weather. There was a daily debate in the kitchen whether to wait another weekend for the *vendemmia*. On the weekends Adamo's sons, as well as other relations, would come to help him and Maria with heavy jobs. Even the small wine harvest of the old farm was too big a task for Adamo and Maria alone. The farm had, for hundreds of years, supported a modest family, but one of several generations. Now that the young men worked in the city, Adamo had to plan his time to a town as well as a country clock. He went out each day among the vines, which were grouped in small plantings in various places on the farm, tasting a grape here and there, and occasionally clipping a particular bunch which was in a more favorable position and had ripened sooner. "An experienced farmer knows when a grape is ripe by the taste," he said.

There are two stages to the grape harvest. It began with the gathering of the *scelti*, the selection of the finest bunches, which were brought in first, followed then by the general picking or the *vendemmia*. The reserved grapes were divided between the red and the white, and Adamo was already bringing them into the house with great care and arranging them in the storeroom on the big bamboo racks, or *stoia* (from *Passatoia*, which literally means footbridge). The *stoia* were racks stretched between posts like a fourposter bed with five or more "decks". The red grapes would remain there for two weeks, then to be added to the new wine to help the fermentation and increase the sugar content; this was the traditional method for making *Chianti*. The white grapes he treated with even greater care, lifting each cluster from the basket and setting it apart on the rack so that the grapes would not be bruised or the skins ruptured. These were to be the grapes for the *Vin Santo*. No one else but Adamo was allowed to pick the Vin Santo grapes. It required a trained eye and complete concentration. "If you do not mind," he would say to me, politely looking the other way when we were down among the vines, "I must pick these grapes for a while by myself." He went over the Sangioveto and the white *trebbiano* vines daily, turning the bunches around, picking off any grapes that looked as if they might spoil. Every now and then he would take his clippers out of the ox-horn sheath at his waist and with the attention of a surgeon sever the stem and deliver the bunch tenderly to the basket. Some of the most promising clusters he would have wrapped in newspaper as they hung on the vine, making a sack tied on with the willow shoots which serve for string on the farm. These bags protected the more exposed bunches from both the birds and the scorching sun.

The Barbera grapes were already sweet and ripe, "good this year for Vin Santo but not for red wine, *un po' scadente*," he said. "There are those that are more spoiled (*vizziati*), weaker, like a person who has weak blood, they are more susceptible to disease. If the weather is too dry, for instance, the grapes fall off. They don't stick. Not even one grape remains. The vine is doing nothing. Like us. If we didn't work, what would happen to us? In general, if people didn't work they would die of hunger. It is not true that work is hateful, to be done by a '*rozzo di contadino*' (uncouth farmer). Everyone has their useful work. *Basta lavorare*. It is enough work. That which is useful is that which bears fruit."

Vin Santo was more important to Adamo than his red wine. He could put up with a quite inferior red table wine in a bad year, diluted as it always was by a splash of water in the glass. Red wine was something that went along with the food, with cooking and preserving; it was part of the meal, and he drank it moderately. Vin Santo was not for the table, however, nor was it ever taken with food. More than an apéritif before a meal, or a digestif afterwards, it was "*una bibita*", something to be sipped at any time of day that the occasion demanded, and there were many possible occasions. Upon the arrival of a guest, or friend, or member of the family from the town, the glasses would be put out on the table after a few minutes of conversation, and the bottle of Vin Santo brought out from the cupboard. "*Prima di metterti in cammino beviti un vinsantino*" Adamo would say to me. (Before you sit by the fire have a little vinsanto.) The glasses were small since all wine was used sparingly, but Vin Santo was drunk neat from the bottom of three or four ounce glasses. It was the offering wine. Adamo said simply, "It is Vin Santo because it is special, different from the red, not for food, *vino piu ommaggio*" (homage). It was also a strengthening wine, and a restoring wine. Before setting out for town on foot Adamo would pour himself half a glass; or in the summer, before going out to reap in the early light, long before the first meal of the day, Adamo would take a glass, "to give me strength". When the men had been working in the fields they would come in, wash their hands at the stone sink, and then go to the table for "*Un bicchier' di Vin Santo*". Vin Santo is a rich wine, amber and slightly cloudy. It differs from farm to farm, soil to soil, but it is a wine light in color in contrast to the "*nero*" which is the inky red Chianti. Vin Santo is not as dry as a white wine, nor as dry as a sherry, although an old Count who was a friend of ours used to claim that when his farmer's Vin Santo failed, it still made a good sherry, though the pity was, he didn't know how. Nor is Vin Santo sweet, if sweet brings to mind dessert wine. Adamo's was consistently a "medium" wine, with a strong bouquet of earth and fruit, rather like a Madeira. Adamo's production was for his own use and not for the landlord. "*La padrona* has different tastes," he explained. Some landlords look on Vin Santo as an inferior drink, associated as it is with the farmhouse, others value it highly. Until recently it was rarely found for sale in a store, most Vin Santo was produced and consumed by each farmer on each separate *podere*. When asked about the name, Adamo shook his head. Vin Santo was Vin Santo because it had always been called that since before the time of his great-grand-parents; because it was special, being squeezed rather than crushed, it didn't need to "boil" or ferment before it was put in the casks, requiring less watching than the red. It was also used in church. "It was especially for the Mass. There has been Vin Santo for as long as there has been Mass said; perhaps even before," he said. "But we never tasted it in church in the old days, you know. At Mass we were given the bread only. There were too many people in our parish at Rignano (where he was born and served as acolyte), maybe 2,000. And the priests, they were not going to give Vin Santo to all those people. That would take too much wine. They liked to drink it themselves. *Egoisti, sa!*" he said with a sharp look to express his consistently low opinion of clergy. Vin Santo is in fact a raisin wine, and is likely a descendant of those sweet wines much favored in the ancient world. Its hospitable and respected role in daily life probably long predates its use in church as the "offering".

The weather was especially important for the *vendemmia*. Signs were watched in the sky, and the clouds, in the direction of the wind and in the moon. One day before the *vendemmia* I came up into the kitchen of the house and found Maria standing by the hearth watching a pot and wiping her eyes with her apron. "It is going to rain today, certainly," she said, "this fire always smokes when it is about to rain." When the rains have begun at this time of the year the chances of a stretch of clear weather returning immediately are uncertain, especially if the change in the weather coincides with a change in the phases of the moon. "We are on the other side of the moon," Adamo would say as greeting on an unexpectedly tempestuous day. For harvesting the grapes of the Vin Santo especially, fine weather was an absolute necessity. "If the grapes are the least damp when they are picked they will spoil when they are placed on the bamboo. After a heavy rain it is not enough to have a few days of sun to dry them off, you must also have a good wind. The big leaves on the vines at this time of year cover the grapes, you see, and keep the sun off."

As the thunder rolled down the chimney over the hearth and the slow, smoky burning fire of olive wood, Adamo was out picking the last bunches of any grapes that could possibly be considered ripe. He was pleased that he had managed to gather nearly all the grapes he would need for the fermentation of the "dark" wine; as well as most of the whites needed for the Vin Santo. On the weekend, if the weather held, his family would be on hand to bring in the bulk of the red for the regular wine. That would be a picking which required no particular precision or talent. By then Adamo hoped to have finished all the "reserve" picking himself, although right until the end of the *vendemmia* he would remain on the lookout for a fine bunch which he might have overlooked, to add to the *scelti*.

Once the grapes for the Vin Santo were picked and laid upon the bamboo racks, that was the end of the Vin Santo production until December when the grapes would be pressed. Being a much less complicated wine to make than the red, Vin Santo does not need to go through the first "boiling" period of fermentation in a vat. The grapes on the racks ferment gently within themselves, evaporating and concentrating at the same time. Left from the *vendemmia* in October until early December in a cool but dry room, the grapes had become slightly "hard". When the proper day came in December, according to the quarter of the moon, Adamo moved the grapes down to the small hand press in the Tinaio and there, in a single day, rapidly expelled in three pressings what juice remained in the grapes and put it into the *barilli*, the small oval wooden barrels. When filled these are then stored on their narrow sides in any room that is dry and cool, to remain with their taps cemented securely for two, three or even four years, if the demand allows it, until they are decanted as needed and put into bottles. In Adamo's house the *barilli* sit against a wall in an upstairs back room which is useless for other purposes now that the center of the floor has caved in. The heavy red tiles slope in from every side over the old weakened floor beams towards a black hole in the middle of the room, but Adamo would say, "Stay close to the walls and it's all right." In a corner opposite the casks Adamo had piled, in defiance of gravity, a heap of potatoes for the winter. A few had rolled down to the edge of the hole. The fact that he had put his precious Vin Santo in that room reassured me somewhat, when I had to go through it to the next.

Adamo made all his wine in the old way, both Vin Santo and the red, with no concessions to new techniques or chemistry. He never seemed to doubt that he would make a drinkable wine, once he had the grapes safely off the vines. If the grapes were good he could be lucky and have a splendid year. He never seemed anxious even about the red wine with its greater number of steps and decisions to be made about fermentation, shifting of casks, etc.

It could be tested along the way to see what was happening and an exerperienced wine maker knew how to make adjustments. In contrast Vin Santo seemed simple, once past the crucial decisions of when and which grapes to pick. When the grapes were dried and squeezed that was it. The casks could not be opened for years. And while the opening of the first barrel of Vin Santo in a given year was a moment of suspense it was also a time of pleasant expectation. Perhaps the landlords, like our friend the Count, wanted more consistency. Adamo's knowledge had been passed down from previous generations and learned from observation. "We have always lived next to a vineyard," he said, meaning that he and his family have always had a vineyard, "I understand how the wine is supposed to taste. I never add anything to the wine, you know the artificial things they use to make the wine boil faster, to make it a higher grade. My wine is always under ten percent. I only use the must from my own grapes. Some years the wine turns out better than others, of course. If it is a very poor year we run out. Then we have to buy. But I have a friend with a good vineyard. I have known him a long time and he always has wine. Unless there is a complete failure. He makes his wine the way I do, so I know it is good."

Adamo's attitude towards home-produced wine arises not just from parsimony. It springs from his broad conviction of the value of what he eats. It directly affects his health, which directly affects his strength, which in turn determines his ability to be a farmer. Health and the weather are the two variables upon which the success of his farming depend and they are both beyond control. Health, however, may be propitiated to some extent by preventive maintenance, by the quality of one's food and wine, hence the profound interest in the value of food. Things grown on one's own land, under one's own eye, by hand, are to be trusted. Adamo in his high seventies for his part remained confident in his own strength, in his ability to produce the oil, bread and wine, the essentials which he consumed. He said, "I still put my hands to it."

In the evening the weather broke with a heavy storm. Adamo watched from the loggia the rain sweeping through the olive grove, and examined the drops splashing off the tiles of the shed below to see if they contained any hailstones. "After the rain the grapes have less sugar, make a weaker wine. If the grapes are wet too long, they become rotten," he said, looking gloomily into the storm. "*Vino scipido*. When the wine is spoiled we give it to the distiller. At least we get something for the grapes. He makes *grappa* from the spoiled grapes. We do not drink it much around here, *La grappa non e amabile*. It is more for those who live in Northern countries, Switzerland, Germany, Austria. They are more accustomed to it." He sighed. "*Pazienza*. Perhaps we shall still be able to pick for the red wine this weekend if this blows over. At least we have brought in most of the Vin Santo."

The rain continued for several days, but the weather cleared up by mid-week. The vineyards were too drenched to be touched, however. Adamo occupied himself with cleaning out and readying the equipment that would be needed for the winemaking. The big fermenting vat, or *tino*, which on a large estate could easily hold a dozen men and would spend its long life in the same *tinaio*, or cellar, on Adamo's farm was small enough to be moved out into the courtyard where it had been left in the rain to fill with water and swell to tighten any loose ribs. Adamo's "*tinello*" was the size of those which, in great vineyards, used to be put on the cart behind the oxen and brought down into the vineyard so that the pickers could empty their grapes directly into it and the workers tread the grapes right there. The vat measured roughly four feet wide by five feet deep. When the water drained out, it was tipped on its side so that Adamo could crawl inside to nail a bunch of straw, tied together like a round whisk, over the bung hole to act as a sieve, so that when the new wine was drawn off, the grape skins and seed and stems would not clog the tap. A screen of any composition would not have been adequate as it would soon become packed; it was the three dimensional feature of the "broom" which was the old secret of its success.

When Adamo's sons came out from town they moved the vat back into the cellar and set it up on supports three feet above the floor, which made it easier to fill the smaller containers when the new wine was drawn. Adamo, standing on the projecting supports and holding on to the edge of the *tinello* with one hand, could just get his other arm over the edge of the vat. This meant he could mash the grapes by hand with a big pestle rather than having to get in and stamp upon them with his feet. The small hand-operated wine press was pushed back into position beside the vat, and then the tall narrow wooden tubs or *bigoncie* into which the grapes would be picked were carried out into the courtyard to be rinsed out in their turn. When Adamo still had his oxen the *bigoncie* made the trip from the vines to the vat in the big cart, now they were crammed into the back of primo's small blue market car which bucketed down the stony track and ground its way slowly back up the hill in first gear. The grapes were picked into these heavy wooden containers so that they could receive a preliminary mashing with the pestle. This *mostatoia* or juice-maker can be recognized by its particular design as the club over the shoulder of Folly or sometimes Hercules in medieval paintings of the vices and virtues. Adamo himself made his own, in the traditional shape of a long bat into which he had cut deep, circular ridges, which increased its mashing efficiency.

On Saturday afternoon Adamo allowed his family to go down to the vines to begin the general picking for the Chianti. His son Ugo, the butcher, had taken the afternoon off, as had Primo, the eldest, who lived at home but was occupied most days with selling in the market. Adamo's cousin, a slender woman his own age, was there and his nephew, Beppino. Ugo's wife, Anna, and their children, came too.

Adamo, Primo, Beppino, Adamo's sister, and Maria picked into the *bigoncie* with Primo's car carrying four at a time up the hill to the vat in the cellar. Watching the little Fiat grinding its way up the hill, Adamo said, "We carried twelve *bigoncie* at a time in the ox-cart, and made five or six trips a day. We took back about 70 *bigoncie* a day." Adamo clipped the grapes, quickly dropping them into a basket beside his feet which he would empty then into the heavy wooden *bigoncie*. There was no need to treat the grapes gently now, as they would be crushed in the *bigoncie* tubs with the wooden bat before they were emptied into the big vat, the *tinello*. Adamo let Primo carry the heavy tubs to the car, while he walked along the row lifting every broad leaf to make sure no clusters of grapes had been overlooked. A trace of the brilliant blue copper sulfate remained in the veins of the leaves. "A hundred years ago we did not need to put copper on the vines. The disease (phylloxera) had not come here yet. It is always worse in wet years. This year was not too bad as it has been dry since July. We have not had it for three years because the last months of the summer have been so dry, but we have to spray anyway as a precaution. The disease comes from the weakness of the earth under the rain or mist. When it was very bad we had some years without wine at all, though there were some dryer parts of the country which could make it." He cupped a big bunch in his hand, the end of it trailing half way up his arm to his elbow. "They are small this year due to the cold spring. We call them *Passerini* [sparrows] in dialect, when they are like this. Not to offend," he added apologetically. "Nature has a hundred names, each one, in Italian, or English, or American, or dialect, has its '*parola scritta*'."

Adamo's son Ugo with his wife and two little girls went down another track instead, to a small group of older vines which strung in the old *arbustum* method between several ash trees that ran along a ditch at the edge of a field. They had with them some of Adamo's small baskets as well as a new one of plastic which they had brought with them, which was the same shape and size, a replica of the old ones. They had as well a big rectangular hamper made of withies. They emptied their baskets into it and when it was full they carried it slowly up the hill between them, leaning slightly out to counter the weight. The girls trotted up and down behind them chatting and laughing to each other in high voices which carried through the olive trees. An echo of the past when all the young people took part in the grape picking.

In the courtyard Ugo and Anna transferred the grapes from the hamper into the open tubs for their preliminary crushing. In the twilight the pestle pumped up and down as though churning butter. The bat came out each time stained scarlet but running with pale pink juice. The oldest daughter ran upstairs to get a glass which her father allowed her to hold under the pestle as he held it high in the air, breaking the rhythm of his steady plunging. Two or three mouthfuls of juice would run into the glass which she would share in sips with her sister, begging again in a few minutes for another taste from her father.

Primo's blue car shot in under the archway on its last trip of the evening and Ugo helped him swing the barrels out of the back. Primo took a turn with the pestle, lifting it high and slamming it down ending with a circular twist in the barrel before heaving it up again. When the contents were well crushed and the juice could be seen bubbling up around the grapes the two brothers carried them to the big vat and tipped them in, reaching up over their heads.

By the time they had finished stripping all the vines the next day, including the extra grapes from the heaving bearing Vin Santo vines, the vat was filled to within a foot of its rim. Adamo then stood upon one of the supporters projecting from beneath the vat and plunged the pestle in, stirring with sweeps as wide as he could reach. He would continue to stir the mixture every few hours for the next week, to make sure that the juice did not sit on the surface where it could turn to vinegar. After the first day the wine began to bubble and foam. In spite of the open door next to the vat and the open window at the end of the cellar there was a pungent breath-taking odour in the room. Adamo kept his head turned aside while he plunged the stick in and out. "The fumes can kill a man," he explained. "People have fallen into vats and have died before anyone could get them out. *E vero*. In the big vats especially, the fumes are terribly strong."

The wine steamed and frothed along for ten days. Adamo waited to be on the safe side of the moon before the fresh wine was drawn off, the remaining pulp pressed through the hand press, and all the liquid carried into the big casks or *caratelli* in the wine cave. These casks were kept in the room in the cellar which was deepest into the hill. It was without a window, being underground on three sides, and the black mold on the moist stone walls absorbed nearly all the light from the one bulb hanging on a wire in the middle. A ladder rested against the shoulder of one of the *caratelli*. As the wine was pressed, it was put into the small casks, the same size as those used for the Vin Santo, and they were carried by a single man as he had to climb the ladder to reach the opening at the top of the *caratello*. "Those small casks hold a *quintale* of wine," said Adamo, "very heavy. They are what we call *un peso morto*. One of them will kill a man if it falls on him. Once I let one go; I dropped the whole thing, a *quintale* of wine. I felt it slipping as I carried it up; it was at Rignano and they had no ladder but a couple of planks which were not very steady. One began to turn under my foot. I knew if I fell with the barrel . . . well . . . so I dropped it. There was nothing to do."

When the juice had all been transferred, the blue grapes that were put by on the bamboo racks upstairs for the fermentation were brought down and stripped of their stems and added, skin and seeds, to the big casks. Then the casks were closed and their waspwaisted glass stoppers set in place on top. By watching the action of the wine in these stoppers Adamo could follow the progress of the wine; when it in turn should be drawn off and transferred to the slightly smaller storage casks in the same long room.

In Adamo's youth the farmers made not only Chianti but by squeezing the grapes again after having drawn off the juice, and mixing them with water, they made a light, fizzy drink for everyday called Acquarello. Stingy landlords reputedly substituted it for the good wine, but Maria and Adamo speak of Acquarello nostalgically. It seems to have been akin to a spritzer. Actually Adamo and Maria almost never drink their good red wine as it comes from the bottle. The wine bottle and the water bottle stand side by side on the table. When wine is poured water follows. Each person pours their own mixture. I was considered rather hard-headed to drink wine straight, at midday, but then it was understood I had no heavy work to do in the afternoon. Nevertheless, I was consuming double. Water stretched the wine the year around. On the other hand, Adamo pointed out, "when you drink wine you eat less bread, you need less. When you drink water with bread you are hungrier." Most of Adamo's wine was drunk young, within the first or second year of the vintage. There was not very much of it to begin with as his vineyard had never been re-established after the phylloxera. Only a dramatic year could produce the quality and the quantity to set some by. Adamo was still nursing a cask of '79, but it would soon be gone.

Although Adamo's wine production was small, supplying just enough wine in good years for himself, his sons and a few relatives, picking the grapes was still a major event in the farm year and a far more pleasant one than the cold gathering of olives from the tops of ladders in December and January. They still had, on the last evening of the *vendemmia*, a meal all together, and it was as much a part of the wine-making process as the heavy work. After carrying baskets up the hill, heaving wooden tubs over the rim of the *tinello* and mashing the grapes with the pestle for several days or a week perhaps, it was with pleasure that everyone sat down in the big upstairs kitchen to one of Maria's dinners. "On the last day of the *vendemmia*, we used to work a little less years ago," Adamo said. "We would celebrate, and enjoy the *bacchi* [grapes], and drink some of the fresh juice, and end the day with a big meal and dancing. Maria's brother would play the accordion."

Maria had cooked much of the meal earlier in the day; the boiled meats and the roast chicken needed only to be reheated, but the vegetables she would cook at the last minute. Before the picking was quite done Maria came up the hill slowly carrying a basket of grapes. She put it down in the courtyard next to a wooden tub and arched her back. Maria was very small, not much more than four and three-quarters foot, but strong and compact as a wine cask. When her family teased her about her size, she answered them with a *"stornello"*:

Amor'non guadar' se son piccina,
Amor'non sta ne l'en grandezza.
In botte piccine ci sta vin buono,
Donna piccina e pien' di gentilezza.

[Love, do not mind if I am small,
For Love has naught to do with size.
As good wine is found in little casks,
A small woman may be filled with sweetness.]

It was getting dark outside when the kitchen began to fill with people. Adamo came in and carried a dipper full of water from the black pot over the fire to the sink to wash. He poured it into a little basin in the large stone sink and then came back for more, his wet hand hissed as he inadvertently brushed the edge of the cauldron over the coals.

Maria was cutting up some enormous mushrooms which Primo had brought home from his hunting expedition. *Porcini di castagno*, these were the big mushrooms that grew near the roots of the chestnut trees in the fall. The most succulent treat from the woods, they have been relished since ancient times. One appears next to a rabbit in a mosaic at Pompeii. They were called *porcini*, "piglets", because they were considered as succulent as meat. Maria sliced them up, three of them were enough for the big group, dipped them in flour and piled them on a plate ready to be fried at the last minute in olive oil. Another three Primo reserved for his market where they would fetch several thousand lira each. Primo had had a successful morning in the woods, he hung by the door a clutch of twenty brightly colored finches. Threaded together by their beaks they made a delicate bundle hardly bigger than a hat.

Maria took the roast chicken out of the wood stove, and put a few more pieces of wood inside. She poured the oil from the roasting pan into a frying pan and set it on the brazier in the counter. The chicken-flavored olive oil was to be used for frying the potatoes. Maria hurried between the tables, the hearth and the brazier. She fried the mushrooms quickly while Anna finished the *crostini*. "It's ready," said Maria at last, and we ate:

Broth from the boiled meats with pastina.

Crostini, little slices of bread moistened with broth and covered with minced rabbit and chicken livers, ground and cooked in olive oil and mashed with anchovies and capers.

Boiled meats, beef and chicken, with home grown artichokes preserved in olive oil and home grown capers pickled in vinegar as condiments.

Roast chicken with a few thrushes, caught early in the week (and we threw the bones to the dog).

Fried potatoes.

Fried porcini.

Salad.

Fruit: peaches, pears, apples, figs, chestnuts roasted in the fire.

As we were finishing the fruit Maria brought the pan of chestnuts from the ashes. "In the old days we started the last day of *vendemmia* with salted herring, bread and nuts," said Adamo. "Then at midday we had black-eyed beans boiled plain with olive oil and sage (*faggioli al uccelletto*) with some boiled greens (*rape*), bread and wine. For dinner we would have broth, and meat; chicken or goose or duck or rabbit, with bread. And for fruit, figs and grapes."

"We didn't do so much cooking in those days," said Maria, taking a chestnut herself. "Here, this is a soft one," she said handing it to Adamo. He shook his head. "Take it," she urged, "the first of the season. It's good and soft." Adamo took the chestnut and peeled it carefully and munched it in several bites. He took up the wine bottle and poured wine for those who had begun to eat chestnuts themselves. "Chestnuts call for wine," he said, "when they are roasted, not so much when they are boiled, or made into bread, but when they are roasted they call for wine."

Glossary

Arbustum	The method dating from Etruscan times of looping vines between live trees or props.
Bacco	Grape, Latin word.
Barillo	Small wooden casks, oval end.
Bigoncie	Narrow wooden tub for carrying and crushing grapes.
Botte	Small wine casks, rounded.
Carattello	Wine casks, round. Also, large wine casks used for storing and aging wine in the *cave*.
Cave	Wine cellar.
Cestino	Small basket with handle into which grapes are picked before putting into *bigoncie*.
Mezzadria	Sharecropping system, prevalent in Tuscany since the Middle Ages.
Mostatoio	Bar or pestle for crushing grapes in *bigoncie* before they are added to *tino*.
Passerini	Nickname for small grape, meaning sparrow or little bird. With feminine sexual connotations.
Podere	Small farm worked generally by one family.
Stoia	Bamboo drying racks.
Scelti	Chosen bunches of grapes used in fermenting wine.

Schiacciata	Flatbread made with oil in round pan.
Tinaio	Cellar or room where *tino* was kept.
Tino	Huge wooden vat for fermenting grapes in wineroom or cellar.
Tinello	Smaller *tino*. Transportable.
Vendemmia	Grape harvest.

8. Competitive beer drinking among the Mambila

Farnham Rehfisch

The Mambila[1] are skilled and enthusiastic farmers, fortunate in having an abundance of fertile land. The result is that they normally produce a considerable surplus of their two staple crops, maize and guinea corn, except in the few bad years when the rains either come very late or are otherwise inadequate. Some of their surplus grain is sold to the town-dwelling Fulani and Hausa as well as to the nomadic cattle-keeping Fulani. The demand being small, most of the surplus is turned into beer for their own consumption. It is my impression backed by statements of many Mambila informants that they could sell a far greater proportion of their grain than is actually the case and run no risk of being left with insufficient supplies for their own use.

In Mambila language the term *bill* refers to the two partners in a relationship of competitive gift exchange. *Bill* also may have the wider meaning of "friend". For the purposes of this paper I shall restrict its usage to the first meaning given above. The terms "host" and "guest" will be employed when it becomes necessary to distinguish between the partner who gives and the one receiving.

At about fourteen to sixteen a boy is said to be old enough to select as a partner a lad of about his own age. Factors influencing his choice will be discussed below. Girls too have this prerogative but little data on this relationship were collected. Gift exchange between women is of far less structural significance than that between men for a number of reasons which cannot be discussed here. It is not possible for a boy to select a girl as a partner, nor a girl a boy. Not all males choose a partner, only about thirty percent of my informants had one. Why such a small number of males establish this type of relationship is not clear though some informants who had not done so said that at the right age they had no specific individual with whom they wished to acquire a link of this sort. It might be tempting to argue that only the wealthy could afford to become involved in gift-exchanges, but this would not fit the facts since there is no important wealth differential between the members of a village. It should be added here that the establishment of such ties is not limited to certain kin groups since any boy is free to select a partner if he so wishes. Quite a large proportion of those who had once had a partner had him no longer. In some cases the partner had died, in others the relationship was broken. One reason frequently given for breaking off such ties was that one of the two had moved to another village too distant for the tie to be maintained. The most common cause of a breach is a serious dispute between the two partners. In one typical case an informant had courted the sister of his partner; the parents of the girl having refused to accept him as a suitor, in a rage he insulted his friend and refused to continue the relationship. Finally it is not customary for a person to have more than one partner during his lifetime.

The relationship is established when a boy offers a pot of beer to another and asks him to become his partner. The pots contain from four to five gallons. No special ceremony takes place on this occasion. The two have probably been friends for some time. The invitation is interpreted as a sign of friendship and not a challenge, even though as we shall see later an element of competition does enter into the relationship. It may be rejected, but this entails the risk that the candidate will be stamped as too mean to wish to give beer to others. Generosity being highly valued in this society no one wishes to have the reputation of being either unwilling or unable to offer drinks to his friends. If the offer is accepted, and it usually is, the proferred beer is shared between the host, his guests and their friends. Normally the guest and his followers sit on one side, facing the others. Either he or one of his friends is in charge of distributing the beverage and special care is taken to see to it that all present have an equal share. If the guest gives too much to his own group the host may become angry and break the relationship. At some future date, one or two years hence, the erstwhile guest invites his partner to come and drink beer with him. The host is expected to provide at least one more pot than was given on the previous occasion. The two take it in turn to entertain each other, each time the host being expected to offer more beer than previously done. While in name the feasts are offered to the guest, the host and his friends are given a share equivalent to that consumed by the guest and his group. The older kinsmen of the partners see to it that exchanges are not made too frequently since this would lead to the amount given becoming large too quickly, that is before the two are old enough to recruit enough persons to help them in brewing sufficient to live up to their obligations. Age is the primary determinant of status in Mambila society and only those enjoying relatively high status are able to rely on the help of a large number of people to assist them on occasions of this kind.

At the outset when the amount of beer given is small, it is expected that it will all be brewed from the surplus stocks of grain belonging to the host. This is usually the case until the partners reach the age of thirty or thereabouts. At this stage the amount given varies from sixteen to twenty pots depending upon the number of exchanges that have taken place. Henceforward a man begins to rely on others for assistance. At first the fellow residents of his compound will help him by preparing beer for the feast. Later the residents of his compound cluster will also contribute. When he is approximately fifty years old his role in the hamlet will be important and therefore it will be considered fitting for all the members of that unit to assist him in fulfilling his obligations vis-à-vis his partner. Later the whole village will be drawn in when he wishes to entertain his guest. It is only at the age of sixty or more that a man has an important enough status in the context of the entire village to expect help from all its inhabitants. If a man of forty or fifty were to ask for it, he would be laughed to scorn, the people saying that while only a "small boy" he was trying to act the role of a "big man".

The partner is usually chosen from among the residents of a neighboring settlement. A member of one's village is not usually selected for three reasons. The first is that it is said to be advantageous to have a partner in settlements visited with some frequency so that one is assured of hospitality. Since a man should always be welcomed when stopping at a compound in his own village, there is no need to establish such ties within it. Secondly fellow villagers should cooperate and not compete against each other as individuals, though under certain circumstances sub-groups of the village, especially hamlets, do in fact act in opposition to each other. If a man selected a fellow villager as a partner, the element of competition in the relationship would be incompatible with that of neighbor. Thirdly, as mentioned above, when the exchange is one of long standing the whole village acts as a unit in preparing beer for the host to offer to his guest. If the feast were to be given for a fellow villager, the former would be both a donor and a recipient on the same occasion, and this is incompatible with Mambila ideals. It would of course be possible for the guest not to make any beer at this time, but then he would not be living up to his obligations as a good neighbor.

While it is said not to be desirable to select a member of one's own local group as a partner, it is sometimes done. In cases of this kind the partnership will be amiably broken before the amount of beer to be exchanged reaches the scale where the entire village must cooperate in its preparation.

Two categories of persons must under no conditions be selected as partners: fellow hamlet members and kinsmen. The former for the reasons given above when discussing the inadvisability of selecting a fellow villager as a partner and the latter because the competitive element inherent in the partnership is incompatible with the type of relationship that should exist between kinsfolk.

The Mambila gave a number of reasons for selecting a specific person as a partner. The first, as mentioned above, is to be assured of hospitality when visiting his village. The second was that the selector liked the individual as a person and wished to establish a close relationship with him. Finally some informants said that they had chosen a boy because he was a close relative of a girl that they hoped eventually to marry. By establishing this link they could anticipate that their partner would support them when courting the girl. As a rule the choice is in the hands of the boy alone, neither his parents nor other senior kinsmen intervening unless the one selected has a very bad reputation or falls into one of the prohibited categories. The fact that the re- lationship is not extended to the kinsmen of the two partners may account for their neutrality on the subject.

While the reciprocal giving of beer is said to be the *raison d'être* of the re- lationship, the ties binding the two partners extend to spheres of social ac- tivities other than feasts. When a man marries, his partner is expected to contribute a small part of the cash required for brideswealth. He should also come to the wedding ceremony and has the exclusive right to joke with, and even fondle, the bride though neither then nor at any other time may he have intercourse with her. He may consult an oracle should his partner fall ill. He should attend his partner's funeral. The two should help each other from time to time in house-building, farming, etc. Gifts are often presented by one to the other with no obligation that a counter-gift be returned.

When one of the two partners dies the relationship is normally broken, but it may be continued by a surviving sibling of the deceased if he so wishes. There is no pressure put on the brother to do so, even should the deceased have been in the position of owing a feast to his partner at his death. The link is never maintained after the death of the two original part- ners.

It should be noted here that while there are a number of possibilities open to a Mambila to establish formal ties with a non-kinsman – as for example by marriages, by the institution of blood brotherhood, or by joining a per- manent cooperative working group – none of these relationships include competitive gift exchanges.

During my stay in the village of Warwar a number of small scale feasts were held as well as one involving the whole village. As a general rule only one or two large scale feasts are held yearly. Here I intend to describe briefly one of the former category and, in rather more detail, the large one.

The first was given by a boy of about eighteen to his partner who lived in Vokude, about four miles away. He announced his intention to his "friend" on the market day preceding the one fixed for the occasion. Four days before the date set he took some maize from his own granary and gave it to his two sisters to grind into flour. He himself brought the necessary water and supervised the brewing. In this he was helped by his two female and two male siblings. In all eight pots of beer were made but only six were given to the guest. The latter was accompanied by seven young men from his own village and the host had eleven friends present. The seven included four kinsmen, while six of the host's group were relatives of his. I was the only person present during most of the festivities who was not between the ages of 16 and 20. At first two pots were brought out and given by the host to the guest. The latter filled a cup and gave it to the host who took a sip and passed it on to the oldest member of his own group. The next cup went to the guest who took a sip and passed it on to the senior of his followers. Before the two pots were empty all had had one or more cups. The members of each group drank in turn. The next two pots were offered by the host who again gave them to the guest who passed them on to the youngest member of his group for distribution and so it went until all the beer was finished. On two occasions persons wandering by were invited to partake by the guest, he being the owner of the beer.

Whenever any food or beverage is available a share should be offered to any passer-by as was done in this case. After the guests had gone one of the remaining pots of beer was consumed by the host and his young friends, while the other was given to the host's father. In almost all cases of beer being prepared for a feast, more is made than is expected to be consumed during the gift-exchange. This will later be drunk by the giver of the feast, his kinsmen and neighbors.

The large scale feast involving the whole village was given by one of the four hamlet heads in Warwar for his partner from Dembe, a settlement only a few miles away. The feast lasted for three days, but the preparations had begun a week earlier. Beer was brewed by almost all the households in the village. Less than five percent of the total number did not prepare any, the reasons given being: they had not enough surplus grain, illness, or absence from the settlement. Even those not on friendly terms with the host brewed beer for him on this occasion. One informant who was at this time involved in a serious dispute with the hamlet head nevertheless made a very large contribution himself and saw to it that those living in his compound cluster did the same. He said that he could not let the village down by refusing to cooperate. His use of the term village in this context reflects the fact that when a gift-exchange reaches the point where all the group cooperates in providing beer for the guest, the reputation of the unit as a whole rests on the ability of the host to live up to his obligations.

On the opening day of the feast about fifty men from Dembe led by the guest arrived during the late afternoon. They were met at the hamlet boundary by the host and some of his kin and friends. Four pots of beer were immediately given to the guest who himself distributed the first pot and asked a younger member of his contingent to divide up the rest. Again here those present were given a roughly equivalent share. The Dembe people sat on one side of the pots and the Warwar group on the other as is always the case except after much beer has been drunk and formality has broken down. After all had been consumed the whole party adjourned to the compound of the host where more beer was consumed. Later on more persons from Dembe arrived including some of the wives of those who had come earlier, more men, and a number of young men and girls. The total number of visitors was now about 120, roughly 80 males and 40 females. Later on small groups straggled in.

That evening chickens were cooked and given to the host who, with the help of some of the older men from Dembe distributed them to all those present. The night was spent chatting, drinking beer, chewing kola nuts, and dancing, the latter mainly by the young of both sexes. Individuals would retire into one of the near-by houses for a cat-nap, but seldom stayed away long, seemingly unable to remain away from the beer and festivities.

The following day the visitors wandered through all the village, were offered beer in the compound where it had been prepared. They had, by this time, broken up into small groups of about ten, and were always accompanied by a roughly equivalent number of local residents. In the afternoon all returned to the host's compound where two live goats, a sheep and a dog were offered to the guest. Goat meat being taboo to him personally, though not to all of the Dembe contingent, only the sheep, the dog, plus a number of chickens were cooked, and the goats were spared. Again the meat was distributed to all present. The night was spent as the previous one, except that fewer people took an active part in the festivities since a large number slept through most of the night. Nevertheless dances and beer drinks were held in many of the compounds of the village, unlike the first night when most of the activities were confined to the host's compound.

On the third day more visits were made, more beer drunk, and more chickens were eaten. Late in the afternoon the guests, accompanied by the majority of the Dembe people, began to wend their way home. But, before leaving, an important part of the feast had to be accomplished. Each time the visitors had been given beer to drink or chickens to eat a small stick was given to the host or in his absence to the most senior Warwar male present. All the sticks had been passed on to the host who proceeded to count them out in the presence of the guest. It was noted that 483 pots of beer, 47 chickens, 1 sheep and 1 dog had been provided during the three days. The kola nuts chewed and the tobacco smoked were not, and are never included in the reckoning. The sticks were given by the host to his guest to serve as a mnemonic device so that, when he returned the feast, he would be certain to know how much should be provided to fulfill his obligations. When feasts reach this size there is no attempt to offer only one more pot of beer than was given on the previous occasion. Rather the practice is to give as much as is required to satisfy those present. The host is able to keep a fairly close track of how much is being given by means of the sticks passed on to him. If as the feast is drawing to a close he becomes aware that he has not supplied the necessary amount, he calls upon all the residents of the village to provide more. Since most people have prepared a few extra pots, which they hoped to consume after the visitors' departure, more will be forthcoming at his call. In the case above, the host did not need to ask for additional help, since when the Dembe partner had given the last feast only some 430 pots of beer and 30 chickens had been consumed. When the Dembe people reached the village boundary the host provided four more pots of beer which was considered to be a very generous gesture since these would not be counted in the total and therefore need not be returned on a future occasion.

All the food and beer offered during the three days was given in the name of the host to the guest, even if neither of the two was present. In their absence the giver would say that he was making the gift for the host to the guest, and the most senior male present from the Dembe group would accept it in the name of the guest.

At the conclusion of the feast I asked the host when he thought that his hospitality would be returned. He answered that he did not know, but probably in a year or two. He added that it might take longer for the Dembe people to acquire a sufficient surplus to brew enough beer. Under normal conditions this would not be the case, since while the amount is quite large it only meant that a relatively small part of the total surplus of grain in Warwar was utilized on this occasion. Dembe, being a much smaller village, would probably utilize a considerably larger proportion of its surplus, but giving such a feast would not risk impoverishing the settlement. The erstwhile host added that he was not certain that his partner would supply as much as he himself had done and, if not, then he and all the Warwar people would laugh at those of Dembe. This is the only sanction used to make a partner live up to his obligations. I later learnt of two instances when a man who had not been able to offer more than he himself had received saw the relationship broken off and himself jeered at. In both cases the scale of the feast was small and did not involve even a hamlet, far less a village. When these large groups become concerned it is of greater importance that the host be able to live up to his obligations since if he does not do so he endangers not only his own reputation but that of the group as a whole. It is important to note that when the Warwar host suggested that perhaps his Dembe partner would not be able to provide an adequate feast he smiled and appeared to derive much pleasure from this speculation. The competitive element however is kept in the background, since no boasting or statements implying that the Dembe people were too poor or mean to be able to provide suitable return gifts were heard during the feast. No comments were made by either side as to the quantity or quality of what was offered.

On other occasions when beer or food is given it is not uncommon for the guest to criticize the amount and/or the quality. For instance beer is given to those who have taken part in communal farm labor or helped a man in building a house. The workers often comment wryly about the amount of beer given to them and insist that more be made available. Similarly when the groom's party offer food and beer to the bride's followers, slurring remarks are often made by the latter.

There are two major factors which help to explain why criticism of the host's offerings is allowed at communal work parties and wedding feasts, but not on the occasion of gift exchange. The first is that on the occasion of gift exchange the host and guest enjoy equal status and hence neither has the right to criticize the other. In the case of bridal feasts and work parties the guests enjoy superior status in the context of the situation and hence it is acceptable for them to make disparaging remarks in reference to what they are being offered. However it should be noted that in the case of a very senior male organizing a work party his offerings are not likely to be criticised since his status is so high that he has not become temporarily subordinated to those helping him.

The second factor which militates against criticism being levelled at the host during a gift exchange, but not on the other two occasions, is that in the first case the two groups are uni-bonded, that is to say linked only by the single tie between the two partners, the host and guest, while the two other types of feasts bring together persons linked by a number of ties. In the case of uni-bonded groups a breach of the tie and fighting is likely to arise if disputes develop, while this is much less likely when the bonds linking the participants are many. The Mambila are well aware of the fact that in the former case large scale feasts may result in fighting. As a precautionary step members of the host's village collect the spears of all the guests upon their arrival and these are not returned until the visitors are about to leave. A brief description of the ties linking the participants in a wedding or work party will show how these occasions differ from those of gift exchange. Work parties are usually made up of persons from the same hamlet or village, and fighting between members of such a unit is deprecated. When outsiders join the group they do so because they already have links with the host, these being for the most part consanguinal or affinal kin ties. Should a dispute arise between kinsmen, fighting should be avoided. In most cases the bride's group will not enjoy kin ties with that of the groom, but links binding it to residents of the groom's village will not only exist, but be emphasized during the festivities. The bride's group will make their first stop in the groom's village at the house of a relative of the bride or of one of her party. If other kin live nearby they also will be visited. This acts as a public recognition of the ties existing between the bride's group and persons inhabiting the groom's settlement. Those visited will be held responsible for seeing to it that disputes do not arise between the bride's and groom's groups, and to act as mediators between the two if needs be. The criticism of the fare offered will also often emphasize previous links. A member of the bride's group when showing dissatisfaction at the amount of food and drink offered will mention that when a male from her own village married a girl from the settlement of the groom much more was offered the guests. At least some, if not many, of the guests at a gift-exchange feast will be related to the host or his neighbors, but these ties seem not to be stressed. Individuals coming to the feast make no attempt to formally visit their kinsfolk. They have come as followers of the guest, residents of his village, and the solidarity of the whole group is maintained vis-à-vis the host's settlement.

In the major feast described above a sister's son of the host, who had settled in Dembe after having previously lived in Warwar for a time, remained firmly attached to the guest's party and acted no differently in relation to his Warwar kinsmen than did any of his neighbors. No effort on these occasions is made to place an individual in an intercalary position to act as mediator in case of strife arising. The fact that the bonds of kinship and neighborhood either do not exist or if they do are ignored in the context of the situation, makes it important, not only for the maintenance of the relationship but also to avoid inter-village fighting from breaking out, that criticism of any kind, a potential source of conflict, be prohibited.

During the festivities described above no beer or food was wasted, nor is it the custom to do so. Several years ago a man from Mang gave a feast and when his guest arrived at the village boundary poured out ten jugs of beer onto the ground. This act was meant to show that the host was so rich that he could afford to waste the beverage and still live up to his obligations. While this act elicited much comment, it has never been repeated. Most informants agreed that it was foolish and should not be done again.

Before analyzing the contribution made by this institution towards maintaining the Mambila village structure, it is important to stress what it does not do. At the incipient stage of the relationship neither the status nor the prestige of the partners is enhanced. It is only when large scale feasts are given that the temporary prestige of the two is moderately increased only inasmuch as they are the focus of the activities, but once the festivities are terminated the added prestige disappears. The advantage to a host is that his name becomes known more widely as a result of having lived up to his obligations with éclat. The fact that two men of roughly the same age, one having a partner and the other not, enjoy the same status within the village indicates that the giving of feasts is not a determinant of status.

However feasts do act to maintain the status system. One prerogative of high status in Mambila society is the right to give orders to those lower on the scale than oneself with the expectation that compliance will follow. In the organizing of a large scale feast not only the host but all the senior males have the right to command their juniors to make beer for the feast. The compound head is responsible for seeing to it that his group makes its contribution, the same applies to the head of the compound clusters and of course the hamlet heads. The feast then is an occasion on which the senior males may activate their authority roles.

The institution plays an important part in the integration of the village itself. There are few occasions on which the settlement acts as a unit. Large scale feasts are one. Here all the residents are made to realize their responsibility towards the group, and the necessity of their sacrificing some of their surplus grain stocks as well as labor for the benefit of the village. All have a common purpose, namely the brewing of enough beer and contributing the requisite number of chickens and animals to be slaughtered. During the feast itself the affiliation of the individual with a village is stressed. It has already been said that residents of the two settlements involved sit apart, one on each side of the pots of beer. An individual obtains his share as a member of the village and for no other reason. When the pots offered at one time are many the guest may immediately divide them up, that is give a certain number to the host's group to be distributed and keep some for his own followers.

The individual's identification with his own local group is also stressed during the dancing. At the outset members of the two villages dance in separate groups and this may continue during the entire feast, but normally after a time the dancers tend to become intermixed. The songs sung to accompany the dancing are also important in this respect. During the time when the large scale feast described above was taking place, the chief of Warwar had been and continued to be unpopular thereafter. On purely local occasions songs were sung voicing the anger of the people at some of his actions and jeering at his inability to obtain from the Native Authority what the villagers believed to be their rights. However when the Dembe people were present only lyrics praising their chief, extolling his virtues and abilities were heard. The strength, wealth, solidarity and large population of Warwar were the themes of others of the songs heard on this occasion. The Dembe contingent of course sung only in laudatory terms of their own settlement. Neither made any slurring references to the other.

Competitive gift exchange plays an important role also in the maintenance of the Mambila economy. It has been said that in all but very bad years a considerable surplus of maize and guinea corn is harvested. However when the rains fail then the yield is considerably lessened. Not a few informants told me they were consciously planting more than they would need for their own families' use in order either to provide a feast for their partner or else help someone do so. When the yields are low due to bad climatic conditions this extra planting may mean the difference between hunger and sufficiency.

These feasts, like other ceremonials and rituals, help to overcome the tedium of everyday life. The day-to-day routine is highly repetitive and acknowledged by the Mambila to be boring. It is only during the festive seasons that excitement reigns and life is lived to the full. When the farm work is demanding on both the time and energy of the people, they are often heard to be discussing with pleasure the festivals to come and those that had taken place already. For months before the feast described above, informants were heard estimating the amount of beer that they would drink on that occasion. A subject of great interest to the young, made obvious by their conversation was what the girls from Dembe who would come would be like; many predicted the amorous exploits in which they would play a part. For months afterwards the feast remained an important subject of conversation and both men and women never seemed to tire of stating the amount of beer that they had drunk and the food they had eaten.

This article was first published in *Cahiers d'Etudes Africaines*, III (1), 9, 1962, 51–103.

Note

1 The Mambila live in Adamawa Province on what is called the Mambila Plateau. They number approximately 18,000 and live in autonomous villages with populations ranging from roughly 200 to 2,000 persons. Most villages have a secular chief, an office introduced under the Native Authority system. All villages are subdivided into hamlets, each with its own headman, an indigenous office. The incumbent is always the oldest male resident. A hamlet includes a number of compound clusters made up of from two to six compounds in spatial proximity one to the other, some of whose male members are usually kin. The residents unite for certain ritual and secular purposes. Here again the oldest male inhabitant is the head. The composition of the constituent compounds is complicated by the fact that there are no fixed residence rules and therefore links binding the residents may be of a number of different kinds. The most usual type of compound houses a core made up of a man, his wife or wives, most of his married sons with their wives and children, and his unmarried sons and daughters.

Short Mambila Bibliography

Meek, C. K., 1931. *Tribal Studies in Northern Nigeria*. London, Kegan Paul, vol. I, pp. 532–82

Meyer, E., 1939–40. Mambila-Studie, *Zeitschrift für Eingeborenen-Sprachen*, 30, 1: 1–52; 30, 2: 117–48; 30, 3: 210–32. Berlin

Migeod, F. W. H., 1925. *Through British Cameroons*. London, Heath Cranton Ltd, pp. 148–66

Rehfisch, F., 1960. The dynamics of multilineality on the Mambila plateau, *Africa* 30, 3: 246–61. London

Schneider, G., 1955. Mambila album, *Nigerian Field* 20: 112–32

III

DRINKS CONSTRUCT AN IDEAL WORLD

9. Symbolic action in Alcoholics Anonymous

Paul Antze

Though a perennial favorite of psychologists and sociologists, Alcoholics Anonymous has thus far garnered scant interest in the anthropological community.[1] There may be a good reason for this. At first glance the organization looks so narrow in purpose and so pragmatic in style as to offer very little to tempt the ethnographer's palate. After all, how much "culture" can there be in a group that exists only to help problem drinkers stay sober?

If we think of culture in the Geertzean sense, as a coherent web of symbols that directs human conduct, then the answer is "quite a good deal". AA makes a fascinating case study in the power of symbols to generate new patterns of action by reconstruing the experience of persons in a standardized way. In truth AA does far more than to help the compulsive drinker shake off a troublesome habit. It also draws him into a community that globally reorders his life. It provides him with a new understanding of himself and his motives as an actor – in effect a new identity. It teaches him to seek fulfillment in different ways. It brings him to revise every phase of his conduct in keeping with a new ethical regimen built around such watchwords as "serenity", "humility", "forgiveness" and "service". While AA is at great pains to insist that it is not a religion, its central teaching is that alcoholics can recover only with the help of "a power greater than themselves" – in effect, a personal deity. Of the famous "Twelve Steps" that constitute AA's plan for sobriety, six make direct mention of God while only one mentions alcohol. AA also relies on such practical mainstays of traditional religion as confessions, prayers, testimonials and regular missions to the unconverted. Thus it is not surprising that when long-term members speak of the group, they ascribe to it the same kinds of ultimate values that one normally associates with religion:

> I came into AA solely for the purpose of sobriety, but it has been through AA that I have found God. (Quoted in AA 1955, p. 192)

> Before I came to this outfit I don't think I had the faintest idea of who I was or what life was all about. Now I'm beginning to see that Somebody out there has a plan for me. (Field notes, AA meeting, Toronto, 1978)

> My religion did not give me AA. AA gave me greater strength in my

religion. [It] has helped me to seek, to listen, and to apply the principles of good living, and I am rewarded with much more excitement and joy than was mine before AA. I have become aware of other gifts available to me as a human being. To get the benefits I need only ask and then use them. (Quoted in AA 1973, p. 4)

Among members of more than a few months' standing AA also seems to elicit an unusually high level of commitment and solidarity. Statistics are hard to gather on this point, especially since the organization keeps neither membership lists nor attendance records. However, a major survey conducted in the mid-1970s (Leach and Norris, 1977) suggests that the typical AA member attends between two and three meetings a week, while some attend as many as six or seven. This does not include the additional hours that most members spend every week on "Twelfth Step" work with drinking alcoholics. Whatever the statistical realities, members at meetings express a strong belief in their mutual commitment, a belief that manifests itself impressively in the warmth they show to newcomers. As one member put it,

Where else but in AA could you find half a million people dedicated to love, and really loving each other? The love of one alcoholic for another is something never seen before in the history of the world. . . . In AA we do unto others what's already been done unto us. We help others as we've been helped. (Quoted in AA 1973, p. 63)

It is perhaps because of such feelings that AA members in urban areas show a strong tendency to drop nonalcoholic friendships and rebuild their social lives wholly within the circle of their fellow "recovered alcoholics" (Bean, 1975, p. 40).

What is fascinating about this organization from a symbolic or cognitive viewpoint is that it draws all the power it displays – the personal changes it induces, the mutual commitment it evokes – from a single and rather slender root: the special relationship that members perceive between themselves and alcoholic beverages. It is this relationship that underlies the new identity that AA confers, and that members reassert at every meeting: "My name is ——————— and I am an alcoholic". Likewise alcohol and its dangers – as AA conceives them – provide the ultimate reason for the ethical regimen that members embrace, and for their tenacious commitment to the round of AA activities. In these respects AA as a social form has a certain "totemic" quality. The group's name, its central preoccupations, its solidarity and power to confer identity all spring from a single substance which members collectively abjure. Furthermore, as with most totemic societies, members avoid the substance not out of moral qualms, but because they see themselves as belonging to a category of persons uniquely endangered by it. One needn't believe literally in totemism to grasp the importance of this phenomenon. AA represents one of the rare modern cases of a group that builds its own self-conception almost wholly out of its beliefs about a comestible substance. And as in most cases where an ingestible thing is used in defining a social one, the relationship is reciprocal; AA's sense of its own nature and purpose does much to shape its way of thinking about the properties of alcohol. Thus an understanding of the logic that binds group to substance and vice versa in this case may well teach us broader lessons about the use of foods and beverages in framing social categories.

The significance of this relationship is more than purely cognitive. There is an impressive feat of persuasion implicit here as well. Somehow, although it takes its point of departure from an extremely narrow concern, AA has enlisted the allegiance of its members to an elaborate symbolic order. The group seems to perform the major social and psychological offices of religion with considerable success: it gives identity and a sense of purpose to members, it schools them in the general conduct of their lives, it binds them into a community. And yet it founds these varied attainments almost wholly on notions it has evolved about a certain class of beverages. How does this happen? By what symbolic alchemy does AA transform the ill-defined "problem with liquor" that most members bring to the group into what it calls with some justice "a whole way of life"?

To pose this question is to call up another analogy from tribal societies, this one more elaborate. In his studies of the Ndembu of Zambia, Victor Turner has given special attention to a group of religious practices which he calls "cults of affliction" (Turner, 1957, 1967, 1975). Such cults embody the typical Ndembu response to bad luck in hunting, reproductive disorders, and a host of other minor ills. According to Turner, the Ndembu ascribe these problems to ancestral shades who have "caught" their living kinsmen for neglecting them ceremonially or for other breaches of traditional morality. The interesting point is that the rituals required to heal these afflictions are more than strictly curative; they also initiate the victim to a specialized community of former-sufferers-turned-healers. As Turner explains,

> The patient in any given cult ritual is a candidate for entry into that cult and, by passing through its rites, becomes a cult adept. The particular shade that had afflicted him in the first instance, when propitiated, becomes a tutelary who confers on him health and curative powers for that particular mode of affliction.... Cult members make up associations of those who have suffered the same modes of affliction as the result of having been seized ... by deceased members of the cults. (1967, p. 362)

The Ndembu cults are like AA in forging lasting bonds among their membership, and apparently for similar reasons: "The affliction of each is the concern of all; likeness of unhappy lot is the ultimate bond of ritual solidarity. The adepts have themselves known the suffering the candidates are experiencing" (Turner, 1957, p. 302). They are also like AA in upholding certain traditional cultural values, and in using mutual confession and the settling of grievances as therapeutic tools (see below, pp. 159–163).[2]

Given all these affinities, the beliefs underlying the Ndembu healing cults take on added interest. In their case, at least, it is easy to see the logic that generates a moral community from a common experience of suffering. The Ndembu regard the shades that bring affliction as ambivalently powerful figures who may help as readily as they hinder. To those who heed the warnings they send through misfortune, these ancestral spirits become friends and protectors. In the words of Turner's informant Muchona, "What hurts you, when discovered and propitiated, helps you" (Turner, 1967, p. 133). Because affliction is one route to new ceremonial powers, in fact, the Ndembu view it as a potential boon:

> I have often heard doctors or diviners reply to the question, "How did you learn your job?" by the words, "I started by being sick myself," meaning that the shade of one of their relatives afflicted them with illness. There is then a double meaning in being caught by a shade. One is punished for neglect of their memory, but at the same time one is chosen or "elected" to be a go-between in future rituals that put the living into communication with the dead. (Turner, 1967, p. 10)

A similar logic appears to govern a great many other healing cults found in traditional societies, especially those devoted to spirit possession. Ioan Lewis (1971) has examined a wide array of these cases in which, as he puts it, "the royal road to divine election lies through affliction" (p. 89). Here again, typically, the afflicting spirit is propitiated or "domesticated" to become a benefactor venerated through cult activity.

In recruiting persons with drinking problems to its own moral community, does AA relay on any comparable notions? Given the social and cultural gulf dividing this modern group from those described by Turner and Lewis, close symbolic parallels would appear unlikely. And yet AA achieves many of the same effects. How does this happen? If there is a way to answering this question, I think it lies in tackling the problem raised earlier, namely the relationship that AA fashions between itself as a social group and the substance its members avoid.

The remainder of the present paper makes an attempt in this direction. It does so largely by considering what AA means by a single word, a word that mediates very nicely between substance and group and that serves to distinguish real or potential members from humanity at large. I mean of course the word "alcoholic". Regular confession to this status ("I am an alcoholic") is one of the few bits of genuine ritual in AA's life. However, its implications are far from obvious, and they are easily obscured by the very familiarity of the term. To understand fully what it means to be an alcoholic from AA's point of view is to see just how the group teaches its members to think of themselves as persons. As will become apparent below, such an understanding also does much to explain the sort of religious commitment that AA engenders. For this reason an attempt to uncover the model of "alcoholic personhood" implicit in AA's thinking must be central to the whole discussion that follows.

Normally when ethnographers undertake studies of this kind, they do so on the basis of "texts" drawn from the speech of informants and from their conduct in typical scenes (Frake, 1962). In the present case such observational materials remain essential, but the primary sources are texts in a more literal sense of the word. As an organization with little structure[3] and a membership that soon became massive, AA has always relied heavily on the printing press to store and transmit its main ideas. The group's only central council is the "General Service Conference", composed of representatives elected by membership regions. One of the GSC's main functions is to approve all literature bearing the AA name, and thus to assure that group publications are consistent with "the common group conscience" as AA puts it. It is because of this body's activity – and only because of it – that we may employ such phrases as "AA says" or "according to AA" with some reliability.[4]

The writings that codify AA beliefs fall into three general classes. First, the group publishes a variety of small pamphlets directed to the general public and to prospective members, pamphlets with titles ranging from "The Woman Alcoholic" and "The Teen-Age Alcoholic" to "A Doctor Looks at AA". Some of these are revealing, but because of their promotional and educational aims, most are of secondary interest. A far more important group of writings are the major expository works that outline AA's methods as well as its history and philosophy for the benefit of members. Foremost among these is the famous "Big Book" simply titled *Alcoholics Anonymous* (1939, revised 1955), which remains the fundamental statement of AA teachings. Others are *The Twelve Steps and the Twelve Traditions* (1953), *AA Comes of Age* (1957), *The AA Way of Life* (1967), and a little breviary of inspirational thoughts drawn from these and other sources, *Twenty-Four Hours a Day* (1962). It would be hard to overestimate the influence of these books. All were mentioned frequently at the meetings I attended, and veteran members showed an impressive ability to quote passages from memory. This was especially true for "The Big Book", which many neophytes seemed to read continually during their early, shaky months in the programme. Writings in the third class are printed anecdotes and life stories told by members. These are also highly influential, since they serve to put many of AA's basic beliefs into vivid narrative form. They appear mainly in the latter part of the revised "Big Book" (1955), in AA's monthly magazine *The Grapevine*, and in the recently published *Came to Believe* ... (1973), a compendium of "spiritual experiences" related by members.

It remains only to point out that the pattern I hope to expose in all these materials is not wholly present at an explicit level. AA's expository works are rich in metaphors, analogies and illustrations that transmit messages of their own, messages that elude any bald summary of the group's official teachings. The same is true in a much greater degree of the stories told by members, whether conveyed orally in meetings or reprinted in AA books. Anyone who listens to even a few of these tales will recognize that they are not flat "objective" reports. Each presents experience from a point of view and thus, overtly or tacitly, serves as an object lesson in collective beliefs. In this sense the stories told by members are very much like religious testimonials. The points of formal similarity uniting them, their common themes and images and turns of phrase, must be seen as important clues to the view of reality that members share.[5] Hence the discussion that follows will attend closely to patterns at this "subtextual" level as well as to AA's overt teachings.

Approaching AA's writings in this manner comes close to treating them as one might a work of literature. Such an approach is not wholly inappropriate given the nature of the message they transmit. In the pages ahead it will become apparent that AA tells the alcoholic who he is, not in the dry manner of a physician or psychologist, but by situating him in a highly dramatic predicament. It makes him the central actor in a play whose plot is largely fixed by the nature of his condition, a play that circumscribes his options and gives clear meaning to his acts.[6] The group does this largely by virtue of the relationship it builds between the alcoholic and two other figures or "powers" in his life: AA's Higher Power and the "power" of the alcohol itself.

"Like men who have lost their legs"

In AA writings and in the speech of its members, alcohol wears a number of different faces. Each of these serves to define the alcoholic in a slightly different way. At the most obvious level AA members seem more than ready to speak of alcohol *in itself* as a harmless or essentially neutral substance. AA is not a temperance organization, and its writings contain none of the diatribes on the evils of rum found in such movements. Indeed, members telling stories in meetings are inclined to summon up their early, prealcoholic drinking exploits with a kind of nostalgic good humor. As the Big Book observes, many even make a point of keeping liquor in their homes for the benefit of nonalcoholic guests.

Hand in hand with this neutral view of alcohol goes the belief for which AA is probably most famous – that persons with serious drinking problems are not morally deficient but victims of a *disease* for which they can scarcely be blamed. As AA explains in one of its pamphlets,

> Alcoholism is an illness, a progressive illness, which can never be cured but which, like some illnesses, can be arrested.... Before they are exposed to AA many alcoholics who are unable to stop drinking think of themselves as morally weak or possibly mentally unbalanced. The AA concept is that alcoholics are sick people.... Once alcoholism has set in there is nothing morally wrong about being ill. (AA 1952, p. 4)

To be an alcoholic is first of all to be a sick person. What does this mean? Today the notion that alcoholism is a disease is so widely accepted that it seems wrong to accord the belief any special significance of an ethnographic nature. One tends to dismiss it as a simple reflection of popular medical knowledge. To do so, however, would be a serious mistake. The disease model of alcoholism was still far from being fashionable when AA first proclaimed its views in 1937. E. M. Jellinek (1960) has shown in fact that this perspective owes much of its current popularity to AA's own therapeutic success, and to the resulting influence that the group has acquired with both physicians and the public at large. Medical research, on the other hand, is still very far from confirming the appropriateness of a disease model in explaining the compulsive drinking syndrome.[7] As for the disease model expounded by AA, analysis shows that several of its basic features are either wholly unsupported by current medical research or directly contradicted by it.[8] Such considerations suggest that AA's views on this point, far from being a reflection of medical knowledge, are more properly seen as elements of a folk system with a logic and coherence of its own. A closer examination of these views is now in order.

AA takes a categorical view of the disease it ascribes to members. It points out that the term "alcoholic" is not one that admits of degrees. As one pamphlet has it, "There's a saying in AA that there's no such thing as being a little bit alcoholic. Either you are or you aren't" (AA 1952, p. 5). Furthermore, AA insists that all who fall into this category face not a single problem but two intertwined ones. The group styles these as "a physical allergy" and "a mental obsession", and each deserves our separate attention.

The "physical allergy" idea originated with an early friend of the AA movement, Dr. William Silkworth, who had theorized that the cells of the alcoholic's body develop a selective intolerance for alcohol akin to other allergic reactions. Since the publication of research in the early 1950s that definitely excluded allergenic processes from alcohol addiction,[9] AA's literature has spoken instead of "a physical sensitivity", though the word allergy still appears in the Big Book. The term in either case is slightly misleading, since it does not identify an observable physical reaction, but a particular way of behaving. It refers to the alcoholic's typical inability to control the *amount* of liquor he consumes. Once he samples that first drink, his "physical sensitivity" condemns him to carry on well past the point of intoxication (AA 1955, p. 22). Thus the true alcoholic, in AA's phrase, is "always one drink away from a drunk". To those unsure that they qualify for this status, AA proposes a simple test:

> Try to drink and stop abruptly. Try it more than once. It will not take you long to decide if you are honest with yourself about it. It may be worth a bad case of jitters if you get a full knowledge of your condition. (AA 1955, p. 32)

The crucial point about the physical sensitivity phenomenon, to AA's way of thinking, is that like most real allergies it is *irreversible*. No exertion of willpower, no period of sobriety, however protracted, will allow the "true alcoholic" to drink normally again.[10]

> The idea that somehow, someday he will control and enjoy his drinking is the great obsession of every abnormal drinker. The persistence of this illusion is astonishing. Many pursue it into the gates of insanity or death. . . .
>
> We know that no real alcoholic *ever* recovers control. All of us felt at times that we were regaining control, but such intervals – usually brief – were inevitably followed by still less control, which led in time to pitiful and incomprehensible demoralization. . . .
>
> We are like men who have lost their legs; they never grow new ones. Neither does there appear to be any kind of treatment which will make alcoholics of our kind like other men. (AA 1955, p. 30)

To be an alcoholic is thus to inhabit a slightly different world from the rest of humanity, and for those who join this world alcohol assumes a different aspect as well. It changes from a harmless or enjoyable substance to "a deadly poison". Indeed, it is more than poison. At a metaphorical level in AA's writings, alcohol for the alcoholic becomes the embodiment of death itself. The Big Book and other sources make repeated use of the phrase "death and insanity" to describe its inevitable effects. They speak of alcoholism as a "fatal malady", likening its victims to cancer patients who require radical surgery if they are to live (AA 1957, p. 61) or to persons under a death sentence with but the slimmest chance of reprieve (AA 1957, p. 105). They also point out that alcohol inflicts a kind of personal death on the alcoholic long before physical death by "poisoning his relationships" (AA 1953, p. 26) or "walling him off from others" (AA 1962, p. 84) until he is wholly alone. The intent of all these images is apparent enough. They are ways of dramatizing AA's central belief that the alcoholic is someone who lives under an absolute prohibition on drinking, a prohibition he violates only at the cost of his life:

I guess the first thing I learned here was that I was an alcoholic. I really *couldn't* control it. For years my doctor would tell me I was killing myself, but it took you folks to convince me. Now I know it's true – if an alcoholic drinks, eventually he will drink himself to death. Sooner or later, this is what happens. The only way you beat it is to skip the first drink. (Field notes, AA meeting, Toronto, 1978)

The curious point, according to AA, is that if someone is "really an alcoholic", he also seems unable to heed this rule. No matter how clearly he realizes his condition, some unknown force within eventually drives him to take that first drink anyway. This is the other side of the affliction, "the mental obsession that condemns us to drink" (AA 1955, p. 30ff.) Although the "mental obsession" idea is a relatively simple one, the Big Book develops it with enormous care. It employs a series of stories to this end (pp. 32–43), each about a person fiercely determined to stay clear of liquor who nonetheless fails to do so. It makes a point of ascribing various strengths to the figures involved, among them "will power", "discipline", "good character", "common-sense" and "self-knowledge". And yet in each of these cases "some insanely trivial excuse" leads to the first drink and the subsequent "bender". A typical mark of such relapse episodes, according to AA, is their completely mysterious character.

Why does he behave like this? If hundreds of experiences have shown him that one drink means another debacle with all its attendant suffering and humiliation, why is it that he takes that one drink? . . . If you ask him why he started on that last bender, the chances are he will offer you any one of a hundred alibis. . . .

Once in a while he may tell you the truth. And the truth, strange to say, is that usually he has no more idea why he took that first drink than you have. (AA 1955, pp. 22–23)

Understandably enough, the Big Book styles the alcoholic's peculiarity in this regard as "a subtle form of insanity". It likens his behavior to that of an habitual jaywalker, already injured several times and well aware of the risks he is taking, who continues to race in front of cars: "Such a man would be crazy, wouldn't he?" (p. 38).[11]

Both the "physical allergy" and "mental obsession" ideas are highly interesting in their own right. While neither is quite accurate in scientific terms, apparently both capture the lived realities of the situation well enough to ring true for a great many compulsive drinkers. But they are also both part of a symbolic scheme that aims to persuade and transform, and their real interest lies at this level. These two notions are bound to have a curious effect on anyone who accepts both of them as accurate descriptions of himself, since they seem to leave him no way out. As Gregory Bateson observed a number of years ago (1971), AA's linking of the allergy and obsession ideas serves to trap the drinking alcoholic in a "double-bind" of classic proportions. It tells him that if he drinks again he will "die or go mad" while also telling him that he has no hope of stopping. Thus it places him under an injunction of life or death importance which he cannot possibly obey. According to Bateson, a key feature of such "impossible" situations is that they promote a loosening of deep assumptions underlying both horns of the dilemma. Depending on circumstances, the results may be destructive – as in a schizophrenic breakdown – or constructive, as in a scientific breakthrough.

From the AA viewpoint, the bind described here is constructive, and in fact essential to recovery. One of the group's central beliefs is that no alcoholic is ready to change until he has passed through an experience of radical despair known as "hitting bottom":

> Few people will sincerely try to practice the AA program unless they have "hit bottom", for practicing AA's Steps means the adoption of attitudes and actions that almost no alcoholic who is still drinking can dream of taking. . . . (AA 1953, p. 24)

Members often invoke this notion to explain the relapse of neophytes: "Well, he hasn't hit bottom yet. What do you expect?" AA's teachings about the two-sided nature of alcoholism are genuine articles of faith among members, but they also have the practical aim of nudging prospects toward this salutary crisis. In a speech before the annual meeting of the New York State Medical Society in 1944, AA's co-founder Bill W. made the group's strategy here explicit.

> When these facts . . . are poured by an AA member into the person of another alcoholic, they strike deep – the effect is shattering. . . . Sometimes his deflation is like the collapse of a toy balloon at the approach of a hot poker. But deflation is just what we AA's are looking for. . . . The more utterly we can smash the illusion that the alcoholic can get over alcohol "on his own", the more successful we are bound to be.
>
> In fact we aim to produce a crisis, to cause him to "hit bottom" as AAs say. . . . This reduces him to a state of *complete dependence* on whatever or whoever can stop his drinking. . . . Better still he becomes sweetly reasonable, truly open-minded, as only the dying can be. (Wilson, 1944)

"A Power greater than ourselves..."

Any problem drinker who has genuinely "hit bottom" will find little difficulty in taking the first of AA's Twelve Steps: "We admitted we were powerless over alcohol – that our lives had become unmanageable". Such an admission, especially if it reflects a deep and heartfelt experience, may not seem the most propitious way to begin a program of therapy. However, when surrender to alcohol happens under AA's tutelage, it never occurs by itself. It is just the first element of a two-sided event, the other half of which is embodied in AA's Second Step: "We came to believe that a power greater than ourselves could restore us to sanity". AA conceives of both these steps under the rubric of "surrender", a word that has broader significance in the everyday language of members. They use it not only to describe a preliminary event, but to identify an ongoing attitude that becomes essential to their sobriety. The essence of surrender as a permanent attitude is best captured in the two most overtly religious of AA's Twelve Steps, the third and the eleventh:

3. We made a decision to turn our will and our lives over to God as we understood Him.
11. We sought through prayer and meditation to improve our conscious contact with God as we understood Him, praying only for knowledge of His will for us and the power to carry that out.

Surrender in this sense of the word lies close to the heart of AA's spiritual teachings, and yet the group believes that it first takes root at the moment of defeat by alcohol. At times, in fact, AA writings convey the feeling that there are not two surrenders, one to the bottle and one before God, but only a single event that is somehow both an admission of defeat and an opening to God. When the Big Book says, "We needed to ask ourselves one short question, 'Do I now believe, or am I willing to believe, that there is a Power greater than myself?'", it does so just after a section on the incurability of alcoholism, so there is some ambiguity about the sort of power in question. Other statements imply that hitting bottom compels the drinker to seek God's help because there are no other options:

We were in a position where life was becoming impossible . . . and we had but two alternatives: one was to go on to the bitter end, blotting out the consciousness of our intolerable situation as best we could; and the other, to accept spiritual help. (AA 1955, p. 25)

When we became alcoholics, crushed by a crisis that we could neither postpone nor evade, we had to fearlessly face the proposition that God is everything or He is nothing. (AA 1955, p. 53)

The most interesting evidence on the two-sided character of surrender in AA comes from accounts of the crucial experience given by members themselves. The most dramatic of these have made their way from one local meeting to the next until they have won a place in AA literature. Such vivid accounts are certainly not typical in a statistical sense, nor are they even likely to be wholly accurate in their own right. However, they are important as carriers of a group mythology that lends meaning to more common and ambiguous episodes. They display a remarkable uniformity of structure that reveals much about the relationship between alcohol and the Higher Power in AA's thinking.

Nearly all the surrender experiences that win renown in AA are classic accounts of death and rebirth. As one might expect, it is alcohol that wears the death's head in these stories, flanked by allusions to such forms of personal death as insanity or utter loneliness. The Higher Power, on the other hand, embodies the forces of renewed life and strength and companionship. The experience itself has three phases, which appear with varying degrees of clarity: 1) The drinker falls into a serious depression. He may feel himself to be on the verge of dying or may even be close to death for good physical reasons. 2) He sees his condition to be hopeless and/or cries out to God for help. 3) A sudden unexplainable feeling of comfort and release sweeps over him, which he recognizes then or later as the entry of the Higher Power into his life.[12] The prototype for these experiences may be found in Bill W.'s own moment of surrender:[13]

> My depression deepened unbearably and finally it seemed to me as though I were at the very bottom of the pit. I still gagged badly on the notion of a Power greater than myself, but finally, just for the moment, the last vestige of my proud obstinacy was crushed. All at once I found myself crying out, "If there is a God, let him show Himself! I am ready to do anything, anything!"
>
> Suddenly the room lit up with a great white light. I was caught up into an ecstasy which there are no words to describe. It seemed to me that I was on a mountain and that a wind not of air but of spirit was blowing. And then it burst on me that I was a free man. (AA 1957, p. 63)

Other accounts follow this pattern. Those in my field notes include the case of a man critically injured in a car accident (the result of drunken driving) whose prayer in the ambulance brought a sudden sense of peace and the knowledge that he would live, along with what turned out to be a permanent loss of his need to drink. In another case a man suffering from extreme d.t.'s awoke drenched with sweat and shivering in his hospital bed to ponder his earlier relapses and a doctor's warning that he would die the next time he drank. His shivering became increasingly violent "until suddenly everything went very still and a voice said to me, 'You have one more chance; help others like yourself'". I also heard two reports of the Higher Power's intervention during suicide attempts, both portraying the crucial moment as the beginning of "a new outlook on life".

The richest and most complete examples of the AA "surrender myth", if I may call it that, appear in the volume *Came to Believe* ... (AA 1973). These stories fairly glow with the polish of repeated tellings, and fit the paradigm outlined above with an almost excessive neatness. Space does not permit a full review of their contents, but for illustrative purposes two quotations may suffice. In the first case the narrator had attended AA while still drinking and then decided to attempt "cold-turkey" withdrawal from alcohol on his own:

> That night I was desperately ill; I should have been in the hospital. About seven o'clock I began to phone everyone I could think of, in and out of AA. But no one could or would come to my aid . . . I knew I was going to die. . . .
>
> I went to bed sure I would never get up again. My thinking had never been clearer. I couldn't really see any way out. I was propped up with pillows, and my heart was pounding almost out of my chest. My limbs started turning numb – first my legs above my knees, then my arms above my elbows.
>
> I thought, "This is it!" I turned to the one source I had been too smart (as I saw it) or too stupid to appeal to earlier. I cried out, "Please God, don't let me die like this!" My tormented heart and soul were in those few words. Almost instantly the numbness started going away. I felt a Presence in the room. I wasn't alone any more.
>
> God be praised I have never felt alone since. I have never had another drink and, better still, have never needed one. . . . Somehow I know that, as long as I lived the way God wanted me to live, I need never feel fear again. (AA 1973, p. 14)

The narrator of the second story had been abstinent in AA for several months but without "getting the spiritual part of the program". One morning around 3 a.m. he awoke alone in his house "with a frightening sense of approaching death". As in the above case, his limbs began turning numb. Kneeling by his bed in a feverish attempt at prayer, he experienced a peculiar hallucination:

> Then, without raising my head or opening my eyes, I was able to "see" the entire floor plan of the house. And I could "see" a giant of a man standing on the other side of the bed, arms folded across his chest. He was glaring at me with a look of intense hatred and malevolence. . . . After about ten seconds I "saw" him slowly turn around, walk to the bathroom and look inside, turn to the second bedroom and look into it, walk to the living room and gaze around, and then leave the house by the kitchen door.
>
> I remained in my original position of prayer. Simultaneously with his departure, there seemed to be coming toward me from all directions, from the infinite reaches of space, a vibrating pulsating magnetic current. In probably fifteen seconds this tremendous power reached me, stayed for some five seconds, and then slowly withdrew to its origin. But the sense of relief given me by its presence beggars description. In

my clumsy way, I thanked God, got into bed, and slept like a baby.

I have not had the desire for a drink of anything intoxicating since that memorable morning twenty-three years ago... (AA 1973, p. 16)

How do AA members conceive of this Power that snatches them from the jaws of alcoholic death? In its official pronouncements AA insists that everyone is free to draw on any notion of the deity that he finds convenient; the point is simply to think of "God as you understand Him" (AA 1955, p. 44ff.). Nonetheless, when members describe the Higher Power in meetings, or in print, all tend to use very much the same language. A few quotations may help to convey its flavour:

In meeting me casually I don't think my strong belief in "the Man Upstairs" shows, but I have no other explanation for the many good things that have happened to me since I have been in AA – they come to me from a Greater Power. These words may be difficult for you to understand now, but be patient and you'll know what I mean. (AA 1955, p. 328)

I had a lot more hell to go through. But what a difference there is between going through hell without a power greater than oneself and with it! ... One night my son, when he was only sixteen, was suddenly and tragically killed. The Higher Power was on deck to see me through, sober. I think he's on hand to see all of us through whatever may come to us. (AA 1955, p. 424)

I have recently made a friend of Someone I wish everyone could know. This Friend is never too busy to listen to me, my problems, my joys and my sorrows. He gives me the courage to face life squarely and helps me to conquer my fears. The counsel I get is always good, for this Friend is wise, patient and tolerant. (AA 1973, p. 79)

In short, the God of AA is essentially a warm supportive figure, the very model, in fact, of a tutelary spirit. (In the informal usage of meetings, "Higher Power" is most often joined to a possessive pronoun, as in "consult your Higher Power" or "I asked my Higher Power".) His primary function is to provide strength and courage in hours of need. Nowhere in the AA literature or in any of the meetings I attended was there any mention of a judging deity, a stern father or lawgiver. In fact the Higher Power as described by members seems almost infinitely ready to forgive mistakes. In these respects the Higher Power bears a strong resemblance to AA as a whole. Both play the same essentially accepting, comforting, guiding roles, both are nonjudgmental, and both assume special importance at moments of crisis. The connection is so close that AA urges alcoholics who balk at religious affirmations to think of the group's combined membership as "the power greater than themselves". Even members with more exalted notions of the deity tend to see AA as a kind of social embodiment of His will. Two observations made by members nicely illustrate this point:

> I know the plan of the Higher Power comes to us through the medium of people. To us alcoholics this does not mean common or garden people but special people, such as other alcoholics. And I am guided to include among the people from whom I receive guidance those who loved me, befriended me and stuck by me, as others stuck by other alcoholics. (Quoted in AA 1975, p. 82)

> In Step Two, the Power greater than ourselves meant AA, but not just the members I knew. It meant all of us, everywhere, sharing a concern for each other and thereby creating a spiritual resource stronger than any one of us could provide. Another woman in my group believed that the souls of dead alcoholics, including those before the time of AA, contributed to this fountainhead of goodwill. . . (Quoted in AA 1973, p. 84)

Expressions of this kind suggest that, as a religion, AA conforms remarkably to the pattern that Emile Durkheim epitomized in the formula, "society is God". It is interesting that Durkheim first discerned this pattern in the totemic societies of Australia, since the material just considered suggests that AA's religious drama may owe something to traditional Western beliefs about its own "totemic substance". It is not hard to identify parallels between the main virtues that AA members ascribe to their deity and those explicitly valued in alcohol by Western drinkers, compulsive and noncompulsive alike. Social ritual and medical folklore have long made alcohol an elixir of life and strength, a reviver of spirits, a promoter of friendship and a spur to courage in times of trial. These are the qualities that Robert Burns celebrated:

> John Barleycorn was a hero bold
> Of noble enterprise
> For if you do but taste his blood
> 'Twill make your courage rise
>
> 'Twill make a man forget his woe;
> 'Twill heighten all his joy;
> 'Twill make the widow's heart to sing,
> Though the tear were in her eye.

Such writers as Samuel Klausner (1964), E. M. Jellinek (1977) and Howard Clinebell (1967) have documented the relationship between the "inspiriting" powers of alcohol and its widespread use in religious rituals. It seems more than an accident that AA members should perceive a similar array of qualities in their Higher Power and to some extent in their group as a whole. Indeed, group literature explicitly urges them to use the Higher Power as a kind of stand-in for the bottle.

> Before he turned to AA, the average alcoholic had already admitted that he could not control his drinking. Alcohol had, for him, become a power greater than himself, and it had been accepted on those terms. AA suggests that, to achieve and maintain sobriety, the alcoholic needs to depend on another Power that he recognizes is greater than himself. (AA 1952, p. 17)

It also seems no accident that AA should make a point of endowing alcohol itself with exactly the opposite traits, so that to the alcoholic this substance becomes a "poison" with the mysterious ability to render him "powerless", to "wall him off from other people", to threaten him with "insanity and death". From a persuasive standpoint the merits of construing alcohol and the Higher Power in this way are obvious enough; such a scheme of things tends to invest the group with the very qualities that might make drink appealing, while assuring that drink itself becomes an object of fear. However, the relationship suggested here has another, more intriguing aspect as well.

AA's darker portrayal of alcohol has its own traditional antecedents, running back at least to the Book of Proverbs (23:32: "Look thou not upon the wine; at the last it biteth like a serpent and stingeth like an adder"). Warnings about the dangers of "ardent spirits" have continued unabated over the centuries, although they probably reached their acme in those lurid sermons about "The Great Destroyer" that were the stock-in-trade of the American temperance movement (Lender and Karchanapee, 1977, pp. 1349–51). The traditional image of alcohol has thus been far from unequivocal. At the level of popular culture this substance has somehow been both a death-dealer and a life-enhancer at once. It is interesting that both of its aspects appear in the drama that AA constructs, but with an important difference. Here they are arranged on opposite sides of the symbolic fence, as it were. Alcohol as the agent of death forces the drinker to surrender, while alcohol's life-giving qualities – "sublimated" or "transfigured" in the Higher Power – appear to rescue him and remove his need to drink. In effect AA has taken the highly ambivalent mix of imagery surrounding the substance and parcelled it between two distinct entities, the one becoming the emblem or "apotheosis" of the group as a whole while the other becomes its nemesis. As a symbolic manoeuver this bears a formal resemblance to the infantile defense that Freudians call "splitting", wherein a parent is divided into good and bad figures, although here, apparently, it occurs to much happier effect.

"A spiritual awakening"

In the chain of beliefs that AA stretches between the affliction of compulsive drinking and its system of religious and ethical ideals, a central link has yet to be considered. This concerns a distinctive personal quality that the group ascribes to every "real" alcoholic. As we saw earlier, AA makes much of the alcoholic's peculiar inability to avoid the first drink even when he knows better, styling it as a "subtle form of insanity". The emphasis is well placed, since AA's beliefs about this tendency are the key to its whole religious-ethical regimen. In effect, AA holds that the alcoholic's lack of defense against drink originates in a deep-seated attitude or approach to life which eludes his direct control; it originates, to use AA's own phrase, in his "spiritual condition".

The relationship between "spiritual condition" and drinking behavior in AA's thinking is perhaps most clearly evidenced in a distinction the group draws between two main forms of abstinence. One of these, known appropriately as "being dry" is an achievement of pure willpower and is by nature very difficult; thus sooner or later the "dry" alcoholic is almost sure to tumble off the wagon. Members use the word "sobriety" to describe the other way of abstaining, the AA way, which they hold to be almost effortless: ("Our new attitude toward liquor has been given us without any effort on our part. It just comes!") (AA 1955, p. 84). The difference is that the dry alcoholic still languishes in an unimproved spiritual condition, whereas the sober alcoholic has undergone what the Big Book calls "a spiritual awakening" (p. 24).

What is it that fuels the "dry" alcoholic's persistent craving for drink? The answer is a surprising one, given AA's well-known view of alcoholism as a blameless disease:

> Selfishness – self-centeredness! That, we think, is the root of our troubles. Driven by a hundred forms of fear, self-delusion, self-seeking and self-pity ... we have made decisions based on self that later placed us in a position to be hurt.
>
> So our troubles, we think, are basically of our own making. They arise out of ourselves, and the alcoholic is an extreme example of self-will run riot, though he usually doesn't think so. Above everything, we alcoholics must be rid of this selfishness. We must or it kills us! (AA 1955, p. 62)

The Big Book never explains exactly how selfishness prompts the alcoholic to drink, but it does argue that this attitude wreaks havoc with his personal life. It likens him to "an actor who wants to run the whole show", who is "forever trying to arrange the lights, the ballet, the scenery and the rest of the players in his own way" (p. 60). When he finds that the world does not respond to his directorial urgings, he falls prey to a group of emotions that bear a more proximate relationship to drinking, among them anger, resentment, depression, fear and self-pity. AA members employ the term "dry bender" to describe an extended bout with any of these feelings, a usage that betrays the common belief in their affinity to the alcoholic binge. The point, in fact, is that any such feeling – resentment for example – has the power to set off a "wet" bender:

> It is plain that a life which includes deep resentment leads only to futility and unhappiness. But with the alcoholic, whose hope is the growth and maintenance of a spiritual experience, this business is infinitely grave. We found that it is fatal. For when harboring such feelings we shut ourselves off from the sunlight of the Spirit. The insanity of alcohol returns and we drink again. And with us, to drink is to die. (AA 1955, p. 66)

AA represents its spiritual and ethical directives as a program designed to relieve the alcoholic of his pathological selfishness, and with it, of the fears and resentments that drive him to drink. In view of the autocratic nature of the impulse to be overcome, it is hardly surprising that the program's watchword should be "surrender". As we noted earlier, this attitude is not simply an admission of defeat by alcohol; it entails the much broader abdication of ego that comes from putting one's life in God's hands.

> This is the how and why of it. First of all, we had to quit playing God. It didn't work. Next, we decided that hereafter in this drama of life, God was going to be our Director. He is the Principal; we are His agents. He is the Father and we are His children. . . (AA 1955, p. 62)

> For we are now on a different basis; the basis of trusting and relying upon God. We trust infinite God rather than our finite selves. We are in the world to play the role He assigns. Just to the extent that we do as we think He would have us, and humbly rely upon Him, does He enable us to match calamity with serenity. (p. 68)

In actual practice, surrender for AA also means the development of a more accepting, less combative approach to the trials of everyday life. The little mottoes that adorn the walls of AA meeting rooms indicate this very clearly – "Live and let live", "Easy does it", "One day at a time". The most revealing expression of the new attitude that members cultivate is probably the famous AA Serenity Prayer: "God grant me the serenity to accept the things I cannot change, courage to change the things I can, and wisdom to know the difference." Surrender in this sense of the word does not come of itself, nor can it be had simply by trying. It requires God's help in the removal of what AA calls "character defects" – the dangerous emotional habits that stem from "selfishness" or "pride". AA's ethical regimen is a systematic exercise in confession, repentance and restitution that is intended to bring this about. Its outlines are conveyed in Steps Four through Ten:

4. [We] made a searching and fearless moral inventory of ourselves.
5. Admitted to God, to ourselves and to another human being the exact nature of our wrongs.
6. Were entirely ready to have God remove all these defects of character.
7. Humbly asked Him to remove our shortcomings.
8. Made a list of persons we had harmed, and became willing to make amends to them all.
9. Made direct amends to such people wherever possible, except when to do so would injure them or others.
10. Continued to take personal moral inventory and when we were wrong promptly admitted it.

The program includes a final step that takes the form of a regular and very concrete activity.

12. Having had a spiritual awakening as a result of these steps, we tried to carry this message to alcoholics and to practice these principles in all our affairs.

Because it is directed to helping others, "twelfth-stepping" is a nice exercise in the kind of selfless attitude that AA considers essential to sobriety; it also provides frequent reminders of the disastrous effects that would follow from a "slip". Thus, as with the other steps cited here, the purpose of twelfth-stepping is mainly therapeutic: "Practical experience shows that nothing will so much insure immunity from drinking as work with other alcoholics. It works when other activities fail" (AA 1955, p. 89). At the same time for many AA members, twelfth-stepping has another and far weightier meaning: It is a mission of intrinsic importance, a mission which only they can perform, and which thus becomes the basis for a new sense of direction and purpose.

I feel myself a useful member of the human race at last. I have something to contribute to humanity, since I am peculiarly qualified as a fellow sufferer, to give aid and comfort to those who have stumbled and fallen over this business of meeting life. (Quoted in AA 1955, p. 229)

The sense of personal importance that members draw from twelfth-stepping and the high seriousness they attach to it may be be surmised from a brief statement widely circulated among local meetings, entitled "Why We Were Chosen: A Message From the Higher Power". It depicts God as saying:

Unto your weak and feeble hands I have entrusted a power beyond estimate. To you has been given that which has been denied the most learned of your fellows. Not to scientists or statesmen, not to wives or mothers, not even to my priests or ministers have I given this gift of healing other alcoholics which I entrust to you.

It must be used unselfishly; it carries with it grave responsibility. No day can be too long; no demands upon your time can be too urgent; no case be too pitiful; no task too hard; no effort too great... You must be prepared for adversity, for what men call adversity is the ladder you must use to ascend the rungs toward spiritual perfection...

You were not selected because of your exceptional talents, and be careful, always, if success attends your efforts, not to ascribe to personal superiority that to which you can lay claim only by virtue of My gift...

You were selected because you have been the outcasts of the world and your long experience as drunkards has made or should make you humbly alert to the cries of distress that come from the lonely hearts of alcoholics everywhere. (Anonymous, no date)

In a slightly less focused way members tend to ascribe a similar intrinsic value to all aspects of the "spiritual awakening" that AA promotes. "Getting the program" at a deep and permanent level, in fact, seems almost identical with seeing it in terms that transcend the therapeutic. Bernard Smith, the nonalcoholic former Chairman of AA's General Service Board, expressed a common sentiment when he proclaimed his belief at the group's 25th anniversary that "those who live by the principles of AA enjoy a greater measure of happiness than any class or group of people to which I have ever been exposed" (AA 1957, p. 277). Smith went on to describe AA members as being doubly lucky, since in addition to escaping alcohol they had also escaped "enslavement to the false ideals of a materialistic society", a society where "millions who are not alcoholics are living today in illusory worlds, nurturing the basic anxieties and insecurities of human existence rather than facing themselves with courage and humility" (p. 279). Speakers in meetings often dwell upon the "added dividends" that come with life in AA:

We are like a man who has bought a farm with the sole thought of raising wheat. And raise the wheat the farm does – the finest of wheat. But as the farmer goes about the task of raising wheat, he finds the most beautiful of flowers springing up in odd quarters; he notices for the first time a grove of stately trees. And as time goes on, he strikes oil in this acre and gold in that... Each day he comes on new comforts, new beauty, new riches; ... each day's discovery sets him atingle for the next. (Quoted in Clinebell, 1967, p. 134)

However, usually when members advance this view, they speak in more personal terms:

I was spiritually bankrupt long before AA entered my life and long before alcoholism took over like a parasite under my skin. I had nothing, no faith at all to cling to. . .

I got sober in AA, and, like a miracle, the warm flood of reality flowed over me, and I was no longer afraid. . . I began, in early sobriety to feel *compassion* for other drunks, then for my children, then for my ex-husband. This compassion . . . opened up the door to a huge fortress within me which had been forever locked. . . .

Now this was the strange thing: I was not, in sobriety, returning to my former state. I was not resuming a "well" state which I had left when I began to drink alcoholically. I was becoming, as I heard it put once, "weller than well". I found a new substance inside me. It had never been there before, even in childhood. I learned my own version of what spirituality is. . . It means I have to be concerned with my fellowman; through this alone can I receive the grace of God, my Higher Power, for, in the words of John Donne, so long before AA, "No man is an island." (AA 1973, p. 119)

"We have two authorities . . ."

However much he exults in spiritual growth for its own sake, the successful AA member also knows that it is not quite a matter of choice. No matter how long he remains sober, he is still an alcoholic, and thus "always one drink away from a drunk". Since AA teaches him that "a spiritual awakening" is his only defense against drink, it remains, for all its benefits, a necessity imposed by alcohol itself. Thus,

It is easy to let up on the spiritual program of action and rest on our laurels. We are headed for trouble if we do, for alcohol is a subtle foe. We are not cured of alcoholism. What we really have is a daily reprieve contingent on the maintenance of our spiritual condition. Every day is a day in which we must carry the vision of God's will into all our activities. (AA 1955, p. 85)

This fact gives alcohol a peculiar position in the thinking of members. Alcohol is in one sense The Enemy, the maddening, lethal poison from which the Higher Power saved them at the moment of surrender. And yet it was the havoc wrought by alcohol that recruited them to the group, and it is the continuing fear of this substance that assures their devotion to its principles. In this sense alcohol is not really the enemy of the group or its deity, but a kind of dark ally. It is always there lurking in the background, waiting to strike down the member who has grown complacent, who has allowed "self" back into his life, who has neglected his prayers or moral inventory or Twelfth-Step activity. At points in the AA literature, in fact, alcohol emerges as the chief guardian – and a very jealous one – of the moral order the group has constructed. Bill W. put this view very clearly in a major address given in 1956:

> Many people wonder how AA can function under such a seeming anarchy. Other societies have to have law and force and sanction and punishment, administered by authorized people. Happily for us we found we need no human authority whatever. We have two authorities which are far more effective. One is benign, the other malign. There is God, our Father, who very simply says, "I am waiting for you to do My will". The other authority is John Barleycorn and he says, "You had better do God's will or I will kill you". And sometimes he does kill. So when the chips are down we conform to God's will or perish. At this level the death sentence hangs over the AA member, his group, and AA as a whole. . . For us, it is do or die. (AA 1957, p. 105)[14]

When this strand of AA thinking is juxtaposed with the high intrinsic value that members impute to their "spiritual awakening", the resulting picture becomes very interesting. If alcohol compels certain people to face themselves, to acknowledge their limitations, to develop in positive directions, then in spite of the trouble it brings (or maybe for exactly that reason) it stands as a kind of benefactor. AA veterans show a strong tendency to look back on "John Barleycorn" as a harsh but valuable teacher, perhaps even an instrument of God's will. Testimonials to the spiritual edification conferred by an extended bout with alcoholism are not hard to come by.

> Faced with alcoholic destruction, we soon become as open-minded on spiritual matters as we had tried to be on other questions. In this respect alcohol was a great persuader. It finally beat us into a state of reasonableness. (AA 1955, p. 48)

> To the intellectually self-sufficient man or woman, many AAs can say, "Yes, we were like you – far too smart for our own good. We loved to have people call us precocious. We used our education to blow ourselves up into prideful balloons. . . Since we were brighter than most folks (so we thought) the spoils of victory would be ours for the thinking. The god of intellect displaced the God of our fathers.
> But John Barleycorn had other ideas. We who had won so handsomely in a walk turned into all-time losers. We saw that we had to reconsider or die." (Quoted in AA 1967, p. 60)

> [Even before becoming an alcoholic] I could not, or would not, admit I was wrong. My pride would not let me. And yet I was ashamed of me. Caught in this conflict, I banished God from my life. . . .
> I had to be beaten to a pulp physically, mentally and emotionally, become bankrupt in all facets of my being, before I could give up pride and admit defeat. . . . I needed the trials and tribulations I have had so

I could surrender and give up self. Only in complete acceptance of the utter defeat of my pride and ego could I *begin* to win. (Quoted in AA 1973, p. 86)

The same essential perception also takes a more extravagant form: If addiction to alcohol was needed to prepare members for things spiritual, then perhaps it should be viewed as a *felix culpa*, a happy weakness that serves divine ends. It would be wrong to assume that all members believe this explicitly. And yet the theme reasserts itself from time to time in meetings, and it has found a number of important published expressions as well. It carries with it the thought that God may be the secret author of the alcoholic's trials and that alcohol itself may be the guise He puts on to humble certain persons and draw them into His service. From this viewpoint alcoholism ceases to be a mere disease and becomes a "divine malady", a special manifestation of God's grace. An anonymous writer took this view some years ago in a *Grapevine* article that has since been widely quoted and reprinted.

> AA members should consider themselves extremely fortunate, not only because they have found a sober way of life that brings them happiness without alcohol, but because they have been afflicted with a disease whose recovery *compels them to become spiritual*, to seek God and make contact with Him. . . In the light of this no AA member need be ashamed that he is an alcoholic.
>
> On the contrary they can, with good reason, consider themselves a chosen people – chosen by God to suffer, to lose the way, to call for help, to be turned against the light, and chosen by Him to be dependent on His grace for their sobriety, their happiness and their salvation. ("Alcoholism – Divine Malady?", *Grapevine*, May 1968, p. 16)

A slightly different version of this idea appeared in a speech given at AA's Twenty-Fifth Anniversary Meeting by Father Edward Dowling, a long-time associate of the group's founders. After pointing out that "most people get to heaven by backing away from hell", Dowling suggested that the trials of compulsive drinking were but a means used by God in "his loving chase" for the alcoholic. He likened the alcoholic to the hero in Francis Thompson's poem, "The Hound of Heaven", ending his speech with a series of quotations from the poem. The Hound – in this case alcohol – pursues his victim through life's highways and byways, gradually bringing him to ruin. Finally, the chase having reached its denouement, a mysterious Voice addresses the shattered hero:

> "How little worthy of any love thou art!
> Whom wilt thou find to love ignoble thee
>   Save Me, save only Me?

All which I took from thee I did but take,
    Not for thy harms,
But just that thou mightst seek it in my arms."

And the hero, with dawning insight, begins to see his pursuer differently.

Halts by me that footfall:
Is my gloom, after all
Shade of His hand outstretched caressingly? (Quoted in AA 1957, pp. 260–61)

Conclusion: AA and the Protestant paradigm

Addiction to alcohol is both an emotion-laden experience and one marked by deep ambiguities. To the problem drinker and those around him the lines between volition and compulsion, between physical affliction and moral failing are seldom very clear. AA succeeds in part by offering a scheme of meaning that erases these ambiguities. It interprets the alcoholic experience in such a way as to give members a clear position in life, a sense of who they are and what they must do. As I noted earlier, alcohol assumes a number of faces in AA's thinking. Each of these confers its own element of identity on the compulsive drinker and its own bit of sense upon his problem. As a neutral substance harmless to the population at large, alcohol reveals him to be "an alcoholic", the victim of an irreversible disease. As a "deadly poison" which for all his efforts he cannot avoid, it defines him as someone powerless to save his own life and thus in need of "a power greater than himself". As a substance whose irresistible qualities depend on a certain "spiritual condition", it shows him to be proud and selfish and thus in need of surrender. As a force so powerful that it *compels* surrender and leaves him no option but to "grow along spiritual lines", a force perhaps allied with the Higher Power, it bestows retroactive purpose on his suffering and shows his life to be a matter of divine concern. In effect, then, AA has construed alcohol and the member's difficulties with this substance in such a way as to make its own religious program the only possible response. To the extent that it succeeds in this effort, of course, the group also harnesses much of the emotional stress generated by compulsive drinking – the guilt and anxiety as well as the craving – in ways that build an intense commitment to its ideals.

This pattern suggests that the logic underlying AA is indeed very much like that found in tribal cults of affliction and possession. While AA members do not literally worship the substance that gave them so much trouble, their deity is a tutelary figure who embodies many of the qualities they valued in that substance. What is more they "turned their lives over" to this deity only because of the threat imposed by alcohol. How do they interpret that threat? On the one hand they imply that alcohol "caught" them, not because of ceremonial breaches to be sure, but because of their habitual selfishness. On the other, they see the resulting crisis as having "elected" them to a unique therapeutic mission. When we consider this pattern in the light of materials presented by Turner, Lewis and others, it is hard not to believe that we are dealing here with a response to suffering so deeply satisfying that it has emerged in a number of very different human contexts. No other way of explaining the parallels appears plausible.

At the same time, such parallels do not arise *ex nihilo*. As both George Devereux (1958) and Robin Horton (1967) have argued, the way in which any group responds to affliction depends intimately on the "thought models" already available in its culture. In Western societies most attempts to grapple with suffering have borne the impress of the Judeo-Christian tradition, and AA is no exception. This fact takes on importance in view of certain formal affinities between this tradition and cults of affliction, especially the notion that suffering may operate as a form of religious election. In any case, an attempt to specify the traditional religious "thought model" that informs the teachings of AA seems essential to explaining their underlying logic. It may also provide a final way of grasping the special role accorded to alcohol in the AA system.

That AA's whole outlook owes a major debt to Christianity is obvious enough. Indeed, the group's emphasis on an experience of radical despair leading to a "spiritual awakening" (an experience that Martin Luther called *metanoia*) indicates that the operative model may be more narrowly a Protestant one. And yet AA departs sharply from those countless and mostly ill-fated attempts by Protestant evangelical groups to rescue sinners from the clutches of demon rum. As a number of observers have pointed out (Stewart, 1955; Clinebell, 1967; Petrunik, 1972) AA's "theology" differs from that of evangelical religion in fundamental ways. In addition to the fact of its specialized purpose, there is none of the moral fervor so obvious in evangelical preaching. AA does not treat drinking as a sin; indeed the group says nothing against drinking *per se* and makes no mention of sin. Likewise, AA has no use for such evangelical standbys as hellfire, the Last Judgment or the Ten Commandments. To put the crucial difference in theological terms, evangelical thought has always conceived of God as a two-sided figure, a "God of Wrath" who makes moral demands and punishes transgressions, and a "God of Mercy" who offers help in times of need (Althaus, 1966, p. 173). By contrast, as I noted earlier, AA's God deals only in mercy, and the group as a whole takes much the same attitude. There is some reason to believe that AA's resolutely nonjudgmental posture is important to its success, since as Cohen has argued (1964, pp. 622–25), alcoholics as a group are notoriously resistant to moral suasion. An important study comparing AA to the Salvation Army and rescue missions, in fact, has cited this difference as a key reason for AA's superior therapeutic record (Clinebell, 1967, pp. 144–47).

All these considerations notwithstanding, I should like to argue that

AA's teachings draw their essential logic from Protestant theology of a very traditional kind. Once certain substitutions are made, in fact, there is a point-by-point homology between AA's dramatic model of the alcoholic's predicament and the venerable Protestant drama of sin and salvation. A terse review of the core beliefs found in both schemes may help to make this clear.[15]

1) A fundamental tenet of all orthodox Christian belief, both Protestant and Catholic, is that the ills afflicting the human race spring from a deep and permanent flaw in man's nature known as Original Sin. As a result of this condition man is not permitted to act as he chooses; rather, he stands under a series of divine injunctions and prohibitions known collectively as "The Law". To break the Law is to face the threat of "eternal death", for "the wages of sin is death".

AA's view of the compulsive drinker offers a direct secular analogue to these beliefs. AA holds that the ills afflicting such persons also have their origins in a permanent flaw – the "disease" of alcoholism. As a result, they too may not act as they please, but stand under an absolute prohibition on drinking. They violate this rule at the cost of their lives, since as the Big Book has it, "for us to drink is to die".

2) Protestant theology in its orthodox or evangelical versions is marked by a deep pessimism about man's unaided ability to meet the demands of The Law. In Luther's famous image, man's puny attempts at righteousness are "as but filthy rags" before God. One reason for this view is that Protestant orthodoxy has adhered closely to the Pauline belief in the essential corruption of man's "free will" as a result of the Fall. Again, Luther's words express the basic view. "What conclusion is possible", he asks, "but that Free Will is at its worst when at its best, and that the more it tries the worse it becomes and acts?" (Quoted in Althaus, 1966, p. 278)

In a similar vein, AA is at great pains to show that the true alcoholic has no hope of resisting alcohol on his own. Neither self-knowledge nor strength of character can protect him from the impulse to drink, and injunctions to rely on "willpower" may do more harm than good. Thus AA's alcoholic and the Protestant sinner are in an identical dilemma: each finds that his survival (of body in one case, of soul in the other) hangs on strict adherence to a rule which – by his very nature – he cannot possibly obey.

3) Protestant theology is also noted for its emphasis on pride or ego-centrism as the foremost of human sins. This view stems in part from Luther's original contention that the First Commandment ("Thou shalt have no other gods before me") is the fundamental one from which all others arise, and that man's sinfulness is essentially a matter of putting himself ahead of God. According to Luther, human nature

> is concerned only with itself, seeks only its own advantage and always ignores anything that might get in its way. . . . It puts itself in place of

everything else, even in place of God Himself and seeks only its own purpose and not God's. (Quoted in Althaus, 1966, p. 147)

Luther's words find an obvious parallel in the Big Book's depiction of the alcoholic as "an extreme example of self-will run riot". When AA traces the alcoholic's troubles to his propensity for "playing God" or for being "an actor who wants to run the whole show"', or when it points out that for him "the god of intellect had replaced the God of our fathers", it is doing more than taking note of a psychological quirk. It is also giving secular and specialized form to an old Protestant notion about the dynamics of sin.

   4) As I noted earlier, evangelists of both Lutheran and Calvinist persuasions have held that salvation arises most readily from a deep and despairing experience of "conviction under The Law". When accompanied by the saving message of the Gospel, they have held, such an experience gives way almost automatically to an awakening of faith. To this end the great evangelists like Jonathan Edwards and John Wesley made a point of first preaching the terrors of "The Law" as vividly as possible, and only then offering their audiences the consolations of the Gospel. As Edwards wrote of this technique,

> Persons are first awakened with a sense of their miserable condition by nature; the danger they are in of perishing eternally; and that it is of great importance to them that they speedily escape and get into a better state. Those that before were secure and senseless are made sensible how much they were in the way to ruin. . . . (Edwards, 1829, p. 52)

The evangelist's approach to conversion is precisely the one that AA employs when it stresses the importance of "hitting bottom", an approach that includes its own attempt to hasten the process with words about the danger of perishing. However, it is also at this point that AA seems to break most clearly with the evangelical tradition. For the evangelist the force that reduces the sinner to despair is ultimately that of God Himself, the "God of Wrath" who placed him under the Law in the first place. From the traditional Protestant viewpoint, in fact, God created the Law precisely in order to expose man's weakness, to break his high pretentions and restore him to a proper state of humble dependence on divine grace. Luther expressed the basic idea in a famous passage:

> God is the God of the humble, the miserable, the oppressed . . . and his very nature is to comfort the broken-hearted, to justify sinners, to save the very desperate and damned. Now that pernicious and pestilent opinion of man's own righteousness which will not be a sinner, unclean, miserable and damnable, but righteous and holy, suffereth God not to come into his own natural and proper work. Therefore God must take this maul in hand (The Law, I mean) to beat in pieces and

bring to nothing this beast with her vain confidence, so that she may so learn at length by her own misery that she is utterly forlorn and damned. (Quoted in James, 1905)

As Luther and others have emphasized, the dangers embodied in the Law are not a mere preliminary to conversion but a permanent state of affairs. They apply equally to those who drift away from the faith as to those who never find it. For the traditional Protestant, in other words, God's posture toward man is one of eternal threat as well as eternal promise.

The contrasts between this two-sided deity and AA's wholly benign Higher Power have already been emphasized. And yet by now it should be apparent that both the threat and the promise of Protestant theology have their counterparts in AA as well. The difference is that while Protestant thought has made both functions the work of a single figure, AA "splits" them between two entities in much the fashion that it appears to split the benign and dangerous qualities of alcohol. It has not erased the threatening aspect of the Protestant God, but merely relocated it in the very object of the alcoholic's desire. Thus it is alcohol, rather than God, that "beats" members "into a state of reasonableness"; it is alcohol that breaks their self-reliant pride and compels them to seek the help of "a power greater than themselves". It is also alcohol whose destructive effects take on a providential quality when viewed in retrospect. In effect, then, AA has retained the essential structure of Protestant teachings while avoiding the implicit moralism, the appeal to heavenly authority that repels so many compulsive drinkers.

If within the AA scheme alcohol and the Higher Power are the common structural heirs to a single traditional deity, then we should not be surprised that members experience the moment of their conversion as a double-edged event, and that surrender to the former becomes an opening to the latter as well. The cultural program is still the old one; only the *dramatis personae* have changed. Working together, these two figures still place the alcoholic in precisely the bind that evangelical theology reserves for its sinners. The Higher Power stands on one side, promising "spiritual riches" exactly as the God of Mercy does. On the other side stands its partner, a substance that threatens "death and madness", that humbles the proud and teaches surrender, that watches like a grim executioner over the faith of the group, a God of Wrath in the unlikely shape of a bottle.

Notes

1 The Classified Abstract Archive of the Alcohol Literature enumerates nearly 200 scholarly articles in which AA figures as a major topic. There is no hope of summarizing this material here, but it is interesting to note that nearly all of it falls under a relatively small number of headings: 1) articles introducing AA and its techniques to a specialized audience (e.g. psychiatrists, social workers,

clergymen); 2) studies assessing the practical value of AA as a treatment for alcoholism, either alone or in conjunction with hospitals and other helping institutions; 3) investigations into social dimensions of AA like organizational structure, class composition, and affiliation processes; 4) theoretical discussions linking AA to various conjectures about the dynamics of alcoholism. The only consideration of AA by an anthropologist that has come to my attention is a highly original contribution by Gregory Bateson (1971), but his article is much more an application of cybernetic theory than an exercise in the analysis of symbols.

2 In the *Ihamba* ritual described by Turner, confession and the setting of long-standing grudges are considered essential to the healing process. There is a general belief that the "tooth of *Ihamba*" afflicting the patient will not allow itself to be extracted until members of the village have all "made their livers white" by airing their hostilities and expressing a wish to live peaceably.

AA also holds that long-term hostilities are a serious impediment to recovery. Since these normally lie between the member and persons outside the group, the method used to end them is necessarily more individualized. It involves the repeated taking of a "personal inventory" enumerating a member's general faults and his specific offenses toward others, confession of his wrongs "before God and another person" and restitution to persons harmed wherever possible.

3 The official relationship between AA and its members is *laissez-faire* in the extreme. According to the group's statement of purpose, "The only requirement for membership is a desire to stop drinking", and according to a widely quoted maxim, "anyone is a member of AA who says he is". Joining AA does not entail obedience to any body of rules, not even the rule of abstinence. The basic organizational unit is the local group or meeting, which is more or less autonomous. The General Service Conference and its executive arm, the General Service Office have only the power to "make suggestions", and then only in matters bearing on relations between groups or on a group's relationship to AA as a whole. This loose arrangement is very much in keeping with the non-demanding character of all AA's teachings; the rationale behind it is a strong belief that alcoholics do not submit readily to any form of mandatory rule.

4 Of course it hardly suffices to rely only on printed sources for this purpose. Observation at meetings provides an essential check on the relative importance that various teachings assume in the thinking of members, as well as clues to the ways in which they understand those teachings. My own observation at about two dozen meetings in Chicago and Toronto indicated a high degree of uniformity in the way members viewed such central issues as the nature of alcoholism or the meaning of the Twelve Steps and a fairly direct correspondence between their ideas and those found in AA literature. However to assure that quotations used here are in some sense typical of AA as a whole rather than of just a local sample, I have drawn these almost entirely from printed sources.

5 The telling of stories is actually the dominant activity of all AA meetings. These occasions do not adhere to any single rigid plan, but usually after a reading from the Big Book and a few business announcements, one member, the designated speaker for the evening, tells his life story at length. Then, if the group is not large, all participants comment on the lessons to be learned from his account, often providing further anecdotes of their own. The meeting usually closes with

a recital of the Lord's Prayer. The amount of time that AA members spend in sharing and discussing personal stories suggest that these must be understood as essential vehicles for the transmission of group beliefs.

6 This inquiry owes an indirect debt to Kenneth Burke's "dramatistic" approach to the study of belief systems. Burke has argued that ideologies generate motives (and thus shape actions) by employing "strategies for encompassing situations" similar to those employed by the dramatist in shaping a play. My concerns here reflect a similar general viewpoint, but I have found it easier to pursue them without drawing on Burke's somewhat cumbersome terminology.

7 Critics of the disease model of alcoholism (MacAndrew, 1968; Reinert, 1968) point out that it faces the same kinds of objections often leveled against disease models of mental illness. First, as most medical authorities concede, the only viable operational definition of alcoholism is a purely social one. For example, according to the American Psychiatric Association (1967), the alcoholic is "a person who as the consequence of consuming excessive amounts of alcohol follows patterns that substantially impede his vocational, social, and psychological adjustment". Secondly, as E. L. Jellinek (1960) has established, there is not one alcoholism but at least four, each appearing in different cultural milieux and having a different prognosis. Finally, there is still no consensus about the biological basis for any of these alcoholisms. Indeed, the APA manual on this subject (1967) noted that "the overwhelming majority of persons working in the field oppose the view that alcoholism has any *direct* biological basis at all".

8 See Notes 9 and 10.

9 See Robinson and Voegtlin (1952).

10 A number of well-conducted studies have shown that many persons apparently addicted to alcohol can learn to drink normally again, at least for periods of as long as a year or two. The most thorough of these investigations (Armor *et al.*, 1976) reported a rate of recovery to social drinking (sustained over an eighteen-month period) of better than 30%. Other studies (Davies, 1962; Kendell, 1968; Smart, 1978a) describe results consistent with these figures.

11 According to several reports (Gerard *et al.*, 1962; Armor *et al.*, 1976; Smart, 1978b) significant numbers of apparent alcohol addicts do abstain completely from drinking for periods of several years without the help of AA or any other therapeutic program. Thus while the "mental obsession" may be a reality for some alcoholics, it is certainly not universal in its effects.

12 All of the surrender experiences on which I have been able to gather information took place well after the drinker had made his initial contact with AA and usually after he had struggled for some time to abstain. Thus it seems likely that they are not purely spontaneous experiences (if such things exist) but responses to circumstances and expectations generated by the group itself.

13 The likely prototype for Bill's "surrender" in turn, may be found in the many conversion stories that appear in *The Varieties of Religious Experience* (James, 1905), a book that Bill had read carefully in the weeks prior to his experience.

14 The other major statement on authority in AA is the third of the group's Twelve Traditions: "For our group purposes there is but one ultimate authority – a loving God as he may express himself in our common group conscience. Our leaders are but trusted servants; they do not govern." Here again the Durkheimian theme is striking. However the intent of this statement is more political

than theological; it urges members to take their decisions by consensus rather than coercion. The same phrase is also used in encouraging members to become actively involved in governance functions. A campaign to this end took place at regional conferences in 1978 under the slogan, "Our ultimate authority: The Common Group Conscience". Seen in the light of statements like these, Bill's words come very close to making AA's "totemic substance" – exactly because of the dangers it poses – into a force protecting the vitality of the *conscience collective*.

15 This summary hardly does justice to the variety and subtlety of Protestant thought. However the aim is simply to take note of a skeletal pattern shared by a whole array of sects whose main concerns are "evangelical" – that is, with matters of sin and salvation. Although I have found Luther a convenient spokesman for several of the major themes, they appear to be part of the Calvinist tradition as well.

References

Alcoholics Anonymous, 1952. *Forty-Four Questions*. New York, AA World Services
    1953. *The Twelve Steps and the Twelve Traditions*. New York, AA World Services
    1955. *Alcoholics Anonymous*. New York, AA World Services (1939, revised 1955)
    1957. *Alcoholics Anonymous Comes of Age*. New York, AA World Services
    1962. *Twenty-Four Hours a Day*. New York, AA World Services
    1969. *The AA Way of Life*. New York, AA World Services
    1973. *Came to Believe . . .* New York, AA World Services
Althaus, P., 1966. *The Theology of Martin Luther*. Philadelphia, Fortress Press
American Psychiatric Association, 1967. *The Treatment of Alcoholism*. Baltimore, Pridemark
Armor, D. *et al.*, 1976. *Alcoholism and Treatment*. Santa Monica, Rand Corporation
Bateson, G., 1971. The cybernetics of "self": a theory of alcoholism, *Psychiatry* 34(1): 1–18
Bean, M., 1975. *Alcoholics Anonymous*. New York, Insight Communications
Burke, K., 1962. *A Grammar of Motives, and a Rhetoric of Motives*. Cleveland, World Publishing
Cohen, F., 1962. Personality changes among members of Alcoholics Anonymous, *Mental Hygiene* 46: 427–37
    1964. Alcoholics Anonymous principles and the treatment of emotional illness, *Mental Hygiene* 48: 621–26
Clinebell, H., 1967. *Understanding and Counselling the Alcoholic Through Religion and Psychology*. Nashville, Abingdon Press
Davies, D. L., 1962. Normal drinking in recovered alcohol addicts, *Quarterly Journal of Studies on Alcohol* 22: 94–104
Devereux, G., 1958. Cultural thought models in primitive and modern psychiatric theories, *Psychiatry* 21

Durkheim, E., 1915. *The Elementary Forms of the Religious Life*. New York, Allen and Unwin

Edwards, J., 1829. *A New Narrative of the Revival of Religion in New England with Thoughts on That Revival*. Glasgow, Wm. Collins

Frake, C., 1962. The ethnographic study of cognitive systems, in T. C. Gladwin and W. Sturtevant, eds., *Anthropology and Human Behavior*. Seattle, Anthropological Society of Washington

Gerard, D. *et al.*, 1962. The abstinent alcoholic, *Archives of General Psychiatry* 6: 83–95

Horton, R., 1967. African traditional thought and Western science, *Africa* 37 (1 & 2): 50–71 and 155–87

James, W., 1905. *The Varieties of Religious Experience*. New York, Crowell

Jellinek, E. L., 1960. *The Disease Concept of Alcoholism*. New Haven, College and University Press

—— 1977. The symbolism of drinking: a culture-historical approach, *Journal of Studies on Alcohol* 38, 5: 849–66

Kendell, R., 1968. Normal drinking by former alcohol addicts, *Quarterly Journal of Studies on Alcohol* 24: 44–60

Klausner, S., 1964. Sacred and profane meanings of blood and alcohol, *Journal of Social Psychology* 64: 27–43

Leach, B., and Norris, J., 1977. Factors in the development of Alcoholics Anonymous, in B. Kissin and H. Begleiter, eds., *The Treatment and Rehabilitation of the Chronic Alcoholic*. New York, Plenum Press

Lender, M. E., and Karchanapee, K. R., 1977. "Temperance tales"; antiliquor fictional American attitudes toward alcoholics in the late 19th and early 20th centuries, *Journal of Studies on Alcohol* 38(7): 1347–70

Lewis, I. M., 1971. *Ecstatic Religion: An Anthropological Study of Spirit Possession and Shamanism*. Baltimore, Penguin Books

MacAndrew, C., 1968. On the notion that certain persons who are given to drunkenness suffer from a disease called alcoholism, in S. Plot and R. Edgerton, eds., *New Concepts in Mental Illness*. New York, Doubleday

Petrunik, M., 1972. Seeing the light: a study of conversion to Alcoholics Anonymous, *Journal of Voluntary Action Research* 1: 31–5

Reinert, R., 1968. The concept of alcoholism as a disease, *Bulletin of the Menninger Clinic* 32: 21–25

Robinson, M., and Voegtlin, W., 1952. Investigations of an allergic factor in alcohol addiction, *Quarterly Journal of Studies on Alcohol* 13: 196–200

Smart, R., 1978a. Characteristics of alcoholics who drink socially after treatment, *Alcoholism: Clinical and Experimental Research* 2: 49–52

—— 1978b. Spontaneous recovery in alcoholics: a review and analysis of the available research, *Quarterly Journal of Studies on Alcohol* 38: 123–64

Stewart, D., 1955. The dynamics of fellowship as illustrated in Alcoholics Anonymous, *Quarterly Journal of Studies in Alcohol* 160: 251–62

Turner, V. W., 1957. *Schism and Continuity in an African Society: A Study of Ndembu Village Life*. Manchester, Manchester University Press

—— 1967. *The Forest of Symbols: Aspects of Ndembu Ritual*. Ithaca, Cornell University Press

1975. *Revelation and Divination in Ndembu Ritual*. Ithaca, Cornell University Press

Wilson, W., 1944. Basic concepts of Alcoholics Anonymous, *Proceedings of the Annual Meeting, Medical Society of the State of New York*

10. The Kava ceremonial as a dream structure[1]

Elizabeth Bott

I am convinced that a knowledge of unconscious mental processes gained from the practice of psychoanalysis can deepen and enrich understanding of social behavior. But I have not written this paper to prove or even to illustrate this conviction. I have written it in an attempt to understand a particular event, the kava ceremony of the Kingdom of Tonga in the South Pacific. This ceremony is a social event and as such involves groups, roles, and social differentiation as well as conscious and unconscious feelings. In order to understand it to my satisfaction I found I had to use ideas derived both from social anthropology and from psychoanalysis.

What I am saying, in effect, is that the problem in question should take priority over one's loyalty to a particular profession or professions, whether that problem is concerned with the understanding of a patient, of a ceremony, of social stratification, of political behavior, or whatever it may be. Of course professional training shapes one's interests and limits one's selection of topics for study. In view of my double training as an anthropologist and a psychoanalyst it is not surprising that I have selected a problem that concerns both professions. The analysis of ceremonies falls within the traditional domain of anthropology, but it has also stirred many psychoanalysts to speculative efforts in applied psychoanalysis.[2]

In the course of trying to understand and interpret the kava ceremony it has repeatedly occurred to me that a ceremony has much in common with a dream. A dream is a condensed and disguised representation of unconscious thoughts and wishes. A ceremony is a condensed and partially disguised representation of certain aspects of social life. A dream and a ceremony both serve a double and contradictory function: they release and communicate dangerous thoughts and emotions; but at the same time they disguise and transform them so that the element of danger is contained and to some extent dealt with. An effective ceremony protects society from destructive forms of conflict; an effective dream protects the sleeper from anxiety.

Of course there are important differences between a dream and a ceremony. A dream is the product of an individual; a ceremony is the product of a group. Dreams reflect unconscious thoughts. Some of the ideas and emotions expressed in ceremonies are unconscious, but many others are not so much unconscious as unformulated. Just as one can speak a language correctly without being able to formulate its grammatical rules, so one can play one's part in social life and in a ceremony without understanding how all the parts and principles fit together. Further, many of the symbolic statements made in a ceremony concern social norms and values of which the participants are consciously aware.

The basic events of the kava ceremony are very simple. A group of people pound up the root of a kava plant, mix it with water, and drink it. But all this is done according to a fixed ceremonial procedure that has hardly varied for at least 160 years. We have a good description of the ceremony dating from 1806 (Mariner, 1818, vol. 2, pp. 172–96) and the verbal orders and the actions performed have hardly changed at all, with one important exception. The kava root used to be chewed and then mixed with water, whereas nowadays it is pounded with stones.

The botanical name of the kava plant is *Piper methysticum*. It contains several chemical constituents and there is considerable controversy about their physiological effects. The general conclusions are that it has a slight tranquilizing and anaesthetic action, though the effects are very mild. Tongans, however, treat kava as if it were strong stuff. And so it is, but the strength comes from society, not from the vegetable kingdom.[3]

Before I describe the ceremony, here are a few background facts about the Kingdom. Tonga is a Polynesian society consisting of about 150 small islands with a population of about 70,000 people in 1960. It has a Treaty of Friendship with Great Britain, but has always been independent, never a colony, a fact of which Tongans are very proud. The people have been Christian for 130 years and virtually everyone can read and write. Tongans practise subsistence farming on small holdings, with coconuts and bananas as the main cash crops. There are no extremes of wealth or poverty. For the past 100 years government has assumed the form of a constitutional monarchy. Anyone who saw Queen Sālote of Tonga at the coronation of Queen Elizabeth in 1953 will not be likely to forget her. She is as memorable in Tonga as she is in Britain. She died in December 1965 and was succeeded by her eldest son, the present King Taufa'ahau Tupou IV.

Description of the ceremony

The basic form of the kava ceremony is always the same, though it may vary from a small informal gathering of four or five people to a huge assemblage of several hundred people. It can be dressed up or down as the occasion requires. It takes place on many different sorts of occasion: when men visit each other just to talk; when welcoming home relatives who have been away; in courtship; at weddings; at certain points in a funeral; at the appointment of a king and later on at his coronation; and similarly at the appointment of a chief and on the occasion when he first presents himself and his villagers to his King.

Figures 10.1 and 10.2 show the seating at an informal and at a formal ceremony. The participants sit cross-legged, with the chief whose title is genealogically the most senior at the head of the circle. He has an official called a matāpule on either side of him. These matāpule are the hereditary ceremonial attendants of chiefs, their duties being to conduct their chief's kava ceremony and to give and receive gifts on his behalf. The matāpule have never held political authority. The chiefly title holders, on the other hand, used to have political authority, though nowadays much of it has been transferred to the central government.

The rest of the main circle ('alofi) is composed of other chiefs and matāpule sitting alternately. There are always more matāpule than chiefs, however, so that after the first few places matāpule sit next to one another. In the part of the main circle nearest the bowl (fasi tapu and fasi tou'a) some chiefs and matāpule sit in pairs, and some minor chiefs sit on their own.

In theory the seating of the various chiefs in the main circle demonstrates the genealogical position of their titles relative to that of the presiding chief. The title of the presiding chief is supposed to be genealogically senior, and the other chiefly titles in the main circle are supposed to have been derived from his line at later points in time. Although each chiefly titleholder sits as an individual, he also represents the village over which he had titular authority. In Tongan idiom he is more than a representative; the title is the embodiment of the village and its history.

In a large formal ceremony all the people in the main circle have to have been formally appointed to chiefly or matāpule titles. Women, who do not normally hold titles or wield political authority, thus do not sit in the main circle. (The Queen, who held the ruling title, Tu'i Kanokupolu, was of course an exception to this general rule. In the traditional system kings and chiefs were almost invariably men, but British rules of succession to the kingship were adopted in 1875.) In a small informal ceremony the people in the main circle do not have to have been formally appointed to titles; they can use the name of a matāpule title they are descended from, or, failing that, they can use their personal names. Women can therefore sit in the main circle on such informal occasions if they want to.

The kava bowl is opposite the presiding chief. The bowl is three or four yards away from the chief in a small ceremony, some two hundred yards away in a large royal ceremony. The kava maker sits behind the bowl with an assistant on either side of him. There is a group of people behind the bowl who help to make and serve the kava (the "outer group" – tou'a). In a small informal ceremony the outer group is often very small. It is sometimes reduced to the bare minimum necessary to carry out the ceremony – the kava maker, one assistant, and someone to serve the kava. In a large formal ceremony the outer group is larger and more elaborately structured.

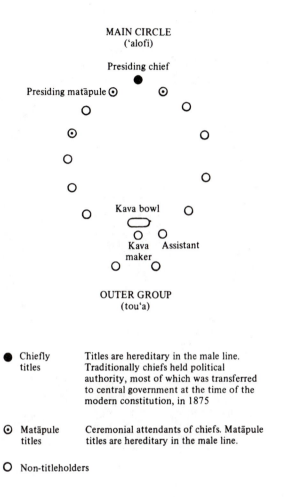

Fig. 10.1: Schematic diagram of seating at small informal kava ceremony.

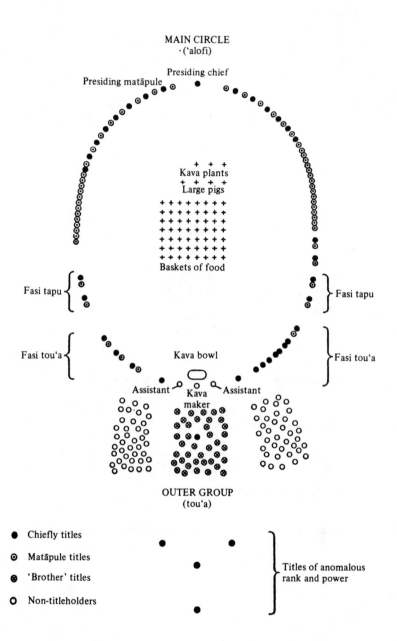

Fig. 10.2: Schematic diagram of seating at formal royal kava ceremony.

In a very large royal kava ceremony, such as that represented in Figure 2, the outer group is divided into three parts. In the center group sit men who are the holders of minor titles that stand in the relation of "younger brother" (*tehina*) to certain of the titles in the main circle. It is the titles that are brothers, not the men. In the beginning, when the titles are supposed to have originated, the first titleholders are said to have been actual brothers, and this relation has continued to exist between the titles even though the men who hold the titles may no longer be linked by kinship. "Our titles are brothers but we are not related", as Tongans put it.[4]

The right-hand portion of the outer group (that is, the portion to the right of the presiding chief) is composed of people without titles. In theory anyone can sit in the outer group at a kava ceremony, but at a formal ceremony most of those who attend are the "children" (*fānau*) of the titles in the main circle, meaning that they are descendants of former holders of the titles. Some of the people who sit in this part of the outer group serve the kava during the ceremony. Others are called "grandchildren of high rank" (*makapuna 'eiki*). This means that they had a grandfather who held one of the titles in the main circle, and their kinship relation to the present titleholder is such that they have higher personal rank than the current titleholder. They play an important part in the ceremonial distribution of food during the ceremony. Many of the "children" and "grandchildren" in this part of the outer group are women.

The left-hand portion of the outer group is also composed of "children" of the titles. Most of the people in this group are men, and they do the heavy work of the ceremony – carrying the kava, pigs, and other food in and out, dividing the food for distribution, and so forth. The path between this group and the central group is called the "path of work" (*hala ngāue*), whereas the path between the right-hand group and the center group is called the "sacred path" (*hala tupu*).

Finally, at a formal royal ceremony, there are certain very important chiefly titles that are seated right at the back, behind the outer group (see Figure 10.2).

To summarize the salient facts about the seating: the chief whose title is genealogically senior sits at the head of the main circle; the rest of the main circle is made up of formally appointed titleholders, chiefs and matāpule, sitting alternately. The titles of the chiefs in the main circle are supposed to be genealogically junior to the title of the presiding chief. The outer group is composed, first, of men who hold minor chiefly titles that stand in the relation of "younger brother" to the titles in the main circle and, second, of men and women without titles who are the "children" and in a few cases also the "grandchildren" of the titles in the main circle.

The first thing that happens in the ceremony is that people come in and seat themselves. Kava plants and sometimes food are presented to the presiding chief and placed in the center of the circle (see Figure 2). The traditional food to go with the kava is sugar cane, but vast quantities of pigs and other cooked food are presented along with it. Nowadays the sugar cane is often omitted. In a formal ceremony the food is meticulously counted and thanks for it are chanted by the matāpule. Then the presiding matāpule tells someone on the outer group to take a kava plant from in front of the presiding chief down to the bowl end, where it is split up, cleaned, and then pounded by the kava maker. (Traditionally small bits of the kava root were handed to people in the outer group who chewed it, spat it out neatly on to a leaf, and then handed it back to the kava maker who put it in the bowl.) The kava maker puts the pounded kava root in the bowl and begins to knead it with his hands, and water is poured in by the kava maker's assistants – all of these actions being carried out according to fixed ceremonial orders chanted by the presiding matāpule. The pouring in of the water is one of the most sacred moments of the ceremony and all conversation stops. Then the matāpule calls out to mix the kava and to strain it. While the kava maker is straining the kava conversation is resumed, speeches may be made, and if there is food some of it is ceremonially divided and distributed to each titleholder in the main circle. The titleholders do not eat their food, however. They call for their respective "grandchildren of high rank" to come from the outer group and take the portions of food away. Then all the remaining food is ceremonially given to the matāpule on the left of the presiding chief, who orders men from the outer group to take it away. After the ceremony is over this food is divided among the participants.

Eventually, after the flurry of activity in distributing and removing the food, the kava maker's assistant calls out that the kava is clear and the matāpule gives the order for servers to come from the outer group with cups. A cup of kava is taken to each person in the main circle and to several in the outer group. Generally when the serving is completed the ceremony is ended. It may be continued, but in this case the second serving is directed by the matāpule on the chief's left. An informal kava ceremony may go on all night, alternating from right to left.

To recapitulate the sequence of ceremonial operations: the participants seat themselves; kava and food are presented and counted; a kava root is pounded and placed in the bowl; the kava is kneaded and water is poured in; the kava is strained, to the accompaniment of conversation or speeches and the distribution and clearing away of food; finally, cups of kava are served.

The first kava ceremony I saw was a small informal one, so informal that I did not realize it was a ceremony. I noticed an old man mumbling away from time to time – in fact he was giving ceremonial orders – and I saw that there were occasional lulls in the conversation, but I thought they were natural pauses not especially sacred moments in a ceremony. The first royal ceremony I saw was an entirely different affair. From the first moment when the food and kava were brought in with cries of "Tue, tue, tue, tue, tue – e – e", and the matāpule chanted their thanks, the atmosphere was electric – charged with an intense feeling of being together in a group. The kava, the ceremony, and the group were sacred – *tapu*. I have never felt anything like it in our own society except at the coronation of Queen Elizabeth, where it seemed to me that our mutual indifference to anything outside our own little circle was lost for a moment in a common feeling of being one nation.

How does one set about understanding such a ceremony? It is not much use asking people point-blank what it means any more than it would be useful to ask an individual what his dream means. To such questions Tongans reply politely, "It is our custom," and that is the end of the matter. What one should not do, either with a dream or a ceremony, is plunge headlong into arbitrary interpretations of symbolism. While this may be a useful intellectual exercise for the anthropologist or the psychoanalyst, it does not bring him much closer to the new and unique bit of reality he is trying to understand. It would be like trying to interpret a dream without knowing anything about the dreamer – no associations, no transference, no background knowledge of the dreamer's current life and childhood.

To understand a ceremony one needs to know something about the social context. One can also learn a lot by listening to what people say spontaneously and following up their leads. One can ask certain direct questions, such as why people sit where they sit, why the kava is used instead of another plant, or what the properties of kava are, without running into the blank wall of "It is our custom." One can ask people to explain the differences between one type of kava ceremony and another. I think this process of exploration is analogous to the use of patients' associations to dreams.

In the course of talking around the ceremony several informants told me the myth of the origin of kava, which proved to be a useful lead. I recorded two versions of the myth and there are others in the literature (Gifford, 1924, pp. 71–5). Their points of similarity and difference helped to clarify the central theme of the myth but I only have time for one version, which is the one recorded by the late Queen Sālote.

The myth of the origin of kava

One day the King of Tonga went fishing with a friend. They did not catch anything, and as they were tired and hungry they called in at the little island of 'Eueiki to get something to eat. At that time there was only one couple living on the island and they had one child, a daughter, whose name was Kava'onau. (In some versions the name is abbreviated to "Kava".) She had leprosy. It was a time of famine and the only food the couple had left was a large kape plant (*Alocasia macrorrhiza*) which stood near the beach. When the King landed he sat down to rest against this plant. When the couple re-alized who their guest was they set about making an earth oven, but when they came to get their sole remaining food plant they could not use it because the King was leaning on it. The King's friend saw the couple hit something in their house and bring it to be baked in the earth oven. He saw that they had killed their daughter because they had nothing else to give their King. The King's friend told the King what the couple had done. The King was deeply moved by their sacrifice. He rose up immediately and returned to the main island, telling the couple to bury their child properly.

Two plants grew from the grave, one from the head and one from the foot. One day the couple saw a mouse bite the first plant, stagger a bit, and then bite the second plant, after which he recovered his balance.

One day Loʻau came to the island and the couple told him all that had happened. (Loʻau is a figure who turns up in Tongan legend and mythology at times when social institutions are being established or changed. He tells the people how to organize their social life and then fades from view. He is thought of as human, not a god, and he is called the "carpenter of the land", which, freely translated, means the establisher of social customs.)

When Loʻau heard the couple's story he sat in silence for a time, deeply moved, and then he spoke in poetry telling them what they should do. They must take the two plants to the King and give him Loʻau's instructions about how the plants should be used. The one from the head was to be used to make a drink, and that was the kava, and the other was to be eaten with the drink, and that was the sugar cane. The couple did as Loʻau had told them. At first the King thought their plant might be poisonous. He had one of his matāpule taste it first. But on finding it was all right he directed the people to carry out Loʻau's instructions.

And so kava was made for the first time and the rules and procedures for making it were established.

Tongans say that the origin of the kava from the leprous girl explains some of its properties. The shoots of the kava plant grow, split, and become limey and grey like the skin of a leper, and the skin of those who drink too much kava becomes grey and scaly like the skin of a leper. There are other linguistic links with the idea of kava as a poison. *Kavafisi* and *kavahaha* are creepers used as fish poisons. The word "*kavahia*" means to be nauseated. Some informants told me that they felt nauseated when they drank strong green kava, and nausea is said to have been the Tongan reaction to attempts to copy the Fijian custom of *actually* eating human flesh.[5] At the same time, in other contexts Tongans said that kava loosened the tongue and made one feel pleasantly relaxed. Thus there is a series of associations between kava, tranquility, leprosy, poison, nausea, and cannibalism. It may seem odd that tranquility should appear alongside ideas of poison, nausea, and cannibalism, but I hope the reasons for this strange juxtaposition will become clearer as the exposition proceeds.

Interpretation

The first point is that *the kava ceremony is one of a series of ceremonies that clarify social principles and social roles*. In the kava ceremony the principle of stratification by titles is marked off as clearly as possible from all other forms of social differentiation. This aspect of the ceremony is conscious and explicit. Many Tongans told me, "Everything in the kava ceremony goes by titles."

In the traditional political system, chiefly titles carried formal political authority. A chiefly titleholder had the right and obligation to rule and to represent all the inhabitants of a given territory. The kava ceremony displayed the political relationships of titles to one another.

This emphasis on titles only makes sense when one knows that in the traditional system, and to a considerable extent today as well, there were two other systems of social differentiation that were very important in everyday life though they played a very minor role in the kava ceremony; these two other systems of social differentiation were political power and personal rank.[6]

Any man who could gather about him a large and industrious group of relatives and friends could become a political leader in the traditional system. This dimension of political power cut across the system of titles. Some powerful leaders did not hold titles. Some chiefly titleholders were strong leaders of large and powerful local groups; others were politically unimportant.

The third system, that of personal rank, is the same today as it was in the traditional system. The rewards of high rank are gifts of food and elaborate gestures of deference from people of lower rank. By and large, high rank is more highly esteemed than political power or political authority. Power and authority mean work and responsibility; high rank means pure privilege.

Personal rank depends not on whether one holds a title, but on sex, seniority, and descent. Sisters have higher rank than their brothers; elder siblings have higher rank than younger siblings; and the descendants of sisters have higher rank than the descendants of their brothers. Unlike a system of social class such as we are familiar with in our society, the Tongan system of rank is such that no two individuals can have the same rank. The society is not divided into ranked groups or categories; rather the conception is one of a line from the person of highest rank at the top to the person of lowest rank at the bottom. Moreover, personal rank is relative to the relationships involved. A man may be an "aristocrat" (*'eiki*) at one funeral and a lowly kitchen worker at another, depending on how he is related to the deceased.

Unlike titles, which are normally inherited in the male line, personal rank is inherited from both parents. To be a great aristocrat means that one is descended, preferably through a line of eldest sisters, from the eldest sister of the former sacred King, the Tu'i Tonga, a title that is now defunct. Even the principles of rank in themselves may sometimes conflict. If a man marries a woman who is a great aristocrat and his sister marries a lowly commoner, the children of the respective marriages will be in a contradictory situation. According to one principle the children of the sister will have higher rank than the children of her brother, but according to the other principle (that descent from the Tu'i Tonga's sister confers high rank) the children of the brother will have higher rank. The resolution of such contradictions depends on the situation and the people involved, and gives rise to much gossip, ill-feeling, and amusement.

Like the dimension of political power, personal rank cuts across the other dimensions of stratification. This tendency was very marked in the traditional system. Many men of high rank did not hold titles or political power. Some titleholders were of high rank, some of low rank. Some powerful leaders were of high rank, others of low rank.

The discrepancy between rank and political power was incorporated into the traditional political hierarchy. The sacred king, the Tu'i Tonga, held the most senior title and was of very high personal rank; only his sisters and their children were of higher personal rank. But this political power was very limited. Secular authority was wielded by a second king, the Tu'i Kanokupolu, which is the title of the present ruling line. The Tu'i Kanokupolu title was genealogically junior to that of the Tu'i Tonga, and the individual incumbents of the Tu'i Kanokupolu title were of much lower personal rank than the sacred king, but their political power was much greater. They were supposed to rule the kingdom on behalf of the Tu'i Tonga. The recurrent practice of a particular type of marriage between the two royal houses ensured that the sacred king continued to be of higher personal rank than the secular king; personal kinship ties thus reinforced the relationship between the titles.

In the traditional system the object of the social and political game was to use one's standing in one system to increase one's standing in the others, marriage being one of the main devices for doing so. The process took several generations. Increasing the rank of one's descendants was the ultimate goal, but it was unwise in the long run to concentrate on rank alone. The disappearance of the former sacred kingship is a case in point. The kava ceremony provided a snapshot of the process; it showed where the maneuvering for position had got to at any particular moment, at least as far as the system of formal titles was concerned.

In the modern social and political system the principle of independent but overlapping dimensions of stratification has been retained, though the content has changed. The system of personal rank continues unaltered. Education, however, has supplanted the old system of power and unofficial political leadership. Education is the new pathway to political authority and to higher rank for one's descendants.

The system of chiefly titles and political authority has also changed. In 1875 at the time of the Constitution most of the authority of the chiefly title-holders was transferred to the central government. In compensation for their loss, about forty of the more important and powerful chiefs were given the new European title of "noble" (*nopele* in Tongan) and were given a special position in the central government. They could elect seven of their peers to the legislative assembly. At the present time being a noble gives one a considerable initial advantage in acquiring political authority, though one must also be educated.

The system of noble titles thus provides a link between the old and the new systems of formal government. The kava ceremony has changed accordingly. It used to be a ceremonial statement of political authority; now it is a statement of continuity between the new political system and the old. As before, principles of personal rank and political power are almost entirely excluded from the ceremony. People are seated and served according to their titles, not according to their personal rank, education, or position in government.

In the beginning I found the constant contradictions of rank, titles, and government authority difficult to grasp. Tongans assured me it was perfectly simple if one had grown up with it. But one thing that helps to keep it simple is ceremonies. Ceremonies mark off one social principle from the others and keep each principle clear in everyone's mind. At government feasts people are seated primarily according to their position in government; a commoner of low rank who is a Cabinet minister will be seated at the Queen's table. At funerals, duties depend mainly on the principles of kinship and personal rank. In the kava ceremony titles are what matter, and power and personal rank play a very minor role. Thus, if the same set of people were involved in the three types of ceremony, they would assume different positions and would have very different relationships with one another in each ceremony. Hence the kava ceremony cannot be understood on its own; it is part of a complex of ceremonies.[7]

I have repeatedly said that power and personal rank are "virtually" excluded from the kava ceremony. The qualifying objective needs explanation. Although titles are dominant in the ceremony and are supposed to be seated and served according to their genealogical seniority, there are certain features of the seating and the ceremonial procedure that link the system of titles to the principles of political power and personal rank.

Certain important titles are in an anomalous relation to the present kingship. Two of these titles were originally senior to the title of the present king. A third title had a good claim to the throne at one period. A fourth title, although always junior to the present ruling line, had a remarkably able and ambitious series of incumbents in the eighteenth and early nineteenth centuries. One of them broke away from the secular king (the Tu'i Kanokupolu) and became a virtually independent ruler of the northern islands. The power of this particular titleholder, in other words, far out-stripped the official political authority of his title. By a series of marriages to aristocratic women, the line increased the personal rank of its incumbents until, in the late nineteenth century, the personal rank of the current incumbent was considerably higher than that of the King himself. In the royal ceremony at the present time, all four of these titles are seated far away at the back, twenty yards or so behind the outer group (see Figure 2). Both their distinctiveness and their anomalous position are thus emphasized. They do not fit in.

There is one event in the ceremonial procedure itself that draws attention to the principle of personal rank. This is the moment when the "grandchil-dren of high rank" are called from the outer group to collect the portions of food allocated to the titleholders in the main circle. It is a reminder to all concerned that although the chiefs and nobles hold the titles, they have relatives who are of higher personal rank.

The kava ceremony thus displays the system of titles, with passing references to the two other principles of social differentiation, personal rank and political power. It demonstrates the separateness of the three principles and at the same time shows how they co-exist.

We have no historical information on how this particular form of differentiated social principles developed. It was in full flower at the time of Captain Cook's visits. He confessed himself bewildered by the system, though he gives a clear description of behavior from which the operation of the three principles of authority, power, and rank can be inferred.

Although the historical development of the system remains obscure, some of its effects can be observed in operation. It preserves social continuity while at the same time providing opportunities for flexibility and individual initiative. For individuals it provides a ready-made defence and a mode of adaptation to a general problem that Freud outlined long ago in *Totem and Taboo*: how are subordinates to reconcile themselves to the fact that they hate and envy the authority ("father") whom they also need and love. In the Tongan system "authority" is split up and dispersed so that no one, not even the King, can be on top all the time. However great a man may be in one dimension, someone else will be greater in some other dimension of some other context. What you lose on the swings you gain on the roundabouts. Further, the system is such that it is difficult, even today, to mobilize consistently opposed groups of "haves" and "have-nots". But it would be a mistake to regard the splitting of authority, rank, and power as a "solution" to the problem of ambivalent feelings towards authority, for it seems very likely that each of the three systems generates its own complex of envy and rivalry. The system may generate more hatred than it disperses.

There are many indications in everyday life that Tongans are very sensitive about problems of authority and conflict. People avoid open expression of disagreement, while at the same time seeing to it that the authorities concerned find out indirectly about the issues involved. For example, people will agree to fulfil what they consider to be unreasonable demands by a person in authority or a person of high rank, but they will then fail to carry out the desired activity. If confronted by their lack of conformity, they disappear, or find a reasonable excuse or say they did not understand what was required of them. "They have been leading us around for generations" as one eminent noble put it.

Possibly one factor in this general sensitivity to conflict and avoidance of open expression of it is that Tonga is an island, or rather a group of islands in close communication with one another. In a comparatively isolated group of islands more of an effort has to be made to contain and resolve internal conflicts than on a large land mass where dissidents and persecuted groups can move away without actually leaving the society. And if the controls break down and violence actually breaks out on an island, as it did in Tonga in the early nineteenth century, the island is in for a blood bath that few can escape.

The second major point about the kava ceremony is that *it is a conserving and conservative institution*. This aspect of the ceremony is less explicit than the emphasis on titles. It is unformulated though certainly not unconscious.

The seating and serving order of the kava ceremony are a partial substitute for a written history, for the seating of each title, especially in the royal kava ceremony, is supposed to be explainable in terms of actual historical events. I was so intrigued by this aspect of the ceremony that I spent many months asking titleholders why they sat where they did in the royal kava ceremony. My husband and I were frustrated and puzzled to find that many titleholders did not know why they sat where they did. Eventually it dawned on us that this in itself was the significant point. Forgetting is selective. The seating of titles that are still politically important is known and understood. The reasons for the seating are forgotten if the titles are politically unimportant today.

Personal rank and political power can change very quickly in Tonga; it takes a long time for the titles and the kava ceremony to catch up. Two or three generations of "bad" marriages can drastically reduce the personal rank of the man who holds a title, but the title itself and its position in the kava ceremony are hardly affected. Once a drop in personal rank is combined with a drop in the political power and influence of the titleholder, however, the rank of the title and its position in the kava ceremony gradually begin to decline as well. People start to forget the reasons for the seating of the title. Its position in the circle may be changed to accommodate a more important title. Eventually unimportant titles cease to be appointed and even their ceremonial place is forgotten.

Occasionally there is a massive reshuffle of seating arrangements to take account of changes in political power. This happened after the death of the last sacred king in 1865. While the sacred kingship was still in existence, the kava circle of the secular king, the Tuʻi Kanokupolu, included only those titles that were derived from the Tuʻi Kanokupolu line and were genealogically junior to the Tuʻi Kanokupolu title. But when the sacred kingship lapsed in 1865 and the Tuʻi Kanokupolu became the sole king, the titles derived from the Tuʻi Tonga line had to be fitted into the Tuʻi Konokupolu's kava circle, even though many of these titles were genealogically senior to the title of the Tuʻi Kanokupolu. This conflict between actual political power and the genealogical seniority of titles was surmounted by a sort of legal fiction. Before he died the last Tuʻi Tonga transferred his sacred prerogatives to the Tuʻi Kanokupolu. There is some doubt, however, about how he disposed of his kava prerogatives. Some say that he handed these over to the "King of the Second House," a very ancient title that stands in the relation of "brother" to the Tuʻi Tonga title. The difficulty was solved by a marriage between the Tuʻi Kanokupolu line and the "King of the Second House" line, the end result being that the "King of the Second House" title is now held by the Royal Family, and the present incumbent is the King's younger brother.

Thus the kava ceremony changes to take account of changes in the power of titles, but it changes more slowly than the rank and power of individuals, and the changes are phrased as much as possible in the idiom of titles and their genealogical seniority.

The third major point about the ceremony is that *it expresses a fundamental contradiction*. We were first alerted to this aspect of the ceremony by comparing the many different social contexts in which it takes place. One thing all these social situations have in common is a confrontation of people of different status. In everyday life these people can be expected to harbour feelings of jealousy and resentment about their differential privileges. At the same time, in spite of the antagonisms, during the ceremony there is a strong feeling of being at harmony together in a group. As Tongans put it, "You do not drink kava with an enemy."

In brief, the ceremony says, "We are all united," but it also says, "We are all different." And the element of difference contains another contradiction, for it makes two contrary communications. It says, "We are differentiated and interdependent," but it also says, "We are unequal. Our titles differ in seniority. And some of us do not have titles at all." In other words the kava ceremony expresses ambivalence – the simultaneous presence of contradictory feelings. I do not mean that each participant in the ceremony becomes consciously aware of the sort of emotional ambivalence that I have described. Most people seemed to be more aware of feelings of unity and harmony than of feelings of antagonism and rivalry – or at any rate more willing to talk about feelings of unity and harmony. The feelings of antagonism showed themselves more in what people did than in what they said. At formal ceremonies we observed many minor breaches of *tapu*. One's hands should be clasped in one's lap throughout the ceremony, for example, but our photographs show that people often moved their hands about. Similarly people are not supposed to talk in a very formal ceremony, but people were whispering away almost all the time – usually uncomplimentary remarks about the way the ceremony was being conducted.

Within the prescribed events of the ceremony there is only a little scope for the formal expression of conflict, envy, and jealousy. For example, there is one titleholder whose duty it is to see that the kava is well prepared and that everyone behaves properly. In 1959 the incumbent of this title was a man of comparatively low personal rank; he aimed his sharpest reprimands at two titleholders of very high personal rank, men whom he would never have dared to challenge in any other social context. But he was not alone; all the men of low rank relished his performance. Even in this case, the titleholder concerned was not ceremonially obliged to abuse the men of high rank. What he did was left to his own initiative.

In other words, the formal, prescribed events of the ceremony emphasize unity and harmony. Rivalry, jealousy, and envy are widely and consciously felt, to varying degrees, but their expression is either unofficial or is left to individual initiative.[8]

The myth of the origin of the kava helps to elucidate the contradictory attitudes implied in the ceremony. When the late Queen was reflecting on this myth she said it expressed the mutual sacrifice and understanding between ruler and subjects that was essential to keep Tonga united and strong. It was this mutual sacrifice and understanding the kava ceremony was commemorating. I agreed with this interpretation, but said I thought the myth also expressed suspiciousness and hostility between ruler and subjects. The couple sacrificed their most precious possession, their daughter, but she did have leprosy; eating her might have harmed the King. The King's refusal to eat her was partly an act of generosity, but he was also protecting himself. And when the couple brought in the plant, he thought at first that it might be poisonous. If I had thought of it at the time, I might have added that the couple's sacrifice was an insult to the King, for to call someone a "man eater" is a common insult in Tonga. And, in addition to everything else, spitefulness is implied in the couple's heroic act. It is as if they were saying to their King, "Look at the dreadful thing you have made us do."

After some discussion the Queen said that such suspiciousness between ruler and subjects was probably inevitable and natural. Perhaps what the myth and the ceremony meant was that mutual understanding and sacrifice was possible in spite of doubt and suspicion.

This was as far as I got with the myth while we were still in Tonga. After we left I wished I had asked many other questions about it, for it now seems to me that there are many other levels of meaning and feeling in it. If I were doing the study again I would ask why the little island of 'Eueiki? Why the famine, the cannibalism, and above all, the leprosy, all of which are known in Tonga but have always been rare? Why the particular food plant, the kape, and what of the many different triangular situations mentioned in the various versions of the myth? There is one issue that I think worth including even though I did not explore it fully at the time. The myth seems to deal with the progression of psychic experience from a very primitive level in which good and bad are confused and contaminated to one in which good and bad are better differentiated, so that it becomes possible to distinguish the symbol from the object. The burial, in other words, transforms the contaminated, sacrificed girl into the two plants, the kava, which is still potentially poisonous, and its antidote, the sugar cane.[9]

The kava myth helps to understand what the plant symbolizes and why Tongans regard it as strong stuff, but it does not throw much light on the actual events of the ceremony – the pounding, pouring in of water, serving, etc. For this we must turn, very briefly, to another myth that almost paraphrases some of the events of the kava ceremony. The explicit claim of this myth to relevance in connection with the kava ceremony is that it is concerned with the origin of the system of titles that the kava ceremony ceremonially displays. None of my informants pointed out the close parallel between the events of the kava ceremony and the events of the myth, though I was told the myth in the context of discussing the ceremony so that there was obviously an associative link. I myself was only half aware of the connections between the myth and the ceremony while I was still in Tonga, I think this half-awareness is similar to Tongans' feelings about the myth. A connection is dimly felt without being explicitly thought out.

The story of the myth is simple and melodramatic. A god from the sky has intercourse with a woman of the earth and a son is born, called 'Aho'eitu. When he grows up he wants to see his father and, following instructions from his mother, he climbs up to the sky by a giant ironwood tree. 'Aho'eitu is enthusiastically welcomed by his father, who thinks at first that 'Aho'eitu is a god of even higher rank than himself. The father then sends his newfound son, without introduction, to see his other sons in the sky, presumably the sons of sky mothers. When 'Aho'eitu's half-brothers see everyone admiring 'Aho'eitu because of his beauty, and when they hear rumours that he is their father's son, they tear 'Aho'eitu to pieces and eat him up. The father suspects what they have done. He calls for a wooden bowl and makes his sons vomit into it. This is very reminiscent of the former custom of chewing the kava, of the statements that kava sometimes makes people feel like vomiting, and of the linguistic association with nausea. The sons vomit up 'Aho'eitu's flesh and blood, they confess, and the father sends people to collect the bones and the head, which are also put in the bowl. Water is poured into the bowl, as in the kava ceremony. The pouring in of the water, as I have noted above, is one of the most sacred moments of the ceremony.

After some time 'Aho'eitu begins to take shape and finally sits up in the bowl. Then the father calls all his sons together and tells them that 'Aho'eitu will go back to the earth to become the first king of Tonga, the first Tu'i Tonga. At this point, the myth says, affection awakens in the hearts of the brothers, and they plead with their father to be allowed to go with 'Aho'eitu. The father agrees. Four of the brothers go down to earth to serve 'Aho'eitu as his matāpule. The fifth and eldest brother cannot be king, the father says, because he is guilty of murder, but he will be the King of the Second House (Tu'i Fale Ua). If 'Aho'eitu's line should die out then the King of the Second House will become King. (This is the rationale for the belief, mentioned above, that the last Tu'i Tonga bequeathed his kava prerogatives to the King of the Second House.) There are several other myths and legends that purport to show that all through Tongan history the descendants of the King of the Second House tried to murder 'Aho'eitu's descendants in order to wipe out his line.

Using the leads provided by this myth, I think that the chewing or, nowadays, the pounding of the kava is a symbolic repetition of psychic cannibalism, representing a desire both to get possession of the qualities of the beautiful envied brother and son and to destroy him. This mixture of admiration, greed, and destructive envy is a familiar theme from the analysis of the cannibalistic fantasies of patients. But of course in the ceremony it is kava that is pounded or chewed, not a person; this symbolic transformation is taken up in the kava myth.

The idea that the pounding of the kava may represent cannibalistic destruction of an envied object, a brother or son, is consistent with the fact that the people in the outer group, who used to chew and now help to pound the kava, stand in the relation of "child" or "younger brother" to the titleholders of the main circle.[10] In other words, the kava plant is presented to the presiding chief as 'Aho'eitu was presented to his father. The father then sends the kava/son to be destroyed. The destruction is carried out by "children", though perhaps also by "younger brothers" (of the 'father') – an indication that people in the "father" category are involved in the destruction. The father's envy and destructiveness are hinted at in the myth, for the father at first thinks his son is of higher rank, and then sends him to his other sons without introduction. He immediately suspects his other sons of murder and cannibalism, as if the thought were not far from his own mind. So far as I could discover none of this is conscious. That is, participants in the ceremony are aware to some extent of their envy and jealousy of one another, and most of them know the two myths, but they do not consciously link the two sets of knowledge.

In the 'Aho'eitu myth incorporation and destruction are followed by healing water and the awakening of good feeling. Once this has taken place the kava is served, that is, the experience can be re-incorporated in a form that is soothing and tranquilizing. But the transformation is not always successful, for strong green kava sometimes makes people want to vomit. In other words, the method of preparing the kava can be seen as an effort to convert envy and jealousy into remorse and affection, to change poisonous feelings into feelings of tranquility and harmony. But other myths and legends make it clear that envy and jealousy can never be overcome entirely and permanently, just as they can never be eradicated from everyday life. The feelings appropriate to cannibalism are here to stay. Envy, greed, and jealousy are always with us, but so are admiration and remorse. Conflict is inevitable. The kava ceremony states the particular Tongan variant of this general human dilemma and tries to communicate the idea that the forces of love can be made stronger than the forces of hate, at least temporarily. Once again, people do not think all this out consciously. They feel there is something good about the ceremony, something healing, but no one phrases it in terms of reparation to a damaged object and the re-incorporation of the whole experience.

As with the kava myth, there are many other possible interpretations of the 'Aho'eitu myth. One version of the myth, for example, goes into considerable detail about the way the brothers threw 'Aho'eitu's head into a bush, which caused the bush to become poisonous. Perhaps this is a way of talking about castration, with the customary theme of power residing in the cut-off head/phallus. There is a great deal of ambiguity in the myth about who is killing whom. Obviously the half-brothers kill 'Aho'eitu, but he is the father's favorite so they are attacking the father as well. The father himself sends 'Aho'eitu to his death, as I have indicated above. And what of the mother far away in Tonga? 'Aho'eitu is her only son, so she is being attacked and perhaps destroyed. But it is she who tells 'Aho'eitu how to get to heaven in the first place. And what of the link with the kava myth itself in which a daughter is destroyed? Is it a daughter only or also a mother in disguise?

I do not think one can select any particular interpretation as the "right" one. None of them can be "proved" or "disproved", at least not by the methods appropriate to the consulting-room, nor by any other method that I could think of at the time. In the consulting room, where the two partners to the relationship are supposed to be discovering psychic truth, however painful and improbable, one can make interpretations about unconscious cannibalism or unconscious desires to castrate a brother, and judge from the patient's reactions whether the interpretations are close to home or wide of the mark. One always has the transference situation, of which one has direct experience, as a yardstick against which the manifest content of the patient's material can be compared. In Tonga I was often aware of transference, especially of the more obvious aspects of it: the attitude that I was a foreigner with whom a cultural "front" had to be kept up; attempts to "use" me in one way or another to gain some social end; the feeling that I was a sympathetic outsider with whom emotional burdens could be shared.

But I never felt it appropriate to interpret the transference. I found I was prepared to raise such issues as the likelihood of hostility between rulers and subject, particularly with a very secure and much-loved monarch, but I was not prepared to try out interpretations of cannibalism or castration with anyone, so unprepared, in fact, that I could hardly think of such interpretations intellectually until I had left the field. The social situation I was in did not sanction such endeavors.

From among the many possible interpretations, I have emphasized the theme of cannibalism and reparation, of the destruction and restoration of a brother/son, because it seemed to me the most obvious, the most consistent with the events and the status differentials of the ceremony, and the most in accord with constellations of envy and rivalry in other aspects of Tongan social life. It helped to order the facts in a new and comparatively simple pattern that I have not seen before. But it seems very likely that at various times and to various Tongans any or all of the variants described above might be unconsciously meaningful. The ambiguity of myths and ceremonies is part of their point. It gives individuals some leeway to play with experience, to make culture their own possession.

The particular beauty of the kava ceremony, at least for me, is that it deals with problems on so many different levels at the same time. It clarifies social principles and roles. It puts a temporary brake on certain types of rapid change. It states and partly resolves problems of dependence and envy, and of interdependence and rivalry, some aspects of which are generated by the peculiarly Tongan system of social stratification, and some by the universal human attributes of having a capacity for thinking and feeling and being brought up in a society.

Small-scale societies tend to have multidimensional ceremonies of this type more frequently than we do. This suggests that time and continuity of shared experience are needed to build a ceremony that can transmit messages on many different levels at the same time. A long history of interpersonal contact and conflict makes possible the development of a symbolic statement in which universal human experiences are meaningfully linked with unique social circumstances.

Notes

1 The paper was originally given in 1967 as one of the Winter Lectures on Psychoanalysis to members of the general public interested in psychoanalysis. It was first published in 1968 (Sutherland, 1968). The Foundations Fund for Research in Psychiatry generously provided me with a fellowship to analyze and write up the material. I am deeply indebted to the many Tongans who helped me to record and understand the ceremony and to the several colleagues with whom I have discussed the interpretations of it, especially Miss Pearl King, Miss Isabel Menzies, Mrs T. T. S. Hayley, and my husband, James Spillius.

2 Many anthropologists, especially in Britain, do not share my view that under-

standing of unconscious mental processes is relevant to the analysis of social events. They are particularly apprehensive that psychoanalysts will attempt to explain social events in terms of individual needs. Their attitude is paralleled by the psychoanalyst's conviction that the complex events of the consulting room cannot be reduced to the level of neuro-anatomy. See especially Leach (1958); Lévi-Strauss (1964), especially Chapter 3; Gluckman (1964); Turner (1964); and Fox (1967).

3 For discussion of the chemical constituents and physiological action of kava see especially Keller and Klohs (1963). Dr C. R. B. Joyce, Reader in Psycho-Pharmacology at the University of London has very kindly reviewed the literature for me and reports the following conclusions: "All in all, my impression remains firm that this substance is not remarkable for its pharmacological activity; that such active properties as it contains have not been isolated so far (there is more activity on animals in the watery or chloroform extract, for example, than in any so far identified substance); and that the whole situation is a remarkable example of the placebo phenomenon in a wide and important social setting." Personal communciation, May 1967.

4 A similar institution is found among certain Bantu tribes. A. I. Richards (1950) calls it "positional succession"; I. Cunnison (1956) calls it "perpetual kinship".

5 Tongans say that cannibalism was not indigenous to Tonga, but that early in the nineteenth century groups of young Tongan warriors visited Fiji, adopted the practice of eating slain enemies, and continued to practise this custom when they returned home to Tonga. The new custom was not adopted with enthusiasm and was soon abandoned.

6 The analysis of these three principles of social differentiation, political authority (titles), political power, and personal rank was first worked out by my husband, James Spillius, and was presented to the Tenth Pacific Science Congress at Honolulu in 1961 in a paper entitled "Rank and Political Structure in Tonga".

7 This complex of ceremonies is a striking example of what Max Gluckman has called the "ritualization" of social relations in small-scale ("tribal") societies. He attributes this "ritualization" to "... the fact that each social relation in a subsistence economy tends to serve manifold purposes ... it is from this situation that I see emerging the relatively great development of special customs and stylised etiquette to mark the different roles that a man or woman is playing at any one moment" (Gluckman, 1962, pp. 26–7).

8 In recent years anthropologists have devoted much attention to conflict and ambivalence and their expression in religion and ritual as well as in everyday affairs. See especially Fortes (1959); Gluckman (1955), (1963) especially the Introduction and Chapter 3 entitled "Rituals of Rebellion in South-East Africa" and (1965), especially Chapter 6 entitled "Mystical Disturbance and Ritual Adjustment"; Leach (1965); Turner (1957) and (1964).

One problem of particular relevance is that some rituals incorporate conflict directly into the prescribed events of the ritual whereas others, like the kava ceremony, imply conflict but do not prescribe its enactment. But a comparative discussion of this topic would lead me too far from the immediate problem of the kava ceremony.

9 On the differentiation of "good" and "bad" as part of normal psychic development, see especially W. R. Bion (1957), (1958), and (1962). See also Hanna

Segal (1964). On the differentiation of symbol from object see Hanna Segal (1957).

10 The early accounts of kava ceremonies in which the kava was chewed instead of pounded do not specify whether the chewing was done only by the "children" in the outer group or also by the "younger brothers". All we know is that the people who did the chewing were in the outer group and that a considerable number of them took part in the chewing. Nowadays only the kava maker does the actual pounding.

References

Bion, W. R., 1957. Differentiation of the Psychotic from the Non-Psychotic Part of the Personality. *International Journal of Psychoanalysis* 38
  1958. On Hallucination. *IJP* 39
  1962. The Psycho-Analytic Study of Thinking. *IJP* 43
Cunnison, I., 1956. Perpetual Kinship. A Political Institution of the Luapulu Peoples. *Rhodes–Livingstone Journal* No. 20
Fortes, M., 1959. *Oedipus and Job in West African Religion*. Cambridge, Cambridge University Press
Fox, R., 1967. *Totem and Taboo* Reconsidered. In E. R. Leach (ed.), *The Structural Study of Myth and Totemism*. ASA Monograph 5. London, Tavistock
Freud, S., 1913. *Totem and Taboo*. In *The Standard Edition of The Complete Psychological Works of Sigmund Freud* Vol. 13. London, Hogarth
Gifford, E. W., 1924. *Togan Myths and Tales*. Bernice P. Bishop Museum Bulletin 8, Honolulu
Gluckman, M., 1955. *Custom and Conflict in Africa*. Oxford, Blackwell
  1962. Les Rites de Passage. In M. Gluckman (ed.), *Essays on the Ritual of Social Relations*. Manchester, Manchester University Press
  1963. *Order and Rebellion in Tribal Africa*. London, Cohen & West
  (ed.) 1964. *Closed Systems and Open Minds*. Edinburgh and London, Oliver & Boyd
  1965. *Politics, Law and Ritual in Tribal Society*. Oxford, Blackwell
Keller, F., and Klohs, M. W., 1963. A Review of the Chemistry and Pharmacology of the Constituents of Piper methysticum. *Lloydia* 26 (1)
Leach, E. R., 1958. Magical Hair. *J. Roy. Anthrop. Inst.* 88 part 2
  1965. The Nature of War. *Disarmament and Arms Control* 3 (2)
Lévi-Strauss, C., 1964. *Totemism*. (Trans. R. Needham). London, Merlin Press
Mariner, W., 1818. *An Account of the Natives of the Tonga Islands*. (2nd edn.) 2 vols. (ed. John Martin.) London, John Murray
Richards, A. I., 1950. Some Types of Family Structure amongst The Central Bantu. In A. R. Radcliffe-Brown and D. Forde (eds.), *African Systems of Kinship and Marriage*. London, Oxford University Press
  1956. *Chisungu: A girls' initiation ceremony among the Bemba of Northern Rhodesia*. London, Faber & Faber
Seagal, H., 1957. Notes on Symbol Formation, *IJP* 38
Segal H., 1964. *Introduction to the Work of Melanie Klein*. London, Heinemann

Spillius, J., 1961. (Unpublished paper.) Rank and Political Structure in Tonga presented to the Tenth Pacific Science Congress, Honolulu

Sutherland, J. D. (ed.), 1968. *The Psychoanalytic Approach*. London, Baillière, Tindall, & Cassell

Turner, V. W., 1957. *Schism and Continuity in an African Society*. Manchester, Manchester University Press

    1964. Symbols in Ndembu Ritual. In M. Gluckman (ed.), *Closed Systems and Open Minds*. Edinburgh and London, Oliver and Boyd

Reprinted from *The Interpretation of Ritual: Essays in Honour of A. I. Richards*, edited by J. S. La Fontaine. London, Tavistock, 1972. Published therein as "Psychoanalysis and ceremony."

11. Holding time still with cups of tea

Haim Hazan

Introduction

The occasion of tea drinking in English culture is so linked to certain divisions of the day that the notion of temporality seems to be imbued in its essence. Tea time or just "tea", a night cup or a morning cup, serve for some people as temporal codes almost as accurate and recurrent as mechanically set markers. Unlike arbitrary commonly accepted means of indicating time, tea drinking is socially generated and hence is more manipulable and versatile than other time reckoning devices. The main theme of this chapter is that behavior related to tea drinking can serve to organize temporal experience.

The anthropological and sociological study of temporal behavior has been mainly geared to deal with the relations between such phenomena and social systems,[1] cultural orientations[2] or ecological conditions.[3] Nevertheless, the exploration of temporal properties in a set of specific symbols as an analytic unit has only been scantly investigated. Except for Roth (1963), Zerubavel (1977) and a few other studies, the nature of the basic symbolic ingredients of the management of social time remains uncovered. Hence the task of processing and decoding temporal symbols is still a field of inquiry for which pretested analytic tools are not readily available. Indeed, references to symbols of time have been casually made,[4] but no research concentrates on this issue as its focal point. This chapter will endeavor to understand a few of the problems involved in the study of temporal symbolic behavior.

A starting point for such an attempt might be Leach's (1971) metaphorical distinction between linear time and cyclical time. Both modes of time are embedded in cultural values and behavior and as such are almost indivisible. Nonetheless, certain social contexts are impregnated with symbols predominantly oriented to either form. Conventional tea drinking is essentially of a cyclical nature and I would maintain that this particular property qualifies it to serve as a prevalent symbolic code in the constitution of situations where the general structure of the time universe is nonlinear.

In its frequency, regularity, universality and uniformity, drinking tea is an established cultural pattern deeply entrenched in the daily life of English people. Douglas has observed that "now that the child–adult contrast no longer dominates in the family, tea has been demoted from a necessary, place in the daily sequence of meals to an irregular appearance among week-end drinks and no rules govern the accompanying solids" (Douglas 1975: 255). However, there is more to be said.

To begin with, the knowledge necessary for the procedures of preparing, serving and drinking tea is common and requires no special training or skills, and the same applies to the normative behavior related to that knowledge. This is not to say that there are no variations in structure and ingredients of the custom but the essence remains accessible to almost everybody who wishes to partake in it.

The range of meanings imparted explicitly or implicitly to tea-drinking is as wide as the specific personal and social contexts existing in each tea-drinking event. Although there are some popularly accepted vague interpretations attributed to tea, they are flexible and non-committal and thereby do not delimit the symbol to any specific contexts. Furthermore, this diffuse quality of conventional tea drinking makes it amenable to the unstructured rules of Simmel's timeless sociability[5] (Wolff 1964:42–57) or even to the elevated antistructure of Turner's concept of communities as being "in and out of time" (Turner 1969:96).

This last property of timelessness might be considered as contradicting the observation made earlier that tea drinking serves as a time-reckoning device. However, bearing in mind the two dimensions of time – the cyclical and the linear – they could be easily reconciled. The social event of drinking tea would not normally be regarded as an element constituting reciprocal relationship,[6] i.e., one invitation for tea is not necessarily conditioned by a previous similar occasion nor does it call for a future gathering. Each occasion of taking tea is engendered by another set of social situations and interests and hence is a concomitant of other realities. By itself, however, the social consumption of tea is in Luscher's terms (Luscher 1974) an element in a sequence of events, but not a part of a duration – a meaningful progressive temporal pattern.[7]

These characteristics would suggest that tea drinking is a highly versatile, rather unstructured symbol which could be smoothly transferred from one setting to another and from one realm of meaning to an alternative one. Yet, it would retain its shared essence within the configuration of English culture. Moreover, I would like to argue that the lack of linear properties endows tea drinking with qualities of a connective symbol, namely a code of conduct which could be employed to create a sense of continuity where old normative structures and value systems cease to function as meaningful guidelines. The following case study will demonstrate how taking tea operates as an organizer of newly acquired experience on the one hand, and as a bridge between it and the remains of the old existential world on the other hand.

The Day Centre people – an overview[8]

The population under study consisted of about 400 members of a Day Centre for elderly Jewish residents in one of the poorest boroughs of London. Tracing the stages of their life histories within the context of their socio-economic background would unfold a continuous process of deterioration and disintegration accelerating rapidly towards the later phases of their life course.

Being the second generation of East European immigrant Jews who settled in the East End of London at the turn of the century, the members of the Centre were subjected to poverty, illiteracy and social alienation. The low income earned from unsteady employment in semi-skilled occupations was supplemented by support donated by charitable organizations.

Nonetheless, the organization of the community which had been founded on close-knit networks of extended families and ex-compatriots, provided a thriving system of institutions for mutual support. Following the destruction of the East End during World War II, the Jewish inhabitants of the area were evacuated to the north-east of London where community life had undergone a major transformation. Children and well-to-do contemporaries moved to more affluent districts of the metropolis leaving behind an ageing population suffering from growing dearth of community life, decreased standard of living and the scourges of social isolation. Increased restriction in mobility and general functioning due to ill-health also contributed to the fundamental experience of alienation and deterioration.

This change was not anchored in a corresponding set of social definitions which could constitute their interpretation of the process and regulate their behavior. The sequestration of the members of the Day Centre from their former social environment – contemporaries, children, public institutions and interests – also engendered a state of disenchantment and a growing discrepancy between the values of the non-aged society and the meaning attached to their own existence.

Furthermore, their everyday experience of the outside world revealed another incongruity. The external social conceptions of old age as communicated to them by various agents – social workers, welfare administrators, volunteers and relatives – made a sharp contradiction between the social image of the aged and their actual daily experience. This image, upon commonly accepted preconceptions and taken-for-granted stereotypes, presents the elderly as a stagnant category disengaged from the dynamics of social life and confined within the boundaries of essential physical and material needs. Thus the isolation of the Day Centre community was interrupted only by catering for daily necessities, liaising with welfare organizations and seeking guidance as to the most effective means to utilize social services.

The gap between social conceptions and personal experience engendered among members a strong sense of the arbitrariness and inadequacy of old associations and commitments and thus set the bounds for a viable alternative reality, focused on the Centre. The main constituent of this reality was the reconstruction of their time universe.

In the Day Centre they created a present-bound, change-arresting reality, founded on a new set of values obliterating parts of the past and forestalling the future, and on a set of relations between events which by its structure and form maintained the reality of the "eternal now" of the Day Centre.

Members refused to refer to their previous socio-economic differences[9] and selected from their past only those parts reenacting situations of egalitarian comradeship and care. Thus membership in friendship clubs, service in the army, periods of hospitalization and participation in the anti-fascist demonstrations of the thirties were all cherished reminiscences. Alternative solutions to their problems, such as old age homes, geriatric wards or even returning to family care were regarded as undesirable. The imminent possibility of death was also denied by means of equating it to a departure from the Day Centre and hence removing it from their everyday environment.

The Day Centre became a total setting demarcated rigidly from its external surroundings by an internal code of behavior reflecting an inverted configuration of values and structure. Thus the notion of care and help was elevated to a fundamental criterion for assessing human conduct. The relevance of that moral code to the emergence of a present-bound society rests with the structure of its practices rather than with its content. The interactional patterns developed in the Day Centre denied reciprocity of giving and taking; participants were not classified as either "helpers" or "helped". Hence, those who had something to spare – time, attention, advice or material objects – passed it on to the first individual in need regardless of their personal relationship. Any pre-existing relations, for example by virtue of marriage, previous life-long friendship, were placed under insuperable pressure to be belittled and disintegrated. Participants dissociated their roles in the care system of the Day Centre from any long or short term considerations, plans or memories; so much so that assistance was often offered to a previously unacquainted person who seemed to need help. Furthermore, a hierarchical order of helpful versus helpless participants was avoided by the dual nature of one's position in the Day Centre, namely the constant interchange between being a helper and being helped. Even participants who did not feel in need of help were expected to play the role of a potential recipient of it. They were evidently engaged in constructing an undifferentiated, change-proof society.

It is my contention that taking tea was an added dimension of the change-proof universe in the Day Centre. By its structural properties the symbol of social tea drinking reinforced and maintained the boundaries of the Day Centre as opposed to its external environment.

The procedures of tea serving

Tea was served at the Day Centre twice a day for a nominal charge of 2p. Morning tea was prepared separately on each floor whereas the four o'clock tea was brewed and served in the dining area downstairs. The procedures constituting tea time involved three groups of activities; brewing, serving and cleaning-up, all of them performed and supervised by a group of participants who invested themselves with the title of "tea volunteers". These were mainly able-bodied women who had joined the Day Centre in order to escort their incapacitated husbands or in the capacity of "helpers" – a self-bestowed status designed to distinguish them from ordinary members. Social gatherings always preceded the distribution of tea. Thus planned activities such as talks, discussions, meetings or a dance, as well as card-playing, small-talk or sing-along groupings, were held in the dining room in anticipation of the serving of tea. At the same time other parts of the building were evacuated by their occupiers and the full number of the daily attendants were present together downstairs without any physical visible barrier between them. Even the more handicapped participants who used to spend most of the day marooned in armchairs in the lounge attached to the dining room, made an effort, aided by others, to have their tea in company with the rest.

The procedures of serving the tea started when all the members were seated. Cups of unsweetened, brewed milky tea were handed over in an orderly, impartial fashion. Meanwhile one of the "volunteers" would discreetly collect the tea-money from the participants. Biscuits and sugar were portioned off separately and although restricted, requests for second helpings were invariably granted.

That set of activities was seemingly a straightforward operation designed to serve a limited specific purpose. Indeed it appeared that the management was almost flawless and the expressed satisfaction of the drinkers was complete. Nonetheless, such an impression should be revised if the utterances and the interactions related to tea drinking are to be considered.

Tea time and the construction of reality in the centre

Among the various means maintaining the boundaries of the Day Centre time universe, tea-taking occupied an important place. Firstly it touched upon almost every sphere of life in the Day Centre and thus became the most holistic symbol in the construction of that reality. Secondly it appeared to encompass a wide gamut of different situations and actions. Thirdly, in its uniformity and relative immutability the behavioral code for tea played a major role in stabilizing and regulating a set of seemingly precarious, unstructured relationships. This section will attempt to elucidate the various manifestations of that role by describing and analyzing the function of tea time embodied in a number of such sets. Each interactional pattern discussed will also be treated on the merits of its temporal properties.

1.

The participants' everyday experience was rife with events engendered by crisis situations such as illness and death. The nature of the pre-Centre state of existence depicted at the Day Centre was one of confusion, disorientation and alienation. Hence, while relating to everyday difficulties or critical turning points in their lives, participants reiterated emphatically their inability to make sense of that reality or to adjust themselves to its daunting impositions. However, in all references of that kind tea drinking was recurrently mentioned as an act reflecting stability, order and familiarity. A woman participant, when recalling her friend's last minutes, ended the description by saying "and of course, just before she went she had a nice cup of tea". Another participant who joined that conversation related a "mugging" incident which ended as the victim, having returned to her home, "made a cup of tea for herself and went to bed".

Their recollections also drew on a general conception of pre-Centre world as a shattered reality where even tea procedures were in disarray. A participant who wanted to describe the incoherent experience of his previous life stated that "when I was younger people knew how to serve a cup of tea, before I came to the Centre they had forgotten even this". Another commented on the status transformation he had undergone in his synagogue congregation. He maintained that he would not enter his synagogue again as the new warden "does not know me and won't even give me a cup of tea". The speaker, who once enjoyed a position of high social esteem in his community, was emphasizing that at present in the outside world he was no longer regarded as even worthy of the everyday gesture of respect and amicability embedded in tea drinking.

Associations between tea and outside social reality did not confine themselves to the spheres of past meanings. On various occasions participants commented on the future possibility of sheltered, institutionalised life in an old-age home or a geriatric ward where the range of controlling one's life was considerably curtailed. In all such discussions the ultimate demonstration of an absolute dependency was the fact that "in an old age home you can't even make yourself a cup of tea". It is noteworthy that participants acknowledged the fact that tea drinking in itself was not in jeopardy nor was the scheduling of the act. What represented the lack of individual autonomy was the inability to perform the ritual of tea making and to select the participants with whom one could share the preparation and the drinking.

2.

Although tea time was a cherished landmark in the scheduling of the day at the Centre and in that respect fulfilled a parallel function to meal time or dancing-time, there were occasions when those temporal boundaries were encroached. Such breaches occurred when participants were so absorbed in an extra Day Centre time world which thus created a complete disengagement from the routine pattern of repetitive, predictable behavior. Incidents such as "forgetting" to attend the tea-service or overtly foregoing it could be analysed as products of a certain disorder in the normative relations between boundaries; for example, tea-drinking habits during sessions of the local therapy group: the conception of the Centre as a therapeutic environment was a predominant feature of the social worker's view of the purposes and benefits of the establishment. This approach took a practical turn with the setting up of a special framework for participants who experienced emotional distress more than others and showed psychological difficulties in coping with recent bereavements or severe loneliness. People were invited by the supervisor on a personal basis to take part in the discussions and the membership consisted of participants who confessed to being unhappy and depressed together with others who took an explicit interest in "helping" them.

Although conducted by the supervisor, there were no rules as to the manner of speaking and the subjects for discussion. The only strictly watched, unanimously accepted rule was that of confidentiality, namely that no information should be allowed to leak from the group to non-members. This represented a sharp contrast to the normal lack of internal barriers characterizing the Centre and consequently evoked excessive interest and manufactured rumours about the group proceedings. The fact that participants were encouraged to express their individuality instead of submerging their differences and identities into the Centre's collective melting pot was quite a novelty and unsurprisingly the possibility of breaking out of the Centre's mould seemed to be quite intriguing as well as threatening.

The meetings of the group were scheduled to end so as to coincide with tea time. However, the nature of the discussions and the deep involvement of the members seldom allowed the session to break up in time for tea. On such occasions the leader of the group would offer the choice of joining the rest of the participants or carrying on over tea time. Invariably the response was unanimously in favour of the second alternative.

Other ad-hoc discussion groups followed the same pattern. Whenever a subject of prime relevance was broached and debated participants would show their engrossment by overlooking tea time and hence indicating the existence of a tentative boundary between the Day Centre routine and the other reality into which they were submerged. Such was the case with religious issues, death and bereavement and problems of institutional care – all of which were germane to counter realities outside the Centre world. Nonetheless, tea time was never missed when a discussion on seemingly marginal matters such as holidays and everyday trivialities was held.

3.

The manipulation of tea codes was interwoven not only with the encroachment of out-Centre boundaries into the participants' world, but also, as manifested in the case of the therapy group, with social rules of exclusion and inclusion. The issue of participation or non-participation in a certain tea-setting could be construed in terms of gaining access to or being barred from interactional arenas embedded in the Day Centre reality. Thus differentiation between both members of staff and participants and among participants themselves were often expressed through relationships which revolved around the setting of tea time.

Although the spontaneous system of care among participants was based on a set of principles requiring unconditional help according to need and irrespective of other relationships, the attachment and commitment of participants to the Day Centre is varied. Different participants strike different balances between their life in the Day Centre and other external involvements. This multiple experience also generates a variety of groups within that world. Participants who come to the Day Centre merely to seek a day sanctuary or even just to enjoy a cheap hot meal are regarded by others as being in the periphery of participation and hence are treated as outsiders, precluded from some of the informal activities. This rule of entry applied to various kinds of conceived participation is namely that the proximity to the core of the Day Centre life is determined by the degree of centrality of one's involvement in the Day Centre in proportion to involvement in an out-centre life, or, in temporal terms – to involvement in an external time universe.

The norms of tea-drinking differentiation are governed by the above principle. Participants who considered others as only loosely associated with the Centre world would also avoid having tea with them. This exclusion could go as far as asking the "borderline cases" to have their tea somewhere else simply by moving to another unoccupied space in the Day Centre. On a few occasions certain participants had their tea sent to them a few minutes prior to tea time so the possibility of them coming down to join the rest of the participants could be averted. An invitation to join a group of participants for tea was regarded as granting a right of access to that group on other occasions. However, imposing one's company on an established group for tea uninvited would be usually frowned upon and the cost of such an attempt would be a heavy one to bear.

A few events concerning one defined group of participants could illustrate that normative pattern: Five participants who showed no other interest in their lives but the Day Centre, established a close-knit set of relationships among themselves – they spent most of their time in one anothers' company and would organize daily activities such as discussion groups and afternoon entertainment. Tea time always presented them with the opportunity to appear together as an outstanding clique as three incidents which occurred during tea time will demonstrate.

A drama group set up by those five participants started rehearsing for a light-hearted show. The rehearsals took place in the afternoon and were scheduled to finish at tea time. Nonetheless the members of the group insisted on having their tea during the course of the activity – a demand which signified social, physical and temporal exclusion since the tea was served in the upper hall just for the group and a short while before it was served to the remainder of the participants.

The second incident occurred when a participant who was renowned as the "local pauper" and who used to spend only a little time at the Day Centre, tried to join the group for tea by way of initiating a conversation with them. The reaction to this was instant and conclusive – he was sternly asked not to involve himself with them and to "go and beg for your tea somewhere else". Being "social cases" themselves, the risk of identification as "beggars" by association with the "pauper" had to be forestalled. This was done symbolically and publicly by avoiding his company for tea.

A reverse case happened when the group decided to look after newcomers to the Day Centre and to introduce them to the way of life of the participants. Such new members were taken care of by a member of the group who would initiate them to the social world of the Day Centre through partaking in the tea ritual. Thus, new participants enjoyed the privilege of having their tea with the members of the group. Nonetheless, it should be noted that no durable interactional pattern was established between the group as a social unit and any of the "novices". Relationships with individual members of the group, however, were usually maintained.

4.

Tea-time behaviour is stricter than at other daily social gatherings at which sanctions are not directed against uncalled-for involvements and intrusions are tolerated. Hence the rules of tea time embody a fundamental code for inclusion and exclusion. Even more emphatically this applies to the relationship between participants and members of staff whose careers and social priorities are anchored in the mobile changeable outside world.

Priority in serving tea to members of staff was often made an issue for discontent among participants who viewed such incidences as violations of the principle of equal rights in the Day Centre. Normally the staff would

honor the arrangement of impartial tea serving by mingling with participants waiting for their turn. However, on rare occasions when some members of staff preferred to confine themselves to the office during tea time,
tea was brought in by a participant after everybody else had been served.
On one occasion a turmoil erupted when a newcomer to the Day Centre, ig-
norant of that rule, gave preference to staff. The criticism was not
addressed to the participant who had misbehaved, but rather to those who
were regarded as his instructors to the Day Centre reality – i.e. to those veteran participants who committed themselves to introduce the novice to the
normative world of participation. Again tea-time conduct seems to occupy
a highly significant place as a symbol of appropriate interaction.

An even more outrageous breach of the law of equal privileges was demonstrated when members of staff asked participants for a cup of tea other
than at tea time. Invariably this request was bluntly refused. Here the two
different images of power in the Centre were overtly placed in sharp contradiction, revealing a continuous struggle over resources and authority in the
Day Centre. The use of tea procedures as a delineation of boundaries between staff and participants is evident in the following case:

Participants were well aware of the fact that members of staff, however
devoted to the Day Centre and good at their jobs, were still passers-by in
the establishment which was no more than a training transit in the course of
making progress in their careers. Furthermore, there was the awareness
that members of staff hinged their lives around their families and the out-
centre environment. This presented a sharp contrast to the Centre-centered
participant – a contrast which was sometimes looked upon unfavorably and
even with resentment.

The danger of a confrontation with staff was limited by different techniques of "obliterating" the presence of staff as such, even though physically and formally, of course, the staff members concerned remained
unaffected. Thus some participants insisted that most members of staff
spent their day in the office doing paper work, although objectively the
crammed room could hardly accommodate more than four people standing,
let alone sitting down.

They also persistently maintained that the "Centre runs itself" and the
engagement of staff there was merely an unnecessary nuisance. As Alan,
one of the leading spokesmen, put it "the Centre is so successful because we
are nice people – friendly and helpful – it has got nothing to do with the
staff". He also added that there was no doubt in his mind that given the opportunity, the participants would run the Centre better than the staff, they
would inaugurate extended activities in the evenings, install an elevator between floors to enable better integration and show more concern about the
participants' out-Centre problems. He accused staff of not having the Day
Centre's interests at heart and of using it merely to promote their own position in the head office of the organization.

Direct confrontations were averted by the fact that most members of staff were busy on the ground floor aiding the handicapped, preparing lunches and holding discussion groups, keep-fit classes and other activities. The upper hall, therefore, remained a staff-cleared territory and apart from the external instructors and the craft assistant, there was only one member of staff in an organizing capacity in charge of the whole floor. During the field-work period there were two people filling that function and both underwent some significant adjustments to the role allocated to them by participants.

The first one, a young unqualified social worker, identified himself with the participants to an extent of sitting with them, doing craft work and engaging in small-talk and gossip. He developed personal friendships with a number of them, inviting them to his home and seeing to their problems far beyond his duties as a member of staff. In staff meetings he invariably took sides with the participants' views and was in constant opposition to any suggestion to monitor or supervise their activities. The participants themselves saw him as an uprooted person (being a bachelor immigrant from New Zealand with no relations or affiliations in England) who had no other career but the Centre and who, therefore, was in the same position as themselves. Hence his partaking in tea-time groupings was taken for granted and gave rise to no questioning or conflict. His share in preparing the tea was also accepted as it would be from any participant.

His replacement, Joan, however, found herself accused of remoteness and uninvolvement. Twenty-one years old, an ex-model and a Gentile, Joan could hardly be classified as a typical participant and her views on the appropriate relationship between staff and participants only increased the distance. Joan maintained that a distinct line should be drawn between the work in the Day Centre and her private life. She, therefore, declined to release any such information in response to participants' queries concerning her out-Centre life and made it quite clear to the staff that apart from special occasions, she would not stay in the Day Centre for any longer than the official working hours. Her determination to separate her out-Centre life from her job was at first ignored by the participants and later became the subject for snide remarks such as "go and make the tea, you are not good for anything else" (making the tea is an accepted task of the volunteers).

Discussion

The repetitive pattern of tea-related behavior as an organizer of the social reality in the Centre is by no means the only symbolic device adopted by participants to reconstitute their world. A scanning look through other activities taking place in the Centre would indicate a similar correlation between the pattern embodied in each activity and the general structure of the present bound reality.

Thus, games such as chess and cards were voided of their competitive nature by regarding them as teaching situations; so were general individual achievements and expressions of creativity which were dismissed as insignificant and worthless. Dancing and singing recurred cyclically without enough novelty or innovation to form a progressive duration of events. All those activities were previous modes of behavior adapted and moulded by participants as part of the new temporal edifice constituted in the Centre.

Nonetheless, tea drinking represented a different social mechanism. Here adaptation and trimming were unnecessary. For tea-related conduct was transferred from the outside world unchanged and unmanipulated. It was a symbol which required no modification, neither in content nor in form. Inversely, it was found better suited to the participants' new world than to their pre-Centre state. In de Beauvoir's terms, the symbol invested them with "ontological security" (de Beauvoir 1972:697) or as she asserts: "If some ritual – the ceremony of tea among the English for example – is an exact repetition of that which I observed yesterday and I shall observe tomorrow, then the present moment is the past brought to life again, the future anticipated" (*ibid.*:696).

Tea drinking therefore is a somewhat paradoxical symbol anchored in the past and constitutes the present so that it is detached from the past. Shmuel – a member of a California Jewish Day Centre for the aged, depicted by Barbara Myerhoff – maintains that: "When I drink my tea with the spoon in it all those things from my childhood come along with me. I carry with me all the life of that little town to this day" (Myerhoff 1979:67). Unlike this assertion, tea drinking in our Centre draws selectively on the past, only in its form not in its content. That quality endows the symbol with a unique sense of continuity, divorced from shared substances and composed of common structure.

Observations on other sets of symbolic behavior among participants single tea drinking out as a device of prime importance for structuring the time universe of the Day Centre. It is beyond the scope of this chapter to offer an extensive analysis of all aspects of Centre society. However, one example of a seemingly similar behavior might illustrate the issue.

Mealtime – namely lunchtime – seems to possess an analogical quality to tea time at least in as much as they both include a consumption of edible substances by the same group of people. Nonetheless, the content, the order and hence the importance of lunchtime activities represent an opposite behavioral pole to that of tea time.

Lunch was served in two sittings in a crowded, noisy but well organized manner. The order of entry and exit and the rules of distributing the courses were observed by members of staff assisted by a group of volunteers. The various health-conditioned gastric requirements of participants were catered for by preparing a few diet meals. The conduct of participants during lunchtime was invariably a reflection of individual idiosyncracies and personal quirks. Participants found the food distasteful, the order of setting disagreeable and the manner of serving offensive. Some of them complained incessantly of unpleasant company, inconsiderate staff and lack of privacy. In other words, the feeling of communality and solidarity so prevalent in the ritual of tea drinking was replaced by factionalism and individualism.

A brief analysis of the meaning of lunch in the life of the participants would reveal that communal meals, being a stigmatic sign of destitution and social failure, were regarded as poignant reminders of the uncherished past. The participants' position as recipients of charity could not have been more bluntly symbolized than in the need for cheap meals.

Furthermore, the introduction of that symbol of social denigration and self-disdain into the hard-core of Centre life was a potential threat to the past-disengaged society of participants. Thus, lunchtime seemed to be encapsulated in an enclave of time and social relationships which did not penetrate other aspects of the participants' world. As soon as the hurried meal was over and the tables were cleared, the atmosphere in the place re-transformed itself to one of convivial comradeship completely untouched by the previous discontent.

The symbolic code of lunch was therefore not only unfit to operate as a boundary-maintaining device but posed a danger of sapping the barriers of separation from the outside world. To put it in terms of our argument, lunchtime conduct did not contribute to the insulated cyclical time universe to which behavior referred. Lunch symbolized a linear deterioration stemming from the past and accelerating towards a grim future.

This study is based on ethnographic material gathered during 1974–5 for a PhD thesis in the Department of Anthropology in University College London. I am most indebted to Professor M. Douglas, Dr. M. Gilsenan and Dr. A. Kuper for their invaluable guidance throughout the research. I am also grateful to my colleague, Professor S. Deshen, Professor E. Marx and Professor M. Shokeid of the Department of Sociology and Anthropology in Tel Aviv University who read the manuscript and added their useful comments.

Notes

1 See for example: Kolaja 1969 and Gurvitch 1964. For a review of the literature see Zerubavel 1976; Maxwell 1972; and Blau 1973.
2 For example Kluckhohn 1953; Hall 1966; Bohannan 1953; and Beidelman 1963.
3 An extreme view of time-reckoning systems as reflections of nature could be found in Nilsson 1920; Malinowski 1927, and to a lesser extent in Hallowell 1937 and Evans-Pritchard 1939; 1940.
4 Rites of passage are rife with temporal symbols – see for example Turner 1967. In everyday life one might assign this concept to what Goffman 1967 labelled "untoward events".

5 For a similar analytic approach see Roy 1959.
6 The assumption that the notion of time is implicit in the structure of reciprocity appears in discussion of the gift relationship. See M. Mauss 1925 [1966]:34 and also in Titmuss 1973:82.
7 Townsend 1957:297–313 cites the daily timetables of a few elderly men and women. Tea time and tea drinking seem to constitute an important part in the sequence of their routine events, but nonetheless do not show any characteristics of marking a "duration".
8 For a detailed ethnography of the Centre see Hazan 1980.
9 Colson 1977 also found that day-Centre members tend to construct their social relationships around common denominators of the present, while overlooking past socio-economic differences.

References

Beidelman, T., 1963. Kaguru time reckoning: an aspect of the cosmology of an East-African people, *Southwestern Journal of Anthropology* 19: 9–20
Blau, Z. S., 1973. *Old Age in a Changing Society*. New York, New Viewpoints
Bohannan, P., 1953. Concepts of time among the Tu of Nigeria, *Southwestern Journal of Anthropology* 9: 251–62
Colson, E., 1977. The least common denominator, in S. Moore and B. Myerhoff (eds.), *Secular Ritual*. Amsterdam, Van Gorcum, pp. 189–98
de Beauvoir, S., 1972. *The Coming of Age*. USA, Warner Communication Co.
Douglas, M., 1975. *Implicit Meanings*. London, Routledge and Kegan Paul
Evans-Pritchard, E. E., 1939. Nuer time reckoning, *Africa* 12: 189–216
    1940. *The Nuer*. Oxford, At the Clarendon Press
Goffman, E., 1967. Where the action is, in his *Interaction Ritual*. New York, Anchor Books, 149–70
Gurvitch, G., 1964. *The Spectrum of Social Time*. Dordrecht, S. Reidel Co.
Hall, E., 1966. *The Hidden Dimension*. Garden City, Doubleday
Hallowell, I., 1937. Temporal orientation in Western civilization and in preliterate society, *American Anthropologist* 39: 647–70
Hazan, H., 1980. *The Limbo People: A Study of the Constitution of the Time Universe among the Aged*. London, Routledge and Kegan Paul
Kluckhohn, F., 1953. Dominant and variant orientations, in F. Kluckhohn, H. A. Murray and D. H. Schneider (eds.), *Personality in Nature, Society and Culture*. New York, A. A. Knopf
Kolaja, S., 1969. *Social Systems and Time and Space*. Pittsburgh, Pittsburgh University Press
Leach, E., 1971. Cronus and Chronos, in his *Rethinking Anthropology*. London, Athlone Press, pp. 124–32
Luscher, K., 1974. Time: a much neglected dimension in social theory and research, *Sociological Analysis and Theory* 4: 101–17
Malinowski, B., 1927. Lunar and seasonal calendars in the Trobriands, *Journal of the Royal Anthropological Institute* 57: 203–15
Mauss, M., 1925[1966]. *The Gift*. London, Routledge and Kegan Paul

Maxwell, R., 1972. Anthropological perspectives, in H. Yaker, H. Osmond and F. Cheek (eds.), *The Future of Time*. New York, Anchor Books, pp. 36–72

Myerhoff, B., 1979. *Number Our Days*. New York, Sutton

Nilsson, M., 1920. *Primitive Time Reckoning*. Lunsk, C.W.K., Gleerup

Roth, S., 1963. *Timetables*. Indianapolis, Bobbs-Merril

Roy, D., 1959. Banana time: job satisfaction and informal interaction, *Human Organization* 18: 158–68

Titmuss, R., 1973. *The Gift Relationship*. London, Penguin

Townsend, P., 1957. *The Family Life of Old People*. London, Penguin

Turner, V., 1967. *The Forest of Symbols*. London, Cornell University Press
    1969. *The Ritual Process*. London, Routledge and Kegan Paul

Wolff, K. (ed.), 1964. *The Sociology of Georg Simmel*. New York, The Free Press

Zerubavel, E., 1976. Timetables and scheduling: on the social organization of time, *Sociological Inquiry* 46: 87–94
    1977. The French republican calendar: a case study in the sociology of time, *American Sociological Review* 42: 868–77

12. Maigret's Paris, conserved and distilled

Lisa Anne Gurr

In 1930, Simenon wrote *The Strange Case of Peter the Lett*, which introduced Jules Maigret, Chief Inspector of the Quai des Orfèvres in Paris; the last Maigret story appeared in 1972 (see Appendix A for those cited in this essay). Few other detective novelists wrote so much so well, and particularly so well about drink; Maigret appears in 102 books and short stories.[1]

Any work of fiction seeks to create a world; a good novel succeeds.[2] The world, to be believable, must be properly formed and structured, and ordered with a logical system of rules. This is not to say that the novel's world is always familiar; it need only be coherent.

Simenon wrote of a Paris – of its *bistros* and *quartiers*, of its Chief Inspector, criminals and policemen, and of its landladies, shopkeepers, and waiters – that did not exist. But it is patterned on a real world; the archetype is Paris of the 1930s. So this Paris is frozen; it is the same a decade before World War II as it is just after Viet Nam. It is a Paris that existed only in memory for most of the years that saw the publication of the Maigret stories. Dennis Porter, writing about the detective novel genre, calls this "unchangeability in radically changed times."[3] The social rules of Maigret's world are discernable because the behavior is patterned. The social order is the same throughout all the books, and the rules that form the social order are also the same.

The behavior that most clearly indicates the social structure is drinking. The other classes of things that people do that might have served the same purpose for Simenon – to give clues to what to expect – are not nearly as well developed as the drinking habits. Food and dress are not often mentioned in these books, and very rarely in any detail. Drinking is used by Simenon as "a class of behavior which makes regular responses to changes in the world."[4] Drinking is not only physically functional. Its social functions are perhaps less apparent, but also important. Drinks occur within and denote a social system. They indicate groups: the social classes, the sexes, foreigners, and outsiders. The principles of inclusion and exclusion are apparent in the rules of hospitality and in other rules of drinking. Drinks also form a sequence that begins with the morning coffee, includes the apéritif before dinner, and ends with the bedside water. Simenon pays very close attention to the structure, the social system. As Porter says, the Maigret novels are "characterized by notations on manners that make sharp distinctions between the social strata of French life."[5] Maigret says: "Our job is to study men. We take note of some of the facts. We try to establish others."[6] This is, no more and no less, anthropology's job, too. Maigret seeks to understand the whole of the milieu. He gathers his impressions, and then he ponders; he is not analytic, but rather imaginative. He goes deeply into the local mores, tries to unravel a system of rules. The clues, the details, are infinite, and few are directly related to any crime. But they are the atmosphere of the criminal and the crime. And if Maigret can succeed in understanding the atmosphere, he knows who the criminal is. His purpose is

> To know the milieu in which a crime has been committed, to know the way of life, the habits, morals, reactions of the people involved in it, whether victims, criminals, or merely witnesses.[7]

We are looking at a variety of levels of observation, and it would be helpful to keep them separate in our thoughts: Simenon creates and observes Maigret and the other characters; Maigret observes other characters; and we observe the whole lot of them. Simenon has created a world, and left clues; we, and Maigret, seek to decipher the clues, and the biggest clues for us are the drinks.

An amazing variety of drinks in great quantity are named in these books. Maigret and many other characters drink an awful lot, but are rarely described as being drunk. A list of the drinks and the frequency with which they are mentioned or are drunken may be seen in Table 1. It gives a good idea of the variety of drinks being consumed by a variety of characters. (Appendix B is descriptions of some of the less obvious drinks.) Table 2 is of the actual number of drinks that Maigret consumes or mentions. These lists are a starting point for distinguishing the social classes. Table 3 gives some characteristics of most of the drinks, including the class with which they seem to be associated.

The social classes in Maigret's Paris are the same in 1942 as they are in 1969. The lines are clear, and the crossover rare. The main divisions are the working class, the *petite bourgeoisie*, the *haute bourgeoisie*, and the aristocracy. The distinction between the *petite* and the *haute bourgeoisie* is economic, not ideological. Maigret is entirely committed to upholding the entire system. His commitment as a policeman and a detective is to order, to uphold the order.

Simenon pays most attention to the *bourgeoisie* and most fully describes it, and his central character is bourgeois. Maigret's father was bailiff to the

Table 1. *Frequency of use of drinks*

Coffee	47
Café crème	1
Coffee	43
Coffee and brandy (listed twice)	2
Turkish coffee	1
Brandy	46
Armagnac	3
Brandy	16
Brandy and water	2
Calvados	8
Coffee and brandy (listed twice)	2
Cognac	1
Kirsch	1
Marc	3
Napoléon brandy	1
Plum brandy	7
Raspberry brandy	2
Beer	42
Wine (excluding named wines)	37
Champagne	6
Red wine	7
White wine	17
Wine	7
Miscellaneous alcoholic drinks	26
Apéritif	4
Gin and tomato juice	1
Martini	3
Rum (straight)	5
Scotch	2
Toddy (or hot grog)	4
Whiskey	7
Liqueurs	15
Absinthe	1
Chartreuse	6
Liqueur	2
Mandarin-Curaçao	1
Pastis	2
Sloe gin	3
Drink (not specified)	14
Non-alcoholic drinks (excluding coffee)	11
Herb tea	3
Tea	5
Vichy water	3

Table 2. *Number of Maigret's drinks*

Beer	34*
Brandy	24
Armagnac	1
Brandy	7
Brandy and water	2
Calvados	7
Marc	1
Plum brandy	5
Raspberry brandy	1
Coffee	19
Wine	15
Red wine	0
White wine	14
Wine	1
Liqueurs	10
Chartreuse	4
Mandarin-Curaçao	2
Pastis	2
Sloe gin	2
Miscellaneous alcoholic drinks	10
Apéritif	2
Martini	2
Rum	2
Toddy (or hot grog)	2
Whiskey	2
Non-alcoholic drinks (excluding coffee)	2
Herb tea (while ill)	2
Drink (not specified)	7

*"More than one," "several," and "many" are counted
as two.

Table 3. *Characteristics of some drinks: who drinks what*

Drink	Sex Men or women	Lower	Middle	Upper	Foreign	Maigret
Coffee	both	—	—	—	–*	regularly
Brandy	men	—	—	—	—	regularly
Armagnac	men			—		when offered
Calvados	men		—			regularly
Kirsch	men		—			never
Marc	men	—	—			regularly
Napoléon brandy	men				—	never
Plum brandy	men		—			regularly
Raspberry brandy	men		—			regularly
Beer	men		—			regularly
Wine (ordinaire)	men	—	—	—	–	regularly
Champagne	both			–	—	never
Red wine	men	—				rarely
White wine	men		—			regularly
Miscellaneous Alcoholic drinks						
Apéritif	men		—			occasionally
Gin and tomato juice	men				—	never
Martini	men				—	when offered
Rum (straight)	men	—				never
Scotch	men				—	when offered
Toddy (hot grog)	men		—			occasionally
Whiskey	men				—	when offered
Liqueurs						
Absinthe	men		—			never
Chartreuse	both		—			when offered
Mandarin-Curaçao	men		—			when offered
Pastis	men		—			occasionally
Sloe gin	men		—			occasionally
Non-alcoholic drinks						
Herb tea	women		—			when ill
Tea	women		—	—	–	not by choice
Vichy water	both	–	—	–		not by choice

* Likely, but there is no evidence

count and the château of Saint-Fiacre in Allier in central France. Maigret says that his father was of an intermediary social class:

> the estate of which my father was manager was one of seven and a half thousand acres and included no less than twenty-six small farms.
>
> Not only was my grandfather . . . one of these tenant farmers, but he followed at least three generations of Maigrets who had tilled the same soil.[8]

Maigret's grandfather was a peasant; Maigret's father was one half step up; and Maigret himself has reached the *petite bourgeoisie*: "I belong to the social group, of course, to what are known as respectable people."[9] His personal, not professional, loyalties lie with the lower-middle class. Describing his arrival in Paris as a young man, he says

> I was all alone in the world. I had just landed in an unfamiliar city . . .
>
> Two things struck one: that wealth on the one hand, and that poverty on the other; and I belonged to the second group . . .
>
> Now not for one moment did I feel tempted to rebel. I did not envy them. I did not hope to be like them one day.[10]

By his class loyalty and his commitment to the social system as a whole, Maigret conforms to the social ideal. John Raymond comments that "Maigret has his own firm ideas about the social order."[11] His work reflects his desire to maintain the order; his commitment is to the status quo.

The word *maigret* means thin, spare, scarce. Maigret is by no means thin, but he disapproves of any form of ostentation, of display. He is bourgeois in manner, in expectations, and in tastes. His drinks of choice are beer, brandy, coffee, and wine. Beer seems to be the lowest common denominator of drinks for Maigret and men of his class. The brandy category includes a wide range of brandies, which have many different meanings. Maigret drinks coffee for the same reasons as everyone else; coffee has no particular meaning for Maigret except that he occasionally has to be up all night. It is interesting that Maigret never orders red wine for himself. He drinks white wine much as he drinks beer, though less often.

Maigret is not a peasant, and his drinking marc (a coarse, mediocre brandy) is a regional distinction. Marc is made in Bourgogne, less than fifty kilometers from Maigret's birthplace near Moulins.

Other regional loyalties are also demonstrated. In *Maigret's Memoirs*, Maigret is writing a letter to Simenon, making a few corrections to the Maigret stories:

> Simenon has mentioned a certain bottle which we always had in our sideboard . . . and of which my sister-in-law, according to a hallowed tradition, brings us a supply from Alsace on her annual visit there.
>
> He has thoughtlessly described it as sloe gin.

Actually, it is raspberry brandy. And for an Alsatian, apparently, this makes a tremendous difference.[12]

Incidentally, not only did the sloe gin become raspberry brandy, but the raspberry brandy later underwent a final transformation into plum brandy, which is, however, still Alsatian.

Maigret is the symbol of his class, and the great majority of Simenon's Parisians are bourgeois, including many of the criminals. Maigret visits a woman in the Rue Mouffetard to tell her that her son, a burglar whom Maigret had known for many years, had been killed in the Bois de Bologne. They have a drink of plum brandy together from her sideboard (Maigret's people often drink at the news of a death and at funerals). When Maigret gets home, he notices that his sideboard also holds a bottle of white spirits.[13]

Simenon's distinction between drinks and between classes is very clear. The *haute bourgeoisie* and the aristocracy are set apart from the *petite bourgeoisie* by their drinks. Tea is treated as a sign of upper-class and foreign habits. Maigret visits two women one day in the course of an investigation; the first is a *bourgeoisie*, the second a princess. "Alain Mazeron's wife, in the Rue de la Pompe, had offered him some beer. Here it was tea."[14] Tea reappears as a sign of social class in another investigation.[15] A lower-class prostitute describes seeing a man visiting a house across the street from her room:

> "He never stays long. If I remember rightly I've never seen him late in the evening. About five o'clock, that's more his style. For afternoon tea, I expect."
>
> She seemed delighted to show off her knowledge of the fact that, in a world remote from her own, there were people who took tea at five o'clock.[16]

Maigret never drinks tea. Tea is not masculine, it is a mark of those aspiring to a higher class, and it is foreign. Maigret compares himself to another high-ranking inspector: "Superintendent Danet probably took afternoon tea now and then; whereas Maigret had lunched at a *bistro* with a paper tablecloth, in the company of workmen and Algerians."[17] Maigret sets himself firmly against social climbing of all kinds.

The upper classes (the upper-middle class and the upper class) often pride themselves on their discrimination and taste. Maigret visits a lawyer of the highest level of the *bourgeoisie*. The lawyer, Parendon, offers Maigret a drink: "'The cognac isn't particularly good, but I have a forty-year-old armagnac...'"[18]

In the Maigret stories there is very little naming of wines, and no overt gourmet appreciation of wine. Maigret would consider the gourmet approach to wine upper-class and affected. Although wines are mentioned 42 times, there are only seven individual wines named, and only eleven

Table 4. *Named wines*

Wine*	Number of times mentioned	Number of times Maigret drinks it
Beaujolais	2	2
Chavignol	1	2
Pouilly-Fuissé	2	1
Pouilly-Fumé	1	1
Saint-Emilion	3	3
Sancerre	1	1
Vouvray	1	1

* Interestingly, only the Beaujolais and the Saint-Emilion are red wines.

times are wines even named at all (see Table 4). Only one named wine – the Saint-Emilion – is described, and then simply as "unforgettable."[19] The bouquet, aroma, or body of a wine is rarely mentioned. Although Maigret "remembered the white wine which left an aftertaste that recalled some country inn,"[20] this is a personal and not a gourmet description.

When Maigret is first made a detective, he goes with his new colleagues to the Brasserie Dauphine to celebrate. The Brasserie Dauphine is hard by the Quai des Orfèvres, and is patronized by the detectives. The Brasserie Dauphine also delivers; the waiter carries up countless trays of beer and sandwiches to the offices.

> In our old corner we used to drink half-pints of beer, seldom an apéritif. Obviously that wouldn't do for this table.[21]

Maigret buys several rounds of the unfamiliar and potent mandarin-Curaçaos, and spends his first day as a detective drunk. This is the only time Maigret is ever described more than a little tipsy. He does not usually indulge in oddities. He sticks to his beer and pipe.

The working men drink red wine more than anything else, but not many are described. At a bar, the clientele is described as "mainly men in blue work-clothes or old men from the surrounding district who came in for their glass of red wine."[22] Workers do not ever drink beer or white wine in this Paris.

Maigret, in the course of his work, comes into contact with people of many different social classes. He follows their social rules and drinks what they drink. When he is in the company of people of a higher class than he, he sometimes needs to show his own class loyalty, to indicate that he is not trying to rise socially. But with people of the working class, he is comfortable and doesn't need to differentiate himself. For example, in an expensive hotel where a murder has occurred, Maigret tries to order a beer at a tea-dance. The waiter answers, "'We don't serve...'" Maigret interrupts, tells the waiter who he is, and is served a beer.[23] After leaving the home of the wealthy bourgeois lawyer and his family, he goes into a *bistro*: "He wondered what he would drink, and ended up by ordering a pint of beer. The atmosphere of the Parendons still stuck to him."[24] Later on, in the same household, he is offered a choice of wines:

> What did it matter? In the state he was in, vintage Saint-Emilion or some ordinary red wine . . .
> He didn't dare say that he would have preferred the ordinary red.[25]

In one story, Maigret investigates the death of an aristocrat. He is ill-at-ease and unsure of himself. He is with people with whom he is unfamiliar and whom he holds in awe.

> He had made contact . . . with a world which was not only very exclusive but which for him, on account of his childhood, was situated on a very special level.[26]

And when he leaves their home, he "literally plunged into the fuggy atmosphere of a cafe and ordered a beer"[27] to regain his equilibrium.

Maigret is investigating a murder among the international jet set and is rather disgusted with the members of this group and their way of life. Drinks indicate a group or a class. Often, the group and the drink are stereotypes. Americans drink whiskey and gin, the working class drinks inexpensive red wine, and the aristocracy drinks tea.

> Maigret had intentionally taken a Calvados after his meal out of sheer contrariness, because he was about to re-enter a world where one did not drink Calvados, much less marc, but only whiskey, champagne, or Napoléon brandy.[28]

Another time, Maigret goes to Monte Carlo to speak to a wealthy American, and as they are talking, "A waiter whom nobody had rung for brought in a misted glass of some transparent liquid, presumably a Martini." Maigret is curious, and has one too.[29] The American is unknown to Maigret, but Maigret can nonetheless guess what the man drinks, simply because he is a rich American.

Maigret's efforts in an investigation are always directed towards learning, towards understanding. His bourgeois Paris is not a sophisticated, urbane place. In his encounters with the exotic, he is always curious. Maigret visits a Turkish criminal, and sits "on the edge of the sofa, examining the little Turkish coffee cups with interest."[30]

Maigret also reacts against drinks which have a gender rather than a class identification. A landlady from whom Maigret rents a room serves him chartreuse: "He had always hated liqueurs. Mademoiselle Clément, on the contrary, seemed to delight in them."[31] Maigret does on occasion drink liqueurs, but here he is reacting to the sweetness, the false gentility of the drink. While working on this case, he rebels against the cloying atmosphere by drinking beer,[32] white wine, and also "calvados, as a protest against the chartreuse he had drunk the night before."[33]

Although the most obvious use of drinks is in the denotation of social classes, Simenon also uses them in other ways.

Only four women are ever described drinking alcohol. One is the landlady already mentioned above. Another is a prostitute whom Maigret buys a drink in exchange for information. The two others are alcoholics. One woman, a wealthy bourgeoise, is a secret drinker. Her husband is murdered, and when Maigret tells her, she does not react, although she did not kill him:

> he was certain the woman facing him had been drinking, not merely before she went to bed, but that morning already, and a strong smell of alcohol still hung about the room.[34]

Maigret sees her drink out of a bottle (we are not told what she drinks); he is repulsed, and leaves her bedroom quickly.[35]

Another Frenchwoman, a very wealthy countess and a member of the international jet set, also drinks, but not as secretly. Her drinking and her choice of drinks – champagne (Krug '47) often, and whiskey occasionally[36] – reflect her special, high status. She withholds information from Maigret; she had discovered the corpse, and had not notified the police.

Otherwise, none of the other women with whom Maigret comes into contact are ever described drinking alcohol. Presumably, the Frenchwomen in Maigret's world do drink wine at meals, but they are only described drinking coffee, tea, and mineral water. Maigret is very aware of this, and when an elderly woman is to go to the Quai for questioning, Maigret orders a bottle of mineral water for her from the Brasserie Dauphine along with the usual bottles of beer.[37]

The only woman who reappears in the stories, Maigret's wife, never seems to drink alcohol at all. The only drink Madame Maigret is ever described drinking besides coffee is a tisane: "[Maigret] treated himself to a glass of calvados and his wife had a verbena tisane."[38]

This Paris may entertain a prejudice against women drinking alcohol. The tacit exclusion of women from the *bistros* then would be a means of preventing women from drinking, especially publicly. Women are not especially prominent in Maigret's Paris, and would not then be bound to the social system in the same way men are, which is in part through the use of alcohol beverages.

Social groups can be identified by their drinks. Between individuals, imitation can be sincerest flattery. Lucas, one of Maigret's trusty inspectors,

> had come to copy his boss in his slightest habits, in his attitudes, in his expressions, and this was more striking here [in the Maigrets' apart-

ment] than in the office. Even his way of sniffing at the glass of plum brandy before putting his lips to it . . .[39]

In an effort to understand a new situation, Maigret sometimes imitates the people in a case. A very young man of good family is shot one night in a poor district after drinking a brandy in a *bistro*.[40] The next day, Maigret "ordered a brandy, since there had been a lot of talk about brandies the previous evening."[41] Later on in the investigation, the killer, a psychopath, calls Maigret on the phone. He tells Maigret that he has had a few brandies. A little later, Maigret and another one of his inspectors, Janvier, go to the Brasserie Dauphine: "'A brandy,' ordered the superintendent, which made Janvier smile."[42] A story often centers on a single home or a very small area of Paris where there are well-established patterns. The pattern of drinking there, the prevalence of a single drink in a story often adds a unifying thread to the story. Simenon is not interested in random, violent crime, crime without reason, without background, without locale. There must be a context in order for the crime to be understood.

The principles of inclusion and exclusion which are the foundation of the division between the social classes and the sexes, are also demonstrated in the display of hospitality. Offering or accepting a drink is an indication of a social relationship, the acknowledgement of social obligation. Hospitality has its rules.

A woman who keeps a lower-class *bistro* reproaches Maigret: "'. . . you forget that in the old days you sometimes came to my bar for a drink, and you weren't above picking up the bits of information I could give you.'"[43] He is obliged to her because he accepted both the information and the drink.

A wealthy American offers Maigret and his inspector a whiskey; Maigret accepts. However, Lapointe, "out of tact, merely took a glass of beer."[44] Lapointe was not the real object of the offer, but the offer had to include him and he had to accept the offer, according to the rules of social drinking. But he chooses a lesser drink appropriate to his more minor role.

The obligations which are implied in accepting a drink can be manipulated. There is a handsome, red-haired prostitute from whom Maigret wants some information. He buys her a drink because she "felt slightly mistrustful."[45] Thus, he forces her to be obliged to him, and he also displays good will. She does give him the information, and helps him trap a murderer.

The Maigrets have a house in the country which they use on the weekend, and to which they later retire. One weekend, they arrive in the village: "They are welcomed at the inn with open arms and they had to have a drink with everyone, for they were considered almost as belonging there."[46]

In one case, a gesture of hospitality not offered is a clue. An elderly diplomat is found dead in his study, and Maigret is thinking:

Supposing the former ambassador had let somebody in the flat ...
Somebody he knew, since he had sat down again at his desk, in his
dressing-gown ...

In front of him, a bottle of brandy and a glass ... Why hadn't he
offered his visitor a drink?[47]

It would have to be someone well known to the diplomat, but someone he
did not like – and so it was.

On another level, drinks point to a time of day, or to a location in the
week or year. Even though the Maigret stories are not fast-paced, there is
still a need to indicate the time, the day of the week, and holidays. The most
regular indicator, or clock, is coffee; it is drunk by men and women of all
social classes in the morning, after dinner and supper, and as a stimulant
late at night. A great many of the stories contain an almost identical scene:

As on every other morning, his first contact with life was the smell of
coffee, then his wife's hand touching his shoulder, and finally the sight
of Madame Maigret, already fresh and alert, wearing a flowered
housecoat, holding his cup out to him.[48]

This scene starts the vast majority of Maigret's days. But Sundays and holidays, "he was supposed to lie in bed till late in the morning."[49] But Maigret
hates staying in bed, he likes his weekday routine. Anything out of the ordinary makes him grumble.

Maigret drinks coffee at home before he goes to the Quai. He arrives a
little before nine. After nine, and for the rest of the morning, he drinks, for
the most part, beer and white wine. The beer is often sent up by the Brasserie Dauphine. Maigret also very often drinks in the *bistros* in the Paris
neighborhoods. He drinks coffee after the midday meal, before going back
to the Quai. In the afternoons and evenings, Maigret mostly drinks brandy.
He drinks coffee again after the evening meal, along with brandy, and late
at night if he must be up late.

There is evident in the cycle of drinks the cycle of the day and of the calen-
dar. The owner of a bar describes his daily pattern of business:

There's never a lot of people except in the morning for their coffee and
croissants, or a Vichy water. About ten o'clock or ten thirty, workmen
come in for a break, when there's some work going on anywhere
nearby. I'm busiest when people come to have a drink before lunch or
before dinner.[50]

It's difficult to tell when Maigret is having a drink before a meal, because he
does drink so often, but it would be safe to guess that he uses this part of the
pattern too.

If one knows the time or the day, one can predict the drinks. If one
observes the drinks, one can guess the time or the day. On one Christmas
day, Maigret is restless because he is on holiday, because he is not at the

Quai. He is glad when an odd occurrence in the neighborhood relieves him of having to do nothing.[51] There is, on this day, "wine and cakes on the table, the bottle of liqueur ready to hand on the sideboard."[52] Several people come to the Maigrets' apartment that day in the course of the investigation, and are given liqueur – plum brandy – in honor of the holiday.[53] But again, Maigret wants the old order: "After all, perhaps [he] too felt like a glass of cool beer."[54] On another Christmas morning, "a large proportion of the population was still sleeping off the wine and champagne drunk at last night's réveillon suppers."[55]

The norm and the deviation from the norm are very important in Maigret's world. Maigret's duty is to defend the order, and crime lies outside the social order. Not only is the crime itself an anomaly, but the clues which lead to knowledge of the crime are also anomalies in the system. Maigret pays very close attention to anything out of the ordinary. Both actions and individuals can be usual or unusual.

The ordinary world is regulated by habits performed with little or no thought. For Maigret

> Nine times out of ten an investigation would fling him at a moment's notice into an unfamiliar setting, confronting him with people of a set about which he knew little or nothing, and everything had to be learnt, down to the most trivial habits and mannerisms of a social class with which he was unacquainted.[56]

For it is only within the context of the normal – the habits – that the anomaly – the clue – becomes apparent. A burglar who watched homes he planned to rob from the windows or terraces of *bistros*, was caught because "they had picked up his trail in this way, finding that he had become a sudden and temporary habitué of various local cafés."[57]

The landlady who drinks chartreuse rents Maigret a room so that he can investigate a murder which occurred in the street outside. In the middle of the night, he goes downstairs to go across to the cafe to get a beer because the chartreuse annoyed him so much. He finds the landlady making coffee and sandwiches. The sandwiches are not surprising; the coffee is. He discovers that she is hiding a young robber under her bed and feeding him by night.[58] The boy, however, has nothing to do with the murder.

Changes in habit can innocently reflect a change elsewhere in the system. When Maigret's wife goes on a visit to her sister's, he has two apéritifs instead of one.[59] When he's at home, "as he passed the sideboard, he decided to pour himself a drink, something he could do today without exchanging a glance with his wife."[60]

When the burglar's corpse is found in the Bois de Bologne, Maigret is called on the 'phone in the middle of the night. He grouses to himself, "Why did the coffee always taste differently on winter nights when he was woken up like this?"[61]

There are five characters whose drinking habits reflect their anomalous status. In Maigret's Paris men drink and women don't. Both the two women who drink too much do not report a murder. And of the three men who are abnormal because they do *not* drink, two are murderers.

Maigret talks on the telephone with the psychopath who killed the young man who drank brandy.

> "Have you been drinking?"
> "How did you know?"
> He spoke more forcefully.
> "I had two or three brandies."
> "You don't usually drink?"
> "Only a glass of wine with meals, rarely a drink by itself."
> "Do you smoke?"
> "No."[62]

Maigret talks with another man – another murderer – who has been a fugitive for many years, and the conversation is very similar:

> "Do you smoke?"
> "No, thank you. I haven't smoked in years now."
> "And you don't drink either?"
> They were getting to know each other, little by little . . .
> "I don't drink any more, no."
> "You once drank a lot?"
> "Once upon a time."[63]

Another man, the husband of the fugitive's mistress, does not drink but this time because his father was a drunkard: "'he's always had such a horror of drink . . . Some people laughed at him.'"[64] This man is not a murderer, but an outsider all the same.

A small piece of information is often much more than it seems. That information can point to a lot within a context. The problem of course is knowing a context well enough to see the direction in which it points.

Appendix A. *Citation of the Maigret stories*

In citing the Maigret stories, I have used the date of the edition in English. These are the dates of the first publication in French.

	French publication	English edition
Maigret and the Hotel Majestic	1942	1978
"The Evidence of the Altar-Boy"	1947	1976
Maigret's Memoirs	1950	1978
Maigret Takes a Room	1951	1978
"Maigret's Christmas"	1951	1976
"Seven Little Crosses in a Notebook"	1951	1976
Maigret's Failure	1956	1973
Maigret and the Millionaires	1958	1974
Maigret in Society	1960	1973
Maigret and the Lazy Burglar	1961	1973
Maigret Hesitates	1969	1970
Maigret and the Killer	1969	1971

Appendix B. *A Description of Certain Drinks*

Absinthe	a strong liqueur flavored with wormwood
Armagnac	a dry brandy from the southwest of France
Calvados	a brandy made from cider; from Normandy
Chartreuse	an aromatic liqueur made in the southeast of France
Hot grog	a mixture of hot water and liquor
Kirsch	a cherry brandy from Alsace, West Germany, and Switzerland
Mandarin-Curaçao	a liqueur flavored with orange peel
Marc	a brandy of middling quality made from the residue of grapes; from Burgundy
Martini	a cocktail made with gin or vodka and dry vermouth
Pastis	a liqueur flavored with aniseed
Raspberry brandy	from Alsace
Sloe gin	a liqueur flavored with sloe, the fruit of the blackthorn
Tisane	an herb tea
Toddy	a sweetened mixture of liquor and hot water

Notes

1 Becker 1977: Preface. For this paper, I have used eight novels and three short stories (although the lengths of the novels and the short stories are not very different). I have also used one book written in Maigret's voice, *Maigret's Memoirs*; it is not a mystery, but rather a collection of reminiscences. The publication dates of these twelve stories range between 1942 and 1969. The citation dates are the dates of the edition I quote, not the dates of the original French publication. See Appendix A for the latter.

2 In this essay I am gratefully following I. Schapera's model of the use of fiction as ethnographic text as he developed it in "Kinship Terminology in Jane Austen's Novels", 1977.

3 Porter 1981: 211
4 Douglas 1984: 28
5 Porter 1981: 213
6 Simenon 1978b: 64
7 Simenon 1978b: 76
8 Simenon 1978b: 32
9 Simenon 1978b: 77
10 Simenon 1978b: 41
11 Raymond 1968: 157
12 Simenon 1978b: 81
13 Simenon 1973a: 236
14 Simenon 1973b: 158
15 Simenon 1973a
16 Simenon 1973a: 248
17 Simenon 1973a: 256
18 Simenon 1970: 20
19 Simenon 1973a: 213
20 Simenon 1978c: 114
21 Simenon 1978b: 71
22 Simenon 1971a: 39
23 Simenon 1978a: 97
24 Simenon 1970: 96
25 Simenon 1970: 179–80
26 Simenon 1973b: 118
27 Simenon 1973b: 167
28 Simenon 1974: 136
29 Simenon 1974: 71
30 Simenon 1978a: 150
31 Simenon 1978c: 107
32 Simenon 1978c: 127
33 Simenon 1978c: 125

34 Simenon 1973c: 45
35 Simenon 1973c: 46
36 Simenon 1974: 3, 100
37 Simenon 1973b: 184
38 Simenon 1971a: 120
39 Simenon 1976a: 36
40 Simenon 1971a
41 Simenon 1971a: 60
42 Simenon 1971a: 148
43 Simenon 1973a: 287
44 Simenon 1974: 50
45 Simenon 1974: 158
46 Simenon 1971a: 132
47 Simenon 1973b: 172
48 Simenon 1970: 112
49 Simenon 1976a: 1
50 Simenon 1971a: 33–4
51 Simenon 1976a
52 Simenon 1976a: 24
53 Simenon 1976a: 30, 36, 41
54 Simenon 1976a: 41
55 Simenon 1976b: 53
56 Simenon 1976a: 24
57 Simenon 1973a: 229
58 Simenon 1978c: 110, 115–16
59 Simenon 1978c: 87
60 Simenon 1978c: 88
61 Simenon 1973a: 203
62 Simenon 1971a: 146
63 Simenon 1978c: 165
64 Simenon 1978c: 141

References

Becker, Lucille F., 1977. *Georges Simenon*. Boston, Twayne Publishers

Douglas, Mary (ed.), 1984. *Food in the Social Order*. New York, Russell Sage Foundation

Porter, Dennis, 1981. *The Pursuit of Crime*. New Haven, Yale University Press 1968

Raymond, John, 1968. *Simenon in Court*. London, Hamish Hamilton, Ltd.

Schapera, I., 1977. Kinship terminology in Jane Austen's novels, *Occasional Paper No. 33*. London, Royal Anthropological Institute of Great Britain and Ireland

Simenon, Georges, 1970. *Maigret Hesitates*. New York, Harcourt, Brace, Jovanovich

1971a. *Maigret and the Killer*. New York, Harcourt, Brace, Jovanovich

1971b. *When I was Old*. New York, Harcourt, Brace, Jovanovich

1973a. *Maigret and the Lazy Burglar*, collected in *A Maigret Trio*. New York, Harcourt, Brace, Jovanovich

1973b. *Maigret in Society*, collected in *A Maigret Trio*. New York, Harcourt, Brace, Jovanovich

1973c. *Maigret's Failure*, collected in *A Maigret Trio*, New York, Harcourt, Brace, Jovanovich

1974. *Maigret and the Millionaires*. New York, Harcourt, Brace, Jovanovich

1976a. Maigret's Christmas, collected in *Maigret's Christmas: Nine Stories*. New York, Harcourt, Brace, Jovanovich

1976b. Seven little crosses in a notebook, collected in *Maigret's Christmas: Nine Stories*. New York, Harcourt, Brace, Jovanovich

1976c. The evidence of the altar-boy, collected in *Maigret's Christmas: Nine Stories*. New York, Harcourt, Brace, Jovanovich

1978a. *Maigret and the Hotel Majestic*. New York, Harcourt, Brace, Jovanovich

1978b. *Maigret's Memoirs*, collected in *Georges Simenon*. London, Heinemann/ Octopus

1978c. *Maigret Takes a Room*, collected in *Georges Simenon*. London, Heinemann/Octopus

Zeldin, Theodore, 1984. *The French*. New York, Vintage Books

IV

ALCOHOL ENTRENCHES THE ALTERNATIVE ECONOMY

13. The alternative economy of alcohol in the Chiapas highlands

Thomas Crump

The radical changes, which have occurred in the course of the present century, in the political and economic factors governing the demand for, and supply of rum in Chamula, and other neighbouring Indian *municipios*[1] in the Mexican state of Chiapas, provide the background to the present chapter. Chamula, with a present population of some forty to fifty thousand, is the largest of the Indian municipios in the extensive highland area to the north of the old state capital of San Cristobal.[2] Since its southern confines extend almost to the outskirts of San Cristobal, it is not only relatively accessible to the Ladino[3] economy of the state, but, because of adverse demographic and agronomic factors, it has long been dependent upon it for its survival. At the same time Chamula controls the access to most of the other Indian municipios of the highlands. These in turn, being better able to maintain their traditional subsistence economies based upon the cultivation of maize, and having, therefore, relatively little need for commerce with the outside world, have always been of much less interest to the Ladino economy based on San Cristobal.

Three historical periods must be considered. The first may be taken to start in 1900, when the coffee plantations in the mountains overlooking the Pacific coast of Chiapas first began to recruit Indian labour in the relatively densely populated, but economically undeveloped, central highlands (Wasserstrom 1983:116). Although a meagre wage was paid for this labour, the sale of rum to the highland Indians played an essential part in the process of recruitment. The period may be taken to have come to an end in the late 1930s, when a general state prohibition on the sale of alcohol to Indians became effective. During the second period, which then lasted until the end of the 1950s, certain members of the religious hierarchy[4] in Chamula, exempted from the general law, enjoyed an official monopoly for the sale of alcohol at fiestas. This second period gradually led into the third, in which the manufacture of the alcohol sold to the highland Indians became an effective monopoly of illegal stills owned and operated by Chamulas in the remoter parts of the municipio. The fieldwork upon which this chapter is based took place in this period, and was mainly concerned with the financial network supporting this manufacture. The material relating to the first two periods comes from historical sources.

The important point, in relation to all three periods, is that the consumption of rum is a part of every local Indian culture. Within the household, rum is consumed, according to a pre-ordained ritual, on occasions relating to the cure of sickness and the celebration of certain *rites de passage*. Much more important, however, in terms of quantity, is its consumption in the course of the public celebration of religious festivals, inherited from the Catholic Church but transformed to accord with local beliefs, which occur at intervals throughout the year.

To appreciate what this involves, something must be said of the traditional exchange economy of the Indian municipio. Although the Indian populations live in small hamlets, distributed more or less evenly across the whole area, every municipio has a "centre", consisting of a church, a market place, some shops (traditionally owned and run by Ladinos (see note 3), and a number of houses occupied by religious officials at the time of festivals. In Chamula the centre has always been politically important because, having the only church, it was the only possible site for festivals, but economically relatively unimportant, simply because the large open market in San Cristobal was only 10 km away.[5] On the other hand, until about 1940, the few Ladino shops in Chamula centre were the only source of rum, which accounted for the greater part of their trade. Without any surplus from the subsistence cultivation of maize to offer in exchange, the Chamulas were forced to seek a part of their livelihood outside the municipio.

Rum had been sold, at native fiestas and markets, since early colonial days. In the early 1840s small numbers of Ladino immigrants began to set up as farmers in the Indian municipios. They soon found, however, that the sale of liquor to the Indians was far more profitable, and that this was best combined with setting up shop in the municipal centre. As a result, Indian consumption increased enormously (Wasserstrom 1983:130), to a level reminiscent of eighteenth-century London. Although some of the rum may have been imported from outside Chiapas, a substantial part was distilled in one of the twenty-odd *barrios* – or suburbs – into which San Cristobal is divided. The Ladinos involved in the traditional production of rum supplied their product directly to the retailers in the Indian municipios.

By the beginning of the twentieth century production in San Cristobal was confined to a number of families, of which one, headed by Moctezuma Pedrero, was much the most important. Pedrero owed his dominant position (which eventually gave him a near monopoly of the trade) to the fact that he was not only a distiller, but had set up also as an *enganchador*, that is as a labour contractor to the coffee plantations down towards the coast, once they had begun to recruit Indians from the highlands.

The two operations were combined in the following way. An Indian was recruited for plantation labour by means of an *enganche* or hook. This was no more than a debt, incurred by the Indian, which the enganchador would pay off, in exchange for a first claim for the amount owing on the wages to be earned by the Indian on the coffee plantation. This sum, together with a fee for the contract payable to the enganchador, was paid at the time the Indian was recruited. The system obviously worked best – at least for the enganchador and the plantation owners – when a high level of indebtedness was sustained among the Indian population, and what better means was there of achieving this result than to ensure that such little cash as the Indians disposed of was squandered on alcohol? An enganchador who doubled as a distiller had the best of all possible worlds, and it is not surprising that Pedrero came to be the richest man in the highlands. At least in Chamula, the debts taken over by Pedrero, and other enganchadores – for he never monopolized this line of business – were incurred primarily with the Ladino shopkeepers in the centre, whom the system provided with a positive incentive to sell their goods on credit.

By the 1930s the depredations of the combined forces of Pedrero (and one or two others like him), the plantation interests whom they served and the Ladino shopkeepers in Chamula centre, had reduced the ordinary population to a state of almost complete destitution. In four hundred years almost the only economy which the Ladinos in San Cristobal had been able to develop was based upon living parasitically on the large Indian population of the hinterland (Aguirre-Beltran 1953:98 and Pozas and Pozas 1971:162f). The Chamulas, being so close to San Cristobal, and having an agricultural economy in a state of chronic deficit (Wasserstrom 1978:140), were particularly vulnerable to such exploitation,[6] and the picture of their trials given above is far from complete.[7]

The night is darkest just before dawn, and in the last years of the 1930s, under the presidency of Lazaro Cardenas (1934–40), a wave of reform swept over Mexico. This marks the beginning of the second period considered in the present chapter. It is surprising, perhaps, that Cardenas' reforms were effective even in such a remote and isolated area as the Chiapas highlands, particularly in view of the fact that their concern for the welfare of the Indian population represented an unmistakable threat to the traditional Ladino economy. But then Cardenas, in his last three years as president, was supported by a state governor, Efrain Gutierrez, and a *presidente municipal*, Erasto Urbina, of San Cristobal, who had the will to enforce his policies against all local opposition. Not only were steps taken at national level, to restrict the abuses of contract labour (Wasserstrom 1983:162), and the system of debt slavery[8] which it supported, but a specific reform programme was carried out in Chamula.[9] Its basis was to appoint, from among the handful of young Chamulas who were literate in Spanish,[10] a number of municipal scribes, whose job it would be to supervise the supply of labour to the coffee plantations, at the same time defending the local population "against the depredations of unscrupulous planters and enganchadores" (Rus and Wasserstom 1979:15).

The results of this enlightened policy proved to be far-reaching. The appointment of the scribes coincided with the state prohibition on the sale of alcohol in the Indian municipios. In the course of time this led the Ladinos in Chamula centre to give up their shops, which were taken over, in at least two cases, by scribes. This broke an essential link in the chain of operations which enabled Pedrero, and others like him, to maintain the institution of debt slavery. In due course the scribes, in addition to maintaining their role as state officials, began to play an active part in the internal politics of Chamula, and by the 1950s they had become the principal members of the ruling oligarchy.

Now the basis for the political organisation of every Indian municipio is to be found in the local round of festivals. The celebration of a festival is the responsibility of a number of ranked officials specifically associated with it. These officials, who hold office for a year at a time, constitute a religious hierarchy (see note 4), which in Chamula, the largest of the municipios, now has about a hundred members, although the number was certainly less at the beginning of the century. The way in which these officials are recruited varies from one municipio to another.[11] The working of the system ensures that almost every adult male will sooner or later serve a year in a religious office, but in practice the service of the majority is confined to low-ranking offices associated with relatively minor festivals. The minority, however, who achieve high office in relation to the major festivals, constitute the political leadership of the municipio. This is particularly the case in Chamula, where it is permissible, after a period of years, to return to an office already served. The result, in recent times, has been that a number of the more important offices have been more or less taken over by a group of individuals constituting a recognized oligarchy, which – subject to a fair level of internal dissension – effectively controls the nominations to every office in the hierarchy.

In the festival cycle the economic dimension is as important as the political. The organizers of a festival are personally responsible for the considerable costs involved in its celebration. The highest ranking officials carry a financial burden far beyond the resources of any economy based on the household. They must depend, therefore, on some institutionalized means of finance. Different expedients have been adopted in almost every municipio, but the problem was always particularly acute in Chamula, where, on the occasion of the major festivals, provision had to be made for the entertainment of the largest Indian population in the highlands. In 1937 the state government granted the highest ranking officials the monopoly of the sale of alcohol at the time of the festivals for which they were responsible (Rus and Waserstrom 1979:16). The object was essentially fiscal. The office-holders were, in effect, governors of a corporation responsible for providing certain traditional services to the local community. The monopoly granted to them provided the necessary funds. True, this particular reform did conflict with the general ban on the sale of alcohol, but then it would at least reduce consumption, by confining it to the periods of the festivals.

In this institutional framework, Chamula politics, in the course of the 1950s, became polarized into two fractions, both led by Indians, with on the one side, Salvador Gomez Ozo, and on the other, Salvador Lopez Castellanos. Both maintained their power by ensuring that certain key religious offices were held, in every year, either by themselves, or by their nominees. Gomez Ozo, by adhering closely to government policy, was also several times elected Presidente Municipal. He became, at the same time, a substantial landowner, concentrating on market gardening in the hamlets close to the centre – an activity which fits in very well with the government's development policy. This has been a profitable venture, for this part of Chamula "since the early 1950's, has enjoyed direct road communication with San Cristobal" (Wasserstrom 1977:458).

Lopez Castellanos, in contrast to Gomez Ozo, chose to deviate from official policy, and his story dominates the third historical period dealt with in this chapter. To understand what he has achieved one must go back to the point when the departure of the Ladino shopkeepers from the centre, and the effective enforcement of the laws governing contract labour, deprived Chamula of its traditional supply of both credit and alcohol. The secret of Lopez Castellanos' success is that he realized that whatever may have happened to the supply, in neither case had demand been eliminated. The problem was to satisfy it.

A number of factors made it next to impossible simply to continue the operations of the departed Ladino shopkeepers. In the first place neither their official duties as scribes, nor their political position within the municipio, would allow the Indians who took over the shops to collaborate with enganchadores. If, therefore, they were to supply credit, it would have to be entirely at their own risk. Unless, however, their economic base were to be strengthened in some way, the risk of default by debtors was one the shopkeepers could not afford to carry.[12] As for retailing rum – to which the law turned a blind eye – the opening up of the highlands, following the construction of the Pan-American Highway, meant that the national excise duties could effectively be imposed upon local production, leading to a drastic increase in price. This might have been fatal for Pedrero's operation, had he not by this time lost all interest in supplying rum to the Indian municipios – having developed new ventures focussed on the national market.[13]

The problem facing Lopez Castellanos, therefore, was how to replace Pedrero as the chief supplier of alcohol, and indirectly of credit, to Chamula in particular, and the Indian highlands in general. Since neither operation was of itself sufficient to maintain an adequate economic base, Lopez

Castellanos had to look elsewhere. He found the solution to his problems in providing the truck transport necessary to enable Chamula to take advantage of the new road network opened up in the highland after the construction of the Pan-American Highway. The suppliers of the trucks, were needless to say, Ladinos. If, at first, Lopez Castellanos was content with third-hand vehicles, bought from a local owner for a capital sum to be paid off by instalments, he was soon able to afford new vehicles, acquired with hire-purchase finance arranged by the official dealers, who in such a matter see no reason to discriminate against Indians. Intensive use of the fleet, which now goes under the name of *Sociedad de Pequenos Agricultores*, maintains a cash-flow sufficient to provide finance for other ventures, including the illegal manufacture of rum at many different points in Chamula, and its distribution throughout much of the highland area.

It is not certain whether Lopez Castellanos himself ever engaged in the illegal manufacture of rum. He may well have done so originally, if only to be able to supply the customers who came to his shop in Chamula centre. If this is the case, his distillery was almost certainly given up at an early stage. The industry has for a long time been divided up between a number of separate distillers, who operate in limestone caves in the inaccessible, densely wooded area, in the neighbourhood of the highest mountain in central Chiapas. To maintain their operations, two factors are essential to these distillers, transport and credit. Both are supplied by Lopez Castellanos.

The transport problem is simply stated. Sugar-cane, the essential raw material for the manufacture of rum, cannot be grown in Chamula, simply because the climate is wrong. The vast new plantations, developed at Pujiltic in the valley of the Grijalva river, some fifty kilometres to the south, have no interest in supplying the Chamula distillers, whose demand for their product is not only small, but also illegal. The traditional Ladino sugar-planters, in the area around Las Rosas on the upper slopes of the escarpment leading down to the Grijalva valley, are ready to supply Chamula – at a price – but they are not able to supply their own transport. Lopez Castellanos will do so, provided his margin of profit is more than sufficient to cover such incidental costs as bribing the police who inspect the trucks as they make their way along the Pan-American Highway, from the turn-off to Las Rosas, back to San Cristobal. It is not certain whether Lopez Castellanos operates only as a transport contractor, or as also a wholesaler in sugar. In either case the distillers need finance to bridge the time gap between paying the Ladino planters in Las Rosas, and being paid for their finished product by the retail network in the highlands. This finance is also provided, at least indirectly, by Lopez Castellanos. The retail network cannot use truck transport: the area served, including the caves where the stills are located, is only passable for mules, and Lopez Castellanos is not involved in this form of transport.

The financial network is maintained by *agentes* in almost every one of the hundred-odd hamlets in Chamula. These tend to be past holders of minor offices in the festival hierarchy, who had to borrow from Lopez Castellanos to tide them over their period of office. Loans are granted for comparatively short periods, seldom longer than six months, and at rates of interest varying between 10 and 20 per cent per month. No security is required, but the social pressure to repay is almost irresistible. The only cases of default appear to occur when a debtor fails to return from a season on the coffee plantations. There is no evidence, either way, as to whether loans to distillers are a separate case, but they are almost certainly larger in amount than the loans granted to other individuals.

The facts recited above invite a comparison between the scale and objectives of the business activities of Pedrero, in the first period, and Lopez Castellanos, in the third. For this purpose one must first recognize the boundaries of the systems in which these activities have taken place. It is significant here that Pedrero's economic horizon extended, at every stage, as far as the economy of Chiapas, and more particularly its basic infrastructure, allowed. Until about 1950 this factor confined him to a circuit extending in one direction to the coffee plantations in the coastal region, in a second to the sugar plantations on the escarpment above the Grijalva river, and in a third to the Indian populations of the San Cristobal hinterland. The fact that the reforms introduced under Cardenas in the last ten years of this period somewhat cramped his style is significant for demonstrating that his operation always remained legitimate in terms of the Mexican culture to which he belonged. When he lost all interest in the Indian highlands it was because the economic frontiers of the area open to his operations had been effectively extended to embrace the whole nation. The fact that Pedrero, initially, almost certainly resisted these changes (Rus and Wasserstrom 1979:14), does not alter the fact that he, in the end, profited enormously from them. His objective was simply to increase his wealth by whatever means were open to him, at the same time maintaining the political contacts – largely at national level – necessary to protect his interests.

Lopez Castellanos' horizon never extended beyond the Indian highlands, whose boundaries defined the furthest extent of the only culture to which he ever belonged. It never mattered to him that the trade in alcohol, on which his commercial and financial operations depended, was, in terms of the Mexican national culture, a part of the unofficial economy.[14] The trade was only competitive in the highland area because no excise duty was ever paid. It was, none the less, just as legitimate, in terms of the local culture, as any operation carried on by Pedrero. From this perspective it is Gomez Ozo whose response to the policies of the state government must be regarded as deviant. The market gardens, which extend in almost every direction from Chamula centre, with their neat rows of cabbages, represent a transformation of the traditional economy – with official government support – not equalled by anything achieved by Lopez Castellanos. It could be argued, indeed, that the stills in the limestone caves are a factor contributing to the survival of the traditional subsistence agriculture.

The concentration of economic power in the hands of a single individual is also significant in the case of both Pedrero and Lopez Castellanos. Economic history no doubt provides support for the proposition that distilling is a trade which lends itself readily to the formation of monopolies. A uniform product, for which there is a universal demand, with relatively low carrying costs, and whose manufacture offers considerable economies of scale, is characteristic of business monopolies.[15] If, at the present time, the actual production of rum in Chamula is far from being a monopoly, its fragmentation into independent concerns is the result of exceptional political and geographic factors.[16] On the other hand there is no doubting Lopez Castellanos' monopoly in the provision of the finance essential to the whole operation.

Any comparison made between the scale of Pedrero's operations in Chamula before, say, 1940, and that of Lopez Castellanos' after, say, 1960, suggests a pronounced fall in the level of consumption of rum. In the former period, in the face of grinding poverty and unremitting exploitation, the Chamulas found in alcohol almost their only solace. They found in rum what Hogarth's London found in gin. In the latter period they have had more than their share in the economic development of the state, and the despair of the earlier days has been replaced by some sense of opportunity. At the same time, where before the 1930s there were no effective restrictions upon supplying cheap rum to any part of the highlands, including San Cristobal, since 1940 the legal restrictions upon its sale in the Indian municipios, combined with effective enforcement of the excise law, have undoubtedly contributed to reduced consumption. In more recent times the state government has done much to encourage the consumption of soft drinks in the highlands, with the distribution franchise being allocated to one of Gomez Ozo's sons. Today one has almost the impression that the part played by rum in the festival cycle is being taken over by Coca-cola.[17] The fact is that the constraints upon the manufacture of rum in Chamula make the whole operation highly inefficient, so that it probably never had the potential to maintain supplies at the level achieved by Pedrero in the 1930s.

To make sense of any comparison between Pedrero and Lopez Castellanos, one must take into account the fact that for the latter, the nation is not the correct unit of analysis. As Seers (1963:85) has pointed out,

> If fiscal and monetary systems are very tenuous, geographic or racial or religious barriers may seal off parts of the nation into virtually self-contained sub-economies.

Lopez Castellanos is only rich and powerful according to the standards of Chamula, which contains less than 2 per cent of the population of Chiapas, and accounts for a very much smaller share of the state economy. Outside his own area he is known only to those who concern themselves in Indian affairs. Pedrero, in contrast, has always been a dominant figure in the politics and economy of the state, and is not without influence in Mexico City. One of the problems about integrating Chamula into the national economy is the pronounced absence of "fit" between the numerical factors which apply within the municipio and the indices established at national level.[18] The Chamula rate of interest, already referred to, at 10 to 20 per cent per month, provides but one example. On this basis the price charged for the local bootleg liquor, although but a fraction of the retail price in San Cristobal, has a much better "fit" with the local economy.

The Chamula sub-economy was never perfectly self-contained, and with the spectacular economic development of the state it becomes less so with every day that passes. Whatever the price indices may be for local products, including alcohol, consumed within the municipio (whose economy is highly diversified), the truck-dealer in Tuxtla-Gutierrez will make no price concessions to an Indian buyer. The same is largely true of the soft drinks which are a serious threat to the market in Chamula rum.

If time is running against Lopez Castellanos, as, in Chamula, it did against Pedrero some forty to fifty years ago, what is the lesson to be learnt from the operations, relating to the supply of alcohol, conducted by both of them? In answering this question one may take it for granted that any given social or cultural order establishes a more or less inelastic demand for one recognized form of alcohol, gin in eighteenth-century London, rum in twentieth-century Chamula. One major factor in determining the level of this demand is the degree of social and economic degradation of the consumers, so that any significant change in one of these factors will be reflected in the other. On this analysis those concerned in the supply of alcohol are bound, in their own interests, to be opposed to social and economic reform. The commitment of this sector of the economy to reactionary politics is familiar to the historian (Trevelyan 1944:570). One expects, however, the conservative to be also a realist, and the truth of this is reflected in the career of Pedrero. The same may be true of Lopez Castellanos, but what other options are open to him? In the convoluted politics of Chamula – which are often marked by violence – it is difficult to make a final judgment.

Notes

1 The *muncipio* is the smallest administrative unit in Mexico, but the scale of operations varies very greatly from one municipio to another. The administrative structure of the Indian municipios is rudimentary, and their authority extremely restricted. They have no taxing power, and the only paid official is the part-time *secretario municipal*, who is invariably a Ladino (see note 3).

2 Since 1880 Tuxtla-Gutierrez, in the lowland area of the state, and some eighty kilometres away, in the direction of Mexico City, has been the state capital.

3 In the culture area which includes Chiapas, and much of Guatemala, the Spanish-speaking population, of mixed Spanish and Indian descent, are known as Ladinos (Pitt-Rivers 1969).

4 This has nothing to do with the official hierarchy of the Catholic Church, whose members are exclusively Ladinos and expatriates.

5 Other Indian municipios may be more than a day's journey away from San Cristobal, which many Indians may never even have visited.

6 It is significant that many Ladinos in San Cristobal refer to almost any Indian as a "Chamula".

7 In the realm of fiction Traven (1971) gives a most graphic picture of the hard life of the average Chamula at this time.

8 In 1914 the revolutionary governor of Chiapas, Gen. Jesus Agustin Castro, promulgated the *Ley de Obreros* (Workers' Law), which abolished debt servitude and regulated many other aspects of plantation labour. The enactment appears to have been of little effect until the time of Cardenas.

9 There is a very extensive literature on Cardenas reforms, but for their effect on Chamula see particularly Wasserstrom (1983: 162–7).

10 At this time only a small minority of Chamulas would even have spoken Spanish. Their own language, Tzotzil, they share with a number of other municipios in the highlands.

11 The process is described in detail for Zinacantan, which is adjacent to Chamula, in Cancian 1965, chapter 4.

12 The same point is made, and the reasons for it given, in Leach's (1968:131) study of the village of Pul Eliya in Ceylon.

13 The trade was also no longer important to Pedrero's operations as an enganchador, which for these had more or less come to an end as a result of Cardenas' reforms.

14 A study of Lopez Castellanos' operations from this perspective is to be found in Crump 1985.

15 For an elementary treatment of this point, see Robinson and Eatwell (1977:157), where the particular cases of matches and electric light bulbs are cited. Braudel's (1973:170–8) treatment of distilling, although thorough in other respects, does not make this point.

16 But compare the organization of the trade and manufacture in London in the first half of the eighteenth century (George 1966:41f.).

17 It is amusing to compare the position with eighteenth-century England, where, after the turn of the century "tea became a formidable rival to alcohol with all classes" (Trevelyan 1944:343).

18 In the last five years a high rate of inflation has also played havoc with the national "indices", but for the twenty-five years from 1955 to 1980 which more or less define the third period considered in this chapter the Mexican peso was remarkably stable.

References

Aguirre-Beltran, G., 1953. *Formas de gobierno indigena*. Mexico, D. F. Coleccion Cultura Mexicana

Braudel, F., 1973. *Capitalism and Material Life 1400–1800*. London, Weidenfeld and Nicolson

Cancian, F., 1965. *Economics and Prestige in a Maya Community*. Stanford University Press

Crump, T., 1985. Geld, koffie en rum: ontwikkelingen in de informele sektor in het hoogland van Chiapas, Mexico. In P. van Gelder and T. Crump (eds.), *De informele sektor in de landen van de derde wereld*. Amsterdam, AWIC & CANSA, pp. 103–14

George, M. D., 1966. *London Life in the Eighteenth Century*. London, Peregrine Books

Leach, E. R., 1968. *Pul Eliya*. Cambridge University Press

Pitt-Rivers, J., 1969. Mestizo or Ladino? *Race* 10: 463–77

Pozas, R., and Pozas, I. H. de, 1971. *Los indios en las clases sociales de Mexico*. Mexico, D. F. Siglo Veinteuno Editores S.A.

Robinson, J., and Eatwell, J., 1977. *An Introduction to Modern Economics*. London, McGraw Hill

Rus, J., and Wasserstrom, R., 1979. *Civil-Religious Hierarchies in Central Chiapas: a Critical Perspective*. 43rd International Conference of Americanists. Vancouver, B.C. (August)

Seers, D., 1963. *The Limitations of the Special Case*. Institute of Economics and Statistics, Oxford. Bulletin No. 35, No. 2, pp. 77–98

Traven, B., 1971. *March to the Monteria*. New York, Hill & Wang

Trevelyan, G. M., 1944. *English Social History*. London, Longmans

Wasserstrom, R., 1977. Land and labour in central Chiapas: a Regional Analysis. *Development and Change* 8: 441–63

   1978. Population growth and economic development in Chiapas, 1524–1975. *Human Ecology* 6: 127–43

   1983. *Class and Society in Central Chiapas*. Berkeley, University of California Press

14. Alcohol monopoly to protect the non-commercial sector of eighteenth-century Poland

Hillel Levine

In Poland, between the end of the sixteenth century and the end of the eighteenth century, there was a dramatic increase in the manufacture and sale of grain-based intoxicants. While income from the manufacture of alcohol accounted for .3% of the overall income of royal properties in 1564 and 6.4% about a century later, in 1764 it accounted for 37.6% of the overall income. By 1789 the proportion of revenues from the sale of alcohol reached 40.1 percent.[1] In view of the large growth in total income during this period, this increase in the proportion of the income derived from alcohol sales indicated an even larger growth in the actual quantity of alcohol manufactured. While precise figures are unavailable for other types of estates, there is little reason to assume that the pattern varied considerably.

There is good reason to believe that the primary customers for this drink were the enserfed peasants. This is corroborated by frequent reports of peasant intoxication.[2] However, the extent to which the consumption of alcohol among the serfs actually increased in this period cannot be demonstrated. These serfs may have used part of their own grain to produce home brews, at least in the earlier period. What is indicated by the increased revenue from alcohol is greater success in institutionalizing the monopoly on its manufacture and distribution within the economy of feudal estates and the increased quantities of grain which landlords deployed particularly for this purpose. This monopolistic enterprise came to be known as the *Propinacja (Propinatio)*.

This directs our attention to the organization of supply rather than to the possible psychological motivations and needs reflected by increased demand. It was the gentry and landowning clergy which claimed and upheld this monopoly both on their estates and in their private towns.[3] However, the manufacturer, wholesalers, and retailers of intoxicants were often drawn from a different segment of the Polish population – the Jews.

The Jewish inn was a part of everyday life in the Polish towns and countryside of this period. A traveler's account of the 1830s gives us a sense of how these taverns, which had hardly changed from the previous century, appeared:

250

It was principally in his capacity as innkeeper that I became acquainted with the Polish Jew. The inn is generally a miserable hovel . . . partitioned off in one corner of a large shed, serving as a stable and yard for vehicles; the entrance is under a low porch or timber; the floor is dirt; the furniture consists of a long table or two or three small ones in one corner, a bunch of straw, or sometimes a few raised boards forming a platform with straw spread over it for beds; at one end a narrow door leads into a sort of hall filled with dirty beds, old women, half-grown boys and girls not overburdened with garments, and so filthy that however fatigued, I never felt disposed to venture among them for rest. Here the Jew, assisted by a dirty-faced Rachel, with a keen and anxious look, passes the full day in serving out to the meanest customer beer and hay and corn; wrangling with and extorting money from intoxicated peasants. . .[4]

Jewish sources likewise capture the ambiance of the inn.[5] Jewish folklore is replete with stories taking place in provincial taverns; the purveyor of drink is a prominent personality type. The scant demographic and economic data that we have of this period, albeit of questionable reliability, provides further support for the important role of Jews in different facets of the *Propinacja*. In the middle of the eighteenth century, it was reported that 20–30% of the Jewish population was involved in some aspect of alcohol production. According to the census of 1764–65, a majority of Jews in villages, as well as 15% of the Jews living in towns, were involved in alcohol-related enterprises.[6]

There are additional attestations to the participation of Jews in the *Propinacja*. From the second half of the eighteenth century on, the role of the Jews in the *Propinacja* was sharply criticized. Liberal reformers, conservative anti-Jewish politicians, Polish nationalists trying to save the declining Polish state, and Russian bureaucrats trying to consolidate Tsarist rule in newly annexed territories all concurred in pointing to the Jews' involvement in this enterprise as evidence of their limited economic utility. As suppliers of drink, Jews came to be blamed for the serfs' poor standard of living, their low productivity, their rebelliousness and destructiveness. Jewish modernizers, while quick to point out the limited economic opportunities of their coreligionists, echoed the condemnatory tones of the publicist literature. Even contemporary Jewish historians have been delicately apologetic for Jewish involvement in the *Propinacja*.[7]

The *Propinacja* has been viewed as a reflection of, and even as a contributor to, the problems of the Polish economy in general and to the decline of serfdom in particular. But what explains the development of the *Propinacja* itself and how do we account for the high incidence of Jews in this branch of the Polish economy?

This paper will survey recent studies which shed light upon the crystallization of feudalism in Poland and will consider Polish micro- and macroeconomics in relation to commercial and industrial developments in the West. It will focus on the *Propinacja* as a mechanism used by the landed classes to respond to problems which threatened to undermine the feudal order which they had established: the declining profitability of their single-crop economy and the increasing instability of their labor force. Using this understanding of Polish feudalism and the *Propinacja*, we will try to move beyond polemics and apologetics in assessing the significance of Jewish involvement in the *Propinacja*. We will show how this involvement is connected to the Jews' position in the medieval Polish economy; what it reflects of the relations between the gentry, the Jews, the clergy, and the serfs in the early modern period; and what repercussions it had for the largest and most concentrated Jewish community in Europe precisely at that moment in the late eighteenth century when the Enlightenment and the French Revolution were beginning to transform the position of their coreligionists in the West.

II

The *Propinacja* developed and took on increasing significance within the demesne economy, which was based on the labor of enserfed peasants. The legal foundation of this system was adumbrated in the late fifteenth century, but what has been called the "second serfdom" did not become an institutional reality until the second part of the sixteenth century.[8] To understand the origins, features, and impact of this newly emerged Polish feudalism, it must be related to contemporaneous developments in western and eastern Europe, particularly the rise of absolutism. The relationship of feudalism to political centralization and the rise of the Absolutist State has been well summarized in Perry Anderson's recent study:

> The Absolutist State in the West was the redeployed political apparatus of a feudal class which had accepted the commutation of dues. It was a compensation for the disappearance of serfdom in the context of an increasingly urban economy which it did not completely control and to which it had to adapt. The Absolutist State in the East, by contrast, was the repressive machine of a feudal class that had just erased the traditional communal freedoms of the poor. It was a device for the consolidation of serfdom in a landscape scoured of autonomous urban life or resistance. The manorial reaction in the East meant that a new world had to be implanted from above, by main force. The dose of violence pumped into social relations was correspondingly far greater. The Absolutist State in the East never lost the signs of this original experience.[9]

Within this typology, Poland, a country at the crossroads of East and West, stands as an anomaly. The development of its agrarian feudalism neither preceded (as in the West), nor was it accompanied by (as in the East), the development of political centralization within the framework of an Absolutist State. The *Propinacja* as a device by which serfdom in Poland was sustained is therefore of particular interest.[10]

The "second serfdom" manifested features of the feudalism which had developed at an earlier date in eastern and western Europe, including large-scale land ownership and small peasant production. The peasant's freedom was limited by extra-economic modes of coercion; and surplus was extracted from him in the form of labor services, deliveries in kind, and, to a lesser extent, rents in cash. Consequences of this expanding demesne economy included a severely restricted commodity exchange and labor mobility, a low level of monetization, and a high interest rate. These made most investments, including those for agricultural improvements, financially unfeasible. The low level of money in circulation resulted in the shrinkage of trade and thus contributed to the decline of towns and urban centers. This came in the wake of widespread interregional and international commerce in the Middle Ages. It had a particularly severe effect on the economic positions of Jews and burghers, increasing the antagonism between them.[11]

However, there were features of this "second serfdom" peculiar to its development in Poland. The consolidation of feudalism occurred in a period during which the central institutions of Poland were still somewhat powerful. Poland expanded in the direction of its eastern borders, incorporating large numbers of seminomadic Pravoslavian peasants. These were enserfed partly by force and partly by the absorption of their leaders into the Polish aristocracy. Nevertheless, religious tensions continued to undergird class conflict. Both contributed to the periodic incitement of marauding Cossacks and Tartars, whose political loyalties vacillated and who received occasional assistance from the rulers of Muscovite Russia. The shifting spheres of political influence in these eastern border regions, the decreasing level of Polish political and military control, and the existence of vast uninhabited territories further to the east to which serfs could escape made for an unreliable labor force on the feudal estates that were being carved out of the Ukraine. Large-scale peasant rebellions, particularly from the middle of the seventeenth century on, resulted in frequent devastation in grain-growing regions.

Despite the unstable conditions under which the eastern expansion took place, the acquisition of new lands became a necessity. Because of the scarcity of capital for any kind of improvement or investment, farming techniques remained rudimentary, the land became exhausted, and the agriculture of the feudal demesne had to be extensive rather than intensive. Indeed, within the economic calculations made by the Polish gentry, land and labor were considered abundant, if not unlimited.

Developments beyond Poland at the same time made the grain crop particularly valuable, spurring the growth of demesne agriculture at the very moment of its institutionalization in the second part of the sixteenth century. As explored in the recent work of Immanuel Wallerstein, the links in economic development between East and West point to the incentives to increase grain production for Poland, a peripheral area in relation to the developing European world-economy. The religious wars and destruction which took place in the West created serious food shortages. This presented tremendous opportunities for Poland to supply grain at high profits to the floundering areas of western Europe. Indeed, Poland was a breadbasket during the early stages of western urbanization and industrialization.

By the second quarter of the seventeenth century, however, the trend of increasing exports of Polish grain with profitable returns reverses itself. This reversal relates to complex international changes, including price fluctuations and improved yields of other granaries which could supply western Europe.[12] The long-term trend may be described in the following manner. The early stages of industrial revolutions, to which Poland had contributed necessary grain and, therefore, a modicum of political stability, had now succeeded in such a way that the results could be applied to agriculture and food provision; this undercut the marketability and profitability of Polish grain. Domestic instability in the seventeenth century created difficulties in the production and transportation of Polish grain, worsening its position in the international economy.[13]

III

Having surveyed the macroeconomic forces related to the consolidation of the "second serfdom" and the system of demesne agriculture, we must now look at how these forces shaped the various groups' efforts to improve, or at least maintain, their relative and absolute economic positions. Some measure, however speculative, of the impact of these economic conditions and fluxes over some time is suggested by Witold Kula's calculations of the relative terms of trade of the upper nobility, lower nobility, and peasants between 1550 and 1750.[14] An examination of grain profits in the period 1550–1600 indicates an improvement in the economic positions of both the magnate and the serf. However unevenly the windfall profits of the second part of the sixteenth century were distributed, this short-lived, but absolute, improvement in the peasant's standard of living might have provided the conditions for voluntary enserfment. The temporary reversal, followed by the undramatic growth in the terms of trade of the lower nobility, may account for the rising frequency of bankruptcy within that class and the increase of magnates' land concentration.[15] What is most striking about these calculations, however, is the steady decline in the terms of trade of the now-enserfed peasantry.

Changes in terms of trade for social groups

	1550	1600	1650	1700	1750
Upper nobility	100	276	385	333	855
Lower nobility	100	80	144	152	145
Peasant	100	205	169	118	51

Using the relative economic positions of 1600 as the base line for calculations, the decline in the economic position of the serfs in the ensuing century and a half appears even more striking.

Changes in terms of trade for social groups

	1600	1650	1700	1750
Upper nobility	100	139	121	310
Lower nobility	100	180	190	181
Peasant	100	82	58	25

This deteriorating economic condition of the serf may provide the background for the escape, rebelliousness, low productivity, and even malicious destructiveness – *dezolacja* – of the dispirited and the undernourished. It might even outline the psychological climate in which an increase in drunkenness among the serfs took place and the political environment in which the lord made greater quantities of intoxicants available. Drunken peasants are more easily beaten into sullen obedience.

However, there are additional socioeconomic factors in the feudal system of seventeenth- and eighteenth-century Poland that suggest the economic utility of the *Propinacja* and point to the suitability of the population from which its manufacturers and managers were recruited. Here a glance at the microeconomy of Polish feudalism, as outlined by Kula, is most illuminating. A distinctive feature of Polish feudalism is the sharp bifurcation which it creates and seeks to regulate between the commercial sector and the noncommercial sector – suggestively called the natural sector – of the economy. The natural sector was made up of the small productive units of the feudal estates in which the peasants worked the lord's land a certain number of days per week and fed his work animals in exchange for the right to live on and to till a small strip of land. From the grain that the peasant and his family raised, he would have to provide food, pay additional cash rent to the lord, pay tithes to the church, and market any possible surplus for the money to meet those fixed obligations as well as to buy whatever commodities he could not produce. These might include salt, wax, nails, and cloth, as well as beer and vodka. The peasant sought to maintain this relationship to the commercial sector of the feudal economy independent of crop conditions. To increase the possibility of having a surplus, even in bad years, the peasant might try to move landmarks to increase his arable area, cultivate his lands more intensively than those he worked for the lord, or even skimp on the food that the lord gave him to feed the work animals. In years of drought or war, when crops were not very successful, it was particularly difficult for the peasant to sustain himself, let alone to have a surplus with which to maintain a market relationship.

The primary consideration of the lord was to market the grain from his lands and the grain paid to him by his serfs at a sufficient profit. He would then be able to buy luxury items, mostly from abroad, and thus maintain his standard of living. In years when war did not ravage the countryside, the large magnates had the resources and sufficient surplus to move their grain to the interior rivers and from thence to the international ports, such as Danzig, where the grain trade was more profitable. There they also had their agents, who procured luxury items, paper, condiments, coffee, sugar, fine clothing, French wines, and art objects, for their town houses and provincial estates. The peasants and lower gentry – and even the magnates in bad years – had to depend on local markets and middlemen to exchange their grain. It was in these markets that the economic interests of the gentry and the peasants could clash. Especially at times of shrinking demand, the peasants were at a relative advantage in being able to find purchasers for their small quantities of grain in local and regional markets. Since their expenses were more modest than the lord's, they could afford to sell at a lower price.[16] Because of this competition, the lord was forced to redouble his efforts to move his grain to more distant markets, thus increasing transportation costs. As the profitability of grain sales on the international market decreased, beginning in the second quarter of the seventeenth century, the gentry was in greater need of local and regional outlets which it could control. Consequently, the participation of peasants in local and regional markets had double-edged outcomes for the overall economic interests of the lord.

Kula note, with no small measure of amazement, the tenacity and resourcefulness of the peasants in producing the surplus needed to maintain the market relationship, regardless of prevailing agricultural and economic conditions. He also notes that the gentry showed equal resourcefulness in controlling this surplus. It was the gentry's management, rather than the increased profitability of demesne production, which was a major factor in the rise of the gentry's overall income at the end of the seventeenth century and during the eighteenth century.[17]

But beyond economic interests connected to the serfs' surplus production, the lord had other reasons to seek to impede, or at least to control, the market relationship that the peasant so much sought to have. For feudalism in Poland was not only an economic relationship; it also described a set of patriarchal social relations canonized in Sarmatian culture, which the lord tried to preserve even when there were economic incentives for its transformation.[18] When it could, the gentry opposed the development of a labor market and agriculture based on rent payments rather than on feudal service. The limited efforts at industrialization in the second part of the eighteenth century, which, when made, were undertaken within the feudal organization of labor and markets, further illustrate the concern of the gentry to preserve these patriarchal social relations.[19] The availability of free-floating currency which could loosen the social structure was consequently seen as harmful to the idealized structuring of the relations between gentry and serf.[20] But beyond that, according to the gentry's economic theories, which supported maximum autarky and self-sufficiency of productive units, any cash expenditure was frowned upon. As a late sixteenth-century writer on economic organization and bookkeeping for feudal estates put it, "It is not only harmful but shameful to buy with money, as a result of neglectfulness, what could be had without expense."[21] That peasants might have surplus cash which could be used to purchase goods produced outside the estate was thought by the gentry to deplete its own wealth. That the lord himself removed exorbitant sums from this economy for luxury items was not seen as a contradiction.

It is in this regard, as Kula indicates, that the manufacture of alcohol operated as a siphoning-off mechanism.[22] Cash that the peasant would somehow succeed in accumulating, which could be spent off of the feudal estate and which could solidify, and even strengthen, his position in relation to local markets had to be siphoned off and allowed to circulate within the idealized microeconomy of the feudal estate. These siphoning-off mechanisms would preserve both the economic and patriarchal social relations of the estate as idealized by the gentry. The usefulness of the *Propinacja* is illustrated by records that we have of estates in the eighteenth century actually requiring serfs to purchase a minimum amount of alcohol as a part of their obligations to the landlord. Thus, what the gentry tried to create within the autarky of the feudal economy and its idealization of patriarchal relations was a mechanism of closed monetary circulation, a *perpetuum mobile*.

This *perpetuum mobile* might have worked, at least for a while longer, were it not for the ultimate falsity of two assumptions upon which it was based: that the supply of cheap labor was unlimited, and that the demand for Polish grain at increasingly higher prices was unchanging. With the decline of dependable labor supplies and stable market outlets for grain, conditions prevailing in the sixteenth century, when Polish feudalism was institutionalized, the *Propinacja* took on additional functions.

The declining prices of grain on the world market from 1625 on, the increasing frequency and severity of peasant rebellions and foreign invasions from the mid-1600s on, and the political vicissitudes of eighteenth-century Poland all reduced the profitability of grain and made the shipment of grain to international markets more difficult. And while these same events might have increased the demand for grain on local markets, the prices that the landlords, particularly the large magnates, might fetch would not be adequate to provide the surplus necessary for imported items and thereby to facilitate consolidation of their economic position under these turbulent circumstances. The *Propinacja* provided an important solution to these crop, shipping, and marketing problems by producing a profitable end product for Polish grain. The profits yielded from grain-based intoxicants far exceeded the profits derived from selling that same quantity of grain on the open market. The *Propinacja* created an expanding and stable local market which did not involve problems of transportation, although it might occasionally need some priming. This aspect of the *Propinacja*'s economic significance is registered in the following statement of an eighteenth-century member of the upper gentry, Prince Joseph Czartoryski, in his essay, "My Opinion on the Principles of Economics"; "Without the sales of the *Propinacja*, we would not be able to assure ourselves of a regular income in currency. In our country the vodka distilleries could be called mints because it is only thanks to them that we can hope to sell off our grain in years when there is no famine."[23] That the *Propinacja* contributed to the ruination of the peasants was not a cost that had to be considered by the gentry as long as labor was viewed as other than a finite resource. But the contradiction between immediate profit and the expense of long-range losses eventually did confront the gentry. Here the involvement of the Jews was beneficial beyond economic utility and administrative exigencies.

IV

Having examined the social and economic forces which contributed to the increased manufacture and marketing of grain-based intoxicants, the question remains: Why the Jews? Are there any factors other than historical accident and economic opportunity which explain their recruitment into this enterprise?[24]

On first glance, the administration of the *Propinacja* can be considered as a mere part of the larger set of economic relations that had developed between the Jews and the landed classes in the sixteenth century, prior to the development of the *Propinacja* as a significant source of income. Within the set of economic relations known as the *arenda*, or leasing-out system, the owners of estates or private towns would grant concessions to Jews who managed parts of their enterprises or entire estates in exchange for a set fee and often an additional commission on revenues.[25]

The managerial position of Jews in developing the estates of the gentry and harnessing the Ukrainian peasants into a servile labor force evoked consternation among Jews from its very beginnings. As early as 1580, there are edicts in Jewish communal records forbidding Jewish participation in the *arenda*.[26] It was correctly assumed that Jews would be wrongly identified with the entire system, that they would antagonize the peasants, and that they might become targets of peasant wrath. Indeed, this happened in the increasingly frequent peasant rebellions. A particularly severe and protracted series of peasant attacks in 1648, which came to be known in Jewish memory and historiography as the Chmielnicki Massacres, was believed even by contemporaries to have been a reprisal for the Jews' role in the *arenda*. However, the frequency with which the prohibition against Jewish involvement in managing feudal estates was reiterated is some reflection of the magnitude and intractability of the involvement.

The skills of Jews in these positions, and their availability and willingness to manage and organize peasant labor, might account for their recruitment and promotion by the gentry. A further advantage of promoting Jews, rather than members of the lower gentry, was that Jews would be less able and less likely to use their economic position to organize intrigues.

Consequently, it may have been merely as a result of their prior involvement in the *arenda* that Jews were recruited to organize the increasingly important monopoly on the production and sale of alcohol. The *Propinacja* became one of the concessions that could be given over directly to Jewish lessees or subcontracted by Jews who managed entire estates. Only the wealthier purveyors may have had the requisite capital to establish breweries and distilleries. These might have been associated with a network of Jewish tavernkeepers in the countryside who would distribute the liquor. On the small estates, contact between the landlord and the tavernkeeper may have been more direct. Viewed from this perspective, the *Propinacja* does not seem to call for special attention, it being part and parcel of a larger and already existing set of exchanges between gentry and Jews.

However, there were other advantages to Jewish involvement in the *Propinacja* that cannot be overlooked. One of the noted effects of the development of feudalism is deurbanization. Towns and cities, aside from providing shelter for fugitive serfs, established markets which the feudal masters could not quite control and which, under certain circumstances (discussed above), could undermine the profitability of the gentry's grain sales. The peasants' efforts to maintain a market relationship were facilitated by Jewish merchants in the towns and Jewish peddlers in the countryside. This undermined the autarky of the feudal estate, and, according to the economic calculations of the gentry, removed wealth from the estate.

Before the sixteenth century, the gentry promoted Jewish merchants and artisans against Christian burghers as a way of breaking the guilds' cartel and of lowering prices on imported goods. But now the gentry saw that it was in its interest to further weaken the towns by eliminating the Jews. From the mid-1550s on, the absorption of increasing numbers of Jews into the economy of the gentry's feudal estates and private towns not only provided economic opportunities for the Jews and a chance for the gentry to obtain managerial skills, but it also afforded the gentry control over a population whose economic activities could potentially weaken the developing feudal economy. The crippling of Jewish trade was accompanied by the elimination of Jews from the crafts. Jewish craftsmen could no longer be supplied with raw materials by tradesmen whom they would then compensate with partnership in the finished product.

This transfer of increasing numbers of Jews from free towns and areas under the jurisdiction of the monarchy to the feudal economies of the gentry had important implications for the organization of the Jewish community. It became far more difficult to protect and promote Jewish interests under many separate and uncoordinated jurisdictions. At the same time, the efforts of the gentry to control the Jews were related to the same contradictory economic forces which influenced their efforts to subordinate the serfs. For the same class, the gentry, which considered the local markets to be interfering with the feudal autarky of their estates also created an economic system which required local markets. The peasants needed local markets to obtain consumer goods which the estate could not manufacture and to raise money for their cash rents and tithes. It was their success in growing a surplus of grain which determined their ability to sustain a market relationship. But in order to change this into cash, there had to be local markets.

Here we see the important role played by Jews in linking the natural and commercial sectors of the economy and in providing the mechanisms by which the economic contradictions inherent in feudalism could be transcended and the fictions of Sarmatian autarky could be sustained. By purchasing peasant grain, the Jews provided the peasants with money to buy goods not manufactured on the feudal estate and to pay the lord's rent, which the serf had to pay to fulfill his part of the feudal contract but for which the theory of Sarmatian autarky never accounted. The problem for the gentry resolved itself into the following terms: How to accentuate the advantages and reduce the disadvantages of this economic relationship between serfs and Jews. It was the *Propinacja* that provided the perfect solution. Encouraging the serfs to spend their surplus on drink would keep the money within the natural sector of the feudal economy; siphoning off their surplus would preserve feudal autarky. At the same time, it would absorb Jews into an enterprise which would limit their development of local markets that were not controlled by the gentry. The peasants would be induced to raise a surplus, but this surplus would still be beneficial to the feudal lord even if it had to pass through the hands of the Jewish innkeeper. The *Propinacja* as a siphoning-off mechanism was a remedy for the inefficiencies and failures of the devices of coercive surplus extraction. It was a feeble effort of the gentry to maintain their profits despite uncertain returns on grain, while preventing the Jews and serfs from gaining the modicum of freedom that participation in exchange markets allows.

V

If the *Propinacja* is to be seen as a siphoning-off mechanism which compensated the gentry for the shortcomings of feudal measures of surplus extraction, and which insured that the adaptive modes of the other economic actors would ultimately work in the gentry's interests, the prominent position of Jews within this enterprise might be considered a masking device by which some of the internal contradictions of the system were concealed. Jewish candidacy for this position was based not only on availability and suitability, but on roles heretofore played within the Polish economy. Removed from their position at the interstices of local and international markets that they had maintained as tradesmen in the Middle Ages, they now were promoted into a position at the interstices of the commercial and noncommercial sectors – where the personalized system of production met the impersonal system of exchange. In this position, Jewish economic activities masked the efforts of the gentry to dominate the serfs personally and to exploit them economically. At the same time, these activities were calculated to compensate the gentry financially for the undesirable outcome of demesne agriculture and the feudal social and economic systems, the precipitation of peasant rebellion and sabotage. The strains inherent in the Jews' new role, masking as it did both contradictions within the system and conflicts between different groups, led to emotional outbursts. These frequent attacks upon Jews were not merely hostile uprisings against the middleman or the outsider, particularly one that dominates. They also functioned as safety valves for societal tensions. But the selection of certain allegations from the classical and medieval stockpile may imply a closer link between the sources of strain and the dramatic forms in which they were expressed.

In this period there was a notable and tragic resurgence of the accusations that Jews clandestinely stabbed Communion wafers, causing them to bleed; that they murdered Christian children for ritual purposes; that they mixed their victims' blood with grain to make the Passover wafers that celebrated Jewish freedom; and that they used Christian blood as sacramental wine. A Christian child missing, or found dead, was sufficient cause to raise the specter of the blood libel. These accusations incited murderous pogroms and trials by torture.[27] It might be speculated that symbolic associations were made between grain and sustenance; blood and vitality; wine and intoxicants used ritually by Jews for spiritual elevation; and grain-based intoxicants and the debasement of the serfs. These associations provided the expressive forms for the attacks that dramatized the economic relations of gentry, Jews, and serfs.[28] Other classes of Polish society injured by the enserfment of the peasantry and the gentry's subsequent economic measures could find a plausible explanation for their new economic problems in the Jewish management of the *Propinacja*, and would eagerly collude in attacks upon the Jews. The burghers could rage against the Jews for two reasons: they had been bypassed as possible agents for this profitable concession; and their economic position further declined because they could sell fewer imported and manufactured goods to peasants who drank away their money. The clergy could blame the Jews for leaving the peasants without the resources to pay tithes. The Christian clergy were particularly instrumental in orchestrating attacks because they controlled, and therefore could invoke, the religious symbols used to legitimate the blood libel. Thus, resentment against the Jews could be incited and organized to the satisfaction of the burghers and the serfs and would often have the enthusiastic cooperation of the gentry.

That the *Propinacja* was an integral part of the gentry's efforts to compensate for the declining profitability of grain sales and to "save the system" – the idealized notion of social order, which included an economy based on personal obligation and the squandering of surplus – was overlooked. The gentry, who profited most from this arrangement, could join the other classes of Polish society, with which they were at economic odds, in harmonious denunciations of the Jewish exploiters. They could pass on both the risk and the blame to their Jewish agents in exchange for having given them their meager opportunity to sustain themselves and to pay the high taxes which they were pledged to pay to the increasingly impotent monarch. The possibilities for short-term profit did not exclude the chance for the gentry to vent their self-righteous moral indignation at Jewish expense. However, when the siphoning-off mechanism, which was to save the system, itself began to falter in its economic functions and its harmful side effects became more salient, the Jews, whose participation in the feudal system by way of the *Propinacja* no longer succeeded in masking the internal contradictions of that system, were subjected to attacks which were translated from the sphere of dramatic representation to that of public discourse.

VI

Jewish involvement in the *Propinacja* became a focus of attention among Polish parliamentarians and pamphleteers in the discussions of the "Jewish problem", which occurred during the second half of the eighteenth century and culminated in the proposals made before the Four-Year Sejm, 1788–92.[29] Resolutions to reform the Jews, sounded in certain circles of the better-educated and Western-oriented gentry, echoed the public discourse taking place at this time in the West regarding the amelioration of the Jews' position in an "Enlightened" or otherwise transformed new society.[30] However, the conclusions drawn were often quite different. At the very moment that futile debates on the "Jewish problem" were being held at the Sejm in Warsaw, similar debates were being conducted in Paris, on the eve of the French Revolution. Most Parisian publicists viewed the preservation of the legal disabilities endured by the Jews under the *Ancien Régime* as incompatible with their program to eliminate the Estates that was integral to the desired political changes. More generally, those Western reformers at all favorably disposed toward Jews argued that government usurpation of

Jewish communal authority and the extension of economic and even civil rights to individual Jews would curtail their "harmful" traits and eventually make them productive and loyal citizens. It was even hoped that they would soon join the majority religion as a result of this good treatment. Although Polish reformers could no longer ignore the precipitous decline of the Polish Republic, they almost all avoided a direct and constructive confrontation with the social, political, and economic problems reflected by the *Propinacja*. In the eleventh hour, when Poland was threatened by internal dissolution and by the territorial and political avariciousness of its neighbors, Polish reformers and "men of the Enlightenment" preferred to indulge in condemning the Jews for involvement in the *Propinacja*, holding them responsible for its pernicious effects and even implying at times that Poland's backwardness was attributable to the unproductive economic roles Jews chose for themselves. Some members of the upper gentry may have joined the condemnation of Jewish involvement in the *Propinacja* for greed's sake rather than reform's. They hoped to wrest a larger proportion of this profitable business from the lower gentry, who still required the investments and the managerial skills of Jewish agents.

This mounting criticism of Jewish involvement in the *Propinacja* soon received an infusion from Russian officials supervising the newly annexed Polish territories, who themselves derived no immediate economic benefit from the *Propinacja* but who wished to exert greater political and economic control over the Polish gentry. After the First Partition of Poland (1772) and for a good part of the nineteenth century, any Russian investigation of peasant discontent – often initiated after crop failures and peasant rebellions – pointed an accusing finger at the odious Jewish producers and purveyors of peasant misery. But in painting dark pictures of evil Jews who withheld grain from starving peasants because it was more profitable to use it for liquor than to sell it for bread, neither Polish reformers nor Russian bureaucrats sought to investigate the forces which created and sustained the *Propinacja*. Haranguing about its effects seemed to preclude sober analysis of its causes. Provocative rhetoric now replaced dramatic representation as the device by which the internal contradictions of the crumbling Polish feudal system could be masked.

VII

In conclusion, we must ask: Besides the general and irrational need to have a scapegoat, what political and economic motives were behind the myopic view of the *Propinacja*? How did they limit the impact even of well-intentioned programs designed to improve the situation of Jews in a revitalized Poland?

Answers to these questions may be seen in the desperate efforts to preserve the feudal social structure against the cumulative effects of its internal contradictions. The feudal system limited the perspectives and narrowed the options of all involved, and the political and economic motivations of their actions within that system determined the forms of protests and reactions alike. As Kula so cogently argues,

> The system ... was created by men, by the recurrence of certain of their modes of behaviour and of their reactions. Once created, it dominated them for a long time. Since it was full of internal contradictions, it produced many effects which were involuntary or even contrary to its existence. Of these, the most important were class distinctions. While dominating men, the system also brought forth against itself their rebelliousness. If there actually existed within the system factors which, as their cumulative effect, would have led to its collapse, the primary one was represented by the actions of the peasant masses scattered over hundreds of thousands of square kilometers: sabotage of forced labour, escapes, and struggles to have relations with the market. While uncoordinated and spontaneous, these actions are all oriented in the same direction because they are determined by a substantially identical class situation.[31]

The Polish gentry, including the reformers among them, as well as the Russian civil servants, who had their own problems with serfdom, saw agrarian and economic problems as results rather than causes of peasant rebelliousness. Therefore, whatever explanations and proposals they made could not undermine the legitimacy of feudalism, of its institutionalization of gentry privilege and serf labor. Rather than confront the problems and contradictions intrinsic to the social system, they made well-meant, but wholly insufficient, appeals for minor changes – crop rotation and fertilization, and the use of serf labor in cottage industries and in the small-scale exploitation of such natural resources as coal and wood. At the same time, they pointed to the deleterious effects of Jewish economic activities and blamed the Jews for the failures of serfdom.

The proposals to reform the Jews of Poland and, following the partitions, those areas annexed to or controlled by Russia, must be seen in relation to the stronger commitment to preserve the feudal social structure in spite of its problems of political control and its economic inefficiency. Even Polish reformers advocating otherwise far-reaching programs of change shied away from tampering with its fundamental provisions.[32] The effort to preserve feudalism severely limited the possibilities of increasing the economic productivity of Polish Jews, rendering even sympathetic reform proposals inconsequential. This contrasted with the situation in western countries, where important changes in the social structure preceded or accompanied changes in the economic and political integration of the Jews.

Aside from the structural limitations imposed upon Jewish economic enterprise and productivity by the feudal order, however, it might have been the case that conservative and liberal Russian and Polish publicists who sought to preserve serfdom saw the Jews as a new labor force which could gradually replace the more rebellious Tartar and Cossack peasants.[33] Proposals to reform the Jews and increase their productivity argued for the elimination of Jews from the *Propinacja* and from other managerial positions on behalf of the gentry. These proposals urged Jews to invest in manufacturing, which, because of high interest rates and small labor markets, was possible for only a very small financial elite with international connections. The majority of Jews, who grew steadily poorer, were urged to enter agricultural labor. They were to replace serfs, whose further subordination might have led either to an agrarian revolution or to the transformation of labor contracts into cash rents – alternatives which had to be forestalled. To the publicists, the solution to the "Jewish problem" was also the solution to the "peasant problem", since it would press the increasing number of impoverished Jews into a "third serfdom".

All but a few wealthy Jews and fellow-travelers of the Enlightenment resisted reform measures imposed from without. Polish Jews struggled to maintain their positions in familiar enterprises, including the *Propinacja*, in spite of the proven risks and the mounting abuses to which they were subjected. Kula's more general statement may be applied to them: the "uncoordinated and spontaneous" actions of the Jewish masses constrained to live within the Polish and Russian "Pale" were efforts to maintain their position in the *Propinacja* and to resist involvement in agriculture. Caught between the crumbling Polish feudal autarky and the rising Russian autocracy, the masses of Polish Jewry made but an unenthusiastic response to the possibilities of, and proposals for, "reform" – a response that may have reflected their intuitive but profound perception of its more than ambiguous terms.

This article was first published in *Review*, IV, 2 Fall 1980, 223–25 © 1980 Research Foundation of SUNY. The author wishes to thank Professors Yaron Ezrahi, Jerzy Jedlicki, and Immanuel Wallerstein for commenting on earlier versions of this work.

Notes

1 Leskiewicz 1960 quoted in Kula 1976: 134.
2 Fernand Braudel reports that "peasants on the Polish estates consumed up to three litres of beer a day." Braudel 1973: 168.
3 For the purposes of most of this analysis, the interests of the landowning clergy will be considered with those of the gentry because of the class origins of the upper clergy and the compatibility of their interests with those of the gentry. Similarly, the economy of feudal estates belonging to the monarchy will require no special consideration from that of the magnates.
4 Stephens 1838, 11: 189.
5 See the interesting descriptions of the Jewish inn and trade in alcoholic drink in Maimon 1954, 11: 17–18, 56.
6 See Gross, ed., 1975: 132–40 and Tartakower 1959–60.

7 For example, see Dubnow 1923–38, VII: 51–52 and Sheffer 1948: 197.

8 See Anderson 1974: 208 and Wallerstein 1974: 97, n. 112; 101, n. 125.

9 Anderson 1974: 195. For a summary of factors attributed to the differential patterns of development in these regions at this time, see Wallerstein 1974: 97ff.

10 See Jedlicki 1973: 66.

11 See Kula 1976: 19ff.

12 See Braudel 1973: 66–120, esp. 84.

13 See Kula 1976: 129–33, 151.

14 See Kula 1976: 123–24. The calculation of the terms of trade is based upon the purchasing price of the amount of agricultural produce that a member of the upper or lower gentry and a serf are likely to be able to present to the market and what that price is able to procure in terms of the commodities of a hypothetical "basket of goods" that each of these is likely to procure. Though this represents a limited number of variables, it gives some indication of how the standard of living of people within each of these social categories probably changed over the specified period of time.

15 This concentration of land itself might be viewed as an incipient stage of the development of capitalism within Poland. However, because of the efforts of the magnates to keep cash expenditures for everything except their personal luxury items to a minimum and to reduce all commercial transactions in relation to their feudal estates to a minimum, this accumulation and concentration of the means of production can be related only to long-term developments. Neither did the *déclassé* nobility provide the manpower for the growth of a centralized bureaucracy and army – a development which takes place elsewhere in relation to the rise of the Absolutist State. From the seventeenth century onward, the monarchy of Poland was so weak that it could not enlist these bankrupt gentry, who moved to the estates of the more successful magnates, and thus further weakened the political center. In this regard, the Jews, who constituted a high proportion of the general population relative to their proportion in other countries and who were available for taxation by the monarchy, may have inadvertently inhibited the development of a strong political center. Having received their original charters from the monarchy in the thirteenth century, when it was a powerful institution, the Jews, as "Serfs of the Chamber," continued to support the monarchy in an effort to have these charters renewed and extended. This continued long after the king was in any position to enforce those charters. This support of a central institution on a minimal level plus the revenues from the king's estates reduced the need for the mobilization of other strata of Polish society to maintain some semblance of a political center. The gentry was always eager to save money and to pass on the costs of necessary collective action. This arrangement also inhibited the concentration of political power.

16 See Kula 1976: 137–38.

17 See Kula 1976: 128, 140.

18 See Jedlicki 1970: 92ff.

19 See Jedlicki 1968: 221.

20 For an examination of money and the depersonalizing of social relations, see the classic essay of Simmel 1964.

21 Gostomski 1951: 106 quoted in Kula 1976: 141.

22 See Kula 1976: 134–44.

23 See Kula and Leskiewiczowa 1955, quoted in Kula 1976: 137.

24 See Kula 1976: 137. While Kula points to the economic significance of the *Pro-pinacja* as a siphoning-off mechanism (and we follow him in this analysis), he completely overlooks the involvement of Jews – what this might further indicate of the economic utility of the *Propinacja*, or its implications for the social and economic position of Jews. In another of Kula's works, on methodology in economic history, he does call for a consideration of the economic roles and functions of Jews in Polish history. See Kula 1963: 76–77. However, this deletion is by no means unusual in contemporary Polish historiography.

25 See Weinryb 1973: 61.

26 See Halpern (ed.), 1954, II: 242.

27 Weinryb 1973: 152 lists sixty "Blood libels, charges of profanation of the holy wafer and similar accusations" out of a total of 114 attacks occurring between the end of the 1540s and 1787 in Poland, in comparison with three such attacks out of a total of eighteen recorded for the fourteenth and fifteenth centuries (p. 47). He clearly admits that these calculations of the incidence of local attacks are far from complete. However, the record of a higher absolute number and a higher relative number of blood libels and accusations of wafer desecration may be significant and may provide some evidence for the symbolic links between these allegations and Jewish involvement in the *Propinacja*.

28 See Maimon 1954: 20–22, in which he recounts how a blood libel was plotted against his grandfather by a local priest in revenge for having been refused unlimited free drink in the grandfather's inn.

29 For a survey of the proposals made in the Sejm (the Polish parliament), see Ettinger 1972: 20–34. The proposals promulgated particularly in connection with the Four-Year Sejm (1788–92) are collected in Eisenbach, *et al.* 1969: VI. For an assessment of some of the Russian proposals, see Sprenger 1976.

30 A large literature exists on the impact of the western European Enlightenment (and of Western political and economic change) on the position of Jews in western and central Europe in the eighteenth century. For a survey, see the works of Jacob Katz, particularly his most recent study, *Out of the Ghetto* (1974). The assumption of most Jewish historians is that what takes place in the eighteenth century in the West is repeated with some variation in the nineteenth century in the East. However, because of the lag between proposed and actual changes in the Jewish situation in the East, insufficient attention is paid to the influence of western publicistic literature and of actual changes in the western Jewish situation on the discussions taking place in Poland in the second half of the eighteenth century.

31 Kula 1976: 186.

32 See Jedlicki 1970: 94.

33 From this perspective, those reform proposals which suggested the enserfment of Jews should be read not merely as anti-Semitic outbursts, but as economic positions that were connected to the concern to preserve serfdom. See Verte 194: 148–55, 203–13.

References

Anderson, Perry, 1974. *Lineages of the Absolutist State*. London, New Left Books

Braudel, Fernand, 1973. *Capitalism and Material Life, 1400–1800*. New York, Harper & Row

Dunbow, Semen, 1923–40. *Divre yeme 'am 'olam*. Tel Aviv, 11 vols

Eisenbach, A. *et al.*, 1969. *Materialy z historii sejmu czteroletneigo*. Wroclaw

Ettinger, S., 1972. Ha-yesodot weha-megammot be-izuv mediniyyuto shel ha-shilton ha-Rusi kelapai ha-yehudim im ha-lukat Polin, *Heawar* 19: 20–34

Gostomski, Anzelm, 1951. *Gospodarstwo* (1588), Stefan Inglot, ed., Wroclaw, Wydawn. Zakladu Narodowego im Ossolinskich

Gross, Nachum (ed.), 1975. *Economic History of the Jews*. New York, Schocken Books

Halpern, Israel (ed.), 1948–54. Pinkas vad arbah arasot, Art. 1, in Israel Halpern, ed., *Bet Yisrael be-Polin*. Jerusalem, 2 vols

Jedlicki, Jerzy, 1968. State Industrial Economy in the Kingdom of Poland in the Nineteenth Century, *Acta Poloniae Historica* 18: 221–37

   1970. Social Ideas and Economic Attitudes of Polish Eighteenth-Century Nobility: Their Approach to Industrial Policy, in Hermann van der Wee *et al.*, eds., *Fifth International Congress of Economic History*. The Hague, Mouton, I, 89–103

   1973. Native Culture and Western Civilization, *Acta Poloniae Historica* 28: 63–85

Katz, Jacob, 1974. *Out of the Ghetto*. Cambridge, Mass., Harvard Univ. Press

Kula, Witold, 1963. *Problemy i metody historii gospodarczej*. Warszawa, Panstwowe Wydawn, Naukowe

   1976. *An Economic Theory of the Feudal System: Towards a Model of the Polish Economy, 1500–1800*. London, New Left Books

Kula, Witold, and Leskiewiczowa, J., 1955. Ks Jozef Czartoryski: 'Mysli moje o zasadach gospodarskich', *Przeglad Historyczny* 46: 445–52

Leskiewicz, Janina, 1960. Le montant et les composants du revenu des biens fonciers en Pologne aux XVI–XVIII siècles, in *Première conférence internationale d'histoire économique, Stockholm, 1960*. Paris, Ecole pratique des hautes études, 409–14

Maimon, Solomon, 1954. *Autobiography*. London, East and West Library

Sheffer, Isaac, 1948–54. Toldat ha-kalkalah shel yehudi Polin velitah miyemai rishonim vead lehalukat ha-medinah, in Israel Halpern, ed., *Bet Yisrael be-Polin*. Jerusalem, 2 vols

Simmel, Georg, 1964. The Metropolis and Mental Life, in Kurt Wolff, ed., *The Sociology of Georg Simmel*. New York, Free Press of Glencoe, 409–24

Sprenger, A., 1976. Gavriil Derzhavin's Jewish Reform Project of 1800, *Canadian-American Slavic Studies*, 10, I, Spr.; 1–23

Stephens, John Lloyd, 1838. *Incidents of Travel in Greece, Turkey, Russia, and Poland*. New York, 2 vols

Tartakower, Arieh, 1959–60. Polish Jewry in the 18th century, *Jewish Journal of Sociology* 2, 1: 110–14

Verte, M., 1940–41. Hazarot Poloniyot lepitaron teritoriali shel shailot hayehudim, *Zion*, n.s., 6: 148–55, 203–13

Wallerstein, Immanuel, 1974. *The Modern World-System, I: Capitalist Agriculture and the Origins of the European World-Economy in the Sixteenth Century.* New York, Academic Press

Weinryb, Bernard, 1973. *The Jews of Poland: A Social and Economic History of the Jewish Community in Poland from 1100 to 1800.* Philadelphia, Jewish Publ. Society of America

15. Alternative mechanism of distribution in a Soviet economy

Gerald Mars and Yochanan Altman

Introduction

Travellers to Soviet Georgia have often remarked on what seems to be an excessive generosity with which people there treat each other (Maclean 1980). It is regularly noted that Georgians spend considerable time and resources on organizing and consuming large feasts, and of how strangers are enthusiastically welcomed and incorporated into them.[1] It is apparently quite common for diners in a restaurant to send over a couple of bottles of wine or a dish of meat to strangers at another table (quoted in *Samshoblo* 1981), and indeed one of us experienced such generosity at a picnic site outside Tblisi. When this happens the tables are likely to merge, addresses are exchanged and hopes expressed of continuing the relationships that the feast has established. Even before either of us made contact with Georgians, therefore, we were not surprised to hear that at Georgian feasts wine is expected to flow like water and that competitive drinking can reach levels that frequently startle outsiders.

The importance of feasts is indicated not only by the time and resources expended on them, but by the number of people involved in their prior preparation and the degree of formalized behaviour which precedes a feast, dominates it, and continues thereafter. Perhaps the most telling indication, however, is that the Soviet authorities have officially frowned upon Georgian feasts arguing that they not only represent a massive misuse of resources but that as these are often purloined from official sources, represent a misuse of Soviet property and absorb energy that should be put to more socially – that is officially – approved ends (*Ma'ariv* 1982).

The first questions that arise, therefore, have to do with why should Georgians be so hospitable and so generous, and not only to fellow Georgians, but often to complete strangers? We have found both in Tblisi – Georgia's capital – and in Ashkelon – in Israel (which houses some 6,000 recent migrant Jews from Georgia) that the feasts are an important social institution. And while they vary in their social function, size, constituency and spontaneity, feasts in both locations possess similar structures and serve similar ends. We have come to realize that feasting among the Georgians (and this applies equally to Christians, Jews, and those of neither affiliation) is not only interesting in its own right, but that it can offer unique insights into an understanding of Georgian society. It helps to explain how apparent prolific expense on food and drink can be understood as a rational use of scarce resources that serves to maintain and extend prestige and contacts. And it also helps to explain how individualistic concerns can be catered to in a Soviet economy.

Soviet Georgia, though not bordering the Mediterranean, has been much influenced by repeated contacts with Arabic, Persian and Turkish invaders. It is a typical "honour and shame" society, such as anthropologists have observed existing in most of the countries that border the Mediterranean. These are societies largely male dominated where macho values are paramount.

While they trace descent on both sides, Georgian families stress the male line and within it an emphasis on agnates – on the solidarity and mutual obligations of brothers. Honour, and its corollary, shame, are constant preoccupations in Georgia. Within family groups spheres of action are well-defined; they do not overlap and they are non competitive – everyone knows their place. Beyond the family, however, these limitations are reversed. Insecurity, instability and a perpetual ranking and re-ranking of personal relationships is the norm (Peristiani 1965). A male has therefore continually to prove himself as *catso* – a man. He is, in this respect, perpetually "on show" and has constantly to demonstrate his worthiness to public opinion in general and to his colleagues and peers in particular. These require the extravagant use of display and consumption, as well as exhibitions of "manliness". For women, honour is established by sexual modesty, propriety and by the exercise of feminine accomplishments. The feast in its preparation by women and in its associated drinking by men, offers the most common opportunity to test out and exercise these requirements.

The structure of the feast

It might seem at first sight to be stretching rational classification when we include as feasts, events that range from informal ad hoc gatherings of 5 or 6 people, to those that are highly formalized, minutely pre-arranged and, in our experience, have numbered over 1,000. We do so, however, because, under the general title of "feast", we find that all these gatherings possess a common structure. So although feasts may be extensively pre-planned over many months, or are sometimes arranged on the spur of the moment; whether they are composed predominantly of kin or of neighbours or friends; or whether the putative purpose is to welcome a stranger or to cement a deal, they nonetheless all possess the following structural features.

Head of Table

We have between us attended over 40 feasts. Each feast had an appointed Head of Table – the *Tamada*, who is not necessarily the host or the owner of the premises if the feast takes place in a home. It is the Tamada's job to direct the order of the proceedings and in particular to offer the toasts that punctuate the feast from its beginning to its end. He is selected on a number of criteria that ideally emphasize the idea of authority and worthiness: he is always male. Usually he is older than the rest of the company since age is a virtue in Georgia. He may be the most eminent person present, and he should certainly be verbally fluent, spontaneous and witty. In addition, however, and most important, he must be able to hold his drink, since it is he who sets the upper limit. A Tamada, therefore, is one who should naturally be respected by the others, who should be able to elevate the emotions of the audience, who should in fact, be *catso*.

The feast will start with the Tamada calling for order and quiet, which is important as an acknowledgement of the respect in which he is held. Heads of Tables have been known to get quite irritable, and even angry, when they cannot obtain the silence they feel is required, since this reflects upon their inability to establish control – a control that must be maintained throughout the whole feast – and particularly at the feast's conclusion when the Tamada has to decide when to bring the proceedings to an end.[2]

Toasting

The feast is punctuated by toasts which are the central feature of a feast; there might well be as many as twenty or even more toasts in an evening, and some toasts have been known to last as long as an hour. Wine is normally poured into crystal glasses, each person taking his wine from the bottle nearest him though a Guest of Honour will usually be served first – at least at the beginning. There are often different measures of glasses – the normal capacity would be some 150ml. Crystal (or crystal like) glasses are used because they are considered expensive and therefore good for display. But being transparent they also do not enable men to cheat on the amount of alcohol consumed. That is – honour is literally "on the table" and everyone can observe everyone else's standing.

While a toast will always start with the Tamada – he dictates the issues and addresses the first speeches – he will later pass the right to toast and speak to another. He will do this by clinking his glass (prior to emptying it after his speech) against the glass of his nominee who then addresses the company. This second toaster might then in his turn pass the right to a third and so on, which explains why Georgian feasts can last for up to eight hours. At large feasts where there are several tables, such toastings serve to link the tables. One can often observe a toaster rising from a table at one corner of a hall and with a full glass, shouting to someone who is seated at a far corner. The other will also rise – both then greeting each other loudly – and simultaneously emptying their glasses while standing facing each other. In this way, as the evening proceeds, all participants become enmeshed in a matrix of personal linkages.

Feasts are always set in the same framework. At its start the Tamada will announce the first toast, which is always an honouring of those who are the cause of the gathering. They might be the bride and groom, a visitor "who has brought us here in his honour", or as occurred in Tblisi, it might be to honour a girl who had just graduated. The end of the feast is similarly marked by a common toast – the toast honouring the Tamada, who has organized and kept the gathering together.

Focussing and linkages: the toast as integrator

Between the first and last toasts, idealized values of the society and the levels of social organization above the personal network are both brought together and made concrete and manifest through the personalities at the feast. There are thus toasts to the Land of Georgia, and if foreigners are present, to the land of their countries also. If the feast brings together the staff of different institutions these institutions too will be toasted. There is thus a focussing through individuals of ideal and abstract valuations on the one hand, and by treating individuals *as representatives* there is a linking of concrete organizational affiliations on the other.

A typical example of such linkage and focussing through those present, can be gained by considering aspects of the feast that one of us attended in Tblisi to honour a young woman on the occasion of her graduation. The Tamada was the senior professor of her university department and one of the oldest people present. The gathering comprised both sexes and ages from twenty to over seventy, members of both sides of the girl's family, her husband's family, junior professors and staff from her department, a couple of professors and their guests from other university departments, some neighbours, two foreign guests, who were brought by two different visitors, and some of the girl's friends. The second toast was to the girl's parents and to the parents and grandparents, both alive and dead, of all those present; and indeed this toast was then extended to the virtues of parenthood in general.[3] The third toast was to honour two visitors; one of the authors as an Englishman, and an East German; both from countries which had been at war, both now united in friendship at the same feast, both learning that Georgia was a land of peace where over forty nationalities lived in harmony. The toast that followed was to the girl's mother, to motherhood, and to women in general. The Tamada then elaborated on the role of women as providers of beauty and love, both in general and specifically as related to the people present. There then followed a series of toasts to the professor's own department, to its staff and to other departments and their staff, who were represented at the feast.

The twelfth toast, in this feast of twenty toasts, was to Georgian women and Armenian women, particularly significant since this was a mixed gathering of Georgians and Armenians – the girl being honoured having mixed parentage. The Tamada emphasized that Georgian and Armenian women were different, yes, but also similar in their essential femininity. As the evening proceeds, and after everyone present has been toasted, the toasts often become either so widely abstract that they cover everything and everyone such as toasts "to the divine spirit", "to all on our land", or they become so specific that to the sober celebrant they appear quite silly, like drinking "for the electric light, without which we wouldn't be able to see what we are doing here", and which sometimes allow for competitive and excessive bravado. It is at these latter stages of a feast that men might well snatch up a vase or a jug, fill it with wine and attempt to empty it at a single draught. Others present will then be coerced to attempt to match or exceed the feat. It is this type of excess that caused Fitzroy Maclean to describe Georgians as "much, much harder drinkers than anyone else in the world". Such gargantuan revelling can be appreciated as doubly competitive when it is realized that men are not only expected to drink, but are not expected to relieve themselves during the evening and that they are indeed required to stay in the room so that private urinating, purging or vomiting cannot offer any unfair advantage.

One of us sat at a feast in Ashkelon beside a man in his fifties who was bitterly protesting against the "stupid young lads" who had started to compete. "What's the point in it? Now they are like big men and then they'll vomit their souls and it will take them two days to recover", he preached. How surprised we were then when he finally joined the competition himself. And he explained it thus: "I have no choice. This feast will be remembered for days and those who had a go will praise themselves as great warriors while I will be considered feeble." In Ashkelon one can sometimes tell the course a feast has taken by the number of men strolling around the next day – having forcibly had to take the day off work.

Singing, reciting and dancing

Toasts are interspersed with singing and by recitations of poetry both established and spontaneous and, if there is a musical instrument or an orchestra present, with dancing. The songs and the poetry – like the toasts – will be chosen to develop the same principles of linkage and focussing that integrate and incorporate those present into a single fellowship. Thus at the Tblisi feast there was a recitation from Shakespeare to honour one of the present authors, a song by Mendelssohn to honour the East German, and songs that praised Tblisi as a uniquely beautiful city, and Georgia as a land of proud men and lovely women. There was also an attempt to sing an Armenian song which foundered because most of the guests were Georgians and did not know the words. If there is dancing as the evening proceeds, people will not sit where they previously sat but will, after each dance, sit in a new place so that members of the feast shuffle themselves and linkages with new people can be established.

The nature of wine

Wine in the Georgian tradition is strongly associated with manhood and with male friendship.[4] Not only do men make the wine they drink but they have no other involvement with food preparation. And men are largely the sole consumers of their product – the quality of which is used as a competitive marker. Women at feasts normally only drink a single glass towards the end of the feast when they accept the thanks of the men for the feast's preparation. It is unheard of for men to drink alone – the role of wine is essentially social, formalized and specific to the feast.

How the feast relates to Georgian culture

The feast can be understood as an institution reconciling two themes that run through Georgian culture. The first is the great emphasis placed on competition; the second a concomitant need for cooperation.

Both these themes are evident in the selection and role of the Tamada. In keeping order his job is to mediate between conflicting competitive interests, hence his personal qualities are so important, particularly his standing as a drinker and his social situation as a person of some eminence. By his personal standing and his eminence he not only honours the gathering, he is above the general level of competition. But he is also *primus inter pares*, and it is in this dimension of his role that he has to carry out his tasks with grace, elegance and persuasion. A too blatant display of authority has no place at a feast – except possibly in the early establishment of his position.

Competition, as has been indicated, is particularly evident in competitive drinking by men and in the elegance of their speeches when offering and replying to toasts. But it is also evident in the furnishings to be seen crammed into the family lounge or in a room set aside specifically for feasting. Here are displayed in glass fronted cabinets, china, glass cutlery and serving bowls – all items used at feasts. When a couple become engaged, amongst the gifts they are bound to receive are such household items for display and feast-giving. But competition and display are also evident in the way the feast is served, not only in the range of dishes which are brought on in a continuous stream throughout the evening, but because they are served on small plates. These are over-filled and, as the evening proceeds, have to be piled on top of each other thus presenting an image of excess.

If the competitive theme is dominant in men, and the way men behave, the cooperative theme is evident in the role women take in the feast. It is women who are primarily responsible for obtaining the food (particularly delicacies such as caviar not easily obtained outside Moscow); for cooking and serving it and for cleaning up after the feast. For these purposes women need to exploit the network of their kinfolk and their neighbours. The cooking will be carried out cooperatively both in separate kitchens and communally. The table will be laid by a group of women and the serving of guests will be similarly carried out by them as will the clearance of the feast and the cleaning of the kitchen.

It would be a mistake, however, to equate competition solely with men and cooperation, as solely the prerogative of women; though women are less competitive than men, they are competitive. A woman, for instance, will compete on a man's behalf and will gain personal prestige by demonstrating the speed and efficiency with which she can produce a whole range of dishes for an ad hoc feast. And, in a similar way, the feast also permits and encourages a modification of male competition as the evening proceeds. Though broccadacio drinking might well dominate a feast during its early and middle phases, the bonhomie of cooperative fellowship asserts itself in the latter phase of the feast. It is then that elaborate personal valuations are made, friendships are sworn, addresses exchanged, and at the end of the feast men might well be found eating from the same plate and drinking from the same cup. The term for this practise is *megobarebi* which can be translated as "close friends".

The place of networks in Soviet Georgia

So far the feast has largely been considered as an event that operates at a local level; as a gathering of people selected on different bases and coming together in fellowship. But the feast also serves a wider purpose and one well recognized by its participants. It links and binds together people who possess different affiliations, who represent different places, institutions, occupations and kinship linkages. And it is in understanding this role of the feast and the latency inherent in the links it encourages, that we can appreciate why the feast is so important in Soviet Georgia and perhaps too why it should be officially discouraged by the Soviet authorities. This is because it is in the manipulation of such ego-focussed networks that Georgians can and do influence and manipulate the organisations of the State (Mars and Altman 1983, 1984).

When we conceive of the feast in this way – as a network made manifest – we can see how it mediates between the individual in his unremitting search for prestige and the organizations and institutions of Soviet Society with which he has constantly to deal. As we saw in our earlier example, participants in the feast become concrete representatives – "embodiments" – of more abstract entities. We saw that the English and German scholars for instance, became representatives of their respective countries; the professors representatives of their institutions and individuals of their families. Hence both general as well as specific interests become linked and by the same token individuals gain idealistic properties – they become archetypes of their wider affiliations. We can see, therefore, why the toasts for such abstract entities as womanhood or nationhood become highly significant: a failure to meet expectations by an individual reflects adversely on the wider grouping of which he is a representative. A man who cannot consume the right amount of wine not only shames himself but reflects adversely on his wider affiliations.

When we realize that honour and prestige are vitally linked to conspicuous consumption and display, we realize why scarce goods should be highly prized, the more so since consumer goods are in chronically short supply in the Soviet Union. But it is not just in the obtaining of scarce goods that networks are necessary – they are necessary too at all the myriad points of contact which link the Soviet citizen with numerous state organizations. We have details of network links that were vital in obtaining preferred jobs, scarce permits and licences, places at university and which moved our informants out of trouble when they came up against the formal sources of state control. In a very real sense, therefore, expenditure on feasts can be understood – not as a wasteful and profligate misuse of resources, but as the bases of shrewd investment and as representing the conversion of material resources to social ones that in their turn can be reinvested for further and future material return. The feast therefore binds together people into a powerful ego-focussed resource-gathering core which allows it to exploit its environment by capturing significant people on its periphery.

The Soviet authorities, in maintaining economic control over their populations, have used the workplace as the principal source of the scarcest and most demanded of resources. Cars, for instance, which are in great demand in Georgia are largely distributed not through car showrooms on the High Street as in the West, they are instead allocated through the workplace. One of us visited two factories in Georgia. With staffs of 350 and 500 workers respectively, they were allocated 35 cars a year. This was more than enough for the immediate use of their workers. But, cars are not needed to be retained by the workers to whom they are allocated, they can in fact (by a legal fiction – a document allowing use though not permanently changing ownership) be re-distributed through personal networks, to friends, acquaintances and relatives. The same kind of network-based distribution applies to other scarce goods which are also allocated through the workplace, such as particularly fashionable clothes, well-designed and therefore scarce modern furniture and luxury items of food in particular demand, such as caviar.

The Soviet State in denigrating the feast nonetheless needs this institution even if it fails to recognize the nature of the linkage between it and the personal support networks through which it becomes manifest. It is through the personalizing institution of the feast and the networks it represents that the demands of an ego-focussed and competitive culture are able to co-exist alongside an impersonal "meta bureaucracy".

Notes

1 Our enquiries into feasts and feasting in Georgia are part of a wider ongoing enquiry funded by the UK Nuffield Foundation, which is attempting to understand processes of resettlement and to reconstruct aspects of Soviet Georgian society by studying recent migrants to Israel. The method is predominantly anthropological involving among other kinds of enquiry, one and a half years fieldwork in Israel by one author, which has been supplemented with short visits both to Israel and to Soviet Georgia by the other. We have, in addition, constant contact with Georgian residents in the UK and we have access to Soviet and Georgian newspapers.

2 Sometimes criteria for the selection of a *Tamada* conflict, and this is especially so if someone has been selected on the basis of their close kinship link with the prime performer. This, however, is most likely to occur when the feast is kinship-based as at a wedding. These gatherings are usually larger than ad hoc gatherings and are able to be pre-planned. In these cases there is a multiplicity of tables and a sub-Tamada is appointed to each table, which reduces the overall role of the main Tamada who, though he may be selected on the grounds primarily of his close kinship attachments, might fail to impress on the criteria of witty or fluid speech.

3 At one feast we attended the story was recounted of a small child of four who had asked his grandfather "Grandfather – you are very old, when are you going to die?" The reply was "I will die when you die because as long as you live my name will live on at occasions like feasts."

4 The Georgians have a saying "Always prefer old wine and old friends."

References

Ma'ariv, 1982 (Israeli Evening Paper). In Georgia hospitality is under attack, Tel Aviv, 6 Sept.

Maclean, Fitzroy, 1980. Inside the Soviet Union, in *Sunday Telegraph Magazine* no 182, March, London

Mars, Gerald, and Altman, Yochanan, 1983. The Cultural Bases of Soviet Georgia's Second Economy, *Soviet Studies*, vol. 35, no 4: 546–60

Mars, Gerald, and Altman, Yochanan 1987. Free Enterprise in the U.S.S.R: The case of Soviet Georgia. Aldershot, Gower Press

Peristiani, J. G. (ed), 1965. *Honour and Shame – the Values of Mediterranean Society*, London, Weidenfeld and Nicolson
Samshoblo, 1981. 18 (531) (Georgian Compatriots Monthly)

Index